taste of home Cooking School
COOKBOOK

REIMAN MEDIA GROUP, LLC • GREENDALE, WI

taste of home | Reader's Digest

A TASTE OF HOME/READER'S DIGEST BOOK
© 2012 Reiman Media Group, LLC
5400 S. 60th St., Greendale WI 53129
All rights reserved.

Taste of Home and Reader's Digest are registered
trademarks of The Reader's Digest Association, Inc.

Editor-in-Chief: Catherine Cassidy
Vice President, Executive Editor/Books: Heidi Reuter Lloyd
Creative Director: Howard Greenberg
North American Chief Marketing Officer: Lisa Karpinski
Food Director: Diane Werner, RD
Senior Editor/Retail Books: Faithann Stoner
Editor: Christine Rukavena
Editorial Intern: Andrea Mesalk
Project Art Director: Jessie Sharon
Associate Creative Director: Edwin Robles Jr.

Content Production Manager: Julie Wagner
Layout Designers: Emma Acevedo, Nancy Novak,
Catherine Fletcher, Kathleen Bump, Julie Schnuck, Holly Patch
Copy Chief: Deb Warlaumont Mulvey
Copy Editor: Susan Uphill
Recipe Asset System Manager: Coleen Martin
Recipe Testing & Editing: Taste of Home Test Kitchen
Food Photography: Taste of Home Photo Studio
Administrative Assistant: Barb Czysz

Taste of Home Cooking Schools
General Manager: Erin Puariea
Field Staff & Program Manager: Betsy Fryda
Sales & Marketing Manager: Jamie Piette Andrzejewski
Associate Brand Manager: Lauren Scott
National Business Development Specialist: Marc Padron
Experiential Marketing Specialist: Mitch Cooper
Operations Coordinator: Dawn Strzok

The Reader's Digest Association, Inc.
President and Chief Executive Officer: Robert E. Guth
**Executive Vice President, RDA, & President,
North America:** Dan Lagani
President/Publisher, Trade Publishing: Harold Clarke
Associate Publisher: Rosanne McManus
Vice President, Sales & Marketing: Stacey Ashton

For other Taste of Home books and products,
visit us at tasteofhome.com.

For more Reader's Digest products and information,
visit **rd.com** (**in the United States**)
or see **rd.ca** (**in Canada**).

International Standard Book Number (10): 0-89821-945-0
International Standard Book Number (13): 978-0-89821-945-6
Library of Congress Control Number: 2011940520

Cover Photography
Photographer: Rob Hagen
Food Stylist: Diane Armstrong
Set Stylist: Pam Stasney

Pictured on front cover:
Beef Roast au Poivre, page 120
Berry Patch Lattice Pie, page 280

Pictured on back cover:
Berry Patch Lattice Pie, page 280

Pictured on spine:
Mini Scallop Casseroles, page 171

Printed in China.
1 3 5 7 9 10 8 6 4 2

contents

If you'd like to attend a **Cooking School** in your area, please visit our website at **tasteofhome.com/cooking-schools** for a complete program schedule and ticket information. If you're attending one of our **cooking schools, enjoy the show!**

WELCOME

Get ready to learn, have fun and discover new favorites with the experts at *Taste of Home Cooking School!*

Whatever your skill level in the kitchen, **you will learn tricks, tips, secrets, entertaining ideas** and so much more with this **vibrant collection of more than 400 of our best-loved recipes.**

Whether you crave a magnificent lasagna, long for comfort-food classics like barbecued ribs and potato salad, or are making a holiday meal for the very first time, you'll find what you need—and so much more—in the *Taste of Home Cooking School Cookbook!*

The chapters in this volume are organized for the way you want **to cook and entertain.** With the first two chapters, **Appetizers** and **Drinks,** you can plan casual get-togethers with pub favorites like guacamole, mini cheeseburgers and stuffed jalapenos. Or host a cocktail party with more upscale fare and the recipes to make martinis, old-fashioneds, an exciting banana-flavored eggnog and more.

In the next chapter, **you'll take a tasty trip to your all-time favorite restaurants without leaving your own kitchen.** Prepare burger-joint and bistro favorites, delicious, easy Mexican food, pizza-parlor specialties and fabulous Chinese takeout. These foods are so yummy, fresh and affordable you'll quickly see why we call this chapter **Better Than Takeout!**

You'll also find soups, meats, pastas, vegetarian choices and side dishes to make a complete meal.

Then **join us for breakfast** with two dozen tempting recipes that serve one, two or a hungry houseful of overnight guests. You'll find impressive, easy casseroles that are perfect for brunches, holidays and potlucks, too.

Whether you'd like a simple pastry to go with breakfast or to try your hand at making a beautiful loaf of braided challah, the **Baking** chapter is sure to inspire! You'll find rocky road brownies, homemade scones and a variety of savory recipes that help you put homemade bread on the table fast.

No special day is complete without a **sweet, delectable treat.** Whip up adorable cupcakes, make a classic cherry pie with lattice top, learn the secret to perfect creme brulee and **master three easy, no-special-equipment-needed techniques** to create a beautifully frosted cake.

At **Taste of Home Cooking School,** we love **to share our passion for good food with you!** Our culinary specialists demonstrate recipes and share professional techniques with **over 300,000 viewers each year.**

With this beautiful new volume, you can **bring our lessons into your own home.** This is the cookbook you will turn to again and again. Go ahead, grab an apron and join us today!

—*Taste of Home Cooking School*

CHEAT IT! *P.S. Look for the icon throughout this book for low-effort recipes with big rewards!*

MEASURING CORRECTLY: the secret to success!

LIQUIDS
Place a liquid measuring cup on a level surface. For a traditional liquid measuring cup, view the amount at eye level to be sure of an accurate measure. Do not lift cup to check the level. Some newer liquid measuring cups are designed so that they can be accurately read from above.

For sticky liquids such as molasses, corn syrup or honey, spray the measuring cup with nonstick cooking spray before adding the liquid. This will make it easier to pour out the liquid and clean the cup.

SHORTENING
Press shortening into a dry measuring cup with a spatula to make sure it is solidly packed without air pockets. With a metal spatula or flat side of a knife, level with the rim. Some shortenings come in sticks and can be measured like butter.

SOUR CREAM & YOGURT
Spoon sour cream and yogurt into a dry measuring cup, then level top by sweeping a metal spatula or flat side of a knife across the top of the cup.

DRY INGREDIENTS
For dry ingredients such as flour, sugar or cornmeal, spoon ingredients into a dry measuring cup over a canister or waxed paper. Fill cup to overflowing, then level by sweeping a metal spatula or flat side of a knife across the top.

BULK DRY INGREDIENTS
Spoon bulk dry ingredients such as cranberries, raisins or chocolate chips into the measuring cup. If necessary, level the cup with a spatula or flat side of a knife.

BUTTER
The wrappers for sticks of butter come with markings for tablespoons, 1/4 cup, 1/3 cup and 1/2 cup. Use a knife to cut off the desired amount.

BROWN SUGAR
When a recipe calls for brown sugar, it should always be firmly packed when measuring. The moisture in brown sugar tends to trap air between the crystals.

Get Cooking with a Well-Stocked Kitchen

In a perfect world, you would plan out weekly or even monthly menus and have all the ingredients on hand to make each night's dinner. The reality, however, is you likely haven't thought about dinner until you've walked through the door.

With a well-stocked pantry, refrigerator and freezer, you'll still be able to serve a satisfying meal in short order. Consider these tips:

- **Quick-cooking meats** like boneless chicken breasts, chicken thighs, pork tenderloin, pork chops, ground meats, Italian sausage, sirloin and flank steaks, fish fillets and shrimp should be stocked in the freezer. Wrap them individually (except shrimp), so you can remove only the amount you need. For the quickest defrosting, wrap meats for freezing in small, thin packages.

- **Frozen vegetables prepackaged** in plastic bags are a real time-saver. Simply pour out the amount needed. No preparation is required!

- **Pastas, rice, rice mixes and couscous** are great staples to have in the pantry—and they generally have a long shelf life. Remember, thinner pastas, such as angel hair, cook faster than thicker pastas. Fresh (refrigerated) pasta cooks faster than dried.

- **Dairy products** like milk, sour cream, cheeses (shredded, cubed or crumbled), eggs, yogurt and butter or margarine are more perishable, so check the use-by date on packages and replace as needed.

- **Condiments** such as ketchup, mustard, mayonnaise, salad dressings, salsa, taco sauce, soy sauce, stir-fry sauce, lemon juice, etc., add flavor to many dishes. Personalize the list to suit your family's needs.

- **Fresh fruit and vegetables** can make a satisfying predinner snack. Oranges and apples are not as perishable as bananas. Ready-to-use salad greens are great for an instant salad.

- **Dried herbs, spices, vinegars** and seasoning mixes add flavor and keep for months.

- **Pasta sauces, olives, beans,** broths, canned tomatoes, canned vegetables, and canned or dried soups are great to have on hand for a quick meal...and many of these items are common recipe ingredients.

- **Get your family in the habit** of posting a grocery list. When an item is used up or is almost gone, just add it to the list for your next shopping trip. This way you won't completely run out of an item, and you'll also save time when writing your grocery list.

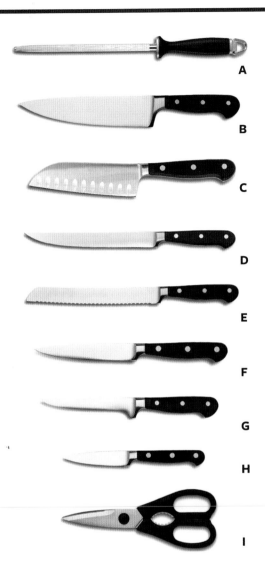

KITCHEN CUTLERY

A basic set of knives is essential to any well-equipped kitchen. There are a variety of knives made from many materials. The best knives, made from high-carbon steel, are resistant to corrosion (unlike carbon steel) and remain sharper longer than stainless steel.

A. STEEL

This long, thin rod with a handle is used to smooth out small rough spots on the edge of a knife blade and to reset the edge of the blade. You can also use a whetstone or electric knife sharpener to sharpen knives.

B. CHEF'S KNIFE

This 8-in. to 10-in. multipurpose knife can be used for such tasks as mincing, chopping and dicing.

C. SANTOKU

This is a Japanese variation of a chef's knife. The 6-1/2-in. to 7-in. multipurpose knife is used for mincing, chopping, dicing and slicing. The blade's dimple design helps reduce drag during slicing.

D. CARVING KNIFE

This 8-in. to 10-in. knife is perfect for slicing roasts and turkey.

E. SERRATED OR BREAD KNIFE

This knife's serrated blade is used for slicing breads, cakes and delicate foods. An 8-in. knife is the most versatile, but a range of lengths is available.

F. UTILITY KNIFE

This 6-in. knife is the right size to slice small foods.

G. BONING KNIFE

This knife's 5-in. or 6-in. tapered blade is designed to remove the meat from poultry, beef, pork or fish bones.

H. PARING KNIFE

This 3-in. to 4-in. knife is used for peeling, mincing and slicing small foods.

I. KITCHEN SHEARS

This versatile tool can be used for a multitude of tasks, from snipping fresh herbs, to disjointing chicken, to trimming pastry, etc.

CARING FOR KNIVES

To keep knives sharp, cut foods on a soft plastic or wooden cutting board. Ceramic, granite, metal and other hard surfaces will dull the blades.

Always hand-wash knives immediately after use. Never let them soak in water or wash in the dishwasher. Store knives in a slotted wooden block or hang them on a magnetic rack especially designed for knives. Proper storage will protect knife edges, keep blades sharper longer and guard against injury. Do not store in a drawer.

USING A STEEL

Rest the tip of the steel on the work surface. Hold your knife at a 20° angle to the steel. Start with the heel of the blade against the steel and draw the blade up across the steel until you reach the tip of the knife. Repeat five times on both sides of knife blade, alternating sides. Repeat as needed.

Cookware

YOUR BASIC COOKWARE SHOULD INCLUDE:

- One Dutch oven, 5 qt. or larger
- One 8-in. or 9-in. saute/omelet pan
- One 10-in. to 12-in. skillet
- Two saucepans with lids
- One shallow roaster

Good cookware should conduct heat quickly and evenly distribute heat over the pan's surface. To help you decide what you need, here's a look at some common materials for cookware:

COPPER
Pros: conducts heat the best
Cons: expensive, reacts with acidic ingredients

ALUMINUM
Pros: conducts heat well, less expensive than copper
Cons: reacts with acidic ingredients

ANODIZED ALUMINUM
Pros: Resistant to sticking, doesn't react to acidic foods
Cons: Can be difficult to clean

CAST IRON
Pros: conducts heat well
Cons: heavy, must be seasoned periodically

STAINLESS STEEL
Pros: durable, looks like new for years
Cons: poor heat conductor

5-QT. DUTCH OVEN

8-IN. SAUTE/OMELET PAN

10-IN. SKILLET

1-QT. SAUCEPAN

ROASTER

Bakeware

A WELL-STOCKED BAKER'S KITCHEN SHOULD HAVE:

1. Two or three 9-in. x 1-1/2-in. round baking pans

2. One 13-in. x 9-in. baking pan or dish (3 qt.)

3. One 10-in. fluted pan

4. One 15-in. x 10-in. x 1-in. baking pan (jelly roll pan)

5. Baking sheets (without sides) in assorted sizes

6. One 9-in springform pan

7. One 9-in. pie plate

8. One 12-cup muffin pan (standard size)

9. Six 6-oz. custard cups

10. Two 9-in. x 5-in. loaf pans and two 8-in. x 4-in. loaf pans

11. One 9-in. x 9-in. and one 8-in. x 8-in. square baking dishes or pans

12. One 10-in. tube pan

FOR THE BEST BAKING RESULTS:

- Use the pan size that's specified in the recipe.
- Use aluminum pans with dull finishes (darker ones can cause overbrowning).
- Use glass or ceramic baking dishes to marinate or for recipes that include tomato sauce.
- If you substitute a glass dish for a metal one, reduce the oven temperature by 25° to avoid overbaking.

APPETIZERS

10-MINUTE ZESTY SALSA

Yield: 1-1/2 cups.

The view from our mountain home includes Pikes Peak, so we frequently eat on our wrap-around porch in good weather. During family get-togethers, we often savor this zippy salsa with chips while we take in the natural beauty all around us. kim morin // lake george, colorado

- 1 **can (10 ounces) diced tomatoes and green chilies, undrained**
- 1 **tablespoon seeded chopped jalapeno pepper**
- 1 **tablespoon chopped red onion**
- 1 **tablespoon minced fresh cilantro**
- 1 **garlic clove, minced**
- 1 **tablespoon olive oil**

Dash salt

Dash pepper

Tortilla chips

In a small bowl, combine the tomatoes, jalapeno, onion, cilantro, garlic, oil, salt and pepper. Refrigerate until serving. Serve with tortilla chips.

EDITOR'S NOTE: We recommend wearing disposable gloves when cutting hot peppers. Avoid touching your face.

Nutrition Facts: 1/4 cup equals 29 calories, 2 g fat (trace saturated fat), 0 cholesterol, 214 mg sodium, 2 g carbohydrate, 1 g fiber, trace protein.

GUACAMOLE

Yield: about 1-1/2 cups.

The lemon or lime juice will keep the dip looking fresh and will prevent discoloration until serving. Or, before chilling, place plastic wrap directly on the dip so there isn't any air between the dip and the wrap. anne tipps // duncanville, texas

- 1 **medium ripe avocado, halved, seeded and peeled**
- 4-1/2 **teaspoons lemon juice**
- 1 **small tomato, seeded and finely chopped**
- 1/4 **cup finely chopped onion**
- 1 **tablespoon finely chopped green chilies**
- 1 **garlic clove, minced**
- 1/4 **teaspoon salt, optional**

Tortilla chips

In a large bowl, mash avocado with lemon juice. Stir in the tomato, onion, chilies, garlic and salt if desired. Cover; chill. Serve with tortilla chips.

Nutrition Facts: 2 tablespoon equals 29 calories, 3 g fat (trace saturated fat), 0 cholesterol, 5 mg sodium, 2 g carbohydrate, 1 g fiber, trace protein.

5-MINUTE GUACAMOLE: Combine 1 avocado, 1 tablespoon salsa, 1 garlic clove and 1/4 teaspoon salt in a food processor; cover and process until guacamole is smooth.

CHOCOLATE FRUIT DIP

Yield: 2 cups.

I usually serve this popular dip with strawberries and pineapple, but it's good with other fruit like apples and melon. Your friends will think this one's really special.
sarah maury swan // granite, maryland

- 1 **package (8 ounces) cream cheese, softened**
- 1/3 **cup sugar**
- 1/3 **cup baking cocoa**
- 1 **teaspoon vanilla extract**
- 2 **cups whipped topping**

Assorted fruit for dipping

In a large bowl, beat cream cheese and sugar until smooth. Beat in cocoa and vanilla. Beat in whipped topping until smooth. Serve with fruit.

Nutrition Facts: 2 tablespoons equals 96 calories, 7 g fat (5 g saturated fat), 16 mg cholesterol, 42 mg sodium, 8 g carbohydrate, trace fiber, 1 g protein.

MANDARIN SALSA

Yield: 4 cups.

Sweet mandarin oranges temper the boldness of cilantro, jalapeno and onion in this salsa, creating an impressive and colorful combination.
yvonne opp // greenville, pennsylvania

- 5 **plum tomatoes, chopped**
- 1 **large sweet onion, chopped**
- 2 **jalapeno peppers, seeded and chopped**
- 2 **tablespoons sugar**
- 2 **tablespoons minced fresh cilantro**
- 2 **tablespoons lime juice**
- 1 **teaspoon salt**
- 1 **teaspoon minced garlic**
- 1 **can (15 ounces) mandarin oranges, drained**

Tortilla chips

In a small bowl, combine the first eight ingredients. Gently stir in mandarin oranges. Chill until serving. Drain before serving if necessary. Serve with tortilla chips.

EDITOR'S NOTE: We recommend wearing disposable gloves when cutting hot peppers. Avoid touching your face.

Nutrition Facts: 1/4 cup (calculated without chips) equals 24 calories, trace fat (trace saturated fat), 0 cholesterol, 150 mg sodium, 6 g carbohydrate, 1 g fiber, trace protein. Diabetic Exchange: 1/2 starch.

LICK-THE-BOWL-CLEAN HUMMUS

Yield: 2-1/2 cups.

Everyone loves hummus, but I enjoy the garlic and onion types so much that I decided to let them shine in this homemade version. I get so many compliments when I serve it!

sarah gilbert // beaverton, oregon

> 2 **large sweet onions, thinly sliced**
> 1/4 **cup plus 1/3 cup olive oil, divided**
> 1 **can (15 ounces) garbanzo beans or chickpeas, rinsed and drained**
> 1/4 **cup plus 2 tablespoons lemon juice**
> 1/4 **cup tahini**
> 4 **garlic cloves, minced**
> 1/8 **teaspoon** *each* **salt and pepper**

Baked pita chips or assorted fresh vegetables

In a large skillet, saute onions in 1/4 cup oil until softened. Reduce heat to medium-low; cook, stirring occasionally, for 30 minutes or until deep golden brown.

Transfer to a food processor; add the beans, lemon juice, tahini, garlic, salt, pepper and remaining oil. Cover and process for 30 seconds or until smooth. Serve with chips.

Nutrition Facts: 1/4 cup (calculated without chips and vegetables) equals 218 calories, 17 g fat (2 g saturated fat), 0 cholesterol, 91 mg sodium, 14 g carbohydrate, 3 g fiber, 3 g protein.

FRENCH QUARTER CHEESE SPREAD

Yield: 8 servings.

Topped with toasty pecans, this sweet-and-savory cheese is simply a hit. Make it ahead of time for convenience, then bring to room temperature and serve.

heidi blaine hadburg // safety harbor, florida

> 1 **package (8 ounces) cream cheese, softened**
> 1 **tablespoon grated onion**
> 1 **garlic clove, minced**
> 1/4 **cup butter, cubed**
> 1/4 **cup packed dark brown sugar**
> 1 **teaspoon Worcestershire sauce**
> 1/2 **teaspoon prepared mustard**
> 1 **cup finely chopped pecans, toasted**

Assorted crackers

In a small bowl, combine the cream cheese, onion and garlic. Transfer to a serving plate; shape into a 6-in. disk. Set aside.

In a small saucepan, combine butter, brown sugar, Worcestershire sauce and mustard. Cook and stir over medium heat for 4-5 minutes or until sugar is dissolved. Remove from the heat; stir in pecans.

Cool slightly. Spoon over cheese mixture. Serve with crackers.

Nutrition Facts: 1/4 cup (calculated without crackers) equals 280 calories, 26 g fat (11 g saturated fat), 46 mg cholesterol, 138 mg sodium, 10 g carbohydrate, 1 g fiber, 4 g protein.

>> HOW TO:

MAKE A CHEESE BALL

1 Keep hands and countertop clean by spooning the cheese mixture onto a piece of plastic wrap.

2 Working from the underside of the wrap, pat the mixture into a ball. Complete recipe as directed.

FESTIVE FETA CHEESE BALL

Yield: 2 cups.

I was inspired to come up with this recipe when I was asked to bring an appetizer to a party. Everyone loved it!

cinde ryan // gig harbor, washington

- **2 packages (8 ounces each) cream cheese, softened**
- **1/2 cup crumbled feta cheese**
- **2 teaspoons ranch salad dressing mix**
- **1/4 cup shredded Parmesan cheese**
- **1/4 cup crumbled cooked bacon**
- **1/2 teaspoon dill weed**

Assorted crackers

In a bowl, beat cream cheese until fluffy. Add feta cheese and dressing mix; mix well. Shape into a ball. Combine the Parmesan cheese, bacon and dill weed; roll cheese ball in Parmesan mixture. Wrap tightly in plastic wrap. Refrigerate for at least 1 hour or until firm. Serve with crackers.

Nutrition Facts: 2 tablespoons (calculated without crackers) equals 122 calories, 11 g fat (7 g saturated fat), 35 mg cholesterol, 313 mg sodium, 2 g carbohydrate, trace fiber, 4 g protein.

MAPLE-GLAZED SNACK MIX

Yield: 7-1/2 cups.

I haven't met a person yet who doesn't love this mix! My three children especially enjoy it for snacks during the school year.

cynthia norris // winnetka, california

- 2 **cups Corn Chex**
- 2 **cups Rice Chex**
- 2 **cups Honey-Nut Cheerios**
- 1 **cup miniature pretzels**
- 1/2 **cup pecan halves, coarsely chopped**
- 1/3 **cup maple syrup**
- 1 **tablespoon butter**
- 1 **teaspoon vanilla extract**

In a large bowl, combine the cereals, pretzels and pecans. In a small microwave-safe dish, combine maple syrup and butter. Cover and microwave on high for 45 seconds or until butter is melted. Stir in vanilla. Pour over cereal mixture and toss to coat.

Transfer to a 15-in. x 10-in. x 1-in. baking pan coated with cooking spray. Bake at 250° for 45 minutes, stirring every 15 minutes. Cool on a wire rack. Store in an airtight container.

EDITOR'S NOTE: This recipe was tested in a 1,100-watt microwave.

Nutrition Facts: 1/2 cup equals 104 calories, 4 g fat (1 g saturated fat), 2 mg cholesterol, 141 mg sodium, 17 g carbohydrate, 1 g fiber, 2 g protein. Diabetic Exchanges: 1 starch, 1/2 fat.

tasteofhome COOKING SCHOOL SECRET

EASY, INFORMAL APPS

An appetizer party is a fun twist on entertaining that's less formal than a traditional sit-down dinner.

When appetizers will serve as the meal, offer five or six different choices (including some substantial selections) and plan on eight to nine servings per guest. If you'll also be serving a meal, two to three servings per person is sufficient.

For most dips, count on using 1/4 cup per serving. Richer dips or cheese spreads will go further; count on 1 cup to serve eight guests.

In order to appeal to everyone's tastes and diets, have a balance of hearty and low-calorie appetizers, as well as hot and cold choices.

So that you can spend more time with guests, look for appetizers that can be made ahead and require little last-minute fuss.

CRESCENT SAMOSAS

Yield: 16 appetizers (3/4 cup sauce).

Tender, buttery crescents are filled with a delicious filling, making these appetizers a real stand-out. No one will guess that they're light!

jennifer kemp // grosse pointe park, michigan

- 1 can (14-1/2 ounces) diced new potatoes, drained
- 1 tablespoon olive oil
- 1/4 cup chopped green chilies
- 1 garlic clove, minced
- 1 cup frozen peas, thawed
- 1-1/2 teaspoons lemon juice
- 1 teaspoon curry powder
- Dash pepper
- 2 tubes (8 ounces each) refrigerated reduced-fat crescent rolls

SAUCE:

- 3/4 cup reduced-fat plain yogurt
- 2 tablespoons minced fresh cilantro
- 1 garlic clove, minced
- 1/2 teaspoon ground cumin
- Dash pepper

In a large nonstick skillet, saute potatoes in oil until lightly browned. Add chilies and garlic; saute 1 minute longer. Stir in the peas, lemon juice, curry powder and pepper. Transfer to a large bowl and coarsely mash.

Separate crescent dough into 16 triangles. Place 1 tablespoon potato mixture on the wide end of each triangle; roll up from wide end. Place point side down 2 in. apart on ungreased baking sheets; curve ends to form crescent shapes.

Bake at 375° for 10-12 minutes or until golden brown. Meanwhile, in a small bowl, combine sauce ingredients. Serve with warm samosas.

Nutrition Facts: 1 appetizer with about 2 teaspoons sauce equals 140 calories, 6 g fat (1 g saturated fat), 1 mg cholesterol, 316 mg sodium, 18 g carbohydrate, 1 g fiber, 4 g protein.

SWEET-TANGY WINGS

Yield: 1-1/2 dozen.

These tender, saucy wings have a hint of sweet and tangy lime flavor. Your guests will devour them!

taste of home test kitchen

- 1/2 **cup reduced-sodium soy sauce**
- 1/2 **cup lime juice,** *divided*
- 2 **garlic cloves, minced**
- 2 **teaspoons minced fresh gingerroot,** *divided*
- 2 **pounds chicken wingettes and drumettes**
- 1/2 **cup apricot jam**
- 1/2 **teaspoon salt**
- 1/4 **teaspoon cayenne pepper**
- 1/8 **teaspoon garlic powder**

Dash onion powder

In a large resealable plastic bag, combine the soy sauce, 1/4 cup lime juice, garlic and 1 teaspoon ginger; add the chicken. Seal bag and turn to coat. Refrigerate overnight, turning occasionally.

Drain and discard marinade. Place chicken on a greased rack in a foil-lined 15-in. x 10-in. x 1-in. baking pan. Bake at 375° for 15 minutes.

Meanwhile, in a small saucepan, combine the jam, salt, cayenne, garlic powder, onion powder, and remaining lime juice and ginger. Bring to a boil. Reduce heat; simmer, uncovered, for 2 minutes. Brush over wings.

Bake 40 minutes longer or until juices run clear, basting and turning every 10 minutes.

Nutrition Facts: 1 serving equals 139 calories, 8 g fat (2 g saturated fat), 38 mg cholesterol, 241 mg sodium, 6 g carbohydrate, trace fiber, 10 g protein.

>> HOW TO:

DISJOINT CHICKEN WINGS

1   Place chicken wing on a cutting board. With a sharp knife, cut between the joint at the top of the tip end. Discard tips or use for preparing chicken broth.

2   Take remaining wing and cut between the joints. Proceed with recipe as directed.

NACHO SALSA DIP

Yield: 7 cups.

This zesty dip is great for any get-together and allows me to spend more time with my guests. I always have requests to bring it when my husband and I attend parties.

sally hull // homestead, florida

- 1 **pound ground beef**
- 1/3 **cup chopped onion**
- 2 **pounds process cheese (Velveeta), cubed**
- 1 **jar (16 ounces) chunky salsa**
- 1/4 **teaspoon garlic powder**

Tortilla chips *or* cubed French bread

In a large skillet, cook beef and onion over medium heat until meat is no longer pink; drain well.

Transfer to a greased 3-qt. slow cooker; stir in the cheese, salsa and garlic powder. Cover and cook on low for 3-4 hours or until heated through. Stir; serve warm with tortilla chips or cubed bread.

Nutrition Facts: 1/4 cup equals 143 calories, 10 g fat (6 g saturated fat), 36 mg cholesterolholesterol, 484 mg sodium, 4 g carbohydrate, trace fiber, 9 g protein.

BRIE PHYLLO CUPS

Yield: 15 appetizers.

Mini phyllo shells from the freezer section hurry along these elegant cups. They look fancy and taste delicious but are a snap to put together for a special occasion.

brenda little // boise, idaho

- 1 **package (1.9 ounces) frozen miniature phyllo tart shells**
- 3 **tablespoons crushed gingersnaps**
- 6 **ounces Brie cheese, rind removed, cubed**
- 1/4 **cup spreadable fruit of your choice**

Place the tart shells on an ungreased baking sheet. Sprinkle about 1/2 teaspoon gingersnap crumbs into each shell; top with Brie and spreadable fruit.

Bake at 325° for 5 minutes or until cheese is melted.

Nutrition Facts: 1 phyllo cup equals 83 calories, 4 g fat (2 g saturated fat), 11 mg cholesterol, 100 mg sodium, 7 g carbohydrate, trace fiber, 3 g protein.

FRUIT COMPOTE WITH BRIE

Yield: 8 servings.

This yummy compote is so versatile. I stir it into yogurt or serve it over cheesecake, ice cream, blintzes and crepes. And of course, it makes Brie taste amazing!

clara coulson minney // washington court house, ohio

- 1 **round (8 ounces) Brie cheese**
- 2/3 **cup golden raisins and cherries**
- 1/3 **cup unsweetened apple juice**
- 1 **teaspoon vanilla extract**
- 1 **tablespoon cherry preserves**

Assorted crackers

Place cheese on an ungreased oven-proof serving plate. Bake at 400° for 8-10 minutes or until cheese is softened.

Meanwhile, in a small saucepan, combine the golden raisins and cherries, apple juice and vanilla; bring to a boil. Remove from the heat; stir in preserves. Spoon over cheese. Serve with crackers.

Nutrition Facts: 1 ounce cheese with about 2 tablespoons compote (calculated without crackers) equals 140 calories, 8 g fat (5 g saturated fat), 28 mg cholesterol, 179 mg sodium, 11 g carbohydrate, 1 g fiber, 6 g protein.

taste of home COOKING SCHOOL SECRET

EVERYONE LOVES BRIE

Buttery and with an edible, slightly salty rind, Brie cheese is ideal for pairing with a fruity compote like Clara's, or with the preserves of your choice in Brie Phyllo Cups (facing page).

For a quick serving idea or a picnic, team up Brie with sliced apples or pears, baguette slices and/or water crackers.

You can substitute Camembert in any recipe that calls for Brie. For a flavor treat, look for St. Andre, a French cheese that is even richer and creamier than its Brie cousin. You'll want to enjoy this one with fresh fruit and bread. It's heavenly!

PREPARE MUSHROOMS FOR STUFFING

1   Hold the mushroom cap in one hand and grab the stem with the other hand. Twist to snap off the stem; place caps on a greased baking sheet. Mince or finely chop stems.

2   Spoon chopped stems onto paper towel and squeeze to remove any liquid.

SAUSAGE-STUFFED MUSHROOMS

Yield: 12-15 servings.

This recipe makes a delicious hot appetizer that's always the hit of the party. You can't go wrong with a classic stuffed mushroom.

beatrice vetrano // landenberg, pennsylvania

- 12   **to 15 large fresh mushrooms**
- 2   **tablespoons butter, *divided***
- 2   **tablespoons chopped onion**
- 1   **tablespoon lemon juice**
- 1/4   **teaspoon dried basil**

Salt and pepper to taste

- 4   **ounces bulk Italian sausage**
- 1   **tablespoon chopped fresh parsley**
- 2   **tablespoons dry bread crumbs**
- 2   **tablespoons grated Parmesan cheese**

Remove stems from the mushrooms. Chop stems finely; set mushroom caps aside. Place stems in paper towels and squeeze to remove any liquid.

In a large skillet, heat 1-1/2 tablespoons butter. Cook stems and onion until tender. Add the lemon juice, basil, salt and pepper; cook until almost all the liquid has evaporated. Cool.

In a large bowl, combine the mushroom mixture, sausage and parsley; stuff reserved mushroom caps. Combine crumbs and cheese; sprinkle over tops. Dot each with remaining butter.

Place in a greased baking pan. Bake at 400° for 20 minutes or until sausage is no longer pink, basting occasionally with pan juices. Serve hot.

Nutrition Facts: 1 stuffed mushroom equals 52 calories, 4 g fat (2 g saturated fat), 10 mg cholesterol, 92 mg sodium, 2 g carbohydrate, trace fiber, 2 g protein.

SWEET & SPICY JALAPENO POPPERS

Yield: 1 dozen.

There's no faster way to get a party started than with these bacon-wrapped poppers. Make them ahead and bake just before serving. Everyone will love them.

dawn onuffer // crestview, florida

- 6 **jalapeno peppers**
- 4 **ounces cream cheese, softened**
- 2 **tablespoons shredded cheddar cheese**
- 6 **bacon strips, halved widthwise**
- 1/4 **cup packed brown sugar**
- 1 **tablespoon chili seasoning**

Cut jalapenos in half lengthwise and remove seeds; set aside. In a small bowl, beat cheeses until blended. Spoon into pepper halves. Wrap a half-strip of bacon around each pepper half.

Combine brown sugar and chili seasoning; coat peppers with sugar mixture. Place in a greased 15-in. x 10-in. x 1-in. baking pan.

Bake at 350° for 18-20 minutes or until bacon is firm.

EDITOR'S NOTE: We recommend wearing disposable gloves when cutting hot peppers. Avoid touching your face.

Nutrition Facts: 1 appetizer equals 66 calories, 5 g fat (3 g saturated fat), 15 mg cholesterol, 115 mg sodium, 3 g carbohydrate, trace fiber, 2 g protein. Diabetic Exchange: 1 fat.

GOAT CHEESE CROSTINI

Yield: 32 appetizers.

My husband got the crostini recipe from a friend at work. At first, I thought the flavors wouldn't work well together, but they blend deliciously!

rebecca ebeling // nevada city, california

- 1 **cup crumbled goat cheese**
- 1 **teaspoon minced fresh rosemary**
- 1 **French bread baguette (10-1/2 ounces), cut into 1/2-inch slices and toasted**
- 3 **tablespoons honey**
- 1/4 **cup slivered almonds, toasted**

In a small bowl, combine cheese and rosemary; spoon over toast slices. Drizzle with honey; sprinkle with almonds.

Nutrition Facts: 1 piece equals 76 calories, 4 g fat (2 g saturated fat), 6 mg cholesterol, 92 mg sodium, 9 g carbohydrate, 1 g fiber, 3 g protein. Diabetic Exchanges: 1/2 starch, 1/2 fat.

BACON-ALMOND CROSTINI: Combine 2 cups shredded Monterey Jack cheese, 2/3 cup mayonnaise, 1/2 cup toasted sliced almonds, 6 slices crumbled cooked bacon, 1 chopped green onion and a dash of salt. Spread over toast. Bake for 5-7 minutes or until cheese is melted. Sprinkle with additional almonds if desired.

TURKEY WONTON CUPS

Yield: 4 dozen.

Convenient wonton wrappers make these cute hors d'oeuvres as fun to make as they are to eat. I sampled them at a party and couldn't believe how tasty they were. They disappeared quickly, and no one ever suspected they used light ingredients.
barbara rafferty // portsmouth, rhode island

- **48 wonton wrappers**
- **1-1/4 pounds lean ground turkey**
- **2 cups (8 ounces) shredded reduced-fat cheddar cheese**
- **1 cup fat-free ranch salad dressing**
- **1/2 cup chopped green onions**
- **1/4 cup chopped ripe olives**

Press wonton wrappers into miniature muffin cups coated with cooking spray. (Keep wrappers covered with a damp paper towel until ready to bake.) Bake at 375° for 5 minutes or until lightly browned. Cool for 2 minutes before removing from pans to wire racks.

In a large nonstick skillet coated with cooking spray, cook the turkey over medium heat until no longer pink; drain. In a large bowl, combine the turkey, cheese, ranch dressing, onions and olives. Spoon by rounded tablespoonfuls into wonton cups.

Place on an ungreased baking sheet. Bake at 375° for 5-6 minutes or until heated through. Serve warm.

Nutrition Facts: 2 wonton cups equals 154 calories, 7 g fat (3 g saturated fat), 34 mg cholesterol, 366 mg sodium, 14 g carbohydrate, trace fiber, 11 g protein. Diabetic Exchanges: 1 starch, 1 lean meat, 1/2 fat.

PORK SATAY

Yield: 20 servings.

Cilantro gives this delightful dish freshness, while the sesame oil and Thai chili sauce add layers of Asian flavors that pair perfectly with peanut butter. taste of home test kitchen

- **1/3 cup reduced-sodium soy sauce**
- **2 green onions, sliced**
- **3 tablespoons brown sugar**
- **3 tablespoons minced fresh cilantro**
- **3 tablespoons Thai chili sauce**
- **2 tablespoons sesame oil**
- **2 teaspoons minced garlic**
- **1 pound pork tenderloin, cut into 1/4-inch slices**
- **1/3 cup creamy peanut butter**
- **3 tablespoons hot water**
- **2 teaspoons lime juice**

In a small bowl, combine the first seven ingredients. Set aside 1/4 cup for dipping sauce. Pour remaining sauce into a large resealable plastic bag; add the pork. Seal bag and turn to coat; refrigerate for 30 minutes.

Drain and discard marinade. Thread pork slices onto 20 metal or soaked wooden skewers. Place skewers on a greased 15-in. x 10-in. x 1-in. baking pan. Broil 3-4 in. from the heat for 3-4 minutes on each side or until meat juices run clear.

Meanwhile, for sauce, combine peanut butter and water in a small bowl until smooth. Stir in lime juice and reserved soy sauce mixture. Serve with skewers.

Nutrition Facts: 1 skewer with 1-1/2 teaspoons sauce equals 73 calories, 4 g fat (1 g saturated fat), 13 mg cholesterol, 172 mg sodium, 4 g carbohydrate, trace fiber, 6 g protein. Diabetic Exchanges: 1 lean meat, 1/2 fat.

MEXICAN CHICKEN MEATBALLS

Yield: about 5 dozen.

These low-fat meatballs taste fabulous on their own, but if you want to take things up a notch, serve with a dip of hot Velveeta cheese and salsa. You could also substitute ground white turkey for the chicken. katrina lopes // lyman, south carolina

- 1/2 **cup egg substitute**
- 1 **can (4 ounces) chopped green chilies**
- 1 **cup crushed cornflakes**
- 1 **cup (4 ounces) shredded reduced-fat Mexican cheese blend**
- 1/2 **teaspoon seasoned salt**
- 1/4 **teaspoon cayenne pepper**
- 1 **pound ground chicken**

Salsa, optional

In a large bowl, combine the first six ingredients. Crumble chicken over mixture and mix well. Shape into 1-in. balls. Place on baking sheets coated with cooking spray.

Bake at 375° for 12-15 minutes or until a meat thermometer reads 165° and juices run clear, turning occasionally. Serve with salsa if desired.

Nutrition Facts: 1 meatball (calculated without salsa) equals 21 calories, 1 g fat (trace saturated fat), 6 mg cholesterol, 49 mg sodium, 1 g carbohydrate, trace fiber, 2 g protein.

>> HOW TO:

MAKE MEATBALLS OF EQUAL SIZE

1 Lightly pat meat mixture into a 1-in.-thick rectangle. Cut the rectangle into the same number of squares as meatballs in the recipe.

2 Gently roll each square into a ball.

MARMALADE MEATBALLS

Yield: about 5 dozen.

I brought this snappy recipe to work for a potluck. I started cooking the meatballs in the morning, and by lunch time they were ready. They disappeared fast!
jeanne kiss // greensburg, pennsylvania

- 1 bottle (16 ounces) Catalina salad dressing
- 1 cup orange marmalade
- 3 tablespoons Worcestershire sauce
- 1/2 teaspoon crushed red pepper flakes
- 1 package (32 ounces) frozen fully cooked homestyle meatballs, thawed

In a 3-qt. slow cooker, combine the salad dressing, marmalade, Worcestershire sauce and pepper flakes. Stir in meatballs. Cover and cook on low for 4-5 hours or until heated through.

Nutrition Facts: 1 meatball equals 73 calories, 4 g fat (1 g saturated fat), 12 mg cholesterol, 126 mg sodium, 6 g carbohydrate, trace fiber, 2 g protein. Diabetic Exchanges: 1 fat, 1/2 starch.

PARTY TIME MINI CHEESEBURGERS

Yield: 10 servings.

Kids and adults alike will love the taste of these mini burgers. Juiced up with pickle relish and topped with cheese slices, these sliders will disappear in no time flat! Be sure to make plenty.
taste of home cooking school

- 1 egg, lightly beaten
- 2 tablespoons dill pickle relish
- 2 tablespoons ketchup
- 2 teaspoons Worcestershire sauce
- 2 teaspoons prepared mustard
- 1/4 cup quick-cooking oats
- 1/4 teaspoon pepper
- 1/8 teaspoon garlic powder
- 1 pound ground beef
- 3 to 4 slices process American cheese
- 10 dinner rolls, split

In a large bowl, combine the first eight ingredients. Crumble beef over mixture and mix well. Shape into 10 patties. Broil 3-4 in. from the heat for 4-6 minutes on each side or until a meat thermometer reads 160° and juices run clear.

Meanwhile, using a 1-in. pumpkin-shaped cookie cutter, cut out 10 shapes from cheese slices or cut slices into thirds. Immediately place on burgers; serve on rolls.

Nutrition Facts: 1 mini cheeseburger equals 217 calories, 8 g fat (3 g saturated fat), 65 mg cholesterol, 387 mg sodium, 21 g carbohydrate, 2 g fiber, 13 g protein.

ANTIPASTO PLATTER

Yield: 14-16 servings.

We entertain often, and this is one of our favorite party dishes. It's such a satisfying change from the usual chips and dip. teri lindquist // gurnee, illinois

- 1 jar (24 ounces) pepperoncinis, drained
- 1 can (15 ounces) garbanzo beans or chickpeas, rinsed and drained
- 2 cups halved fresh mushrooms
- 2 cups halved cherry tomatoes
- 1/2 pound provolone cheese, cubed
- 1 can (6 ounces) pitted ripe olives, drained
- 1 package (3-1/2 ounces) sliced pepperoni
- 1 bottle (8 ounces) Italian vinaigrette dressing

Lettuce leaves

In a large bowl, combine the peppers, beans, mushrooms, tomatoes, cheese, olives and pepperoni. Pour vinaigrette over mixture; toss to coat.

Refrigerate for at least 30 minutes or overnight. Arrange on a lettuce-lined platter. Serve with toothpicks.

Nutrition Facts: 1 cup equals 178 calories, 13 g fat (4 g saturated fat), 15 mg cholesterol, 852 mg sodium, 8 g carbohydrate, 2 g fiber, 6 g protein.

taste of home COOKING SCHOOL SECRET

ANTIPASTO IS AMAZING

Loosely meaning "before the pasta" in Italian, antipasto is a delightful and satisfying first course. Mix it up to include your own favorites; there are no rules. Consider these:

- Salami, sopressata or other Italian deli meats
- Fresh mozzarella cheese or traditional (in a block form) mozzarella, cut into small cubes
- Roasted red peppers or pickled cherry peppers
- A blend of olives from your grocery store's olive bar
- Seasoned zucchini or eggplant that you've grilled yourself
- Finely chopped sun-dried tomatoes, basil or parsley

1 Start on the underside by the head area to remove shell from shrimp. Pull legs and first section of shell to one side. Continue pulling shell up around the top and to the other side. Pull off shell by tail if desired.

2 Remove the black vein running down the back of shrimp by making a shallow slit with a paring knife along the back from head area to tail.

3 Rinse shrimp under cold water to remove the vein.

PICKLED SHRIMP

Yield: about 1-1/2 dozen.

I appreciate this appetizer's ease of preparation, especially during the hectic holiday season. The recipe can easily be doubled for a crowd.

kathi nelson // yorba linda, california

- 1/3 **cup olive oil**
- 1/4 **cup red wine vinegar**
- 1 **tablespoon tomato paste**
- 1-1/2 **teaspoons *each* sugar and celery seed**
- 1 **garlic clove, minced**
- 1/2 **teaspoon coarsely ground pepper**
- 1/4 **teaspoon *each* salt and ground mustard**
- 1/8 **teaspoon *each* crushed red pepper flakes and hot pepper sauce**
- 1 **pound cooked large shrimp, peeled and deveined**
- 1 **small onion, thinly sliced and separated into rings**
- 2 **bay leaves**

In a large resealable plastic bag, combine the first 11 ingredients; add the shrimp, onion and bay leaves. Seal bag and turn to coat; refrigerate for up to 24 hours.

Drain and discard marinade, onion and bay leaves. Serve shrimp with toothpicks.

Nutrition Facts: 3 shrimp equals 132 calories, 6 g fat (1 g saturated fat), 115 mg cholesterol, 153 mg sodium, 3 g carbohydrate, trace fiber, 16 g protein.

STEAMED MUSSELS WITH PEPPERS

Yield: 4 servings.

Use the French bread to soak up the deliciously seasoned broth. If you like food zippy, add the jalapeno seeds.
taste of home cooking school

- 2 **pounds fresh mussels, scrubbed and beards removed**
- 1 **jalapeno pepper, seeded and chopped**
- 2 **tablespoons olive oil**
- 3 **garlic cloves, minced**
- 1 **bottle (8 ounces) clam juice**
- 1/2 **cup white wine *or* additional clam juice**
- 1/3 **cup chopped sweet red pepper**
- 3 **green onions, sliced**
- 1/2 **teaspoon dried oregano**
- 1 **bay leaf**
- 2 **tablespoons minced fresh parsley**
- 1/4 **teaspoon *each* salt and pepper**

French bread baguette, sliced, optional

Tap mussels; discard any that do not close. Set aside. In a large skillet, saute jalapeno in oil until tender. Add garlic; cook 1 minute longer. Stir in the clam juice, wine, red pepper, green onions, oregano and bay leaf.

Bring to a boil. Reduce heat; add mussels. Cover and simmer for 5-6 minutes or until mussels open. Discard bay leaf and any unopened mussels. Sprinkle with parsley, salt and pepper. Serve with baguette slices if desired.

EDITOR'S NOTE: We recommend wearing disposable gloves when cutting hot peppers. Avoid touching your face.

Nutrition Facts: 12 mussels and 1/2 cup broth (calculated without baguette) equals 293 calories, 12 g fat (2 g saturated fat), 65 mg cholesterol, 931 mg sodium, 12 g carbohydrate, 1 g fiber, 28 g protein.

STEAMED CLAMS WITH PEPPERS: Substitute clams for the mussels.

DRINKS

LAVENDER LEMONADE

Yield: 6 servings.

Here's a lemonade that's wonderfully aromatic and refreshing! Its grown-up flavor is perfect for a casual get-together with the girls.
nanette hilton // las vegas, nevada

- 2-1/2 **cups water**
- 1 **cup sugar**
- 1 **tablespoon dried lavender flowers**
- 2-1/2 **cups cold water**
- 1 **cup lemon juice**

Ice cubes

In a large saucepan, bring water and sugar to a boil. Remove from the heat; add lavender. Cover and let stand for 1 hour.

Strain, discarding lavender. Stir in cold water and lemon juice. Serve over ice.

EDITOR'S NOTE: Look for dried lavender flowers in spice shops. If using lavender from the garden, make sure it hasn't been treated with chemicals.

Nutrition Facts: 1 cup equals 139 calories, 0 fat (0 saturated fat), 0 cholesterol, trace sodium, 37 g carbohydrate, trace fiber, trace protein.

BLOODY MARYS FOR TWO

Yield: 2 servings.

With a nice level of pepper and just enough dill from the pickle, these Bloody Marys are sure to please. Fun garnishes make them like a meal unto themselves!
jay ferkovich // green bay, wisconsin

- 1-1/2 **cups Clamato juice, chilled**
- 2 **tablespoons dill pickle juice**
- 1 **tablespoon Worcestershire sauce**
- 1/4 **teaspoon celery salt**
- 1/8 to 1/4 **teaspoon pepper**
- 1/8 **teaspoon hot pepper sauce**
- 1/4 **cup vodka, optional**

Ice cubes

- 2 **celery ribs**
- 2 **pepperoni-flavored meat snack sticks**
- 2 **dill pickle spears**
- 2 **pitted ripe olives**

In a small pitcher, combine the first six ingredients. Stir in vodka if desired. Pour into two glasses filled with ice; garnish with celery, snack sticks, pickles and olives.

Nutrition Facts: 1 serving equals 159 calories, 9 g fat (3 g saturated fat), 20 mg cholesterol, 1,740 mg sodium, 14 g carbohydrate, 1 g fiber, 5 g protein.

MIMOSA

Yield: 1 serving.

A standard offering at brunches, Mimosas are as pretty as they are tasty. Make sure the Champagne is extra-dry, so it doesn't overpower the orange juice.

taste of home cooking school

- **2 ounces Champagne *or* other sparkling wine, chilled**
- **1/2 ounce triple sec**
- **2 ounces orange juice**

GARNISH:

Orange slice

Pour Champagne into a champagne flute or wine glass. Pour the triple sec and orange juice into the glass. Garnish as desired.

EDITOR'S NOTE: To make a batch of Mimosas (12 servings), slowly pour one bottle (750 ml) chilled Champagne into a pitcher. Stir in 3 cups orange juice and 3/4 cup triple sec.

Nutrition Facts: 1 serving equals 119 calories, 0 fat (0 saturated fat), 0 cholesterol, 3 mg sodium, 12 g carbohydrate, 0 fiber, trace protein.

BOTTOMS-UP CHERRY LIMEADE

Yield: 8 servings.

My guests enjoy this refreshing cherry-topped drink. It's just right on a hot Southern summer evening. And it's pretty, too.

awynne thurstenson // siloam springs, arkansas

- **3/4 cup lime juice**
- **1 cup sugar**
- **2 liters lime carbonated water, chilled**
- **1/2 cup maraschino cherry juice**
- **8 maraschino cherries with stems**
- **8 lime slices**

In a large bowl, combine lime juice and sugar. Cover and refrigerate. Just before serving, stir carbonated water into lime juice mixture.

For each serving, place 1 tablespoon cherry juice in a glass. Add crushed ice and about 1 cup of lime juice mixture. Garnish with a maraschino cherry and a lime slice.

Nutrition Facts: 1 cup equals 142 calories, trace fat (trace saturated fat), 0 cholesterol, 2 mg sodium, 39 g carbohydrate, 2 g fiber, trace protein.

NEW ENGLAND ICED TEA

Yield: 1 serving.

While growing up in Massachusetts, my family spent summers at our cottage. The clam bakes on the beach would also include these cocktails for the adults.

ann liebergen // brookfield, wisconsin

- 2 **tablespoons sugar**
- 1 **ounce vodka**
- 1 **ounce light rum**
- 1 **ounce gin**
- 1 **ounce triple sec**
- 1 **ounce lime juice**
- 1 **ounce tequila**
- 1 **to 1-1/2 cups ice cubes**
- 2 **ounces cranberry juice**

Lemon slice, optional

In a mixing glass or tumbler, combine the sugar, vodka, rum, gin, triple sec, lime juice and tequila; stir until sugar is dissolved.

Place ice in a highball glass; pour in the sugar mixture. Top with cranberry juice. Garnish with lemon if desired.

Nutrition Facts: 1 serving equals 493 calories, trace fat (trace saturated fat), 0 cholesterol, 4 mg sodium, 47 g carbohydrate, trace fiber, trace protein.

LONG ISLAND ICED TEA: Substitute cola for the cranberry juice.

MARTINI

Yield: 1 serving.

Martinis can be made with either vodka or gin. Our taste panel's preference was for gin, but try them both and decide for yourself. Be warned, this is a strong drink.

taste of home cooking school

Ice cubes

- 3 **ounces gin _or_ vodka**
- 1/2 **ounce dry vermouth**

GARNISH:

Pimiento-stuffed olives

Fill a mixing glass or tumbler three-fourths full with ice. Add gin and vermouth; stir until condensation forms on outside of glass. Strain into a chilled cocktail glass. Garnish as desired.

EDITOR'S NOTE: This recipe makes a dry martini. Use less vermouth for an extra-dry martini; use more for a "wet" martini. You may also serve the martini over ice in a rocks glass.

Nutrition Facts: 1 serving equals 209 calories, 0 fat (0 saturated fat), 0 cholesterol, 5 mg sodium, trace carbohydrate, 0 fiber, 0 protein.

APPLE MARTINI: Omit vermouth and olives. Reduce vodka to 2 ounces and use 1-1/2 ounces sour apple liqueur and 1-1/2 teaspoons lemon juice. Garnish with a green apple slice.

CHOCOLATE MARTINI: Omit vermouth and olives. Reduce vodka to 2 ounces and use 2 ounces crème de cacao or chocolate liqueur. Garnish with chocolate shavings.

SANGRIA

Yield: 9 servings.

Filled with frozen fruit, this fresh blend is a snap to put together and keep cold. And what a thirst-quenching, elegant beverage for summer parties! Serve over ice if desired.

taste of home cooking school

- 1 **bottle (750 milliliters) red Zinfandel** *or* **other dry red wine**
- 2 **cups diet lemon-lime soda**
- 1/2 **cup orange juice**
- 4-1/2 **teaspoons sugar**
- 1 **cup each frozen unsweetened blueberries, raspberries and sliced peaches**

Ice cubes, optional

In a pitcher, stir the wine, soda, orange juice and sugar until sugar is dissolved. Add the frozen fruit. Serve over ice if desired.

Nutrition Facts: 3/4 cup equals 104 calories, trace fat (trace saturated fat), 0 cholesterol, 9 mg sodium, 11 g carbohydrate, 1 g fiber, 1 g protein.

SPARKLING STRAWBERRY LEMONADE

Yield: 2-1/2 quarts.

Three simple ingredients are all you need to create this fresh and fruity summer beverage. It's bound to become a warm-weather favorite.

krista collins // concord, north carolina

- 1 **package (10 ounces) frozen sweetened sliced strawberries, thawed**
- 2 **liters lemon-lime soda, chilled**
- 1 **can (12 ounces) frozen pink lemonade concentrate, thawed**

Place the strawberries in a blender; cover and process until pureed. Pour into a large pitcher; stir in the soda and lemonade concentrate. Serve immediately.

Nutrition Facts: 1-1/4 cups equals 215 calories, trace fat (trace saturated fat), 0 cholesterol, 31 mg sodium, 56 g carbohydrate, 1 g fiber, trace protein.

SCOTCH OLD FASHIONED

Yield: 1 serving.

This cocktail has satisfied the Scotch drinkers for many generations—it's a real classic.

taste of home cooking school

1 orange slice	1/2 to 2/3 cup ice cubes
1 maraschino cherry	2 ounces Scotch
1/2 teaspoon sugar	Splash club soda
3 to 4 dashes bitters	

In a rocks glass, muddle the orange, cherry, sugar and bitters. Add ice. Pour the Scotch and club soda into the glass.

EDITOR'S NOTE: You may substitute bourbon or rye whiskey for the Scotch if desired.

Nutrition Facts: 1 serving equals 176 calories, trace fat (trace saturated fat), 0 cholesterol, 1 mg sodium, 11 g carbohydrate, trace fiber, trace protein.

MOJITO

Yield: 1 serving.

The traditional Mojito is made with rum, which is both pleasant and mildly sweet. The version made with tequila is more tart and has a more distinctive alcohol taste, but is still refreshing.

taste of home cooking school

1 to 2 lime wedges

2 mint sprigs

2 teaspoons confectioners' sugar

3/4 to 1 cup ice cubes

2 ounces light rum

1/2 cup club soda, chilled

GARNISH:

Mint sprig and lime slice

Squeeze lime wedge into a highball glass; drop lime into the glass. Add mint and confectioners' sugar; muddle. Add ice. Pour rum and club soda into glass; stir. Garnish as desired.

Nutrition Facts: 1 cup equals 149 calories, trace fat (trace saturated fat), 0 cholesterol, 2 mg sodium, 5 g carbohydrate, trace fiber, trace protein.

TEQUILA MOJITO: Substitute silver tequila (such as Jose Cuervo Clasico) for the rum.

>> HOW TO:

MUDDLE A DRINK

Place aromatic ingredients like citrus or herbs in the glass. Add a small amount of sugar or bitters. With a muddler, gently crush and bruise the ingredients until their aromas are released. An ice cream scoop is a good stand-in if you do not have a muddler.

FROZEN STRAWBERRY DAIQUIRIS

Yield: 4 servings.

Blend this refreshing pink drink to serve on a hot summer day, for a barbecue or during a Mexican-themed party.
taste of home cooking school

- **3/4 cup rum**
- **1/2 cup thawed limeade concentrate**
- **1 package (10 ounces) frozen sweetened sliced strawberries**
- **1 to 1-1/2 cups ice cubes**

GARNISH:

Fresh strawberries

In a blender, combine the rum, limeade concentrate, strawberries and ice. Cover and process until smooth and thickened (use more ice for thicker daiquiris). Pour into cocktail glasses.

To garnish, cut a 1/2-in. slit into the tip of a strawberry; position berry on rim of glass. Repeat as desired.

Nutrition Facts: 3/4 cup equals 232 calories, trace fat (trace saturated fat), 0 cholesterol, 3 mg sodium, 36 g carbohydrate, 1 g fiber, trace protein.

BRANDY SLUSH

Yield: 21 servings (about 4 quarts slush mix).

This slush with a hint of citrus keeps you cool on warm days. Even if you're not a tea lover, you'll likely find the mix of flavors especially pleasing.
taste of home cooking school

- **4 individual green *or* black tea bags**
- **9 cups water, *divided***
- **2 cups brandy**
- **1 can (12 ounces) frozen lemonade concentrate, thawed**
- **1 can (12 ounces) frozen orange juice concentrate, thawed**

EACH SERVING:

- **1/4 cup lemon-lime soda, chilled**

GARNISH:

Orange *or* lemon slice

Place tea bags in a small bowl. Bring 2 cups water to a boil; pour over tea bags. Cover and steep for 5 minutes. Discard tea bags. Transfer tea to a large pitcher; stir in the brandy, lemonade concentrate, juice concentrate and remaining water. Pour into a 4-qt. freezer container. Freeze overnight or until set.

For each serving, scoop 3/4 cup slush into a rocks glass. Pour lemon-lime soda into the glass; garnish as desired.

Nutrition Facts: 1 serving equals 129 calories, trace fat (trace saturated fat), 0 cholesterol, 8 mg sodium, 20 g carbohydrate, trace fiber, trace protein.

SPICED POMEGRANATE SIPPER

Yield: 16 servings (about 3 quarts).

This warm and festive drink fills the entire house with a wonderful aroma. It's perfect for a party!

lisa renshaw // kansas city, missouri

- 1 **bottle (64 ounces) cranberry-apple juice**
- 2 **cups unsweetened apple juice**
- 1 **cup pomegranate juice**
- 2/3 **cup honey**
- 1/2 **cup orange juice**
- 3 **cinnamon sticks (3 inches)**
- 10 **whole cloves**
- 2 **tablespoons grated orange peel**

In a 5-qt. slow cooker, combine the first five ingredients. Place the cinnamon sticks, cloves and orange peel on a double thickness of cheesecloth; bring up corners of cloth and tie with string to form a bag. Add to slow cooker. Cover and cook on low for 1-2 hours. Discard spice bag.

Nutrition Facts: 3/4 cup equals 131 calories, trace fat (trace saturated fat), 0 cholesterol, 21 mg sodium, 33 g carbohydrate, trace fiber, trace protein. Diabetic Exchanges: 2 fruit.

>> HOW TO:

MAKE A SPICE BAG

1 Use a spice bag or sachet to contain and then easily discard spices, citrus peel, bay leaves or other items after they've flavored the recipe. Place the seasonings on a double thickness of cheesecloth.

2 Bring up the edges of the cheesecloth and tie securely with kitchen string. If you prefer, a cloth tea sachet (available in tea shops) also makes a great spice bag.

MAKE CHOCOLATE CINNAMON STIRRERS

1 When it's time for a coffee break, stir things up...deliciously. Replace spoons with hand-dipped cinnamon sticks that serve as flavorful stirrers.

2 Dip each cinnamon stick in melted chocolate, then coat in your choice of sweet indulgences such as raw sugar, crushed peppermint, and melted caramel or white candy coating.

MEXICAN HOT CHOCOLATE

Yield: 4 servings.

This delicious, not-too-sweet hot chocolate is richly flavored with cocoa and delicately seasoned with spices. The blend of cinnamon and chocolate flavors is wonderful!
kathy young // weatherford, texas

- 1/4 **cup baking cocoa**
- 2 **tablespoons brown sugar**
- 1 **cup boiling water**

Dash ground cloves *or* nutmeg

- 1/4 **teaspoon ground cinnamon**
- 3 **cups milk**
- 1 **teaspoon vanilla extract**

Whipped cream

Whole cinnamon sticks

Combine cocoa and sugar in small saucepan; stir in water. Bring to boil; reduce heat and cook 2 minutes, stirring constantly.

Add the cloves, cinnamon and milk. Simmer 5 minutes (do not boil). Whisk in vanilla. Pour hot chocolate into mugs; top with whipped cream. Use cinnamon sticks for stirrers.

Nutrition Facts: 1 cup equals 156 calories, 7 g fat (4 g saturated fat), 25 mg cholesterol, 92 mg sodium, 18 g carbohydrate, 1 g fiber, 7 g protein.

CHEAT IT: Give Mexican flair to instant hot cocoa from a mix. Stir a little vanilla extract and ground cinnamon into the prepared cocoa. Garnish with canned whipped cream and a sprinkling of nutmeg if desired.

IRISH COFFEE

Yield: 2 servings.

Creme de menthe adds a festive and colorful touch to the cream. If you prefer, simply top the coffee with a dollop of canned whipped cream. This drink would also be delicious with a little Irish cream liqueur stirred in.

taste of home cooking school

- 2 **teaspoons sugar**
- 2 **ounces Irish whiskey**
- 2 **cups hot strong brewed coffee** (**French** *or* **other dark roast**)
- 1/4 **cup heavy whipping cream**
- 1 **teaspoon green creme de menthe**

Divide sugar and whiskey between two mugs; stir in coffee. In a small bowl, beat cream and creme de menthe until thickened. Gently spoon onto tops of drinks, allowing cream to float. Serve immediately.

EDITOR'S NOTE: You may also use a portable mixer with whisk attachment to thicken the cream mixture in a 1-cup measuring cup.

Nutrition Facts: 1 cup equals 203 calories, 11 g fat (7 g saturated fat), 41 mg cholesterol, 21 mg sodium, 8 g carbohydrate, 0 fiber, 1 g protein.

SET UP A SPECIAL A COFFEE SERVICE

1 Let guests dress up individual cups of coffee. Set out containers of cream, sugar cubes, red-hot candies, cinnamon sticks, purchased chocolate or candy stirrers, vanilla and almond extracts, flavored syrups, and ground cinnamon, nutmeg or ginger.

2 Other stir-in ideas include grated chocolate, whipped cream, cocoa powder, chocolate-covered espresso beans, chocolate syrup, or orange and peppermint extracts, and some biscotti for dipping.

3 To flavor an entire pot of coffee, sprinkle coffee grounds with orange or lemon peel or ground cinnamon, nutmeg and ginger before brewing.

4 The flavor of coffee begins to diminish within an hour after it's made, and leaving coffee on the heating element accelerates the process. To keep coffee fresh and hot, transfer it to a carafe or thermos that's been preheated with hot water.

5 Only make as much coffee as needed and avoid reheating coffee, which can make it bitter. For 12 people, you need about 1/4 pound of coffee and 3 quarts water. For 25 people, you need about 1/2 pound of coffee and 1-1/2 gallons water. For best flavor, start with cold, fresh tap water. If your tap water has an off-taste, use bottled water instead.

TEA 101

There are countless teas on the market, yet all of them (except herbal) come from the same plant. Growing conditions, maturity of leaves when picked and processing techniques contribute to each tea's unique flavor.

Tea comes in four basic styles: black, oolong, green and white. **Black** tea, the most familiar, has a robust, full-bodied flavor and dark color that comes from the process of fermenting the tea leaves. **Oolong** is lighter than black but more intensely flavored than green, due to a partial fermentation of the tea leaves.

Because the leaves don't undergo fermentation for green and white teas, the leaves' high antioxidant content stays intact. **Green** tea has a light amber to pale green color and mild, grassy flavor. **White** tea is the lightest of all, made from immature leaves that have not yet had a chance to open. It has the lowest caffeine content.

BREW THE PERFECT CUP

- Bring fresh, cold water just to a boil.
- For black and oolong teas, pour boiling water over tea and let stand for 3 to 5 minutes.
- For green and white teas, pour slightly cooler water (180° to 190°) over tea and let stand for 1 to 3 minutes.
- To keep the brew from becoming bitter, remove the tea bag or infuser when the tea has reached the desired strength.

CHAI TEA

Yield: 4 servings.

Warm up a chilly evening—or any day at all—with this inviting tea. The spices really come through, and it's even more delicious when stirred with a cinnamon stick.
kelly pacowta // danbury, connecticut

- 4 **whole cloves**
- 2 **whole peppercorns**
- 4 **individual tea bags**
- 4 **teaspoons sugar**
- 1/4 **teaspoon ground ginger**
- 1 **cinnamon stick (3 inches)**
- 2-1/2 **cups boiling water**
- 2 **cups milk**

Place cloves and peppercorns in a large bowl; with a muddler or the end of a wooden spoon handle, crush spices until aromas are released.

Add the tea bags, sugar, ginger, cinnamon stick and boiling water. Cover and steep for 6 minutes. Meanwhile, in a small saucepan, heat the milk.

Strain tea, discarding spices and tea bags. Stir in hot milk. Pour into mugs.

Nutrition Facts: 1 cup equals 92 calories, 4 g fat (2 g saturated fat), 12 mg cholesterol, 49 mg sodium, 10 g carbohydrate, trace fiber, 4 g protein.

WASSAIL BOWL PUNCH

Yield: 3-1/2 quarts.

All ages will enjoy this warming punch. The blend of spice, fruit and citrus flavors is scrumptious. You can assemble it before heading out for a winter activity and sip away the chill when you return. It's ready whenever you are.

margaret harms // jenkins, kentucky

4 cups hot brewed tea

4 cups cranberry juice

4 cups unsweetened apple juice

2 cups orange juice

1 cup sugar

3/4 cup lemon juice

3 cinnamon sticks (3 inches)

12 whole cloves

In a 5-qt. slow cooker, combine the first six ingredients. Place the cinnamon sticks and cloves on a double thickness of cheesecloth; bring up corners of cloth and tie with string to form a bag. Add to slow cooker.

Cover and cook on high for 1 hour or until punch begins to boil. Discard spice bag. Serve warm.

Nutrition Facts: 1 cup equals 143 calories, trace fat (trace saturated fat), o cholesterol, 6 mg sodium, 36 g carbohydrate, trace fiber, 1 g protein.

MULLED MERLOT

Yield: 9 servings.

This delightful recipe is sure to warm up your holiday guests! Keeping it ready to serve in the slow cooker means that you can enjoy the party.

taste of home cooking school

4 cinnamon sticks (3 inches)

4 whole cloves

2 bottles (750 milliliters *each*) merlot

1/2 cup sugar

1/2 cup orange juice

1/2 cup brandy

1 medium orange, thinly sliced

Place the cinnamon sticks and the cloves on a double thickness of cheesecloth; bring up corners of cloth and tie with string to form a bag.

In a 3-qt. slow cooker, combine the wine, sugar, orange juice, brandy and orange slices. Add the spice bag. Cover and cook on high for 1 hour or until heated through. Discard the spice bag and orange slices. Serve warm.

Nutrition Facts: 3/4 cup equals 143 calories, trace fat (trace saturated fat), o cholesterol, 4 mg sodium, 15 g carbohydrate, trace fiber, trace protein.

BANANA NOG

Yield: 11 servings (about 2 quarts).

Amaze your friends with this delicious, offbeat take on old-fashioned eggnog. It's well worth the work, and you can make it ahead. Serve it with cookies and store-bought chocolates, and dessert is done!

jennae lefebvre // aurora, illinois

- 3 **cups milk,** *divided*
- 3 **cups half-and-half cream,** *divided*
- 3 **egg yolks**
- 3/4 **cup sugar**
- 3 **large ripe bananas**
- 1/2 **cup light rum**
- 1/3 **cup creme de cacao**
- 1-1/2 **teaspoons vanilla extract**

Whipped cream and baking cocoa, optional

In a heavy saucepan, combine 1-1/2 cups milk, 1-1/2 cups cream, egg yolks and sugar. Cook and stir over medium-low heat until the mixture reaches 160° and is thick enough to coat the back of a spoon.

Place bananas in a food processor; cover and process until blended. Pour milk mixture into a pitcher; stir in the banana puree, rum, creme de cacao, vanilla, and remaining milk and cream. Cover and refrigerate for at least 3 hours before serving. Pour into chilled glasses. Garnish with whipped cream and sprinkle with cocoa if desired.

Nutrition Facts: 3/4 cup (calculated without garnishes) equals 282 calories, 10 g fat (6 g saturated fat), 95 mg cholesterol, 62 mg sodium, 31 g carbohydrate, 1 g fiber, 5 g protein.

CHEAT IT: Substitute 6 cups of eggnog from the dairy case for the milk mixture prepared in the recipe. Stir the banana puree, rum, creme de cacao and vanilla into the eggnog. Garnish as desired.

ORANGE & COFFEE MARTINI

Yield: 1 serving.

With its pretty jeweled color and complementary orange-coffee flavor, this impressive martini lends an elegant, upscale feel to any occasion.

taste of home cooking school

Ice cubes

- 2 **ounces strong brewed coffee, cooled**
- 1 **ounce vodka**
- 1/2 **ounce orange liqueur**
- 1/2 **ounce hazelnut liqueur**

Fill a mixing glass or tumbler three-fourths full with ice cubes. Add remaining ingredients; stir until condensation forms on outside of glass. Strain into a chilled cocktail glass. Serve immediately.

Nutrition Facts: 1 serving equals 172 calories, trace fat (trace saturated fat), 0 cholesterol, 2 mg sodium, 13 g carbohydrate, 0 fiber, trace protein.

CHEAT IT: Make a large batch of martini mix in advance by combining the coffee, vodka and liqueurs. Refrigerate until the party. Come service time, simply measure 1/2 cup of mix into the tumbler for each cocktail you'd like to make.

>> HOW TO:

BUILD A BAR
FOR ENTERTAINING

To build a bar over time, consider offering wine, beer and one signature cocktail each time you entertain. That way, you'll eventually have a variety of spirits on hand. Basic equipment includes a jigger, shaker, strainer and muddler, plus basic glassware: a rocks glass; highball glass; all-purpose wine glass; and cocktail/martini glass. Add other pieces as your budget allows.

ABOUT THE EQUIPMENT

A jigger is a measuring utensil for liquor. Two popular types are a cup with graduated markings (fig. 1) and a two-sided cup (fig. 2), each side measuring a different amount. A jigger is also a unit of measure; however, the standard measure varies from 1 to 2 ounces. A shot (fig. 3) or pony is 1 ounce.

Shakers are available in two basic types: the three-piece shaker (fig. 1), also known as the cobbler or European shaker; and the two-piece shaker (fig. 2), also known as the Boston or American shaker. The three-piece shaker is often used to make martinis. It has a base, a lid and a cap, which has a built-in strainer under it. The two-piece shaker consists of a mixing glass and a metal shaker that fits over the glass. If you use this type of shaker, you should have a separate strainer.

Strainers are in available two basic styles: the Hawthorn strainer (fig. 1) and the Julep strainer (fig. 2). The Hawthorn strainer has a spiral wire around the edge. The wire allows fruit pulp to flow into the drink while keeping out the ice. It fits into the top half of a two-piece shaker. The Julep strainer is a round strainer with holes in the bowl and a handle. It is used with the bottom half of a two-piece shaker.

Muddlers are available on the end of bar spoons (fig. 1) and as a separate tool (fig. 2). Muddlers are used to crush, grind or mash fruit, herbs and sugar.

COMMON BAR GLASSES

Shown from left to right: hurricane glass; rocks glass; pilsner glass; shot glass; cocktail/martini glass.

Shown from left to right: red wine; white wine; all-purpose wine glass; Champagne flute; Collins glass; highball glass.

BETTER THAN TAKEOUT

BUFFALO CHICKEN WRAPS

Yield: 8 servings.

This fuss-free meal is a favorite, with its tender chicken, tortillas, crunchy vegetables and spicy buffalo wing sauce. Feel free to change the veggies to suit your taste.
sarah gottschalk // richmond, indiana

- 1-1/2 **pounds chicken tenderloins**
- 1 **cup buffalo wing sauce,** *divided*
- 8 **lettuce leaves**
- 8 **flour tortillas (10 inches), warmed**
- 16 **bacon strips, cooked**
- 1 **small green pepper, cut into strips**
- 1/2 **cup ranch salad dressing**

In a large skillet, bring chicken and 1/2 cup buffalo wing sauce to a boil. Reduce heat; cover and simmer for 10-12 minutes or until meat is no longer pink. Remove from the heat; cool slightly. Shred chicken with two forks.

Place a lettuce leaf on each tortilla; spoon about 1/2 cup chicken mixture down the center. Top with bacon and green pepper. Drizzle with ranch dressing and remaining buffalo wing sauce; roll up.

Nutrition Facts: 1 wrap equals 449 calories, 18 g fat (4 g saturated fat), 66 mg cholesterol, 1,749 mg sodium, 35 g carbohydrate, 6 g fiber, 30 g protein.

>> HOW TO:

CUT A BELL PEPPER INTO STRIPS

1 Cut the top and bottom from the pepper and discard. Cut each side from pepper by slicing close to the center and then down. Scrape out the seeds and discard.

2 Cut away any ribs.

3 Place the pepper on the work surface and flatten slightly with your hand. Cut lengthwise into thin strips.

≫ BETTER THAN TAKEOUT

BURGERS & MORE

MAKE YOUR OWN GOURMET CONDIMENTS WITH THE HANDY CHART AT RIGHT

- Start with 1/2 cup each of ketchup, mayo or Dijon mustard
- Dress it up with herbs, spices, hot peppers and more
- Team up your gourmet creation with the sandwiches or fries in this section, or follow our suggestions in the chart

FABULOUS FLAVORED KETCHUPS	To 1/2 cup ketchup, add …	Serve with …
Honey BBQ Ketchup	1/2 cup honey 1/4 cup barbecue sauce 1 tablespoon each cider vinegar and molasses	Veggie burgers Grilled hot dogs
Curry Ketchup	1/4 cup each water and curry powder 1/4 teaspoon each paprika and Worcestershire sauce	Grilled sausages and hot dogs Bagel dogs
Sweet 'n' Sassy Ketchup	1/2 cup packed brown sugar 2 tablespoons prepared mustard	Cocktail franks Grilled hot dogs
GOURMET MAYOS	**To 1/2 cup mayonnaise, add …**	**Serve with …**
Parmesan-Dijon Mayo	2 tablespoons grated Parmesan cheese 1 tablespoon Dijon mustard 1/4 teaspoon dill weed	Grilled chicken sandwiches Roasted veggie sticks Sweet potato or potato fries
Easy "Roasted" Garlic Mayo	6 garlic cloves, peeled and microwaved for 20-30 seconds in 1 teaspoon olive oil or until softened 2 tablespoons plain yogurt 2 teaspoons each lemon juice and Dijon mustard 1/4 teaspoon Worcestershire sauce	Roasted veggie sticks Potato fries Burgers Deli sandwiches Tuna salad sandwiches
Jalapeno Aioli	1 whole garlic bulb, top cut off, wrapped in foil and baked at 425° for 30 minutes or until softened 2 jalapeno peppers, minced 1 tablespoon prepared horseradish	Roasted veggie sticks Grilled fish or chicken Chicken fingers
Cookout Mayo	3 tablespoons each ketchup and sweet pickle relish	Burgers and hot dogs Grilled sausages
YUMMY MUSTARDS	**To 1/2 cup Dijon mustard, add …**	**Serve with …**
Honey Mustard	1/2 cup honey 1/4 cup soy sauce 2 teaspoons sugar	Sandwiches Chicken fingers Chicken salad
Party Mustard	1/2 cup mayonnaise 1/4 cup finely chopped onion 2 tablespoons ranch salad dressing mix 1 tablespoon prepared horseradish	Pretzels Breadsticks Deli tray
Maple-Dijon Mustard	1/4 cup maple syrup 1 tablespoon brown sugar 1/2 teaspoon dried parsley flakes	Ham, fish or chicken sandwiches Pretzels Sweet potato or potato fries

PESTO BLTS

Yield: 2 servings.

BLTs are a tasty way to use up those last, languishing garden tomatoes. These BLTs are especially good served on rustic homemade bread.

robyn larabee // lucknow, ontario

- 2 tablespoons mayonnaise
- 1 tablespoon prepared pesto

Dash pepper

- 4 slices whole wheat bread, toasted
- 2 slices Havarti cheese (1 ounce *each*)
- 2 bacon strips, cooked and halved
- 2 lettuce leaves
- 4 slices tomato

In a small bowl, combine the mayonnaise, pesto and pepper. Spread evenly over one side of each slice of toast. On two slices, layer with cheese, bacon, lettuce and tomato; top with remaining toast.

Nutrition Facts: 1 sandwich (prepared with reduced-fat mayonnaise) equals 379 calories, 23 g fat (9 g saturated fat), 40 mg cholesterol, 738 mg sodium, 31 g carbohydrate, 5 g fiber, 16 g protein.

HOT HAM 'N' CHEESE SANDWICHES

Yield: 2 servings.

These sandwiches are so fast and hassle-free that we end up eating them quite often. They're perfect when you're heading out the door or getting home late.

kathy taylor // mason city, iowa

- 2 tablespoons mayonnaise
- 2 kaiser rolls, split
- 1/4 cup shredded cheddar cheese
- 4 slices cooked bacon strips
- 6 slices deli ham (1/2 ounce *each*)
- 1/4 cup shredded part-skim mozzarella cheese

Spread mayonnaise over rolls. Layer roll bottoms with cheddar cheese, bacon, ham and mozzarella cheese; replace tops.

Wrap sandwiches in foil; place on an ungreased baking sheet. Bake at 350° for 15-20 minutes or until cheese is melted.

Nutrition Facts: 1 sandwich (prepared with reduced-fat mayonnaise and reduced-fat cheddar cheese) equals 409 calories, 20 g fat (7 g saturated fat), 53 mg cholesterol, 1,185 mg sodium, 33 g carbohydrate, 1 g fiber, 24 g protein.

>> HOW TO:

PREPARE STUFFED BURGERS

1 Shape the ground beef into eight 4-oz. portions on waxed paper. Using a fork, press each portion into a 4-in. patty.

2 Top four of the patties with the filling. Cover with remaining patties, making sure to encase the filling between the patties.

3 Seal edges with a fork. Grill to desired doneness.

4 The finished burger holds a delectable surprise.

STUFFED BARBECUE BURGERS

Yield: 4 servings.

These big burgers are almost a meal by themselves. With a delectable cheese and vegetable filling, they'll surely satisfy any crowd.

loretta moe // grafton, north dakota

- 2 **pounds ground beef**
- 1 **cup (4 ounces) shredded cheese of your choice**
- 1/3 **cup finely chopped green pepper**
- 1/3 **cup finely chopped tomato**
- 3 **fresh mushrooms, finely chopped**
- 2 **green onions, finely chopped**
- 1/2 **cup barbecue sauce**
- 1 **tablespoon sugar**
- 4 **hamburger buns, split**

Shape beef into eight patties. In a large bowl, combine the cheese, green pepper, tomato, mushrooms and onions. Top half of the patties with vegetable mixture. Cover with the remaining patties and firmly press edges to seal.

Grill, covered, over medium heat or broil 4 in. from the heat for 3 minutes on each side. Brush with barbecue sauce and sprinkle with sugar. Grill, covered, or broil 5-6 minutes longer on each side or until a meat thermometer reads 160°, basting occasionally. Serve the burgers on buns.

Nutrition Facts: 1 burger equals 714 calories, 39 g fat (18 g saturated fat), 180 mg cholesterol, 777 mg sodium, 32 g carbohydrate, 2 g fiber, 56 g protein.

PROSCIUTTO PROVOLONE PANINI

Yield: 4 servings.

For a quick lunch or supper, try this fancy take on grilled cheese sandwiches. They're fast and easy but sophisticated enough for entertaining. You can substitute the fresh sage with 1 tablespoon of Italian seasoning for a tasty variation.

candy summerhill // alexander, arkansas

- 8 **slices white bread**
- 8 **slices provolone cheese**
- 4 **thin slices prosciutto**
- 3 **tablespoons olive oil**
- 3 **tablespoons minced fresh sage**

On four slices of bread, layer a slice of cheese, a slice of prosciutto and a second slice of cheese. Top with remaining bread.

Brush both sides of sandwiches with oil; sprinkle with sage. Cook in a panini maker or indoor grill until bread is toasted and cheese is melted.

Nutrition Facts: 1 panini equals 404 calories, 25 g fat (10 g saturated fat), 42 mg cholesterol, 986 mg sodium, 26 g carbohydrate, 1 g fiber, 19 g protein.

taste of home
COOKING SCHOOL SECRET

WAYS WITH PANINI

In Italy, "panini" means rolls, but the term is also used to describe sandwiches of any kind. In North America, we think of panini as a dressed-up grilled cheese that is made in a panini maker instead of a skillet. Sometimes, our panini may be so loaded with ingredients that it helps to hold them together when we press them between the panini maker's cooking plates!

An indoor grill or panini maker is a great tool for quickly making pretty, restaurant-quality panini at home.

Don't despair if you don't have a panini maker. Your sandwiches will turn out just as delicious when cooked the old-fashioned way, in a skillet with a little oil or butter. If you want to weigh down the panini, do so with a small cast iron skillet as the sandwich cooks. Just be sure the bottom of the skillet is clean and free of rust.

CRANBERRY CHICKEN SALAD SANDWICHES

Yield: 4 servings.

Cubed cooked chicken speeds assembly of these cute and filling chicken salad sandwiches. Dressed up with cranberries and served in dinner rolls, they're ready in no time and make a deliciously different lunch.

sandra sprinkle // anniston, alabama

- 2 **cups cubed cooked chicken breast**
- 1/2 **cup dried cranberries**
- 1/4 **cup finely chopped onion**
- 1/4 **cup chopped celery**
- 1/2 **teaspoon salt**
- 1/4 **teaspoon pepper**
- 6 **tablespoons Miracle Whip Light**
- 8 **dinner rolls**
- 8 **lettuce leaves**

In a small bowl, combine the chicken, cranberries, onion, celery, salt and pepper. Stir in Miracle Whip.

Cut tops off rolls; hollow out each roll, leaving a 1/2-in. shell. Line each with a lettuce leaf; fill with chicken salad. Replace tops.

EDITOR'S NOTE: This recipe was tested with Miracle Whip Light salad dressing.

Nutrition Facts: 2 sandwiches equals 354 calories, 10 g fat (2 g saturated fat), 83 mg cholesterol, 796 mg sodium, 41 g carbohydrate, 3 g fiber, 25 g protein.

SWEET POTATO DIPPERS

Yield: 4 servings.

A rich and creamy dipping sauce accents the delicious flavor of tender sweet potato slices. Leftover sauce can be served with crackers.

cheryl wilt // eglon, west virginia

- 1-1/4 **pounds sweet potatoes (about 2 medium), peeled**
- 1 **tablespoon olive oil**
- 1/4 **teaspoon salt**
- 1/4 **teaspoon pepper**

DIP:

- 3 **ounces fat-free cream cheese**
- 3 **tablespoons reduced-fat sour cream**
- 2 **teaspoons finely chopped green onion**
- 2 **teaspoons finely chopped seeded jalapeno pepper**

GARNISH:

Additional finely chopped green onion, optional

Cut potatoes into 1/8-in. slices. Place in a large bowl. Drizzle with oil. Sprinkle with salt and pepper; toss to coat.

Arrange in a single layer in two ungreased 15-in. x 10-in. x 1-in. baking pans. Bake at 375° for 25-30 minutes or until golden brown, turning once.

In a small bowl, beat dip ingredients. Serve with potatoes. Garnish with additional onion if desired.

EDITOR'S NOTE: We recommend wearing disposable gloves when cutting hot peppers. Avoid touching your face.

Nutrition Facts: 1 cup dippers with 2 tablespoons dip equals 155 calories, 5 g fat (1 g saturated fat), 5 mg cholesterol, 280 mg sodium, 23 g carbohydrate, 3 g fiber, 5 g protein. Diabetic Exchanges: 1-1/2 starch, 1 fat.

EGGPLANT SNACK STICKS

Yield: 8 servings.

Coated with Italian seasoning and Parmesan cheese, the veggie sticks are broiled so there's no guilt when you crunch into them.
mary murphy // atwater, california

- 1 **medium eggplant (1-1/4 pounds)**
- 1/2 **cup toasted wheat germ**
- 1/2 **cup grated Parmesan cheese**
- 1 **teaspoon Italian seasoning**
- 3/4 **teaspoon garlic salt**
- 1/2 **cup egg substitute**

Cooking spray

- 1 **cup meatless spaghetti sauce, warmed**

Cut eggplant lengthwise into 1/2-in.-thick slices, then cut each slice lengthwise into 1/2-in. strips. In a shallow dish, combine the wheat germ, cheese, Italian seasoning and garlic salt. Dip eggplant sticks in egg substitute, then coat with wheat germ mixture. Arrange in a single layer on a baking sheet coated with cooking spray.

Spritz eggplant with cooking spray. Broil 4 in. from the heat for 3 minutes. Remove from oven; turn sticks and spritz with cooking spray. Broil 2 minutes longer or until golden brown. Serve with spaghetti sauce.

Nutrition Facts: 4 sticks with 2 tablespoons sauce equals 85 calories, 3 g fat (1 g saturated fat), 5 mg cholesterol, 440 mg sodium, 10 g carbohydrate, 3 g fiber, 7 g protein. Diabetic Exchange: 1 starch.

TURKEY REUBENS

Yield: 2 servings.

I have always enjoyed Reuben sandwiches, and I started to make them with smoked turkey a few years ago. These are good to make in summer, when you don't want to heat up the kitchen.
jo ann dalrymple // claremore, oklahoma

- 4 **slices pumpernickel** *or* **rye bread**
- 2 **tablespoons Thousand Island salad dressing**
- 6 **ounces sliced deli smoked turkey**
- 1/2 **cup sauerkraut, rinsed and well drained**
- 2 **slices Swiss cheese**
- 2 **teaspoons butter, softened**

Spread two slices of bread with salad dressing. Layer with turkey, sauerkraut and cheese; top with remaining bread. Butter the outsides of sandwiches.

In a large skillet, toast sandwiches for 3-4 minutes on each side or until heated through.

Nutrition Facts: 1 sandwich equals 411 calories, 19 g fat (8 g saturated fat), 70 mg cholesterol, 1,443 mg sodium, 29 g carbohydrate, 4 g fiber, 29 g protein.

SWEET POTATO WEDGES WITH CHILI MAYO

Yield: 8 servings.

Try this delicious way of enjoying sweet potatoes. It is a great combination of flavors. The spicy seasoning of the mayo sauce pairs well with the delicate taste of sweet potatoes.
raymonde bourgeois // swastika, ontario

- **6 small sweet potatoes, peeled**
- **2 tablespoons olive oil**
- **2 to 3 tablespoons Cajun seasoning**
- **1 cup mayonnaise**
- **4 teaspoons lemon juice**
- **2 teaspoons chili powder *or* chili garlic sauce**
- **2 teaspoons Dijon mustard**

Cut each sweet potato lengthwise into eight wedges; place in two greased 15-in. x 10-in. x 1-in. baking pans. Drizzle with oil. Sprinkle with Cajun seasoning; toss to coat.

Bake at 400° for 30-45 minutes or until tender, turning once. Meanwhile, in a small bowl, combine the remaining ingredients; serve with potatoes.

Nutrition Facts: 6 wedges with 2 tablespoons sauce equals 322 calories, 26 g fat (4 g saturated fat), 10 mg cholesterol, 600 mg sodium, 22 g carbohydrate, 3 g fiber, 2 g protein.

VEGETARIAN BURGERS

Yield: 8 servings.

These do not taste like hamburgers, but they are so good! I made them for my family many years ago when I first became a vegetarian.
julie ferron // wauwatosa, wisconsin

- **3/4 cup unsalted sunflower kernels**
- **1 can (15 ounces) garbanzo beans *or* chickpeas, rinsed and drained**
- **2 cups shredded carrots**
- **1 cup chopped onion**
- **1/2 cup whole wheat flour**
- **2 tablespoons canola oil**
- **8 hamburger buns, optional**
- **Lettuce and tomato slices, optional**

Place sunflower kernels in a food processor; cover and process until ground. Remove and set aside. Place beans in food processor; cover and process until ground. In a large bowl, combine the sunflower kernels, beans, carrots, onion, flour and oil. Shape 1/2 cupfuls into patties.

In a nonstick skillet coated with cooking spray, cook the patties over medium heat for 3 minutes on each side or until lightly browned and crisp. Serve on rolls with lettuce and tomato if desired.

Nutrition Facts: 1 burger equals 195 calories, 11 g fat (1 g saturated fat), 0 cholesterol, 81 mg sodium, 21 g carbohydrate, 6 g fiber, 6 g protein.

RANCH TURKEY WRAPS

Yield: 4 servings.

These hand-held sandwiches make a nice lunch or quick dinner on the go. A great thing about wraps is that, like sandwiches, you can customize each one to suit your taste. emily hanson // logan, utah

- 1/4 **cup cream cheese, softened**
- 1/4 **cup prepared ranch salad dressing**
- 4 **flour tortillas (10 inches), warmed**
- 3/4 **pound sliced deli turkey**
- 8 **slices Monterey Jack cheese**
- 1 **medium ripe avocado, peeled and sliced**
- 1 **medium tomato, sliced**

In a small bowl, beat cream cheese and salad dressing until smooth. Spread over tortillas. Layer with turkey, cheese, avocado and tomato. Roll up tightly; cut in half.

Nutrition Facts: 1 wrap equals 661 calories, 37 g fat (14 g saturated fat), 96 mg cholesterol, 1,719 mg sodium, 41 g carbohydrate, 9 g fiber, 35 g protein.

>> HOW TO:

PIT AND SLICE AN AVOCADO

1 Wash avocado. Cut in half lengthwise, cutting around the pit. Twist halves in opposite directions to separate.

2 Slip a tablespoon under the pit to loosen it from the fruit.

3 To remove avocado flesh from the skin, loosen it from the skin with a large spoon and scoop out.

4 Slice the peeled avocado as desired. Or cut into unpeeled wedges and slide a spoon between the flesh and the skin.

PORTOBELLO BURGERS

Yield: 2 servings.

These grilled portobello mushroom burgers taste like the classic with a meatless twist.

theresa sabbagh // winston-salem, north carolina

- 2 tablespoons balsamic vinegar
- 1 tablespoon olive oil
- 3 garlic cloves, minced
- 1-1/2 teaspoons minced fresh basil *or* 1/2 teaspoon dried basil
- 1-1/2 teaspoons minced fresh oregano *or* 1/2 teaspoon dried oregano

Dash salt

Dash pepper

- 2 large portobello mushrooms, stems removed
- 2 slices reduced-fat provolone cheese
- 2 hamburger buns, split
- 2 lettuce leaves
- 2 slices tomato

In a small bowl, whisk the first seven ingredients. Add mushroom caps; let stand for 15 minutes, turning twice. Drain and reserve marinade.

Moisten a paper towel with cooking oil; using long-handled tongs, lightly coat the grill rack. Grill mushrooms, covered, over medium heat or broil 4 in. from the heat for 6-8 minutes on each side or until tender, basting with reserved marinade. Top with cheese during the last 2 minutes.

Serve on buns with lettuce and tomato.

Nutrition Facts: 1 burger equals 280 calories, 13 g fat (3 g saturated fat), 10 mg cholesterol, 466 mg sodium, 31 g carbohydrate, 3 g fiber, 11 g protein. Diabetic Exchanges: 2 starch, 1-1/2 lean meat, 1 fat.

>> HOW TO:

START A CHARCOAL GRILL (THREE METHODS)

1 **Pyramid Style:** Arrange briquettes in a pyramid in the grill; pour lighter fluid over briquettes. Recap the fluid and place away from grill. Light briquettes.

2 **Electric Starter:** Arrange briquettes in a pyramid in the grill. Insert electric starter in the middle of coals. Plug starter into an outlet. If using an extension cord, use a heavy-duty one. It will take 8 to 10 minutes for ash to form on the coals. At that point, unplug the electric starter and remove it from briquettes. The starter will be very hot, so place it out of the way on a heatproof surface. Continue heating briquettes until they are covered with a light gray ash.

3 **Chimney Starter:** Crumple newspaper or waxed paper and place a chimney starter over the paper on the grill. Fill the starter with briquettes. Light paper. When coals are ready, dump them out of the chimney starter and spread out.

BEEF GYROS

Yield: 5 servings.

Going out to restaurants for gyros can be expensive, so I came up with this homemade version. Usually, I set out the fixings so everyone can assemble their own.

sheri scheerhorn // hills, minnesota

- 1 cup ranch salad dressing
- 1/2 cup chopped seeded peeled cucumber
- 1 pound beef top sirloin steak, cut into thin strips
- 2 tablespoons olive oil
- 5 whole pita breads, warmed
- 1 medium tomato, chopped
- 1 can (2-1/4 ounces) sliced ripe olives, drained
- 1/2 small onion, thinly sliced
- 1 cup (4 ounces) crumbled feta cheese
- 2-1/2 cups shredded lettuce

In a bowl, combine salad dressing and cucumber; set aside. In a large skillet, cook beef in oil over medium heat until no longer pink.

Layer half of each pita with steak, tomato, olives, onion, cheese, lettuce and dressing mixture. Fold each pita over filling; secure with toothpicks.

Nutrition Facts: 1 gyro equals 654 calories, 41 g fat (9 g saturated fat), 57 mg cholesterol, 1,086 mg sodium, 41 g carbohydrate, 3 g fiber, 30 g protein.

ZUCCHINI FRIES FOR 2

Yield: 2 servings.

I often make these fries for my husband and myself—especially when our garden is full of zucchini. The cornmeal coating gives them a nice crunch.

sarah gottschalk // richmond, indiana

- 2 **small zucchini**
- 1 **egg white**
- 1/4 **cup all-purpose flour**
- 3 **tablespoons cornmeal**
- 1/2 **teaspoon** *each* **salt, garlic powder, chili powder, paprika and pepper**

Cooking spray

Marinara *or* spaghetti sauce, warmed

Cut zucchini into 3-in. x 1/2-in. x 1/2-in. pieces. In a shallow bowl, whisk egg white. In another shallow bowl, combine the flour, cornmeal and seasonings. Dip zucchini in egg white, then roll in flour mixture.

Place zucchini on a baking sheet coated with cooking spray; spray with additional cooking spray. Bake at 425° for 18-22 minutes or until golden brown, turning once. Serve with marinara sauce.

Nutrition Facts: 1 serving (calculated without sauce) equals 98 calories, 1 g fat (trace saturated fat), 0 cholesterol, 414 mg sodium, 19 g carbohydrate, 3 g fiber, 5 g protein. Diabetic Exchanges: 1 starch, 1 vegetable.

GREEK-STYLE CHICKEN BURGERS

Yield: 4 servings.

The original recipe for these burgers called for lamb or beef, but I decided to try ground chicken to decrease the fat. The sauce easily doubles as a great dip for veggies and toasted pita chips.

judy puskas // wallaceburg, ontario

- 1/2 **cup fat-free plain yogurt**
- 1/4 **cup chopped peeled cucumber**
- 1/4 **cup crumbled reduced-fat feta cheese**
- 1-1/2 **teaspoons snipped fresh dill**
- 1-1/2 **teaspoons lemon juice**
- 1 **small garlic clove, minced**

BURGERS:

- 1 **medium onion, finely chopped**
- 1/4 **cup dry bread crumbs**
- 1 **tablespoon dried oregano**
- 1 **tablespoon lemon juice**
- 2 **garlic cloves, minced**
- 1/2 **teaspoon salt**
- 1/4 **teaspoon pepper**
- 1 **pound ground chicken**
- 4 **hamburger buns, split**
- 4 **lettuce leaves**
- 4 **tomato slices**

Line a strainer with four layers of cheesecloth or one coffee filter and place over a bowl. Place yogurt in prepared strainer; cover yogurt with edges of cheesecloth. Refrigerate for 8 hours or overnight.

Remove yogurt from cheesecloth and discard liquid from bowl. Stir in the cucumber, feta cheese, dill, lemon juice and garlic; set aside.

In a small bowl, combine the onion, bread crumbs, oregano, lemon juice, garlic, salt and pepper. Crumble chicken over mixture and mix well. Shape into four burgers.

Moisten a paper towel with cooking oil; using long-handled tongs, lightly coat the grill rack. Grill burgers, covered, over medium heat or broil 4 in. from the heat for 5-7 minutes on each side or until a meat thermometer reads 165° and juices run clear.

Serve each on a bun with lettuce, tomato and 2 tablespoons yogurt sauce.

Nutrition Facts: 1 burger equals 350 calories, 12 g fat (4 g saturated fat), 78 mg cholesterol, 732 mg sodium, 35 g carbohydrate, 3 g fiber, 27 g protein. Diabetic Exchanges: 3 lean meat, 2 starch, 1 vegetable.

PARMESAN CHICKEN SANDWICHES

Yield: 2 servings.

For a casual meal, this fast and flavorful sandwich can't be beat. The tender chicken breasts are coated with seasoned bread crumbs and smothered in marinara sauce. Served on a hoagie, it's a real treat!
sue bosek // whittier, california

- **2 boneless skinless chicken breast halves (5 ounces *each*)**
- 1/8 **teaspoon salt**
- 1/8 **teaspoon pepper**
- 1/2 **cup all-purpose flour**
- 1 **egg, lightly beaten**
- 3/4 **cup seasoned bread crumbs**
- 3 **tablespoons grated Parmesan cheese**
- 2 **tablespoons olive oil**
- 2 **slices provolone cheese (1 ounce *each*)**
- 2 **Italian rolls, split lengthwise**
- 1/3 **cup marinara sauce *or* meatless spaghetti sauce**

Flatten chicken to 1/2-in. thickness; sprinkle both sides with salt and pepper. Place flour and egg in separate shallow bowls. In another bowl, combine bread crumbs and cheese. Dip chicken in flour, then egg; roll in crumb mixture.

In a large skillet, cook chicken in oil over medium heat for 4-5 minutes on each side or until no longer pink. Layer chicken and cheese on bun bottoms; spread with marinara sauce. Replace tops.

Nutrition Facts: 1 sandwich equals 721 calories, 30 g fat (10 g saturated fat), 210 mg cholesterol, 1,037 mg sodium, 57 g carbohydrate, 3 g fiber, 51 g protein.

SOURDOUGH CHICKEN SANDWICHES: Prepare chicken as directed. Spread four slices sourdough bread with mayonnaise if desired; top two slices with a lettuce leaf, a slice of Swiss cheese, tomato slice, 1 bacon strip cooked and cut in half, and the chicken breast. Top with remaining bread.

PEPPERY PARSNIP FRIES

Yield: 8 servings.

Looking for creative ways to use parsnips? These crispy bites are a healthier, more interesting take on popular french fries.
sandy abrams // greenville, new york

- **8 medium parsnips, peeled**
- **1 tablespoon olive oil**
- **1/4 cup grated Parmesan cheese**
- **1/2 teaspoon salt**
- **1/4 teaspoon pepper**
- **1/8 teaspoon ground nutmeg**

Cut parsnips lengthwise into 2-1/2-in. x 1/2-in. sticks. In a large resealable plastic bag, combine the oil, Parmesan cheese, salt, pepper and nutmeg. Add parsnips, a few sticks at a time, and shake to coat.

Line two 15-in. x 10-in. x 1-in. baking pans with foil; coat the foil with cooking spray. Place parsnips in a single layer in pans. Bake at 425° for 20-25 minutes or until tender, turning several times.

Nutrition Facts: 1/2 cup equals 156 calories, 3 g fat (1 g saturated fat), 2 mg cholesterol, 210 mg sodium, 31 g carbohydrate, 6 g fiber, 3 g protein. Diabetic Exchange: 2 starch.

TWO-TONE POTATO WEDGES

Yield: 4 servings.

These baked, two-tone fries are a flavorful, zesty crowd-pleaser. They're so easy, they'll be on the dinner table in no time.

maria nicolau schumacher // larchmont, new york

- 2 **medium potatoes**
- 1 **medium sweet potato**
- 1 **tablespoon olive oil**
- 1/4 **teaspoon salt**
- 1/4 **teaspoon pepper**
- 1 **tablespoon grated Parmesan cheese**
- 2 **garlic cloves, minced**

Cut each potato and the sweet potato into eight wedges; place in a large resealable plastic bag. Add the oil, salt and pepper; seal bag and shake to coat. Arrange in a single layer in a 15-in. x 10-in. x 1-in. baking pan coated with cooking spray.

Bake, uncovered, at 425° for 20 minutes. Turn potatoes; sprinkle with cheese and garlic. Bake 20-25 minutes longer or until golden brown, turning once.

Nutrition Facts: 6 each equals 151 calories, 4 g fat (1 g saturated fat), 1 mg cholesterol, 176 mg sodium, 27 g carbohydrate, 3 g fiber, 3 g protein. Diabetic Exchanges: 1-1/2 starch, 1 fat.

PESTO-TURKEY LAYERED LOAF

Yield: 6 servings.

This yummy sandwich is easy and travels well. Make several to feed a crowd, and use any meat, veggies and cheese you like. marion sundberg // yorba linda, california

- 1 **loaf (1 pound) French bread**
- 1 **cup prepared pesto**
- 1 **pound thinly sliced deli turkey**
- 1/2 **pound provolone cheese, thinly sliced**
- 2 **small zucchini, thinly sliced**
- 2 **medium tomatoes, thinly sliced**
- 1 **medium red onion, thinly sliced**

Cut the top fourth off loaf of bread. Carefully hollow out the bottom, leaving a 1/2-in. shell. (Discard removed bread or save for another use.) Spread pesto on the inside of top and bottom of bread. Set top aside.

In bottom of bread, layer the turkey, cheese, zucchini, tomatoes and onion. Gently press the layers together. Replace bread top and wrap tightly in foil.

Place on a baking sheet. Bake at 350° for 25-30 minutes or until heated through. Let stand for 10 minutes before cutting.

Nutrition Facts: 1 serving equals 661 calories, 33 g fat (13 g saturated fat), 73 mg cholesterol, 2,065 mg sodium, 54 g carbohydrate, 4 g fiber, 39 g protein.

MUSHROOM BACON BURGERS

Yield: 4-5 servings.

I grill a lot in the summer. Food just tastes better, and cleanup is much easier. This recipe is a delicious way to dress up plain hamburgers.

gail kuntz // dillon, montana

- 1 can (4 ounces) mushroom stems and pieces, drained
- 4 bacon strips, cooked and crumbled
- 2 tablespoons diced green onions
- 1 teaspoon Worcestershire sauce
- 1 teaspoon soy sauce
- 1/2 teaspoon salt
- 1 pound ground beef
- 4 to 5 hamburger buns

Tomato slices, optional

In a large bowl, combine the first six ingredients. Crumble beef over mixture and mix well. Shape into four or five patties.

Grill, covered, over medium-hot heat or broil 4 in. from the heat for 5-6 minutes on each side or until a meat thermometer reads 160° and juices run clear. Serve on buns with tomato if desired.

Nutrition Facts: 1 burger equals 313 calories, 15 g fat (6 g saturated fat), 64 mg cholesterol, 709 mg sodium, 18 g carbohydrate, 1 g fiber, 23 g protein.

>> HOW TO:

BUY AND HANDLE GROUND BEEF

Ground beef is often labeled using the cut of meat that it is from, such as ground chuck or ground round. (Ground beef comes from a combination of beef cuts.)

Ground beef can also be labeled according to the fat content of the ground mixture or the percentage of lean meat to fat, such as 85% or 90% lean. The higher the percentage, the leaner the meat. Purchase the amount you need: 1 pound of ground beef serves 3 to 4.

Handle the mixture as little as possible when shaping hamburgers, meat loaves or meatballs to keep the final product light in texture. Wash your hands after handling any raw meat.

CHICAGO-STYLE STUFFED PIZZA

Yield: 8 slices.

I rate this hearty double-crust pizza as excellent. Favorite fillings are tucked inside, and tasty tomato sauce tops the pie.

edie despain // logan, utah

- 1 **teaspoon active dry yeast**
- 1 **cup warm water** (110° to 115°)
- 2 **tablespoons canola oil**
- 2 **teaspoons sugar**
- 1-1/2 **teaspoons salt**
- 2-1/2 **to 3 cups all-purpose flour**
- 1/2 **cup yellow cornmeal**
- 1/2 **pound bulk Italian sausage**
- 1 **small green pepper, diced**
- 1 **small onion, diced**
- 3 **garlic cloves, peeled and sliced**
- 2 **cups (8 ounces) shredded part-skim mozzarella cheese**
- 1/3 **cup chopped pepperoni**
- 1/4 **cup grated Parmesan cheese**
- 1 **teaspoon dried oregano**
- 1/4 **cup tomato sauce**

In a large bowl, dissolve yeast in warm water. Stir in the oil, sugar and salt. Add 1-1/2 cups flour and cornmeal; beat until smooth. Stir in enough remaining flour to form a soft dough.

Turn onto a floured surface; knead until smooth and elastic, about 4-5 minutes. Place in a greased bowl; turn once to grease top. Cover and let rise in a warm place until doubled, about 1 hour.

Punch dough down; let rest for 5 minutes. Divide into two portions, one slightly larger than the other. On a lightly floured surface, roll out larger portion to a 12-in. circle. Press onto the bottom and up the sides of a greased 10-in. ovenproof skillet.

In a large skillet, cook the sausage, green pepper and onion over medium heat until meat is no longer pink. Add garlic; cook 1 minute longer. Drain. Stir in the mozzarella cheese, pepperoni, Parmesan cheese and oregano. Spread over crust.

On a lightly floured surface, roll remaining dough into an 11-in. circle. Place over pizza; seal edges. Cut four slits in top. Bake at 375° for 30-35 minutes or until crust is golden brown. Spread with tomato sauce.

Nutrition Facts: 1 slice equals 379 calories, 16 g fat (6 g saturated fat), 35 mg cholesterol, 906 mg sodium, 41 g carbohydrate, 2 g fiber, 17 g protein.

>> HOW TO:

MIX YEAST DOUGH (TRADITIONAL METHOD)

1 Heat liquid to 110° to 115°, using a thermometer. Measure liquid and place in a large mixing bowl. Add active dry yeast; stir until dissolved.

2 Add sugar, salt, fat, eggs (if using) and about half of the flour. Beat with an electric mixer or by hand until smooth.

3 Gradually stir in enough of the remaining flour by hand to form a dough of consistency stated in the recipe.

THREE-CHEESE SPINACH CALZONES

Yield: 4 servings.

My Italian mother used to whip up these yummy dough pockets when I came home from school for lunch. They're easy to pick up and dip in sauce.

marie rizzio // interlochen, michigan

- 1 **package (10 ounces) frozen chopped spinach, thawed and squeezed dry**
- 1 **cup (4 ounces) shredded fontina cheese**
- 1/2 **cup part-skim ricotta cheese**
- 1/2 **cup crumbled Gorgonzola cheese**
- 3 **green onions, chopped**
- 1/4 **teaspoon salt**
- 1/8 **teaspoon pepper**
- 1 **tube (13.8 ounces) refrigerated pizza crust**
- 1 **egg, lightly beaten**
- 1 **teaspoon water**
- 1 **cup spaghetti sauce, warmed**

In a small bowl, combine the first seven ingredients. On a lightly floured surface, unroll pizza crust into an 11-in. square. Cut into four squares. Transfer to a greased baking sheet. Spoon spinach mixture over half of each square to within 1/2 in. of edges.

For each calzone, fold one corner over filling to the opposite corner, forming a triangle; press edges with a fork to seal. Cut slits in top. Combine egg and water; brush over calzones.

Bake at 375° for 12-15 minutes or until golden brown. Serve with spaghetti sauce.

Nutrition Facts: 1 calzone with 1/4 cup sauce equals 549 calories, 22 g fat (11 g saturated fat), 109 mg cholesterol, 1,637 mg sodium, 59 g carbohydrate, 5 g fiber, 28 g protein.

PIZZA-STYLE TOSSED SALAD

Yield: 8 servings.

If you love pizza, you'll adore this salad that tastes just like pizza in a bowl. It's like the salad you'd get at a pizzeria, but without the expense.

pat habiger // spearville, kansas

- 1 **package (10 ounces) Italian blend salad greens**
- 1 **cup (4 ounces) shredded part-skim mozzarella cheese**
- 1 **package (3-1/2 ounces) sliced pepperoni**
- 1 **can (2-1/4 ounces) sliced ripe olives, drained**
- 1/2 **cup Italian salad dressing**
- 1 **cup onion and garlic seasoned salad croutons**

In a large salad bowl, combine the greens, mozzarella cheese, pepperoni and olives. Drizzle with dressing; toss to coat. Sprinkle with croutons.

Nutrition Facts: 1 cup equals 188 calories, 15 g fat (5 g saturated fat), 19 mg cholesterol, 688 mg sodium, 6 g carbohydrate, 1 g fiber, 7 g protein.

THAI CHICKEN PIZZAS

Yield: 4 servings.

A delicate peanut-flavored sauce is topped with cheese, fresh Asian veggies and juicy chunks of chicken to give these unique individual pizzas a deliciously different taste. One bite and this Asian-inspired pizza pie will become a favorite.

taste of home cooking school

- 4 **prebaked mini pizza crusts**
- 3/4 **cup Thai-style peanut sauce**
- 2 **tablespoons creamy peanut butter**
- 1 **to 2 cups shredded *or* cubed cooked chicken**
- 4 **green onions, sliced**
- 1 **cup shredded Italian cheese blend**
- 1/2 **cup canned bean sprouts**
- 1/2 **cup shredded carrot**
- 1/2 **cup sweet red pepper strips**
- 2 **tablespoons chopped cilantro**
- 1 **tablespoon chopped roasted peanuts, optional**

Place crusts on an ungreased 15-in. x 10-in. x 1-in. baking pan. In a small bowl, stir together peanut sauce and peanut butter. Spread over crusts. Top with chicken. Sprinkle with green onions and cheese.

Bake at 425° for 10-15 minutes or until edges are lightly browned and cheese is bubbly. Top with bean sprouts, carrot, red pepper, cilantro and peanuts if desired.

Nutrition Facts: 1 pizza (calculated without peanuts) equals 738 calories, 32 g fat (9 g saturated fat), 51 mg cholesterol, 1,949 mg sodium, 76 g carbohydrate, 5 g fiber, 38 g protein.

BUTTERY PARMESAN GARLIC BREAD

Yield: 4 servings.

Here's a golden-brown crusty loaf that will round out all kinds of dinners in just minutes!

talena keeler // siloam springs, arkansas

- 1/4 **cup butter, softened**
- 2 **tablespoons shredded Parmesan cheese**
- 1 **teaspoon garlic powder**
- 1 **loaf (8 ounces) French bread, halved lengthwise**

In a small bowl, combine the butter, cheese and garlic powder. Spread mixture over cut sides of bread. Place on an ungreased baking sheet.

Bake at 400° for 10-12 minutes or until golden brown. Serve warm.

Nutrition Facts: 1 slice equals 277 calories, 13 g fat (8 g saturated fat), 32 mg cholesterol, 492 mg sodium, 33 g carbohydrate, 1 g fiber, 8 g protein.

KICKIN' HAWAIIAN PIZZA

Yield: 12 pieces.

Pineapple adds pizzazz and honey lends a touch of sweetness to the sauce in this wonderful recipe.

john weakland // lacey, washington

        4   **plum tomatoes, coarsely chopped**
        1   **can (6 ounces) tomato paste**
    1/4   **cup water**
    1/4   **cup chopped roasted sweet red pepper**
        1   **tablespoon dried oregano**
        1   **tablespoon honey**
        2   **teaspoons dried minced garlic**
        2   **teaspoons paprika**
        1   **teaspoon salt**
    1/4   **teaspoon crushed red pepper flakes**
        2   **tubes (13.8 ounces *each*) refrigerated pizza crust**
        2   **cups (8 ounces) shredded part-skim mozzarella cheese**
        1   **cup (4 ounces) shredded Romano cheese**
        1   **package (3-1/2 ounces) sliced pepperoni**
        1   **cup pineapple tidbits, drained**

For sauce, place the first 10 ingredients in a food processor; cover and process until blended. Transfer to a small saucepan; heat through.

Meanwhile, press pizza dough into a greased 15-in. x 10-in. x 1-in. baking pan; build up edges slightly and seal seam. Bake at 425° for 6-8 minutes or until lightly browned.

Spread 1-3/4 cups sauce over crust (refrigerate remaining sauce for another use). Sprinkle with 1 cup mozzarella and 1/2 cup Romano; top with pepperoni, pineapple and remaining cheeses.

Bake for 14-18 minutes or until cheese is melted and crust is golden brown.

Nutrition Facts: 1 slice equals 294 calories, 10 g fat (4 g saturated fat), 20 mg cholesterol, 860 mg sodium, 38 g carbohydrate, 2 g fiber, 14 g protein.

PIZZA CARBONARA

Yield: 4-6 servings.

Convenient refrigerated pizza crust is dressed up with a creamy Parmesan sauce and a topping of Monterey Jack cheese, bacon and green onions in this tasty recipe. It's a deliciously different addition to any pizza party.

sherry keethler // lake st. louis, missouri

1 tube (13.8 ounces) **refrigerated pizza crust**

1/3 cup finely chopped onion

1 tablespoon butter

2 garlic cloves, minced

1 tablespoon all-purpose flour

1/8 teaspoon white pepper

1 cup milk

1/4 teaspoon chicken bouillon granules

1/4 cup grated Parmesan cheese

1/2 pound sliced bacon, cooked and crumbled

1-1/2 cups (6 ounces) shredded Monterey Jack cheese

3 green onions, thinly sliced

Unroll pizza crust. Press onto a greased 12-in. pizza pan; build up edges slightly. Prick dough thoroughly with a fork. Bake at 425° for 7-10 minutes or until lightly browned.

Meanwhile, in a large saucepan, saute onion in butter until tender. Add garlic; cook 1 minute longer. Stir in flour and pepper until blended. Gradually add milk and bouillon. Bring to a boil; cook and stir for 2 minutes or until thickened. Reduce heat; stir in Parmesan cheese. Spread over hot crust. Sprinkle with bacon, Monterey Jack cheese and green onions.

Bake at 425° for 8-12 minutes or until cheese is melted. Let stand for 5 minutes before cutting.

Nutrition Facts: 1 slice equals 417 calories, 21 g fat (10 g saturated fat), 48 mg cholesterol, 903 mg sodium, 36 g carbohydrate, 1 g fiber, 19 g protein.

CHICKEN FAJITA PIZZA

Yield: 6 slices.

Add a fiesta of flavor to homemade pizza with this Italian twist on fajitas. Salsa lovers will be wild about it. Toss together a salad to serve on the side.
iola egle // bella vista, arkansas

1/4 cup lime juice

3 tablespoons olive oil, *divided*

2 garlic cloves, minced

1 pound boneless skinless chicken breasts, finely chopped

1 prebaked 12-inch pizza crust

1 jar (16 ounces) chunky salsa, drained

1 small sweet red pepper, chopped

1/4 cup chopped green pepper

1 green onion, chopped

1-1/2 cups (6 ounces) shredded Mexican cheese blend

Sour cream, optional

In a resealable plastic bag, combine the lime juice, 2 tablespoons oil and garlic. Add the chicken; seal bag and turn to coat. Refrigerate for 15 minutes.

Drain and discard marinade. In a large skillet, saute chicken in remaining oil until no longer pink.

Place crust on an ungreased pizza pan; spread with salsa to within 1/2 in. of edges. Layer with chicken, peppers, onion and cheese.

Bake at 450° for 8-10 minutes or until cheese is melted. Serve with sour cream if desired.

Nutrition Facts: 1 slice (calculated without sour cream) equals 446 calories, 20 g fat (7 g saturated fat), 67 mg cholesterol, 890 mg sodium, 37 g carbohydrate, trace fiber, 29 g protein.

PORK FRIED RICE

Yield: 2 servings.

Here's an all-time classic scaled down for two. The peas and carrots add color and crunch to this savory dinner.

peggy vaught // glasgow, west virginia

- 1 **boneless pork loin chop (6 ounces), cut into 1/2-inch pieces**
- 1/4 **cup finely chopped carrot**
- 1/4 **cup chopped fresh broccoli**
- 1/4 **cup frozen peas**
- 1 **green onion, chopped**
- 1 **tablespoon butter**
- 1 **egg, lightly beaten**
- 1 **cup cold cooked long grain rice**
- 4-1/2 **teaspoons reduced-sodium soy sauce**
- 1/8 **teaspoon garlic powder**
- 1/8 **teaspoon ground ginger**

In a large skillet, saute the pork, carrot, broccoli, peas and onion in butter until pork is no longer pink. Remove from skillet and set aside.

In same skillet, cook and stir egg over medium heat until completely set. Stir in the rice, soy sauce, garlic powder, ginger and pork mixture; heat through.

Nutrition Facts: 1 cup equals 338 calories, 13 g fat (6 g saturated fat), 163 mg cholesterol, 597 mg sodium, 29 g carbohydrate, 2 g fiber, 24 g protein. Diabetic Exchanges: 3 lean meat, 2 starch.

COCONUT SHRIMP WITH DIPPING SAUCE

Yield: 5 servings.

With crispy coconut-cilantro breading and a sweet apricot sauce, these delicious shrimp would be great for any occasion, from an appetizer party to a weeknight dinner.

taste of home cooking school

- 1 **can (14 ounces) light coconut milk,** *divided*
- 1 **jalapeno pepper, seeded and chopped**
- 1/4 **cup minced fresh cilantro**
- 1-1/4 **pounds uncooked medium shrimp**
- 3/4 **cup all-purpose flour**
- 4 **egg whites**
- 3/4 **cup panko (Japanese) bread crumbs**
- 3/4 **cup flaked coconut, lightly toasted**
- 1/3 **cup reduced-sugar apricot preserves**
- 1 **teaspoon spicy brown mustard**

Place 2 tablespoons coconut milk in a small bowl; cover and refrigerate. In a large resealable plastic bag, combine the jalapeno, cilantro and remaining coconut milk. Peel and devein shrimp, leaving tails on. Add to bag; seal and turn to coat. Refrigerate for 1 hour.

Place flour in a shallow bowl. In another bowl, lightly beat the egg whites. In a third bowl, combine bread crumbs and coconut. Drain and discard marinade. Dip shrimp in flour and egg whites, then roll in crumb mixture.

Place on a baking sheet coated with cooking spray. Bake at 400° for 7-9 minutes on each side or until lightly browned. Meanwhile, for dipping sauce, add preserves and mustard to the reserved coconut milk. Serve with shrimp.

EDITOR'S NOTE: We recommend wearing disposable gloves when cutting hot peppers. Avoid touching your face.

Nutrition Facts: about 10 shrimp with 5 teaspoons sauce equals 324 calories, 11 g fat (8 g saturated fat), 168 mg cholesterol, 316 mg sodium, 30 g carbohydrate, 1 g fiber, 23 g protein.

COCONUT SHRIMP WITH PLUM SAUCE: Substitute red plum jam for the apricot preserves.

>> HOW TO:

CUT A JALAPENO

With gloves on, cut the jalapeno in half. Remove the seeds with the tip of a spoon or knife; discard seeds. Chop the jalapeno as directed in the recipe.

RAMEN-VEGETABLE BEEF SKILLET

CHEAT IT!

Yield: 4 servings.

This combination of ingredients is unique and flavorful. Using ramen noodles makes it affordable.

marlene mcallister // portland, michigan

- 1 pound ground beef
- 1-1/2 cups sliced fresh carrots
- 3/4 cup sliced onion
- 1 cup water
- 1 cup shredded cabbage
- 1 cup sliced fresh mushrooms
- 1 cup chopped green pepper
- 3 tablespoons soy sauce
- 1 package (3 ounces) beef ramen noodles

In a large skillet, cook the beef, carrots and onion over medium heat until meat is no longer pink and carrots are crisp-tender; drain.

Add the water, cabbage, mushrooms, green pepper, soy sauce and the contents of seasoning packet from the noodles. Break noodles into small pieces; add to pan. Cover and cook for 10 minutes or until liquid is absorbed and noodles are tender.

Nutrition Facts: 1-1/2 cups equals 379 calories, 18 g fat (8 g saturated fat), 86 mg cholesterol, 1,202 mg sodium, 24 g carbohydrate, 3 g fiber, 29 g protein.

TERIYAKI PORK TENDERLOIN

Yield: 8 servings.

I've made this pleasantly seasoned pork several times for company and received many compliments on it. The recipe is so easy.

debora brown // st. leonard, maryland

- 1/2 cup soy sauce
- 1/4 cup olive oil
- 4 teaspoons brown sugar
- 2 teaspoons ground ginger
- 1 teaspoon pepper
- 2 garlic cloves, minced
- 4 pork tenderloins (3/4 to 1 pound *each*)

Coarsely ground pepper, optional

In a large resealable plastic bag, combine the first six ingredients; add pork. Seal bag and turn to coat; refrigerate for 4 hours, turning occasionally.

Drain and discard marinade. Grill the tenderloins, covered, over indirect medium-hot heat for 25-40 minutes or until a meat thermometer reads 160°. Sprinkle with pepper if desired.

Nutrition Facts: 6 ounces cooked pork equals 216 calories, 6 g fat (2 g saturated fat), 95 mg cholesterol, 859 mg sodium, 3 g carbohydrate, trace fiber, 36 g protein.

BEEF CHOW MEIN

Yield: 2 servings.

This is my basic recipe for stir-fry. I've tried others but always come back to this one. I have also substituted chicken and chicken broth and found it just as good.

margery bryan // moses lake, washington

- 4 **teaspoons cornstarch**
- 1 **teaspoon sugar**
- 4 **teaspoons soy sauce**
- 1 **garlic clove, minced**
- 1/2 **pound beef tenderloin, cut into thin strips**
- 1 **tablespoon canola oil**
- 2 **cups assorted fresh vegetables**
- 1/3 **cup beef broth**

Chow mein noodles *or* **hot cooked rice**

In a large bowl, combine the first four ingredients. Add beef; toss to coat. In a large skillet or wok, stir-fry beef in oil until no longer pink; remove and keep warm.

Reduce heat to medium. Add vegetables and broth; stir-fry for 4 minutes. Return beef to the pan; cook and stir for 2 minutes or until heated through. Serve with chow mein noodles or rice.

Nutrition Facts: 1 serving (prepared with reduced-sodium soy sauce; calculated without rice) equals 296 calories, 16 g fat (4 g saturated fat), 70 mg cholesterol, 643 mg sodium, 12 g carbohydrate, 1 g fiber, 26 g protein. Diabetic Exchanges: 3 lean meat, 2 vegetables, 2 fat.

GINGERED PEPPER STEAK

Yield: 4 servings.

When my mother-in-law shared this recipe with me, she said it cooks up in no time...and she was right! This wonderful meal is a treat even for those not watching their diets.

susan adair // somerset, kentucky

- 2 **teaspoons sugar**
- 2 **teaspoons cornstarch**
- 1/4 **teaspoon ground ginger**
- 1/4 **cup reduced-sodium soy sauce**
- 1 **tablespoon white wine vinegar**
- 1 **pound beef flank steak, thinly sliced**
- 2 **medium green peppers, julienned**
- 1 **teaspoon canola oil**

Hot cooked rice, optional

In a large bowl, combine the sugar, cornstarch, ginger, soy sauce and vinegar until smooth. Add beef and toss to coat; set aside.

In a large skillet or wok, stir-fry green peppers in oil until crisp-tender. Remove and keep warm. Add beef with marinade to pan; stir-fry for 3 minutes or until meat reaches desired doneness. Return peppers to pan; heat through. Serve steak over rice if desired.

Nutrition Facts: 1 cup (calculated without rice) equals 236 calories, 10 g fat (0 saturated fat), 59 mg cholesterol, 579 mg sodium, 10 g carbohydrate, 0 fiber, 26 g protein. Diabetic Exchanges: 3 lean meat, 2 vegetable.

BAKED EGG ROLLS

Yield: 8 servings.

These egg rolls are low in fat but the crispiness from baking will fool you into thinking they were fried!

barbara lierman // lyons, nebraska

Cooking spray

- 2 **cups grated carrots**
- 1 **can (14 ounces) bean sprouts, drained**
- 1/2 **cup chopped water chestnuts**
- 1/4 **cup chopped green pepper**
- 1/4 **cup chopped green onions**
- 1 **garlic clove, minced**
- 2 **cups finely diced cooked chicken**
- 4 **teaspoons cornstarch**
- 1 **tablespoon water**
- 1 **tablespoon light soy sauce**
- 1 **teaspoon canola oil**
- 1 **teaspoon brown sugar**

Pinch cayenne pepper

- 16 **egg roll wrappers**

Coat a large skillet with cooking spray; add the next six ingredients. Cook and stir over medium heat until vegetable are crisp-tender, about 3 minutes. Add chicken; heat through.

In a small bowl, combine the cornstarch, water, soy sauce, oil, brown sugar and cayenne until smooth; stir into chicken mixture. Bring to a boil. Cook and stir for 2 minutes or until thickened; remove from the heat.

Spoon 1/4 cup of chicken mixture on the bottom third of one egg roll wrapper; fold sides toward center and roll tightly. (Keep remaining wrappers covered with a damp paper towel until ready to use.) Place seam side down on a baking sheet coated with cooking spray. Repeat.

Spray tops of egg rolls with cooking spray. Bake at 425° for 10-15 minutes or until lightly browned.

Nutrition Facts: 2 egg rolls equals 261 calories, 3 g fat (0 saturated fat), 27 mg cholesterol, 518 mg sodium, 45 g carbohydrate, 0 fiber, 13 g protein. Diabetic Exchanges: 3 starch, 1 lean meat.

EFFORTLESS EGG ROLLS: Thaw and chop 1 pound frozen stir-fry vegetable blend; cook in a large skillet with 1 pound bulk pork sausage until meat is no longer pink. Stir in 2 tablespoons teriyaki sauce. Fill and bake egg rolls as directed.

CASHEW CHICKEN

Yield: 6 servings.

The cashews add crunch and a sweet, nutty flavor to this recipe. The tasty sauce adds richness to garden-fresh carrots and broccoli.

ena quiggle // goodhue, minnesota

- 1/2 **cup rice vinegar**
- 1/2 **cup sherry**
- 2 **tablespoons sesame oil**
- 2 **teaspoons garlic powder**
- 1-1/2 **pounds skinless boneless chicken, cubed**
- 3 **tablespoons canola oil**
- 3 **cups fresh broccoli florets**
- 1 **cup thinly sliced carrots**
- 2 **teaspoons cornstarch**
- 1/3 **cup soy sauce**
- 1/3 **cup hoisin sauce**
- 1 **tablespoon ground ginger**
- 1 **cup roasted salted cashews**

Hot cooked rice

Combine the first four ingredients. Pour half into a large resealable plastic bag; add chicken. Seal bag and turn to coat; refrigerate 2 hours. Refrigerate remaining marinade.

Discard marinade from chicken. In a wok or large skillet, stir-fry chicken in canola oil for 2-3 minutes or until no longer pink. With a slotted spoon, remove chicken and set aside.

In the same skillet, stir-fry broccoli and carrots for 3 minutes or until crisp-tender. Combine the cornstarch, soy sauce, hoisin sauce, ginger and reserved marinade until smooth; gradually stir into vegetables. Bring to a boil; cook and stir for 1-2 minutes or until thickened. Stir in cashews and chicken; heat through. Serve with rice.

Nutrition Facts: 1 cup equals 454 calories, 27 g fat (5 g saturated fat), 63 mg cholesterol, 1,282 mg sodium, 19 g carbohydrate, 3 g fiber, 31 g protein.

>> HOW TO:

STIR-FRY

1 Chop and measure all ingredients, keeping them close at hand. Begin by stir-frying the meat, poultry or seafood in a small amount of oil.

2 When it's cooked through, remove the meat from the skillet. Cover and keep warm. Stir-fry the vegetables, adding more oil if necessary.

3 Return meat to the pan, add sauce mixture and heat through. Add any last-minute ingredients like peanuts, cilantro or sesame seeds.

TURKEY AND BLACK BEAN ENCHILADAS

Yield: 8 servings.

Hearty and satisfying, these slimmed-down enchiladas with whole-wheat tortillas have a moist and delicious filling you'll love.

sarah burleson // spruce pine, north carolina

- **2 cans (15 ounces *each*) black beans, rinsed and drained, *divided***
- **1 pound lean ground turkey**
- **1 medium green pepper, chopped**
- **1 small onion, chopped**
- **1 can (15 ounces) enchilada sauce, *divided***
- **1 cup (4 ounces) shredded reduced-fat Mexican cheese blend, *divided***
- **8 whole wheat tortillas (8 inches), warmed**

In a small bowl, mash 1 can black beans; set aside. In a large nonstick skillet, cook the turkey, pepper and onion over medium heat until meat is no longer pink; drain. Add the mashed beans, remaining beans, half of the enchilada sauce and 1/2 cup cheese; heat through.

Place 2/3 cupfuls of bean mixture down the center of each tortilla. Roll up and place seam side down in two 11-in. x 7-in. baking dishes coated with cooking spray.

Pour remaining enchilada sauce over the top; sprinkle with remaining cheese. Bake, uncovered, at 425° for 15-20 minutes or until heated through.

Nutrition Facts: 1 enchilada equals 363 calories, 11 g fat (3 g saturated fat), 55 mg cholesterol, 808 mg sodium, 42 g carbohydrate, 7 g fiber, 24 g protein.

BARBECUE CHICKEN BURRITOS

Yield: 4 servings.

I always have the ingredients for these on hand. My husband came up with this recipe, and it turned out to be a hit!

amy dando // apalachin, new york

- 1/2 **pound boneless skinless chicken breasts, cut into 1/2-inch cubes**
- 1-1/2 **cups julienned green peppers**
- 1 **cup chopped onion**
- 4 **tablespoons canola oil,** *divided*
- 1/2 **cup barbecue sauce**
- 1-1/2 **cups (6 ounces) shredded Mexican cheese blend**
- 4 **flour tortillas (10 inches),** **warmed**

Lime wedges, sour cream, shredded lettuce and chopped tomatoes, optional

In a large skillet, cook the chicken, green peppers and onion in 2 tablespoons oil over medium heat for 6-8 minutes or until chicken is no longer pink. Stir in barbecue sauce. Bring to a boil. Reduce heat; simmer for 1 minute.

Sprinkle cheese down center of each tortilla; top with chicken mixture. Fold sides and ends over filling and roll up; seal burritos with toothpicks.

In a large skillet, brown burritos in remaining oil on all sides over medium heat. Discard toothpicks. Serve burritos with lime wedges, sour cream, lettuce and tomatoes if desired.

Nutrition Facts: 1 burrito equals 608 calories, 33 g fat (12 g saturated fat), 69 mg cholesterol, 1,008 mg sodium, 42 g carbohydrate, 8 g fiber, 28 g protein.

TACO PLATE FOR TWO

Yield: 2 servings.

My husband and I enjoy splitting this two-serving taco plate and don't have to worry about leftovers. But the recipe is easy to double if needed.

sue ross // casa grande, arizona

- 1/2 **pound ground beef**
- 1/2 **cup chopped onion**
- 1/3 **cup taco sauce**
- 1/4 **cup chopped green chilies**
- 1/4 **teaspoon salt**
- 1 **cup crushed tortilla chips**
- 1/2 **cup shredded cheddar cheese**

In a large skillet, cook beef and onion over medium heat until meat is no longer pink; drain. Stir in the taco sauce, chilies and salt. Cover and cook over medium-low heat for 6-8 minutes or until heated though. Spoon over chips; sprinkle with cheese.

Nutrition Facts: 1 serving equals 501 calories, 28 g fat (12 g saturated fat), 105 mg cholesterol, 956 mg sodium, 29 g carbohydrate, 3 g fiber, 32 g protein.

BEAN 'N' RICE BURRITOS

Yield: 8 servings.

These hearty and zippy burritos can be whipped up in a jiffy.
kim hardison // maitland, florida

- 1-1/2   **cups water**
- 1-1/2   **cups uncooked instant brown rice**
- 1   **medium green pepper, diced**
- 1/2   **cup chopped onion**
- 1   **tablespoon olive oil**
- 1   **teaspoon minced garlic**
- 1   **tablespoon chili powder**
- 1   **teaspoon ground cumin**
- 1/8   **teaspoon crushed red pepper flakes**
- 1   **can (15 ounces) black beans, rinsed and drained**
- 8   **flour tortillas (8 inches), warmed**
- 1   **cup salsa**

Reduced-fat shredded cheddar cheese and reduced-fat sour cream, optional

In a small saucepan, bring water to a boil. Add rice. Return to a boil. Reduce heat; cover and simmer for 5 minutes. Remove from the heat. Let stand for 5 minutes or until water is absorbed.

Meanwhile, in a large skillet, saute green pepper and onion in oil for 3-4 minutes or until tender. Add garlic; cook 1 minute longer. Stir in the chili powder, cumin and pepper flakes until combined. Add beans and rice; cook and stir for 4-6 minutes or until heated through.

Spoon about 1/2 cup of filling off-center on each tortilla; top with 2 tablespoons salsa. Fold sides and ends over filling and roll up. Serve with cheese and sour cream if desired.

Nutrition Facts: 1 burrito (calculated without cheese and sour cream) equals 290 calories, 6 g fat (1 g saturated fat), 0 cholesterol, 504 mg sodium, 49 g carbohydrate, 4 g fiber, 9 g protein.

HOME-STYLE REFRIED BEANS

Yield: 2-2/3 cups.

Lime juice, cumin and cayenne pepper make these beans so tasty, particularly when compared to the canned variety. I like to dress them up with reduced-fat cheese and salsa.
myra innes // auburn, kansas

- 2/3   **cup finely chopped onion**
- 4   **teaspoons canola oil**
- 4   **garlic cloves, minced**
- 1   **teaspoon ground cumin**
- 1/2   **teaspoon salt**
- 1/4   **teaspoon cayenne pepper**
- 2   **cans (15 ounces *each*) pinto beans, rinsed and drained**
- 1/2   **cup water**
- 4   **teaspoons lime juice**

In a large saucepan, saute onion in oil until tender. Stir in the garlic, cumin, salt and cayenne; cook and stir for 1 minute. Add beans and mash. Add water; cook and stir until heated through and water is absorbed. Remove from the heat; stir in lime juice.

Nutrition Facts: 1/3 cup equals 123 calories, 3 g fat (trace saturated fat), 0 cholesterol, 290 mg sodium, 19 g carbohydrate, 5 g fiber, 5 g protein. Diabetic Exchanges: 1 starch, 1 lean meat, 1/2 fat.

CHICKEN FINGER TACOS FOR TWO

Yield: 2 servings.

Using chicken fingers in this recipe makes for the perfect size taco and also cuts down on prep time. I like to pair it with Spanish rice and refried beans for a complete meal for two.

kathy williams // layton, utah

- 1 **egg, lightly beaten**
- 1/2 **cup seasoned bread crumbs**
- 1/4 **teaspoon salt**
- 1/8 **teaspoon pepper**
- 4 **chicken tenderloins**
- 1 **tablespoon canola oil**
- 4 **corn tortillas (6 inches), warmed**
- 1/2 **cup shredded cheddar cheese**

Salsa, sour cream, guacamole, chopped tomatoes, shredded lettuce and fresh cilantro leaves, optional

Place egg in a shallow bowl. In another shallow bowl, combine the bread crumbs, salt and pepper. Dip chicken in egg, then roll in bread crumb mixture.

In a large skillet over medium heat, cook chicken in oil for 5-7 minutes or until no longer pink. Serve on tortillas with cheese and optional ingredients if desired.

Nutrition Facts: 2 tacos (prepared with reduced-fat shredded cheddar cheese; calculated without optional ingredients) equals 403 calories, 17 g fat (5 g saturated fat), 119 mg cholesterol, 775 mg sodium, 38 g carbohydrate, 3 g fiber, 28 g protein.

>> **HOW TO:**

TRIM CILANTRO

To easily trim cilantro (or flat-leaf parsley) from its stems, hold the bunch, then angle the blade of a chef's knife almost parallel with the stems. With short, downward strokes, shave off the leaves where they meet the stems.

SOUPS

WILD RICE SOUP

Yield: 8 servings (about 2 quarts).

I tasted this thick and hearty soup at a food fair that I helped judge. The original recipe called for uncooked wild rice, but I use a quick-cooking rice blend.
kathy herink // gladbrook, iowa

- **1 pound ground beef**
- **2 cups chopped celery**
- **2 cups chopped onion**
- **3 cups water**
- **1 can (14-1/2 ounces) chicken broth**
- **1 can (10-3/4 ounces) condensed cream of mushroom soup, undiluted**
- **1 package (6.75 ounces) quick-cooking long grain and wild rice mix**
- **5 bacon strips, cooked and crumbled**

In a large saucepan, cook the beef, celery and onion over medium heat until meat is no longer pink and vegetables are tender; drain.

Add the water, broth, soup, rice and contents of the seasoning packet. Bring to a boil. Reduce heat; cover and simmer for 5 minutes. Garnish with bacon.

Nutrition Facts: 1 cup equals 268 calories, 11 g fat (4 g saturated fat), 43 mg cholesterol, 909 mg sodium, 25 g carbohydrate, 2 g fiber, 17 g protein.

SAUSAGE PIZZA SOUP

Yield: 4 servings.

Here's a healthy take on ooey-gooey sausage pizza. You won't believe how delicious this soup really is.
beth sherer // milwaukee, wisconsin

- **1/2 pound Italian turkey sausage links, casings removed**
- **1 medium zucchini, sliced**
- **1 cup sliced fresh mushrooms**
- **1 small onion, chopped**
- **1 can (14-1/2 ounces) no-salt-added diced tomatoes**
- **1 cup water**
- **1 cup reduced-sodium chicken broth**
- **1 teaspoon dried basil**
- **1/4 teaspoon pepper**

Minced fresh basil and crushed red pepper flakes, optional

In a large saucepan, cook the sausage, zucchini, mushrooms and onion over medium heat until meat is no longer pink; drain. Add the tomatoes, water, broth, dried basil and pepper. Bring to a boil. Reduce heat; simmer, uncovered, for 15 minutes. Sprinkle with fresh basil and pepper flakes if desired.

Nutrition Facts: 1 cup equals 128 calories, 5 g fat (1 g saturated fat), 34 mg cholesterol, 528 mg sodium, 9 g carbohydrate, 3 g fiber, 12 g protein. Diabetic Exchanges: 2 vegetable, 1 medium-fat meat.

FRENCH ONION SOUP

Yield: 9 servings (2-1/4 quarts).

I've also made this savory soup in a slow cooker for a fuss-free meal. It cooks on low for 3 to 4 hours.

denise hruz // germantown, wisconsin

- 1/4 **cup butter, cubed**
- 4 **large onions, sliced**
- 1/4 **cup sugar**
- 2 **tablespoons all-purpose flour**
- 2 **cans (14-1/2 ounces *each*) reduced-sodium beef broth**
- 2 **cans (10-1/2 ounces *each*) condensed French onion soup**
- 2 **cups water**
- 1/2 **cup grated Parmesan cheese**
- 9 **slices French bread (1/2 inch thick)**
- 9 **tablespoons shredded part-skim mozzarella cheese**

In a Dutch oven over medium-high heat, melt butter. Add onions; saute until tender. Add sugar; cook and stir until lightly browned. Stir in flour until blended; gradually add the broth, soup and water. Bring to a boil. Reduce heat; cover and simmer for 10 minutes. Stir in Parmesan cheese.

Meanwhile, place bread on a baking sheet. Broil 4 in. from the heat for 2 minutes on each side or until toasted. Sprinkle with mozzarella; broil for 2 minutes or until cheese is melted. Ladle soup into bowls; top each with a cheese toast.

Nutrition Facts: 1 cup equals 192 calories, 9 g fat (5 g saturated fat), 26 mg cholesterol, 875 mg sodium, 22 g carbohydrate, 2 g fiber, 7 g protein.

DRESS UP CANNED SOUP

You can up the nutrition and make any soup feel special by adding these homemade touches:

- Microwave or boil your favorite vegetables until tender; add to beef, vegetable or chicken soup
- Cut tortillas into thin strips and stir them into soup for an instant noodle effect
- Add cubed cooked sausage to bean or potato soup
- Stir cooked tortellini and your favorite herbs into tomato soup

BACON-BEEF BARLEY SOUP

Yield: 7 servings.

Here's a hearty dish that's perfect for hungry boys! Served over creamy mashed potatoes, this quick, comforting soup will really hit the spot.

cathy peterson // menominee, michigan

4 **bacon strips, chopped**	2 **cans (14-1/2 ounces** *each*) **beef broth**
1-1/2 **pounds beef stew meat, cut into 1/2-inch pieces**	1 **can (14-1/2 ounces) diced tomatoes with basil, oregano and garlic, undrained**
1 **medium onion, chopped**	
4 **medium red potatoes, cut into 1/2-inch cubes**	1 **jar (12 ounces) home-style beef gravy**
1-1/2 **cups fresh baby carrots, cut in half lengthwise**	1/2 **teaspoon pepper**
1 **cup frozen corn**	**Mashed potatoes, optional**
1/4 **cup medium pearl barley**	

In a large skillet, cook bacon over medium heat until crisp. Using a slotted spoon, remove to paper towels to drain. In the drippings, cook beef until meat is no longer pink; drain.

In a 5-qt. slow cooker, layer the potatoes, carrots, corn and barley. Top with beef mixture and bacon. Combine the broth, tomatoes, gravy and pepper; pour over top (do not stir).

Cover and cook on low for 8 to 10 hours or until meat and vegetables are tender. Stir before serving. Serve over mashed potatoes if desired.

Nutrition Facts: 1-1/3 cups (calculated without mashed potatoes) equals 319 calories, 10 g fat (3 g saturated fat), 68 mg cholesterol, 1,218 mg sodium, 32 g carbohydrate, 4 g fiber, 26 g protein.

SCOTCH BROTH

Yield: 6-8 servings (2 quarts).

Early in winter, I make up big pots of this soup to freeze in plastic containers. Then I can bring out one or two containers at a time. I heat the frozen soup in a saucepan on low all morning. By lunchtime, it's hot and ready to serve!

ann main // moorefield, ontario

- 2 **pounds meaty beef soup bones (beef shanks** *or* **short ribs)**
- 8 **cups water**
- 6 **whole peppercorns**
- 1-1/2 **teaspoons salt**
- 1 **cup chopped carrots**
- 1 **cup chopped turnips**
- 1 **cup chopped celery**
- 1/2 **cup chopped onion**
- 1/4 **cup medium pearl barley**

In a Dutch oven, combine soup bones, water, peppercorns and salt. Cover and simmer for 2-1/2 hours or until the meat comes easily off the bones.

Remove bones. Strain broth; cool and chill. Skim off fat. Remove meat from bones; dice and return to broth along with remaining ingredients. Bring to a boil. Reduce heat; cover and simmer about 1 hour or until vegetables and barley are tender.

Nutrition Facts: 1 cup equals 155 calories, 7 g fat (3 g saturated fat), 35 mg cholesterol, 499 mg sodium, 9 g carbohydrate, 2 g fiber, 15 g protein.

UPSTATE MINESTRONE

Yield: 8 servings.

If you love vegetables, you'll find this minestrone especially satisfying. Keep the recipe in mind when you have a bounty of fresh garden produce.

yvonne krantz // mt. upton, new york

1   **pound Italian sausage links, cut into 1/2-inch slices**

1   **tablespoon olive oil**

1   **cup finely chopped onion**

1   **cup sliced fresh carrots**

1   **garlic clove, finely minced**

1   **teaspoon dried basil**

2   **cups shredded cabbage**

2   **small zucchini, sliced**

2   **cans (10-1/2 ounces *each*) condensed beef broth, undiluted *or* 3 beef bouillon cubes plus 1-1/2 cups hot water**

1   **can (14-1/2 ounces) diced tomatoes, undrained**

1   **teaspoon salt**

1/4   **teaspoon pepper**

1   **can (15-1/2 ounces) great northern beans, rinsed and drained**

Minced fresh parsley

In a Dutch oven, brown sausage in oil. Add the onion, carrots, garlic and basil; cook for 5 minutes. Stir in the cabbage, zucchini, broth, tomatoes, salt and pepper.

Bring to a boil. Reduce heat; cover and simmer for 1 hour. Add beans; cook 20 minutes longer. Garnish with parsley.

Nutrition Facts: 1 serving equals 196 calories, 10 g fat (3 g saturated fat), 23 mg cholesterol, 1,291 mg sodium, 15 g carbohydrate, 5 g fiber, 11 g protein.

BEEF VEGETABLE SOUP

Yield: 4 servings.

At the end of a long day, put something quick, warm and substantial on the table for your family. This soup always delivers!

d. m. hillock // hartford, michigan

1   **pound ground beef**

1/2   **cup chopped onion**

1   **can (15 ounces) tomato sauce**

1-1/2   **cups frozen mixed vegetables, thawed**

1-1/4   **cups frozen corn, thawed**

1-1/4   **cups beef broth**

1   **tablespoon soy sauce**

1   **tablespoon molasses**

In a large skillet, cook beef and onion over medium heat until meat is no longer pink; drain. Stir in remaining ingredients. Bring to a boil. Reduce heat; cover and simmer for 10 minutes or until hot and bubbly.

Nutrition Facts: 1-3/4 cups equals 318 calories, 11 g fat (5 g saturated fat), 56 mg cholesterol, 1,099 mg sodium, 30 g carbohydrate, 5 g fiber, 27 g protein.

CHICKEN DUMPLING SOUP

Yield: 20 servings (5 quarts).

This soup with light dumplings always brings positive comments. I like to fix it to take to my friends when they're sick.

tami christman // soda springs, idaho

- 12 **green onions, chopped**
- 1/2 **cup butter**
- 1/2 **cup all-purpose flour**
- 10 **cups water**
- 1 **package (16 ounces) frozen peas and carrots**
- 2 **cans (10 ounces *each*) chunk white chicken, drained, *divided***
- 1/3 **cup chicken bouillon granules**
- 1/2 **teaspoon pepper, *divided***
- 5 **cups biscuit/baking mix**
- 2 **tablespoons dried parsley flakes**
- 1-1/3 **cups milk**

In a stockpot, saute onions in butter until tender. Stir in flour until blended. Gradually add water. Stir in the vegetables, one can of chicken, bouillon and 1/4 teaspoon pepper; bring to a boil.

In a large bowl, combine the biscuit mix, parsley and remaining pepper. Stir in the milk just until moistened. Fold in the remaining chicken.

Drop by rounded tablespoonfuls onto simmering soup. Cover and simmer for 15 minutes or until a toothpick inserted in a dumpling comes out clean (do not lift cover while simmering).

Nutrition Facts: 1 cup equals 266 calories, 14 g fat (5 g saturated fat), 27 mg cholesterol, 1,091 mg sodium, 25 g carbohydrate, 2 g fiber, 10 g protein.

taste of home
COOKING SCHOOL SECRET

DUMPLING SUCCESS

Light, fluffy dumplings make chicken soup simply divine. Follow these guidelines to ensure your dumplings are brag-worthy every time:

- Gently mix the dumpling dough just until combined; overmixing will result in a tough dough.
- To keep the dumplings from sinking and getting waterlogged, keep the soup at a bare simmer as you gently drop them onto the soup's surface.
- Cook the dumplings with the soup pot covered and try to avoid peeking, which can deflate the dumplings.

Dress up your dumplings by stirring in herbs, Parmesan or cheddar cheese, or even chopped roasted peppers. They'd be delicious over beef stew, beef barley soup and many other choices. Dumplings are a great way to turn soup into a special and satisfying meal.

>> HOW TO:

MAKE CHICKEN STOCK

1 Remove the excess fat from the cut up chicken. In a stockpot or Dutch oven, combine chicken, vegetables, cold water and seasonings.
2 Bring to a boil over low heat. Skim foam as it rises to the top of the water. Reduce heat; cover and simmer until the chicken is tender, about 1 hour.

3 Remove chicken; let stand until cool enough to handle. Remove chicken from bones; discard skin and bones. Dice chicken; use immediately or cover and refrigerate. Skim fat from broth or chill broth overnight; lift fat from surface of broth and discard.
4 Bring soup to a boil; add noodles. Cook until tender. Stir in reserved chicken; heat through.

GRANDMA'S CHICKEN 'N' DUMPLING SOUP

Yield: 12 servings (3 quarts).

I've enjoyed making this rich soup for over 40 years. Every time I serve it, I remember my grandma, who was very special to me and was known as a great cook.

paulette balda // prophetstown, illinois

1	broiler/fryer chicken (3-1/2 to 4 pounds), cut up
2-1/4	quarts cold water
5	chicken bouillon cubes
6	whole peppercorns
3	whole cloves
1	can (10-3/4 ounces) condensed cream of chicken soup, undiluted
1	can (10-3/4 ounces) condensed cream of mushroom soup, undiluted
1-1/2	cups chopped carrots
1	cup fresh *or* frozen peas
1	cup chopped celery
1	cup chopped peeled potatoes
1/4	cup chopped onion
1-1/2	teaspoons seasoned salt
1/4	teaspoon pepper
1	bay leaf

DUMPLINGS:

2	cups all-purpose flour
4	teaspoons baking powder
1	teaspoon salt
1/4	teaspoon pepper
1	egg, beaten
2	tablespoons butter, melted
3/4	to 1 cup milk

Snipped fresh parsley, optional

Place the chicken, water, bouillon, peppercorns and cloves in a stockpot. Cover and bring to a boil; skim foam. Reduce heat; cover and simmer 45-60 minutes or until chicken is tender. Strain broth; return to stock pot.

Remove chicken and set aside until cool enough to handle. Remove meat from bones; discard bones and skin and cut chicken into chunks. Cool broth and skim off fat.

Return chicken to stockpot with soups, vegetables and seasonings; bring to a boil. Reduce heat; cover and simmer for 1 hour. Uncover; increase heat to a gently boil. Discard bay leaf.

For dumplings, combine dry ingredients in a medium bowl. Stir in egg, butter and enough milk to make a moist, stiff batter. Drop by teaspoonfuls into soup. Cover and cook without lifting the lid for 18-20 minutes. Sprinkle with parsley if desired.

Nutrition Facts: 1 cup equals 333 calories, 14 g fat (5 g saturated fat), 79 mg cholesterol, 1,447 mg sodium, 28 g carbohydrate, 3 g fiber, 22 g protein.

ZESTY TORTILLA SOUP

Yield: 10 servings (2-1/2 quarts).

Because everyone in our family enjoys Mexican food, we find this soup especially appealing. It has just the right amount of zip without being overwhelming.

tammy leiber // navasota, texas

- 1   **medium onion, chopped**
- 2   **tablespoons canola oil**
- 2   **garlic cloves, minced**
- 2   **pounds beef stew meat, cut into 1-inch cubes**
- 2   **cups water**
- 1   **can (14-1/2 ounces) stewed tomatoes**
- 1   **can (10 ounces) diced tomatoes with green chilies, undrained**
- 1   **can (10-3/4 ounces) condensed tomato soup, undiluted**
- 1   **can (10-1/2 ounces) beef broth**
- 1   **can (10-1/2 ounces) chicken broth**
- 1   **tablespoon Worcestershire sauce**
- 1   **teaspoon ground cumin**
- 1   **teaspoon chili powder**
- 1   **teaspoon salt**
- 1   **teaspoon lemon-pepper seasoning**
- 1/2 **teaspoon hot pepper sauce**
- 10 **corn tortillas (6 inches)**

Shredded cheddar cheese, sour cream and sliced green onions, optional

In a Dutch oven, saute onion in oil until tender. Add garlic; cook 1 minute longer. Stir in the next 13 ingredients; bring to a boil. Reduce heat; cover and simmer for 1-1/2 hours or until beef is tender.

Tear tortillas into bite-size pieces; add to soup. Simmer, uncovered, for 10 minutes; let stand for 5 minutes. Garnish individual servings with cheese, sour cream and onions if desired.

Nutrition Facts: 1 cup equals 267 calories, 10 g fat (3 g saturated fat), 56 mg cholesterol, 966 mg sodium, 24 g carbohydrate, 3 g fiber, 21 g protein.

CHUNKY TURKEY SOUP

Yield: 12 servings (1-1/3 cups each).

This hearty soup is the perfect answer to your Turkey Day leftovers. With the zesty flavors of curry and cumin, it will never be mistaken for canned soup!

jane scanlon // marco island, florida

- 1 **leftover turkey carcass (from a 12– to 14-pound turkey)**
- 4-1/2 **quarts water**
- 1 **medium onion, quartered**
- 1 **medium carrot, cut into 2-inch pieces**
- 1 **celery rib, cut into 2-inch pieces**

SOUP:
- 2 **cups shredded cooked turkey**
- 4 **celery ribs, chopped**
- 2 **cups frozen corn**
- 2 **medium carrots, sliced**
- 1 **large onion, chopped**
- 1 **cup uncooked orzo pasta**
- 2 **tablespoons minced fresh parsley**
- 4 **teaspoons chicken bouillon granules**
- 1 **teaspoon salt**
- 1 **teaspoon curry powder**
- 1/2 **teaspoon ground cumin**
- 1/2 **teaspoon pepper**

Place the turkey carcass in a stockpot; add the water, onion, carrot and celery. Slowly bring to a boil over low heat; cover and simmer for 1-1/2 hours.

Discard the carcass. Strain broth through a cheesecloth-lined colander. If using immediately, skim fat. Or cool, then refrigerate for 8 hours or overnight; remove fat from surface before using. (Broth may be refrigerated for up to 3 days or frozen for 4-6 months.)

Place the soup ingredients in a stockpot; add the broth. Bring to a boil. Reduce heat; cover and simmer for 30 minutes or until pasta and vegetables are tender.

Nutrition Facts: 1-1/3 cups equals 175 calories, 2 g fat (1 g saturated fat), 19 mg cholesterol, 595 mg sodium, 24 g carbohydrate, 2 g fiber, 12 g protein. Diabetic Exchanges: 1-1/2 starch, 1 lean meat.

PUREED CARROT SOUP

Yield: 2-1/2 cups.

This bright and creamy soup is fast, easy and makes a perfect amount for two.

robyn larabee // lucknow, ontario

- 2 **cups chopped carrots**
- 1/4 **cup chopped onion**
- 1 **tablespoon butter**
- 1 **can (14-1/2 ounces) chicken broth**
- 1/4 **teaspoon ground ginger**
- 1/2 **cup buttermilk**

In a small saucepan, saute carrots and onion in butter until crisp-tender. Add broth and ginger. Bring to a boil. Reduce heat; cover and simmer for 10-15 minutes or until carrots are very tender. Cool slightly.

Puree the soup in a blender; return to the pan. Stir in buttermilk; heat through (do not boil).

Nutrition Facts: 3/4 cup (prepared with reduced-fat butter and reduced-sodium broth) equals 84 calories, 3 g fat (2 g saturated fat), 8 mg cholesterol, 458 mg sodium, 12 g carbohydrate, 3 g fiber, 4 g protein.

BUTTERY ONION SOUP

Yield: 6 servings (about 1-1/2 quarts).

I developed this recipe when I once had an abundance of sweet onions. I like making it for guests. Sometimes I'll cut the recipe in half to make a little batch just for me!

sharon berthelote // sunburst, montana

> 2 **cups thinly sliced onions**
> 1/2 **cup butter, cubed**
> 1/4 **cup all-purpose flour**
> 2 **cups chicken broth**
> 2 **cups milk**
> 1-1/2 **to 2 cups (6 to 8 ounces) shredded part-skim mozzarella cheese**

Salt and pepper to taste

Croutons, optional

In a large saucepan, cook onions in butter over low heat until tender and transparent, about 20 minutes.

Stir in flour. Gradually add broth and milk; cook and stir over medium heat until bubbly. Cook and stir for 1 minute longer; reduce heat to low. Add mozzarella cheese and stir constantly until melted (do not boil). Season to taste with salt and pepper. Serve with croutons if desired.

Nutrition Facts: 1 cup equals 294 calories, 23 g fat (14 g saturated fat), 66 mg cholesterol, 600 mg sodium, 12 g carbohydrate, 1 g fiber, 11 g protein.

taste of home COOKING SCHOOL SECRET

GARNISHES ADD PANACHE

Add a garnish to soup just before serving to give it added color, flavor and dimension. It's an easy way to make it feel like you've fussed!

Easy garnish ideas include finely chopped green onions or chives, minced fresh parsley, cilantro leaves, cheddar or Parmesan cheese, sour cream and croutons.

CURRIED PARSNIP SOUP

Yield: 6 servings.

My mum used to make this recipe at home in England. It's very aromatic and has a nice bite from the curry and pepper.
julie mathieson // bristol, tennessee

- 1 **large onion, chopped**
- 1 **large carrot, chopped**
- 1 **tablespoon butter**
- 1 **pound parsnips, peeled and chopped**
- 2 **cans (14-1/2 ounces *each*) reduced-sodium chicken broth**
- 1 **teaspoon curry powder**
- 1/4 **teaspoon salt**
- 1/4 **teaspoon pepper**
- 1 **cup fat-free milk**

In a saucepan, saute onion and carrot in butter until tender. Add parsnips; cook 2 minutes. Stir in broth and seasonings. Bring to a boil. Reduce heat; cover and simmer for 12-15 minutes or until parsnips are tender. Cool slightly. In a blender, process soup in batches until smooth. Return all to pan; stir in milk and heat through.

Nutrition Facts: 1 cup equals 113 calories, 2 g fat (1 g saturated fat), 6 mg cholesterol, 513 mg sodium, 20 g carbohydrate, 5 g fiber, 5 g protein.

CURRIED CARROT SOUP: Saute the onion in butter as directed (omitting 1 carrot). Add 1 pound of carrots instead of parsnips and proceed as directed.

BAKED POTATO SOUP

Yield: 2 servings.

I discovered this recipe for our favorite soup in a children's cookbook! Not only is it delicious, but it's easy to prepare and makes a small amount—perfect for my husband and me.
linda mumm // davenport, iowa

- 2 **medium potatoes, baked and cooled**
- 1 **can (14-1/2 ounces) chicken broth**
- 2 **tablespoons sour cream**
- 1/8 **teaspoon pepper**
- 1/4 **cup shredded cheddar cheese**
- 1 **tablespoon crumbled cooked bacon *or* bacon bits**
- 1 **green onion, sliced**

Peel potatoes and cut into 1/2-in. cubes; place half in a blender. Add broth; cover and process until smooth. Pour into a saucepan. Stir in sour cream, pepper and remaining potatoes. Cook over low heat until heated through (do not boil). Garnish with cheese, bacon and onion.

Nutrition Facts: 1 cup equals 277 calories, 8 g fat (5 g saturated fat), 28 mg cholesterol, 1,061 mg sodium, 41 g carbohydrate, 4 g fiber, 11 g protein.

>> **HOW TO:**

PREPARE POTATOES

Scrub potatoes with a vegetable brush under cold water. Remove eyes or sprouts. When working with lots of potatoes, peel and place in cold water to prevent discoloration. Before baking a whole potato, pierce with a fork.

CREMINI & BUTTERNUT SQUASH SOUP

Yield: 8 servings (2 quarts).

This wholesome soup tastes like autumn, with vitamin-rich squash and the earthy flavor of mushrooms. Adding cream makes it velvety smooth.

gilda lester // millsboro, delaware

- 1 **large butternut squash (about 5 pounds)**
- 1 **carton (32 ounces) reduced-sodium chicken broth,** *divided*
- 1 **large onion, chopped**
- 1 **tablespoon olive oil**
- 1/2 **pound chopped baby portobello (cremini) mushrooms**
- 3 **garlic cloves, minced**
- 1 **teaspoon minced fresh thyme**
- 1/2 **teaspoon rubbed sage**
- 1/8 **teaspoon ground nutmeg**
- 1/4 **cup heavy whipping cream**
- 1/4 **cup grated Romano cheese**

Cut squash in half lengthwise; discard seeds. Place squash, cut side down, in a 15-in. x 10-in. x 1-in. baking pan coated with cooking spray. Bake at 400° for 55-65 minutes or until the squash is tender.

Cool slightly; carefully scoop out pulp. Place in a food processor with 1 cup broth; cover and process until smooth.

In a large saucepan over medium heat, cook onion in oil until tender. Add mushrooms; cook 3-4 minutes longer or until tender. Add the garlic, thyme and sage; cook 1 minute longer. Stir in the nutmeg, squash puree and remaining broth. Bring to a boil. Reduce heat; simmer, uncovered, for 20 minutes.

Stir in cream; heat through (do not boil). Ladle soup into bowls; sprinkle with cheese.

Nutrition Facts: 1 cup with 1-1/2 teaspoons cheese equals 167 calories, 6 g fat (3 g saturated fat), 14 mg cholesterol, 403 mg sodium, 26 g carbohydrate, 7 g fiber, 6 g protein. Diabetic Exchanges: 1-1/2 starch, 1 lean meat, 1/2 fat.

>> HOW TO:

PREPARE WINTER SQUASH

1 Wash squash, then pat dry with paper towels. Use a sharp knife to cut in half. Scrape out seeds and fibrous strings.

2 Acorn squash can be cut into decorative rings. Generally winter squash is first cooked, then the flesh is scooped out of the shell. It can be difficult to peel the shell from raw winter squash.

3 To bake winter squash, place cut side down in a greased pan and bake, uncovered, at 400° for 45-65 minutes or until tender. Cool slightly. Scoop squash out of shell; mash. A 1-pound squash will yield about 2 cups mashed squash.

SWISS POTATO SOUP

Yield: 4 servings.

Swiss cheese gives an unexpected gourmet twist to a traditional, thick and rich potato cheese soup.

krista musser // orrville, ohio

5	**bacon strips, diced**
1	**medium onion, chopped**
2	**cups water**
4	**medium potatoes, peeled and cubed**
1-1/2	**teaspoons salt**
1/8	**teaspoon pepper**
1/3	**cup all-purpose flour**
2	**cups 2% milk**
1	**cup (4 ounces) shredded Swiss cheese**

In a large saucepan, cook bacon until crisp; remove to paper towels with a slotted spoon. Drain, reserving 1 tablespoon drippings.

Saute onion in drippings until tender. Add water, potatoes, salt and pepper. Bring to a boil. Reduce heat; simmer, uncovered, for 12 minutes or until potatoes are tender.

Combine flour and milk until smooth; gradually stir in potato mixture. Bring to a boil; cook and stir for 2 minutes or until thickened and bubbly. Remove from the heat; stir in cheese until melted. Sprinkle with bacon.

Nutrition Facts: 1 cup equals 455 calories, 17 g fat (9 g saturated fat), 46 mg cholesterol, 1,218 mg sodium, 57 g carbohydrate, 4 g fiber, 21 g protein.

MAC 'N' CHEESE SOUP

Yield: 8 servings (2 quarts).

I came across this recipe a few years ago and made some changes to suit our tastes. Because it starts with packaged macaroni and cheese, it's ready in a jiffy.

nancy daugherty // cortland, ohio

1	**package (14 ounces) deluxe macaroni and cheese dinner mix**
9	**cups water, *divided***
1	**cup fresh broccoli florets**
2	**tablespoons finely chopped onion**
1	**can (10-3/4 ounces) condensed cheddar cheese soup, undiluted**
2-1/2	**cups 2% milk**
1	**cup chopped fully cooked ham**

Set aside cheese sauce packet from macaroni and cheese mix. In a large saucepan, bring 8 cups water to a boil. Add macaroni; cook for 8-10 minutes or until tender.

Meanwhile, in another large saucepan, bring remaining water to a boil. Add broccoli and onion; cook, uncovered, for 3 minutes. Stir in the soup, milk, ham and contents of cheese sauce packet; heat through. Drain macaroni; stir into soup.

Nutrition Facts: 1 cup equals 263 calories, 9 g fat (4 g saturated fat), 28 mg cholesterol, 976 mg sodium, 32 g carbohydrate, 2 g fiber, 13 g protein.

BROCCOLI MAC 'N' CHEESE SOUP: Double the broccoli and omit the ham for a meatless take on this easy soup.

SPLIT PEA SOUP

Yield: 8 servings (2 quarts).

In less than half an hour, I can have the ingredients for my satisfying pea soup simmering away. It's a treat to enjoy this soup on a chilly night.

heidi schmidgall // hancock, minnesota

- 1 package (16 ounces) dried green split peas
- 2 smoked ham hocks
- 2 quarts water
- 2 medium carrots, halved lengthwise and thinly sliced
- 1 medium onion, chopped
- 1 celery rib, thinly sliced
- 1 garlic clove, minced
- 1 bay leaf
- 1 teaspoon chicken bouillon granules
- 1 teaspoon dried thyme
- 3/4 teaspoon salt
- 1/2 teaspoon garlic salt
- 1/2 teaspoon dried basil
- 1/2 teaspoon dried marjoram
- 1/2 teaspoon pepper

In a 5-qt. slow cooker, combine all ingredients. Cover and cook on high for 4-6 hours or until peas are tender. Skim fat; discard bay leaf.

Set ham hocks aside until cool enough to handle. Remove meat from bones; discard bones and cut ham into small pieces. Return meat to slow cooker; heat through.

Nutrition Facts: 1 cup equals 253 calories, 4 g fat (1 g saturated fat), 14 mg cholesterol, 475 mg sodium, 38 g carbohydrate, 16 g fiber, 18 g protein.

CHEESY HAM CHOWDER

Yield: 10 servings.

This comforting soup is a favorite of my five children. It's full of potatoes, carrots and ham. The best part is that I can get it on the table in about 30 minutes.

jennifer trenhaile // emerson, nebraska

- 10 bacon strips, diced
- 1 large onion, chopped
- 1 cup diced carrots
- 3 tablespoons all-purpose flour
- 3 cups milk
- 1-1/2 cups water
- 2-1/2 cups cubed potatoes
- 1 can (15-1/4 ounces) whole kernel corn, drained
- 2 teaspoons chicken bouillon granules

Pepper to taste

- 3 cups (12 ounces) shredded cheddar cheese
- 2 cups cubed fully cooked ham

In a Dutch oven, cook the bacon over medium heat until crisp. Using a slotted spoon, remove to paper towels to drain. In the drippings, saute onion and carrots until tender. Stir in flour until blended. Gradually add milk and water. Bring to a boil; cook and stir for 2 minutes or until thickened.

Add the potatoes, corn, bouillon and pepper. Reduce heat; simmer, uncovered, for 20 minutes or until potatoes are tender. Add cheese and ham; heat until cheese is melted. Stir in bacon.

Nutrition Facts: 1 cup equals 418 calories, 28 g fat (14 g saturated fat), 76 mg cholesterol, 1,056 mg sodium, 21 g carbohydrate, 2 g fiber, 19 g protein.

ITALIAN-STYLE LENTIL SOUP

Yield: 6 servings.

I like to serve lentils often because they are inexpensive and nutritious. I sometimes add them to my homemade spaghetti sauce and serve over noodles.

rachel greenawalt keller // roanoke, virginia

- 2 medium onions, chopped
- 2 celery ribs, thinly sliced
- 1 medium carrot, chopped
- 2 teaspoons olive oil
- 5-1/4 cups water
- 1 cup dried lentils, rinsed
- 1/4 cup minced fresh parsley
- 1 tablespoon reduced-sodium beef bouillon granules
- 1/2 teaspoon pepper
- 1 can (6 ounces) tomato paste
- 2 tablespoons white vinegar
- 2 teaspoons brown sugar
- 1/2 teaspoon salt
- 2 tablespoons shredded Parmesan cheese

In a large saucepan coated with cooking spray, saute the onions, celery and carrot in oil until almost tender. Stir in the water, lentils, parsley, bouillon and pepper. Bring to a boil. Reduce heat; cover and simmer for 20-25 minutes or until lentils are tender, stirring occasionally.

Stir in the tomato paste, vinegar, brown sugar and salt; heat through. Sprinkle each serving with cheese.

Nutrition Facts: 1 cup equals 122 calories, 2 g fat (1 g saturated fat), 1 mg cholesterol, 420 mg sodium, 21 g carbohydrate, 6 g fiber, 6 g protein. Diabetic Exchanges: 2 vegetable, 1 starch.

YANKEE BEAN SOUP

Yield: 6 servings.

My family really enjoys this hearty soup, which is perfect for a wintry day.

ann nace // perkasie, pennsylvania

- 1-1/2 cups dried navy beans
- 1/2 pound sliced bacon, diced
- 3/4 cup chopped onion
- 1/2 cup chopped carrot
- 1/3 cup chopped celery leaves
- 4 cups water
- 2 cups milk
- 2 teaspoons molasses
- 1-1/2 teaspoons salt

Place beans in a Dutch oven; add water to cover by 2 in. Boil 2 minutes. Remove from the heat; cover and let stand for 1 hour.

Drain and rinse beans, discarding liquid. Set beans aside. In the same pan, cook the bacon over medium heat until crisp. Using a slotted spoon, remove to paper towels; drain, reserving 2 tablespoons drippings.

In drippings, saute onion until tender. Stir in carrot, celery leaves, beans and water. Bring to a boil. Reduce heat; cover and simmer for 1-3/4 to 2 hours or until beans are tender.

Stir in milk, molasses, salt and bacon. Remove 2-1/2 cups of soup; cool slightly. Place in a blender; cover and process until pureed. Return to the pan; heat through.

Nutrition Facts: 1 cup equals 315 calories, 10 g fat (4 g saturated fat), 22 mg cholesterol, 847 mg sodium, 40 g carbohydrate, 13 g fiber, 18 g protein.

>> HOW TO:

MINCE PARSLEY

Here's a simple trimming tip: Don't clean up a cutting board! Simply place parsley in a small measuring cup or glass container and snip sprigs with kitchen shears until minced.

YUM...CHILI!

There are as many scrumptious recipes for chili as there are cooks! From regional favorites, such as Cincinnati (which is served over spaghetti) to a loaded-with-beef Texas version, to white chicken chili, lightened-up turkey and vegetarian, you'll find the perfect chili to meet your needs.

To make chili into a meal, serve Jalapeno Corn Muffins (page 258). Or, toast up a quick quesadilla on the stovetop by sandwiching your favorite shredded cheese between two tortillas. Cook filled tortillas in a skillet coated with cooking spray until lightly browned on both sides.

Freeze small portions of leftover chili for fuss-free future meals. (Do not freeze White Chili, which contains dairy and will appear curdled after freezing.) For easy portioning, place a small resealable plastic bag in a container to hold it upright and fill the bag with chili. Seal and label the bags of chili, which won't take up much room in the freezer and will provide perfect individual portions.

WHITE CHILI

Yield: 12 servings (1 cup each).

My friend and I came up with this delicious slow-cooked chicken chili. It's unusual because it calls for Alfredo sauce.

cindi mitchell // st. marys, kansas

- 3 cans (15-1/2 ounces *each*) great northern beans, rinsed and drained
- 3 cups cubed cooked chicken breast
- 1 jar (15 ounces) Alfredo sauce
- 2 cups chicken broth
- 1 to 2 cans (4 ounces *each*) chopped green chilies
- 1-1/2 cups frozen gold and white corn
- 1 cup (4 ounces) shredded Monterey Jack cheese
- 1 cup (4 ounces) shredded pepper Jack cheese
- 1 cup sour cream
- 1 small sweet yellow pepper, chopped
- 1 small onion, chopped
- 3 garlic cloves, minced
- 1 tablespoon ground cumin
- 1-1/2 teaspoons white pepper
- 1 to 1-1/2 teaspoons cayenne pepper

Salsa verde and chopped fresh cilantro, optional

In a 5- or 6-qt. slow cooker, combine the first 15 ingredients. Cover and cook on low for 3-4 hours or until heated though, stirring once. Serve with salsa verde and cilantro if desired.

Nutrition Facts: 1 cup equals 336 calories, 15 g fat (9 g saturated fat), 69 mg cholesterol, 772 mg sodium, 27 g carbohydrate, 7 g fiber, 24 g protein.

ROOTIN'-TOOTIN' CINCINNATI CHILI

Yield: 4 servings.

Yes, there's root beer in this spicy chili, and it adds a nice touch of sweetness. Serve over spaghetti and let everyone add their own favorite toppings.

holly gomez // seabrook, new hampshire

- 1 **pound ground beef**
- 1 **small onion, chopped**
- 1 **small green pepper, chopped**
- 1 **garlic clove, minced**
- 1 **can (14-1/2 ounces) fire-roasted diced tomatoes, undrained**
- 1 **cup root beer**
- 2 **tablespoons chili powder**
- 2 **tablespoons tomato paste**
- 2 **tablespoons minced chipotle peppers in adobo sauce**
- 1 **tablespoon ground cumin**
- 1 **beef bouillon cube**

Hot cooked spaghetti

Optional toppings: crushed tortilla chips, chopped green onions, and shredded cheddar and parmesan cheeses

In a large saucepan, cook the beef, onions and green pepperover medium heat until meat is no longer pink. Add the garlic; cook 1 minute longer. Drain. Add the tomatoes, root beer, chili powder, tomato paste, chipotle peppers, cumin and bouillon. Bring to a boil.

Reduce heat; cover and simmer for 20-30 minutes to allow flavors to blend. Serve with spaghetti. Garnish with chips, green onions and cheeses if desired.

Nutrition Facts: 1 cup (calculated without spaghetti and toppings) equals 310 calories, 15 g fat (5 g saturated fat), 70 mg cholesterol, 662 mg sodium, 22 g carbohydrate, 4 g fiber, 23 g protein.

>> HOW TO:

COOK SPAGHETTI

Carefully hold spaghetti in boiling water and ease it down into the water as it softens, pushing it around the edge of the pan. When fully immersed in the water, stir the spaghetti to separate strands.

TERRIFIC TURKEY CHILI

Yield: 6 servings (about 2 quarts).

This satisfying chili is full of traditional flavor. I like to keep it light with toppings like fresh cilantro, green onions and reduced-fat cheese.

kim seeger // brooklyn park, minnesota

- 1 **pound lean ground turkey**
- 1 **cup chopped onion**
- 1 **cup chopped green pepper**
- 2 **teaspoons minced garlic**
- 1 **can (28 ounces) crushed tomatoes**
- 1 **can (16 ounces) kidney beans, rinsed and drained**
- 1 **can (11-1/2 ounces) tomato juice**
- 1 **can (6 ounces) tomato paste**
- 1 **can (4 ounces) chopped green chilies**
- 2 **tablespoons brown sugar**
- 1 **tablespoon dried parsley flakes**
- 1 **tablespoon ground cumin**
- 3 **teaspoons chili powder**
- 2 **teaspoons dried oregano**
- 1-1/2 **teaspoons pepper**

In a large saucepan, cook the turkey, onion, green pepper over medium heat until meat is no longer pink. Add garlic; cook 1 minute longer. Drain.

Stir in the remaining ingredients. Bring to a boil. Reduce heat; cover and simmer for 25 minutes or until heated through.

Nutrition Facts: 1-1/3 cups equals 315 calories, 8 g fat (2 g saturated fat), 60 mg cholesterol, 706 mg sodium, 43 g carbohydrate, 11 g fiber, 23 g protein. Diabetic Exchanges: 3 starch, 2 lean meat.

>> HOW TO:

CHOP AN ONION

1. To quickly chop an onion, peel and cut it in half from the root to the top. Leaving the root attached, place flat side down on work surface. Cut vertically through the onion, leaving the root end uncut.
2. Cut across the onion, discarding the root end. The closer the cuts, the finer the pieces will be. This method can also be used for shallots.

SPICY VEGETABLE CHILI

Yield: 8 servings (2 quarts).

This chili makes a comforting meal on cool nights. I love dipping oat bran bread into it.
nancy zimmerman // cape may court house, new jersey

- 1 medium onion, chopped
- 1 medium carrot, thinly sliced
- 1 medium green pepper, chopped
- 1/2 pound sliced fresh mushrooms
- 1 small zucchini, sliced
- 1 tablespoon olive oil
- 4 garlic cloves, minced
- 1 can (28 ounces) diced tomatoes, undrained
- 2 cans (16 ounces each) kidney beans, rinsed and drained
- 2 cans (8 ounces each) no-salt-added tomato sauce
- 1 can (4 ounces) chopped green chilies
- 3 tablespoons chili powder
- 3 teaspoons dried oregano
- 2 teaspoons ground cumin
- 2 teaspoons paprika
- 1/4 teaspoon crushed red pepper flakes
- 1 tablespoon white wine vinegar
- Minced fresh cilantro and fat-free sour cream, optional

In a Dutch oven, saute the onion, carrot, pepper, mushrooms and zucchini in oil until tender. Add garlic; cook 1 minute longer. Add the tomatoes, beans, tomato sauce, green chilies and seasonings. Bring to a boil. Reduce heat; simmer, uncovered, for 35 minutes, stirring occasionally.

Stir in vinegar. Serve in soup bowls; garnish with cilantro and sour cream if desired.

Nutrition Facts: 1 cup (calculated without sour cream) equals 195 calories, 3 g fat (trace saturated fat), 0 cholesterol, 423 mg sodium, 35 g carbohydrate, 11 g fiber, 10 g protein. Diabetic Exchanges: 2 starch, 1 lean meat.

TEX-MEX CHILI

Yield: 9 servings.

I dreamed up this hearty chili with a Tex-Mex twist years ago. It's still everyone's favorite and the go-to recipe in our family cookbook.
martha hook // tyler, texas

- 1-1/2 pounds ground beef
- 1 medium onion, chopped
- 5 garlic cloves, minced
- 1 can (14-1/2 ounces) diced tomatoes, undrained
- 1 cup water
- 1 cup V8 juice
- 1/4 cup brewed coffee
- 2 envelopes chili seasoning
- 1 can (16 ounces) refried beans
- 1 can (15 ounces) Ranch Style beans (pinto beans in seasoned tomato sauce)
- 2 tablespoons ground cumin
- 2 tablespoons chili powder
- 1/4 teaspoon lemon juice

In a large skillet, cook beef and onion over medium heat until meat is no longer pink. Add garlic; cook 1 minute longer. Drain. Stir in the tomatoes, water, juice, coffee and chili seasoning.

Transfer to a 4-qt. slow cooker. Stir in remaining ingredients. Cover and cook on low for 4-5 hours to allow flavors to blend.

Nutrition Facts: 1 cup equals 281 calories, 11 g fat (4 g saturated fat), 51 mg cholesterol, 1,115 mg sodium, 25 g carbohydrate, 8 g fiber, 21 g protein.

RED PEPPER SHRIMP BISQUE

Yield: 2 servings.

Here's a soup that goes nicely with a steak and salad. It's great for special dinners because it feels festive, yet it's surprisingly easy to make.

stephanie buttars // phoenix, arizona

- 1 cup chicken broth
- 1 jar (7 ounces) roasted sweet red peppers, drained
- 1/2 teaspoon sugar
- 1/2 teaspoon paprika
- 1 cup coarsely chopped cooked shrimp (6 ounces)
- 1/2 cup heavy whipping cream
- 1/4 cup grated Romano cheese, *divided*
- 1/4 teaspoon salt
- 1/8 teaspoon pepper

Dash hot pepper sauce

In a small saucepan, bring broth and roasted peppers to a boil. Reduce heat; cover and simmer for 5 minutes. Remove from the heat and cool slightly.

Transfer to a blender; cover and process until pureed. Return to the saucepan. Add sugar and paprika; bring to a boil. Reduce heat; simmer, uncovered, for 5 minutes. Add the shrimp, cream, 2 tablespoons cheese, salt, pepper and hot pepper sauce. Cook and stir for 2 minutes or until heated through. Garnish with remaining cheese.

Nutrition Facts: 1-1/4 cups equals 400 calories, 28 g fat (16 g saturated fat), 224 mg cholesterol, 1,284 mg sodium, 15 g carbohydrate, trace fiber, 24 g protein.

THAI SHRIMP SOUP

Yield: 8 servings (2 quarts).

This tasty soup comes together in minutes, and it's a crowd-pleaser. The ingredients are all available in my little corner store, too.

jessie grearson-sapat // falmouth, maine

- 1 medium onion, chopped
- 1 tablespoon olive oil
- 3 cups reduced-sodium chicken broth
- 1 cup water
- 1 tablespoon brown sugar
- 1 tablespoon minced fresh gingerroot
- 1 tablespoon fish *or* soy sauce
- 1 tablespoon red curry paste
- 1 lemon grass stalk
- 1 pound uncooked large shrimp, peeled and deveined
- 1-1/2 cups frozen shelled edamame
- 1 can (14 ounces) light coconut milk
- 1 can (8-3/4 ounces) whole baby corn, drained and cut in half
- 1/2 cup bamboo shoots
- 1/4 cup fresh basil leaves, torn
- 1/4 cup minced fresh cilantro
- 2 tablespoons lime juice
- 1-1/2 teaspoons grated lime peel
- 1 teaspoon curry powder

In a Dutch oven, saute onion in oil until tender. Add the broth, water, brown sugar, ginger, fish sauce, curry paste and lemon grass. Bring to a boil. Reduce heat; carefully stir in shrimp and edamame. Cook, uncovered, for 5-6 minutes or until shrimp turn pink.

Add the coconut milk, corn, bamboo shoots, basil, cilantro, lime juice, lime peel and curry powder; heat through. Discard lemon grass.

Nutrition Facts: 1 cup equals 163 calories, 7 g fat (3 g saturated fat), 69 mg cholesterol, 505 mg sodium, 9 g carbohydrate, 2 g fiber, 14 g protein. Diabetic Exchanges: 2 lean meat, 1 vegetable, 1 fat.

CASSOULET FOR THE GANG

Yield: 10 servings (4 quarts).

Wine lends a warm background flavor to this satisfying take on a traditional French stew. Use low-fat mashed beans to thicken the broth and boost nutrition.

lynn stein // joseph, oregon

- 1 pork tenderloin (1 pound), cut into 1/2-inch pieces
- 1 pound smoked turkey kielbasa, cut into 1/2-inch pieces
- 1 tablespoon olive oil
- 3 medium carrots, chopped
- 1 large onion, cut into wedges
- 4 garlic cloves, minced
- 2 cans (14-1/2 ounces *each*) no-salt-added stewed tomatoes, cut up
- 1 can (14-1/2 ounces) reduced-sodium chicken broth
- 3 teaspoons herbes de Provence
- 1-1/2 teaspoons garlic powder
- 1-1/2 teaspoons dried basil
- 1/2 teaspoon dried oregano
- 1/4 teaspoon pepper
- 4 cans (15-1/2 ounces *each*) great northern beans, rinsed and drained, *divided*
- 3/4 cup white wine *or* additional chicken broth, *divided*

In a Dutch oven coated with cooking spray, saute pork and kielbasa in oil until lightly browned; drain. Add carrots and onion; saute 4 minutes longer. Add garlic; cook for 1 minute or until crisp-tender. Stir in the tomatoes, broth and seasonings. Bring to a boil. Reduce heat; cover and simmer for 10 minutes.

Place one can of beans in a food processor; add 1/4 cup wine or broth. Cover and process until pureed. Stir into meat mixture. Stir in the remaining beans and wine or broth. Bring to a boil. Reduce heat; simmer, uncovered, for 8-10 minutes or until meat and vegetables are tender.

EDITOR'S NOTE: Look for herbes de Provence in the spice aisle.

Nutrition Facts: 1-1/2 cups equals 316 calories, 5 g fat (1 g saturated fat), 41 mg cholesterol, 959 mg sodium, 40 g carbohydrate, 11 g fiber, 25 g protein.

taste of home COOKING SCHOOL SECRET

SOMETHING SPECIAL: CASSOULET

Pronounced KASS-soo-LAY, this French stew contains white beans and a variety of meats. Our version is a lightened-up take on the classic because it uses leaner meats and isn't thickened with butter and flour.

Serve cassoulet with a green salad and your favorite crusty bread for an informal fall get-together. Brie Phyllo Cups (page 18) are an easy- to-make appetizer that would keep up the theme.

For wine, offer both Pinot Noir and Chardonnay so guests have a choice between red and white wine. This stew goes excellently with either one. If your gang prefers red wine, go ahead and use it in the stew instead of white wine. Cassoulet is a flexible, forgiving dish!

BEEF & PORK

STOVETOP HAMBURGER CASSEROLE

Yield: 6 servings.

This comforting casserole loaded with ground beef, pasta, veggies and cheddar cheese comes together in a jiffy.

edith landinger // longview, texas

- 1 **package (7 ounces) small pasta shells**
- 1-1/2 **pounds ground beef**
- 1 **large onion, chopped**
- 3 **medium carrots, chopped**
- 1 **celery rib, chopped**
- 3 **garlic cloves, minced**
- 3 **cups cubed cooked red potatoes**
- 1 **can (15-1/4 ounces) whole kernel corn, drained**
- 2 **cans (8 ounces *each*) tomato sauce**
- 1-1/2 **teaspoons salt**
- 1/2 **teaspoon pepper**
- 1 **cup (4 ounces) shredded cheddar cheese**

Cook pasta according to package directions. Meanwhile, in a large skillet, cook beef and onion over medium heat until meat is no longer pink; drain. Add carrots and celery; cook and stir for 5 minutes or until vegetables are crisp-tender. Add garlic; cook 1 minute longer.

Stir in the potatoes, corn, tomato sauce, salt and pepper; heat through. Drain pasta and add to skillet; toss to coat. Sprinkle with cheese. Cover and cook until cheese is melted.

Nutrition Facts: 1 cup equals 508 calories, 17 g fat (9 g saturated fat), 76 mg cholesterol, 1,172 mg sodium, 53 g carbohydrate, 5 g fiber, 32 g protein.

BEEF & PORK

TO PURCHASE THE BEST MEAT:
- Look for bright, cherry-red beef and medium to bright-pink pork (with no gray or brown patches).
- The packaging should be cold with no holes, and there should be minimal liquid in the package.
- Check the sell-by date.

TO BE SAFE:
- Cook or freeze the meat before the sell-by date; use leftovers promptly.
- Store uncooked meat on the bottom shelf of the refrigerator so it can't drip onto other foods.
- Cook pork, pork sausage and ground beef until a meat thermometer reads 160°.
- Some cuts of beef like steak and tender roasts may be cooked to your preferred doneness. For medium-rare, cook beef to 145°; medium, 160°; well-done, 170°.

TO DEFROST:
- The thicker the package, the longer it will take to thaw.
- Steaks and chops need 12 to 24 hours.
- Beef and pork packages that are 1 in. to 1-1/2 in. thick need 24 hours.
- Small roasts need 4 hours per pound; large roasts, 6 hours per pound.

FOR COOKING SUCCESS:
- Beef cuts vary a great deal in tenderness, with the most tender cuts coming from the rib and loin. Pork cuts are generally tender, though the shoulders and legs may be less tender.
- To make the most of less-tender cuts, marinate the meat and/or use moist-heat cooking methods, such as braising or slow-cooking.
- Showcase tender meats with simple dry-heat cooking methods—roasting, sauteeing, grilling, broiling and pan-frying.

GO-TO PANTRY MEALS

Good cooks should have a few simple go-to recipes that don't require a special trip to the store. Hamburger Stir-Fry uses pantry ingredients, plus a pound each of ground beef and frozen vegetables... things that you can easily keep on hand. If necessary, simply defrost the beef in the microwave while you prepare the recipe's homemade sauce.

This nutritious, family-pleasing meal is the perfect go-to dinner when you don't have the time or desire to go to the store. Imagine whipping up this stir-fry on a cold and snowy day. You'll feel smart putting a satisfying meal on the table without ever having to leave home!

HAMBURGER STIR-FRY

Yield: 4 servings.

Here's a quick, easy teriyaki stir-fry that uses hamburger instead of the traditional beef strips. It has a nice sauce and is different enough to be a treat for the taste buds.
kathie and john horst // westfield, new york

- 1 **tablespoon sugar**
- 1 **tablespoon cornstarch**
- 1 **tablespoon ground mustard**
- 1/3 **cup cold water**
- 1/3 **cup reduced-sodium teriyaki sauce**
- 1 **pound lean ground beef (90% lean)**
- 1 **package (16 ounces) frozen asparagus stir-fry vegetable blend**
- 1 **medium onion, halved and thinly sliced**
- 2 **teaspoons canola oil**
- 2 **cups hot cooked rice**
- 2 **teaspoons sesame seeds**

In a small bowl, combine the sugar, cornstarch and mustard. Stir in water and teriyaki sauce until smooth; set aside. In a large skillet or wok, stir-fry beef until no longer pink; drain and set aside. In the same pan, stir-fry the vegetable blend and onion in oil until crisp-tender.

Stir cornstarch mixture and add to the pan. Bring to a boil; cook and stir for 1-2 minutes or until thickened. Add beef; heat through. Serve with rice. Sprinkle with sesame seeds.

Nutrition Facts: 1 cup stir-fry with 1/2 cup rice equals 399 calories, 12 g fat (4 g saturated fat), 56 mg cholesterol, 516 mg sodium, 42 g carbohydrate, 3 g fiber, 28 g protein. Diabetic Exchanges: 3 lean meat, 2 starch, 2 vegetable, 1/2 fat.

MEATY SPINACH MANICOTTI

Yield: 14-16 servings.

This hearty stuffed pasta dish will feed a crowd. Tangy tomato sauce tops manicotti that's filled with a mouthwatering blend of Italian sausage, chicken, spinach and mozzarella cheese.

pat schroeder // elkhorn, wisconsin

- 2 **packages (8 ounces *each*) manicotti shells**
- 1/4 **cup butter, cubed**
- 1/4 **cup all-purpose flour**
- 2-1/2 **cups 2% milk**
- 3/4 **cup grated Parmesan cheese**
- 1 **pound bulk Italian sausage**
- 4 **cups cubed cooked chicken *or* turkey**
- 2 **packages (10 ounces *each*) frozen chopped spinach, thawed and squeezed dry**
- 2 **eggs, lightly beaten**
- 1 **cup (4 ounces) shredded part-skim mozzarella cheese**
- 2 **jars (26 ounces *each*) spaghetti sauce**
- 1/4 **cup minced fresh parsley**

Cook manicotti according to package directions. Meanwhile, melt butter in a saucepan. Stir in the flour until smooth; gradually add milk. Bring to a boil; cook and stir for 2 minutes or until thickened. Stir in Parmesan cheese until melted; set aside. Drain manicotti; set aside.

In a large skillet, cook sausage over medium heat until no longer pink; drain. Add the chicken, spinach, eggs, mozzarella cheese and 3/4 cup of the white sauce. Stuff into the manicotti shells.

Spread 1/2 cup spaghetti sauce in each of two ungreased 13-in. x 9-in. baking dishes. Top with manicotti. Pour remaining spaghetti sauce over the top.

Reheat the remaining white sauce, stirring constantly. Pour over spaghetti sauce. Bake, uncovered, at 350° for 45-50 minutes or until a thermometer inserted in the filling reads 160°. Sprinkle with parsley.

Nutrition Facts: 1 serving equals 306 calories, 15 g fat (7 g saturated fat), 90 mg cholesterol, 566 mg sodium, 19 g carbohydrate, 2 g fiber, 22 g protein.

CURLY NOODLE PORK SUPPER

Yield: 4 servings.

This hearty meal-in-one is loaded with tender pork and ramen noodles. Broccoli and red pepper add a fresh-from-the-garden flavor.

carmen carlson // kent, washington

- 1 **pound pork tenderloin, cut into 1/4-inch strips**
- 1 **medium sweet red pepper, cut into 1-inch pieces**
- 1 **cup fresh broccoli florets**
- 4 **green onions, cut into 1-inch pieces**
- 1 **tablespoon canola oil**
- 1-1/2 **cups water**
- 2 **packages (3 ounces *each*) pork ramen noodles**
- 1 **tablespoon minced fresh parsley**
- 1 **tablespoon soy sauce**

In a large skillet, cook the pork, red pepper, broccoli and onions in oil until meat is no longer pink.

Add the water, noodles with contents of seasoning packets, parsley and soy sauce. Bring to a boil. Reduce heat; cook for 3-4 minutes or until noodles are tender.

Nutrition Facts: 1 serving equals 272 calories, 11 g fat (4 g saturated fat), 63 mg cholesterol, 735 mg sodium, 18 g carbohydrate, 2 g fiber, 26 g protein.

ITALIAN SAUSAGE SPAGHETTI

Yield: 5 servings.

Slices of leftover Italian sausage lend plenty of great flavor to this effortless spaghetti sauce.

joyce hostetler // midway, arkansas

- 1 small onion, chopped
- 1 small green pepper, chopped
- 2 teaspoons olive oil
- 3 garlic cloves, minced
- 5 cooked Italian sausage links, cut into 1/4-inch slices
- 1 can (28 ounces) diced tomatoes, undrained
- 1 can (6 ounces) tomato paste
- 1/4 cup water
- 1 teaspoon sugar
- 1 tablespoon Italian seasoning
- 1/2 teaspoon salt
- 1/2 teaspoon pepper

Hot cooked spaghetti

In a large saucepan, saute onion and green pepper in oil tender. Add garlic; cook 1 minute longer. Stir in the sausage, tomatoes, tomato paste, water, sugar and seasonings. Bring to a boil. Reduce heat; cover and simmer for 15 minutes. Serve with spaghetti.

Nutrition Facts: 1 serving equals 364 calories, 23 g fat (8 g saturated fat), 65 mg cholesterol, 1,230 mg sodium, 20 g carbohydrate, 5 g fiber, 19 g protein.

PEPPERONI PIZZAZZ

Yield: 9 servings.

I've fixed this hearty main course for buffets, potluck dinners and even for special dinners at my home.

marge unger // la porte, indiana

- 8 ounces uncooked penne pasta
- 1 jar (28 ounces) spaghetti sauce, *divided*
- 1 package (8 ounces) sliced pepperoni
- 1 jar (4-1/2 ounces) sliced mushrooms, drained
- 1/2 cup chopped green pepper
- 1/2 cup chopped onion
- 1/2 cup grated Parmesan cheese
- 1/2 teaspoon garlic powder
- 1/2 teaspoon salt
- 1/8 teaspoon pepper
- 1/8 teaspoon crushed red pepper flakes
- 1 can (8 ounces) tomato sauce
- 2 cups (8 ounces) shredded part-skim mozzarella cheese

Cook pasta according to package directions. Meanwhile, combine 2-1/3 cups spaghetti sauce, pepperoni, mushrooms, green pepper, onion, Parmesan cheese, garlic powder, salt, pepper and red pepper flakes in a bowl. Drain pasta; add to sauce mixture and mix well.

Transfer to a greased 3-qt. baking dish. Combine tomato sauce and remaining spaghetti sauce; pour over top. Cover and bake at 350° 40-45 minutes or until bubbly. Sprinkle with mozzarella. Bake, uncovered, 5-10 minutes longer or until cheese is melted. Let stand 5 minutes before serving.

Nutrition Facts: 1 serving equals 382 calories, 20 g fat (9 g saturated fat), 41 mg cholesterol, 1,414 mg sodium, 31 g carbohydrate, 3 g fiber, 19 g protein.

MY TAKE ON MOM'S MEAT LOAF

Yield: 4 servings.

Here's a lower-in-fat-and-salt take on my mother's original recipe. I substituted fresh ingredients like garlic, mushrooms and onions for dried onion soup mix and garlic powder. It still tastes like home.

brenda moehringer // gansevoort, new york

- 1 egg white
- 1 tablespoon steak sauce
- 1 tablespoon Worcestershire sauce
- 5 medium fresh mushrooms, finely chopped
- 1/2 cup seasoned bread crumbs
- 1/3 cup finely chopped sweet onion
- 2 tablespoons grated Parmesan cheese
- 2 garlic cloves, minced
- 1 teaspoon dried sage leaves
- 1/2 teaspoon pepper
- 1/8 teaspoon salt
- 1 pound lean ground beef (90% lean)

Barbecue sauce, optional

In a large bowl, combine the first 11 ingredients. Crumble beef over mixture and mix well. Shape into a loaf; place in an 11-in. x 7-in. baking dish coated with cooking spray.

Bake, uncovered, at 350° for 35-40 minutes or until no pink remains and a meat thermometer reads 160°. Let stand for 10 minutes before slicing. Drizzle with barbecue sauce if desired.

Nutrition Facts: 1 serving (calculated without barbecue sauce) equals 264 calories, 11 g fat (4 g saturated fat), 71 mg cholesterol, 503 mg sodium, 15 g carbohydrate, 1 g fiber, 26 g protein. Diabetic Exchanges: 3 lean meat, 1 starch, 1 fat.

TACO MAC

CHEAT IT!

Yield: 6 servings.

Pork sausage, taco seasoning and taco sauce add plenty of zip to easy macaroni and cheese. This zesty dish is just as yummy the next day. Just warm it up and garnish with shredded lettuce, diced tomatoes and cheese.

jolynn fribley // nokomis, illinois

- 1 package (24 ounces) shells and cheese dinner mix
- 1/2 pound bulk pork sausage, cooked and drained
- 1/3 cup taco sauce
- 1 tablespoon taco seasoning
- 4 cups shredded lettuce
- 2 medium tomatoes, chopped
- 1 cup (4 ounces) shredded cheddar cheese, optional

Prepare shells and cheese mix according to package directions. Stir in the sausage, taco sauce and seasoning. Garnish with lettuce, tomatoes and cheddar cheese if desired.

EDITOR'S NOTE: This recipe was tested with Kraft Velveeta Family-Size Shells & Cheese.

Nutrition Facts: 1 serving (calculated without cheddar cheese) equals 465 calories, 20 g fat (11 g saturated fat), 54 mg cholesterol, 1,413 mg sodium, 51 g carbohydrate, 2 g fiber, 20 g protein.

TORTILLA-SALSA MEAT LOAF

Yield: 8 servings.

I'm asked to make this recipe at least once a month during the winter, especially for birthday dinners. My guests like it with asparagus and garlic mashed potatoes.
steven espinosa // salt lake city, utah

- 2 slices day-old white bread
- 2 eggs, lightly beaten
- 1 cup salsa
- 1/2 cup crushed tortilla chips
- 1/2 cup *each* chopped green pepper, onion and celery
- 1 jalapeno pepper, seeded and chopped
- 6 garlic cloves, minced
- 1 teaspoon pepper
- 1/2 teaspoon Italian seasoning
- 1/4 teaspoon seasoned salt
- 1 pound ground beef
- 1 pound ground pork

Place bread in an ungreased 9-in. x 5-in. loaf pan; set aside. In a large bowl, combine the eggs, salsa, tortilla chips, green pepper, onion, celery, jalapeno, garlic, pepper, Italian seasoning and seasoned salt. Crumble beef and pork over mixture and mix well. Pat into prepared pan.

Bake, uncovered, at 375° for 1-1/4 to 1-1/2 hours or until no pink remains and a meat thermometer reads 160°. Invert meat loaf onto a serving platter; discard bread. Let stand for 5 minutes before slicing.

EDITOR'S NOTE: We recommend wearing disposable gloves when cutting hot peppers. Avoid touching your face.

Nutrition Facts: 1 slice equals 315 calories, 18 g fat (7 g saturated fat), 129 mg cholesterol, 319 mg sodium, 10 g carbohydrate, 2 g fiber, 24 g protein.

>> HOW TO:

PEEL FRESH GARLIC

Using the flat side of a chef's knife's blade, crush the garlic clove. Peel away the skin. Chop or mince the garlic as directed in the recipe.

GREEK MEAT LOAVES

Yield: 2 loaves (6 servings each).

Flavored with sun-dried tomatoes and Greek olives, this twist on traditional meat loaf will be a hit, especially when served with a Greek salad and crusty bread. radelle knappenberger // oviedo, florida

- 2 eggs, lightly beaten
- 1/2 cup ketchup
- 1/4 cup 2% milk
- 1 large red onion, finely chopped
- 3/4 cup quick-cooking oats
- 1/3 cup oil-packed sun-dried tomatoes, patted dry and finely chopped
- 1/3 cup pitted Greek olives, chopped
- 2 garlic cloves, minced
- 1 teaspoon salt
- 1 teaspoon pepper
- 2 pounds lean ground beef (90% lean)
- 1/2 cup crumbled feta cheese

In a large bowl, combine the first 10 ingredients. Crumble beef over mixture and mix well. Pat into two greased 8-in. x 4-in. loaf pans.

Bake, uncovered, at 350° for 50-60 minutes or until no pink remains and a meat thermometer reads 160°. Let stand for 5 minutes. Transfer to a serving plate; sprinkle with cheese.

TO MAKE AHEAD: Unbaked meat loaves can be covered and frozen for up to 3 months. Thaw in the refrigerator overnight. Bake as directed.

Nutrition Facts: 1 slice equals 254 calories, 15 g fat (7 g saturated fat), 98 mg cholesterol, 545 mg sodium, 9 g carbohydrate, 1 g fiber, 21 g protein.

taste of home
COOKING SCHOOL SECRET

MMM...MEAT LOAF!

Meat loaf recipes may change over time by using lightened-up ingredients the way My Take on Mom's Meat Loaf (page 103) does. Or they may borrow from other cultures, like Tortilla-Salsa Meat Loaf or the Greek Meat Loaves do. No matter what changes, meat loaf will always be pure comfort food!

Follow these guidelines for success with your meat loaf.

- To ensure a tender loaf, avoid overmixing. Follow the recipe to combine the other loaf ingredients, then crumble the meat over the top and mix just until combined. Gently pat the mixture into a loaf shape.

- Experiment with different meat loaf toppings. Salsa, marinara, barbecue sauce or even jarred olive tapenade could yield tasty results. Add toppings near the end of baking to ensure they do not burn.

- Get a jump on future meals by doubling the recipe and popping an extra loaf in the freezer. Then simply thaw in the refrigerator and bake until done.

- For a classic meal—no matter which loaf you choose—serve Garlic Mashed Potatoes (page 225) and your favorite green vegetable.

- Team up the Tortilla-Salsa Meat Loaf with cooked rice and Home-Style Refried Beans (page 74) for a Southwest-inspired dinner.

GLAZED PORK CHOPS WITH CORN BREAD DRESSING

Yield: 6 servings.

A slightly sweet glaze coats these delicious pork chops that were described by my family as both hearty and homey. A simple corn bread dressing turns this dish into classic comfort food.

dawn kloman // watertown, wisconsin

- 1-1/4 **cups reduced-sodium chicken broth**
- 3/4 **cup chopped onion**
- 3/4 **cup frozen corn**
- 1 **celery rib, chopped**

Dash cayenne pepper

- 3 **cups crushed corn bread stuffing**
- 6 **boneless pork loin chops (6 ounces *each*)**
- 2 **tablespoons brown sugar**
- 2 **teaspoons spicy brown mustard**

In a large saucepan, bring the broth, onion, corn, celery and cayenne to a boil. Remove from the heat; stir in stuffing.

Transfer to a 13-in. x 9-in. baking dish coated with cooking spray. Top with pork chops. Combine brown sugar and mustard; spread over chops.

Bake, uncovered, at 400° for 25-30 minutes or until a meat thermometer reads 160°.

Nutrition Facts: 1 pork chop with 2/3 cup dressing equals 389 calories, 11 g fat (4 g saturated fat), 82 mg cholesterol, 516 mg sodium, 33 g carbohydrate, 2 g fiber, 37 g protein. Diabetic Exchanges: 5 lean meat, 2 starch.

>> HOW TO:

READ MEAT LABELS

Meat labels give you a variety of information. The label states the type of meat (beef, pork, veal or lamb), the wholesale cut (loin, rib, shoulder, leg, etc.) and the retail cut (steak, chops, roast, etc.). The label also states the sell by date, the weight of the meat, coast per pound and total price.

The wholesale cut is an indication of tenderness; for example, a loin or rib chop will be more tender than a shoulder or leg chop. Tender cuts are best cooked with dry-heat methods (grilling, broiling, roasting, pan-frying, pan-broiling and stir-frying). Less-tender cuts are better cooked by moist-heat methods (braising or cooking in liquid).

TACO LASAGNA

Yield: 9 servings.

Loaded with cheese, meat and beans, this layered casserole comes together in a snap. There are never any leftovers when I take it to potlucks.

terri keenan // tuscaloosa, alabama

- 1 **pound ground beef**
- 1/2 **cup chopped green pepper**
- 1/2 **cup chopped onion**
- 2/3 **cup water**
- 1 **envelope taco seasoning**
- 1 **can (15 ounces) black beans, rinsed and drained**
- 1 **can (14-1/2 ounces) Mexican diced tomatoes, undrained**
- 6 **flour tortillas (8 inches)**
- 1 **can (16 ounces) refried beans**
- 3 **cups (12 ounces) shredded Mexican cheese blend**

In a large skillet, cook the beef, green pepper and onion over medium heat until meat is no longer pink; drain. Add water and taco seasoning; bring to a boil. Reduce heat; simmer, uncovered, for 2 minutes. Stir in black beans and tomatoes. Simmer, uncovered, for 10 minutes.

Place two tortillas in a greased 13-in. x 9-in. baking dish. Spread with half of the refried beans and the beef mixture; sprinkle with 1 cup cheese. Repeat layers. Top with remaining tortillas and cheese.

Cover and bake at 350° for 25-30 minutes or until heated through and cheese is melted.

Nutrition Facts: 1 piece equals 448 calories, 21 g fat (11 g saturated fat), 69 mg cholesterol, 1,152 mg sodium, 39 g carbohydrate, 5 g fiber, 25 g protein.

REUBEN CRESCENT BAKE

CHEAT IT!

Yield: 8 servings.

This may not be a true Reuben, but the taste is fantastic and it's so easy. Homemade soup is my favorite accompaniment.

kathy kittell // lenexa, kansas

- 2 **tubes (8 ounces *each*) refrigerated crescent rolls**
- 1 **pound sliced Swiss cheese, *divided***
- 1-1/4 **pounds sliced deli corned beef**
- 1 **can (14 ounces) sauerkraut, rinsed and well drained**
- 2/3 **cup Thousand Island salad dressing**
- 1 **egg white, lightly beaten**
- 3 **teaspoons caraway seeds**

Unroll one tube of crescent dough into one long rectangle; seal seams and perforations. Press onto the bottom of a greased 13-in. x 9-in. baking dish. Bake at 375° for 8-10 minutes or until golden brown.

Layer with half of the cheese and all of the corned beef. Combine the sauerkraut and salad dressing; spread over beef. Top with remaining cheese.

On a lightly floured surface, press or roll second tube of crescent dough into a 13-in. x 9-in. rectangle, sealing seams and perforations. Place over the cheese. Brush with egg white and sprinkle with caraway seeds.

Bake for 12-16 minutes or until heated through and crust is golden brown. Let stand for 5 minutes before cutting.

Nutrition Facts: 1 piece equals 610 calories, 39 g fat (18 g saturated fat), 108 mg cholesterol, 1,905 mg sodium, 28 g carbohydrate, 2 g fiber, 31 g protein.

TRADITIONAL LASAGNA

Yield: 12 servings.

For a casual holiday meal, you can't go wrong with this rich and meaty lasagna. My grown sons request it for their birthdays, too.

pam thompson // girard, illinois

- 9 **lasagna noodles**
- 1-1/4 **pounds bulk Italian sausage**
- 3/4 **pound ground beef**
- 1 **medium onion, diced**
- 3 **garlic cloves, minced**
- 2 **cans (one 28 ounces, one 15 ounces) crushed tomatoes**
- 2 **cans (6 ounces *each*) tomato paste**
- 2/3 **cup water**
- 2 **to 3 tablespoons sugar**
- 3 **tablespoons plus 1/4 cup minced fresh parsley, *divided***
- 2 **teaspoons dried basil**
- 3/4 **teaspoon fennel seed**
- 3/4 **teaspoon salt, *divided***
- 1/4 **teaspoon coarsely ground pepper**
- 1 **egg, lightly beaten**
- 1 **carton (15 ounces) ricotta cheese**
- 4 **cups (16 ounces) shredded part-skim mozzarella cheese**
- 3/4 **cup grated Parmesan cheese**

Cook noodles according to package directions. Meanwhile, in a large saucepan, cook the sausage, beef and onion over medium heat until meat is no longer pink. Add garlic; cook 1 minute longer. Drain.

Stir in the tomatoes, tomato paste, water, sugar, 3 tablespoons parsley, basil, fennel seed, 1/2 teaspoon salt and pepper. Bring to a boil. Reduce the heat; simmer, uncovered, for 30 minutes, stirring occasionally. In a small bowl, combine the egg, ricotta, and remaining parsley and salt.

Drain noodles. Spread 2 cups meat sauce into an ungreased 13-in. x 9-in. baking dish. Layer with three noodles and a third of the ricotta mixture. Sprinkle with 1 cup mozzarella cheese and 2 tablespoons Parmesan cheese. Repeat layers twice. Top with remaining meat sauce and cheeses.

Cover and bake at 375° for 25 minutes. Uncover; bake 25 minutes longer or until bubbly and a thermometer reads 160°. Let stand for 15 minutes before cutting.

Nutrition Facts: 1 piece equals 519 calories, 27 g fat (13 g saturated fat), 109 mg cholesterol, 1,013 mg sodium, 35 g carbohydrate, 4 g fiber, 35 g protein.

LAYERED TORTILLA PIE

Yield: 4-6 servings.

My sister used to serve tortilla pie at the hunting and fishing lodge she operated in Colorado. It was a sure bet to win compliments from the men who came in cold and hungry after spending the day tramping through the woods.

delma snyder // mccook, nebraska

1 **pound ground beef**	1 **can (2-1/2 ounces) sliced ripe olives, drained, optional**
1 **medium onion, chopped**	
1 **can (8 ounces) tomato sauce**	1 **tablespoon butter**
1 **garlic clove, minced**	6 **corn tortillas (6 inches)**
1 **tablespoon chili powder**	2 **cups (8 ounces) shredded cheddar cheese**
1/2 **teaspoon salt**	
1/4 **teaspoon pepper**	1/4 **cup water**

In a large skillet, cook beef and onion until meat is no longer pink; drain. Add the tomato sauce, garlic, chili powder, salt, pepper and olives if desired. Bring to a boil. Reduce heat; simmer for 5 minutes or until thickened.

Lightly butter tortillas on one side; place one tortilla, buttered side down, in a 2-qt. round casserole. Top with about 1/2 cup meat mixture and 1/3 cup cheese. Repeat layers, ending with cheese.

Pour water around the sides of the casserole (not over top). Cover and bake at 400° for 20 minutes or until heated through. Let stand 5 minutes before cutting.

Nutrition Facts: 1 serving (calculated without olives) equals 350 calories, 20 g fat (12 g saturated fat), 82 mg cholesterol, 722 mg sodium, 19 g carbohydrate, 3 g fiber, 24 g protein.

NO-FUSS SWISS STEAK

Yield: 8-10 servings.

I make this dish regularly. My kids love the steak, gravy and fork-tender veggies.

sharon morrell // parker, south dakota

3	**pounds beef top round steak, cut into serving-size pieces**
2	**tablespoons canola oil**
2	**medium carrots, sliced**
2	**celery ribs, sliced**
1-3/4	**cups water**
1	**can (11 ounces) condensed tomato rice soup, undiluted**
1	**can (10-1/2 ounces) condensed French onion soup, undiluted**
1/2	**teaspoon pepper**
1	**bay leaf**

In a large skillet, brown beef in oil over medium-high heat; drain. Transfer to a 5-qt. slow cooker. Add carrots and celery. Combine the remaining ingredients; pour over meat and vegetables.

Cover and cook on low for 6-8 hours or until meat is tender. Discard bay leaf. Thicken cooking juices if desired.

Nutrition Facts: 1 serving equals 246 calories, 8 g fat (2 g saturated fat), 79 mg cholesterol, 477 mg sodium, 10 g carbohydrate, 1 g fiber, 32 g protein.

BARBECUES FOR THE BUNCH

Yield: 16 servings.

This barbecue is an easy way to have dinner ready for a hungry crowd. It's the perfect party food. Just add chips, drinks and your favorite deli salads, and dinner is set!
louise watkins // long key, florida

- 2 **pounds beef top sirloin steak, cubed**
- 1-1/2 **pounds boneless pork loin roast, cubed**
- 2 **large onions, chopped**
- 3/4 **cup chopped celery**
- 1 **can (6 ounces) tomato paste**
- 1/2 **cup packed brown sugar**
- 1/4 **cup cider vinegar**
- 1/4 **cup chili sauce**
- 2 **tablespoons Worcestershire sauce**
- 1 **tablespoon ground mustard**
- 16 **hamburger buns, split**

In a 5-qt. slow cooker, combine the beef, pork, onions and celery. In a small bowl, combine the tomato paste, brown sugar, vinegar, chili sauce, Worcestershire sauce and mustard. Pour over meat mixture.

Cover and cook on high for 6-8 hours or until the meat is very tender. Shred meat in the slow cooker with two forks. With a slotted spoon, serve 1/2 cup meat mixture on each bun bottom. Replace bun tops.

Nutrition Facts: 1 sandwich equals 297 calories, 7 g fat (2 g saturated fat), 53 mg cholesterol, 336 mg sodium, 34 g carbohydrate, 2 g fiber, 24 g protein. Diabetic Exchanges: 3 lean meat, 2 starch.

CHINESE PORK RIBS

Yield: 4 servings.

These yummy ribs will have everyone coming back for seconds.
june ross // belmont, north carolina

- 1/4 **cup reduced-sodium soy sauce**
- 1/3 **cup orange marmalade**
- 3 **tablespoons ketchup**
- 2 **garlic cloves, minced**
- 3 **pounds bone-in country-style pork ribs**

In a small bowl, combine the soy sauce, marmalade, ketchup and garlic. Pour half into a 5-qt. slow cooker. Top with ribs; drizzle with remaining sauce.

Cover and cook on low for 6-8 hours or until meat is tender. Thicken cooking juices if desired.

Nutrition Facts: 1 serving equals 441 calories, 20 g fat (7 g saturated fat), 129 mg cholesterol, 858 mg sodium, 22 g carbohydrate, trace fiber, 40 g protein.

>> HOW TO:

SHRED MEAT FOR SANDWICHES

Remove cooked meat from the pan or slow cooker if the recipe directs. Reserve cooking liquid if called for. Place meat in a shallow pan. With two forks, pull meat into thin shreds. Return meat to the liquid to heat through, or use as the recipe directs.

MOM'S POT ROAST

Yield: 8 servings.

This recipe can feed a crowd, and leftovers are great for sandwiches or a hearty barley soup.

dorothy duder // north hollywood, california

- 3 **tablespoons all-purpose flour,** *divided*
- 1 **teaspoon salt**
- 1/4 **teaspoon** *each* **minced chives, parsley flakes and tarragon**
- 1/4 **teaspoon pepper**
- 1 **boneless beef chuck roast (3 to 3-1/2 pounds)**
- 2 **tablespoons canola oil**
- 8 **cups water**
- 2 **tablespoons beef bouillon granules**
- 2 **tablespoons Worcestershire sauce**
- 1 **large onion, chopped**
- 3 **celery ribs, cut into chunks**
- 3 **garlic cloves, minced**
- 2 **bay leaves**
- 4 **medium potatoes, peeled and quartered**
- 4 **medium carrots, cut into chunks**
- 2 **tablespoons butter**

Combine 1 tablespoon flour and seasonings; rub over roast. In a Dutch oven, brown roast on all sides in oil over medium-high heat. Add the water, bouillon, Worcestershire sauce, onion, celery, garlic and bay leaves. Bring to a boil. Reduce heat; cover and simmer for 2 hours, turning the roast after 1 hour.

Turn roast again. Add potatoes and carrots. Cover and simmer 1 hour longer or until meat and vegetables are tender.

Discard bay leaves. Remove meat and vegetables to a serving platter and keep warm. Pour 2 cups cooking juices and loosened browned bits into a 2-cup measuring cup; skim fat. (Save remaining cooking juices for another use.)

For gravy, in a small saucepan, melt butter; stir in remaining flour until smooth. Gradually stir in cooking juices. Bring to a boil; cook and stir for 2 minutes or until thickened. Serve with roast and vegetables.

Nutrition Facts: 6 ounces cooked beef equals 448 calories, 23 g fat (8 g saturated fat), 118 mg cholesterol, 1,053 mg sodium, 24 g carbohydrate, 3 g fiber, 36 g protein.

OVEN BEEF STEW

Yield: 6 servings.

This is a great cold-weather meal. Add a good loaf of bread and you're all set.
bettina turner // kernersville, north carolina

6	**tablespoons all-purpose flour, *divided***
1/4	**teaspoon salt, optional**
1/2	**teaspoon pepper, *divided***
1-1/2	**pounds boneless beef chuck roast, cut into 1-inch cubes**
1	**tablespoon canola oil**
1	**medium onion, chopped**
3	**garlic cloves, minced**
3	**cups beef broth**
1	**can (14-1/2 ounces) stewed tomatoes, cut up**
3/4	**teaspoon dried thyme**
3	**large potatoes, peeled and cut into 1-inch cubes**
3	**medium carrots, cut into 1/4-inch slices**
1/2	**cup frozen peas, thawed**

In a large resealable plastic bag, combine 4 tablespoons flour, salt if desired and 1/4 teaspoon pepper. Add beef, a few pieces at a time, and shake to coat. In a Dutch oven, brown beef in oil in batches. Set aside. Add onion to pan; cook until tender. Stir in garlic with remaining flour and pepper. Gradually stir in broth. Add beef, tomatoes and thyme. Cover and bake at 350° for 1-1/4 hours.

Add the potatoes and carrots. Cover and bake 1 hour longer or until meat and vegetables are tender. Stir in peas; cover and let stand for 5 minutes before serving.

Nutrition Facts: 1-1/2 cups (prepared with reduced-sodium broth; calculated without salt) equals 439 calories, 13 g fat (5 g saturated fat), 76 mg cholesterol, 426 mg sodium, 50 g carbohydrate, 6 g fiber, 30 g protein.

≫ HOW TO:

BRAISE

1. Season and coat the meat with flour as the recipe directs. In a Dutch oven, brown the meat in oil in batches. To ensure nice browning, do not crowd the meat.
2. Set meat aside and cook vegetables as directed in the recipe. If the recipe directs, add flour and stir until blended.
3. Slowly add broth, stirring to deglaze the pan. If the recipe contains flour, add liquid gradually to allow a lump-free sauce to start to form.

4. Continue adding broth and return meat to the pan. Stir until mixture comes to a boil to prevent lumps.
5. Add other vegetables as the recipe directs.

TRADITIONAL BOILED DINNER

Yield: 6 servings.

Corned beef is a treat to our family any time of the year.

joy strasser // mukwonago, wisconsin

- 1 **corned beef brisket with spice packet (3 pounds)**
- 1 **teaspoon whole black peppercorns**
- 2 **bay leaves**
- 2 **medium potatoes, peeled and quartered**
- 3 **medium carrots, quartered**
- 1 **medium onion, cut into 6 wedges**
- 1 **small head green cabbage, cut into 6 wedges**

Place brisket and contents of spice packet in a Dutch oven. Add peppercorns, bay leaves and enough water to cover; bring to a boil. Reduce heat; cover and simmer for 2 hours or until meat is almost tender. Add potatoes, carrots and onion; cover and simmer for 10 minutes. Add cabbage, cover and cook 15-20 minutes or until tender. Discard bay leaves and peppercorns.

Nutrition Facts: 1 serving equals 282 calories, 11 g fat (2 g saturated fat), 64 mg cholesterol, 1,053 mg sodium, 19 g carbohydrate, 3 g fiber, 28 g protein..

SPICY PEPPER STEAK

Yield: 2 servings.

This surprisingly spicy pepper steak has a bit of Southwestern flair from the green chilies. It's economical and convenient.

ladonna reed // ponca city, oklahoma

- 1/2 **pound beef top round steak, cut into thin strips**
- 1/4 **teaspoon salt**
- 1/4 **teaspoon pepper**
- 1 **tablespoon canola oil**
- 1 **medium green pepper, julienned**
- 1/4 **cup chopped onion**
- 1 **garlic clove, minced**
- 1 **teaspoon beef bouillon granules**
- 3/4 **cup hot water**
- 1 **can (10 ounces) diced tomatoes and green chilies**
- 2 **tablespoons cornstarch**
- 1/4 **cup cold water**
- **Hot cooked noodles, optional**

Sprinkle beef with salt and pepper. In a large skillet, brown beef in oil; remove and keep warm. In the same skillet, saute green pepper and onion until tender. Add garlic; cook 1 minute longer.

Dissolve bouillon in hot water; stir into skillet with tomatoes. Return beef to the pan; bring to a boil. Reduce heat; cover and simmer for 30-35 minutes or until meat is tender.

Combine cornstarch and cold water; stir into meat mixture. Bring to a boil; cook and stir for 2 minutes or until thickened. Serve with noodles if desired.

Nutrition Facts: 1-1/2 cups (prepared with reduced-sodium bouillon granules; calculated without noodles) equals 282 calories, 11 g fat (2 g saturated fat), 64 mg cholesterol, 1,053 mg sodium, 19 g carbohydrate, 3 g fiber, 28 g protein.

GRILLED RIBEYE STEAKS

Yield: 4 servings.

In the summer, I love to marinate these steaks overnight, then grill them for family and friends.

tim hanchon // muncie, indiana

- 1/2 **cup soy sauce**
- 1/2 **cup sliced green onions**
- 1/4 **cup packed brown sugar**
-   2 **garlic cloves, minced**
- 1/4 **teaspoon ground ginger**
- 1/4 **teaspoon pepper**
- 2-1/2 **pounds beef ribeye steaks**

In a large resealable plastic bag, combine the soy sauce, onions, brown sugar, garlic, ginger and pepper; add the steaks. Seal bag and turn to coat. Refrigerate for 8 hours or overnight.

Drain and discard marinade. Grill steaks, covered, over medium-hot heat for 4-6 minutes on each side or until the meat reaches desired doneness (for medium-rare, a meat thermometer should read 145°; medium, 160°; well-done, 170°).

Nutrition Facts: 1 serving equals 700 calories, 45 g fat (18 g saturated fat), 168 mg cholesterol, 1,977 mg sodium, 15 g carbohydrate, trace fiber, 55 g protein.

SIZZLING ANCHO RIBEYES: Combine 2 teaspoons each salt and ground ancho chili powder with 1/2 teaspoon pepper; rub over steaks. Grill as directed. Combine 3 tablespoons softened butter with 3 minced chipotle peppers in adobo sauce; spoon buttermixture over cooked steaks.

THAI STEAK SKEWERS

Yield: 16 skewers (1-1/3 cups sauce).

The combination of peanut butter and coconut milk on these slightly spicy kabobs is delectable.

amy frye // goodyear, arizona

- 1/4 **cup packed brown sugar**
-   2 **tablespoons lime juice**
-   2 **tablespoons reduced-sodium soy sauce**
-   1 **tablespoon curry powder**
-   1 **teaspoon lemon juice**
-   1 **can (13.66 ounces) coconut milk, *divided***
- 1-1/2 **teaspoons crushed red pepper flakes, *divided***
-   2 **pounds beef top sirloin steak, cut into 1/4-inch slices**
-   2 **medium limes, halved and thinly sliced, optional**
- 1/4 **cup creamy peanut butter**
-   1 **tablespoon chopped salted peanuts**

In a large resealable plastic bag, combine the brown sugar, lime juice, soy sauce, curry powder, lemon juice, 1/4 cup coconut milk and 1 teaspoon pepper flakes; add the steak. Seal bag and turn to coat. Refrigerate for 2-4 hours.

Drain and discard marinade. Thread beef onto 16 metal or soaked wooden skewers, alternately threading beef with lime slices if desired. Grill, covered, over medium-hot heat for 6-8 minutes or until meat reaches desired doneness, turning occasionally.

Meanwhile, in a small saucepan, combine peanut butter with remaining coconut milk and pepper flakes. Cook and stir over medium heat until blended. Transfer to a small bowl; sprinkle with peanuts. Serve with steak skewers.

Nutrition Facts: 1 skewer with 4 teaspoons sauce equals 156 calories, 10 g fat (6 g saturated fat), 31 mg cholesterol, 106 mg sodium, 4 g carbohydrate, 1 g fiber, 13 g protein.

CHIPOTLE MUSTARD PORK TENDERLOIN

Yield: 4 servings.

This is one flavorful entree with a lot of kick! The heat from the chipotle really comes through. Serve with plenty of ice-cold lemonade or iced tea.

linda foreman // locust grove, oklahoma

- **1/2 cup honey Dijon mustard**
- **1/3 cup minced fresh cilantro**
- **1/4 cup lime juice**
- **1 tablespoon minced chipotle pepper in adobo sauce**
- **2 garlic cloves, minced**
- **1/2 teaspoon ground cumin**
- **1/4 teaspoon salt**
- **1/8 teaspoon ground cinnamon**
- **1 pork tenderloin (1 pound)**

Chopped honey-roasted peanuts, optional

In a small bowl, combine the first eight ingredients. Pour 1/2 cup marinade into a large resealable plastic bag; add the pork. Seal bag and turn to coat; refrigerate for 8 hours or overnight. Cover and refrigerate remaining marinade.

Drain and discard marinade from pork. Moisten a paper towel with cooking oil; using long-handled tongs, lightly coat the grill rack. Grill pork, covered, over indirect medium heat for 25-40 minutes or until a meat thermometer reads 160°. Let the pork stand for 5 minutes before slicing.

Heat the reserved mustard mixture; brush over the pork before serving. Sprinkle with peanuts if desired.

Nutrition Facts: 3 ounces cooked pork (calculated without peanuts) equals 191 calories, 6 g fat (2 g saturated fat), 64 mg cholesterol, 366 mg sodium, 13 g carbohydrate, 1 g fiber, 24 g protein. Diabetic Exchanges: 3 lean meat, 1 starch.

≫ HOW TO:

PREPARE A CHARCOAL GRILL FOR INDIRECT HEAT

To prepare a charcoal grill for indirect heat, bank half of the coals on one side of the grill and the other half on the other side. Place a foil drip pan in the center if the recipe directs. Replace the cooking grate and place the meat in the center of the grate. Cover and grill according to the recipe.

FLANK STEAK WITH ORANGE SAUCE

Yield: 4 servings.

Tender steak is treated to an orange marinade with a peppery kick in this scrumptious recipe. Try it on the grill with your favorite grilled veggies.

taste of home cooking school

3/4 cup orange juice	1/2 teaspoon coarsely ground pepper
1/4 cup honey	1 tablespoon canola oil
1 tablespoon lime juice	1 teaspoon minced fresh gingerroot
1 tablespoon soy sauce	1 beef flank steak (1 pound)
1 teaspoon minced garlic	

In a small bowl, combine the first six ingredients. Reserve 1/2 cup marinade. Add oil and ginger to the remaining orange sauce; pour into a large resealable bag. Add the flank steak; seal bag and turn to coat. Refrigerate for at least 1 hour or overnight. Cover and refrigerate reserved marinade

Drain and discard marinade from steak. Place steak on a broiler pan. Broil 4 in. from the heat for 7-8 minutes on each side or until meat reaches desired doneness (for medium-rare, a meat thermometer should read 145°; medium, 160°; well-done, 170°).

Meanwhile, in a small saucepan, warm reserved orange sauce until heated through. To serve, thinly slice steak across the grain; serve with orange sauce.

Nutrition Facts: 1 serving equals 289 calories, 12 g fat (4 g saturated fat), 54 mg cholesterol, 298 mg sodium, 23 g carbohydrate, trace fiber, 23 g protein.

>> HOW TO:

GRILL STEAK WITH SUCCESS

Trim steaks to avoid flare-ups, leaving a thin layer of fat if desired to help maintain juiciness. Pat dry with paper towels before grilling—a dry steak will brown better than a moist one.

Avoid grilling at too high a temperature, which will char the outside of the steak before the inside reaches the desired doneness. Grill steaks to at least medium-rare, 145°, but do not overcook.

To test for doneness, insert an instant-read thermometer horizontally from the side, making sure to get the reading in the center of the steak.

BEEF TIPS & CARAMELIZED ONION CASSEROLE

Yield: 8 servings.

The rich flavor of beef sweetened by onions makes this a recipe you'll want to make again and again. It's amazing with mashed potatoes.

linda stemen // monroeville, indiana

- **4 pounds beef sirloin tip roast, cut into 1-inch cubes**
- **1/2 teaspoon salt**
- **1/2 teaspoon pepper**
- **2 tablespoons olive oil**
- **4 large sweet onions, halved and thinly sliced**
- **3 tablespoons butter**
- **4 garlic cloves, minced**
- **2/3 cup all-purpose flour**
- **2 cans (10-1/2 ounces *each*) condensed beef consomme, undiluted**
- **1 can (14-1/2 ounces) reduced-sodium beef broth**
- **2 tablespoons Worcestershire sauce**
- **2 bay leaves**
- **1/2 cup heavy whipping cream**
- **8 slices French bread (1/2 inch thick), toasted**
- **1 cup (4 ounces) shredded part-skim mozzarella cheese**

Sprinkle beef with salt and pepper. In a large skillet, brown meat in oil in batches; drain. Transfer to a greased 13-in. x 9-in. baking dish.

In the same skillet, cook onions in butter over medium-low heat for 25-30 minutes or until golden brown, stirring occasionally. Add garlic; cook 2 minutes longer.

Stir in flour until blended; gradually add consomme and broth. Stir in Worcestershire sauce and bay leaves. Bring to a boil; cook and stir for 1 minute or until thickened. Pour over beef.

Cover and bake at 325° for 1 hour. Carefully stir in cream; discard bay leaves. Bake, uncovered, 25-35 minutes longer or until meat is tender. Place toast over beef mixture; sprinkle with cheese. Bake for 5 minutes or until cheese is melted.

Nutrition Facts: 1 cup beef mixture with 1 slice cheese toast equals 585 calories, 26 g fat (12 g saturated fat), 186 mg cholesterol, 1,039 mg sodium, 29 g carbohydrate, 2 g fiber, 56 g protein.

FRUIT-GLAZED SPIRAL HAM

Yield: 16-20 servings.

The combo of zesty horseradish and tangy mustard creates a delicious glaze perfect for ham. I've used this recipe for years and always get rave reviews.
joan hallford // north richland hills, texas

- 1 **bone-in fully cooked spiral-sliced ham (8 to 10 pounds)**
- 1 **can (8 ounces) unsweetened crushed pineapple, drained**
- 1/2 **cup apricot jam**
- 1 **tablespoon spicy brown mustard**
- 2 **teaspoons prepared horseradish**

Place ham on a rack in a large roasting pan. Cover and bake at 325° for 1-1/2 hours.

Combine the pineapple, jam, mustard and horseradish; spread over ham. Bake, uncovered, for 30-45 minutes or until a meat thermometer reads 140°.

Nutrition Facts: 6 ounces ham equals 248 calories, 4 g fat (1 g saturated fat), 40 mg cholesterol, 1,648 mg sodium, 20 g carbohydrate, trace fiber, 33 g protein.

DIJON-RUBBED PORK WITH RHUBARB SAUCE

Yield: 12 servings (1-1/2 cups sauce).

This moist and tender pork loin roast is served with a rhubarb sauce that's just delicious! It's great for company and makes celebrations special.
marilyn rodriquez // fairbanks, alaska

- 1 **boneless pork loin roast (3 pounds)**
- 1/4 **cup Dijon mustard**
- 6 **garlic cloves, minced**
- 1 **tablespoon minced fresh rosemary *or* 1 teaspoon dried rosemary, crushed**
- 3/4 **teaspoon salt**
- 1/2 **teaspoon pepper**

SAUCE:

- 3 **cups sliced fresh *or* frozen rhubarb**
- 1/3 **cup orange juice**
- 1/3 **cup sugar**
- 1 **tablespoon cider vinegar**

Score the surface of the pork, making diamond shapes 1/4 in. deep. In a small bowl, combine the mustard, garlic, rosemary, salt and pepper; rub over pork.

Coat a roasting pan and rack with cooking spray; place pork on rack in pan. Bake, uncovered, at 350° for 1 to 1-1/4 to hours or until a meat thermometer reads 160°. Let stand 10 minutes before slicing.

In a small saucepan, bring the sauce ingredients to a boil. Reduce heat; cover and simmer for 8-12 minutes or until rhubarb is tender. Serve warm with pork.

EDITOR'S NOTE: If using frozen rhubarb, measure rhubarb while still frozen, then thaw completely. Drain in a colander, but do not press liquid out.

Nutrition Facts: 3 ounces cooked pork with 2 tablespoons sauce equals 181 calories, 6 g fat (2 g saturated fat), 56 mg cholesterol, 308 mg sodium, 9 g carbohydrate, 1 g fiber, 23 g protein. Diabetic Exchanges: 3 lean meat, 1/2 starch.

CARAMELIZE ONIONS

1 Slice root and top off onion; cut in half. Peel and slice. Use a large skillet so the onions are not crowded. Heat oil in the pan over medium heat; add the onions and stir to coat.

2 Cook onions, stirring occasionally from the bottom every 5 minutes. Once onions begin to brown, reduce heat. Continue cooking 20-30 minutes, stirring every 2-5 minutes until onions are golden-brown, adding more oil if needed.

3 When onions reach their desired color, remove from heat to stop cooking. Sprinkle onions with salt, pepper and sugar to enhance flavors if desired.

BEEF ROAST AU POIVRE

Yield: 6 servings.

This beef roast with crushed peppercorns is elegant, delicious and perfect for company. The aroma in your kitchen while it's cooking will be out of this world!

elaine sweet // dallas, texas

- 2 tablespoons *each* whole black and pink peppercorns *or* 1/4 cup whole black peppercorns
- 3 dried chipotle chilies, stems removed
- 1 tablespoon coriander seeds
- 1 tablespoon dried minced onion
- 1 tablespoon dried thyme
- 1-1/2 teaspoons salt
- 1 teaspoon dried orange peel
- 3 tablespoons steak sauce
- 1 beef tri-tip roast (2 to 3 pounds)

ONIONS:
- 4 large onions, thinly sliced
- 3 tablespoons olive oil
- 1/2 cup chardonnay *or* other white wine
- 2 teaspoons dried thyme
- 1/2 teaspoon pepper
- 1/8 teaspoon salt
- 2 tablespoons minced fresh parsley

Place the peppercorns, chilies and coriander in a blender. Cover and process until coarsely ground. Stir in the onion, thyme, salt and orange peel.

Rub the steak sauce and seasoning mixture over the roast; cover and refrigerate for 8 hours or overnight.

Place roast on a rack in a shallow roasting pan. Bake, uncovered, at 425° for 1 to 1-1/2 hours or until meat reaches desired doneness (for medium-rare, a meat thermometer should read 145°; medium, 160°; well-done, 170°).

Meanwhile, in a large skillet, cook onions in oil over low heat for 30-35 minutes or until golden brown, stirring frequently. Stir in wine and bring to a boil. Reduce heat; cook and stir for 1-2 minutes or until liquid is evaporated. Stir in the thyme, pepper and salt.

Transfer meat to a warm serving platter. Let stand for 10 minutes before slicing. Sprinkle with parsley. Serve with onions.

Nutrition Facts: 5 ounces cooked beef with 1/2 cup caramelized onions equals 367 calories, 18 g fat (5 g saturated fat), 91 mg cholesterol, 851 mg sodium, 15 g carbohydrate, 3 g fiber, 33 g protein.

HONEY-MUSTARD PORK ROAST

Yield: 6-8 servings.

Family and friends are surprised when I tell them this impressive-looking roast is easy to prepare. I simply marinate the roast a few hours, then pop it in the oven. The creamy sauce is perfect alongside.
grace brennfleck // clairton, pennsylvania

- 1-1/2 **cups beer** *or* **ginger ale**
- 1 **cup Dijon mustard**
- 2/3 **cup honey**
- 1/2 **cup olive oil**
- 16 **garlic cloves, minced**
- 1/2 **cup minced fresh rosemary,** *or* **4 teaspoons dried rosemary, crushed**
- 1 **boneless pork loin roast (2 to 2-1/2 pounds)**
- 1/2 **cup heavy whipping cream**

In a small bowl, combine the beer, mustard, honey, oil, garlic and rosemary. Pour half into a large resealable plastic bag; add the roast. Seal bag and turn to coat. Refrigerate for at least 2 hours. Cover and refrigerate remaining marinade.

Drain and discard marinade from pork. Place roast on a rack in a roasting pan. Bake, uncovered, at 350° for 55 to 65 minutes or until a meat thermometer reads 160°. Let stand for 10 minutes before carving.

Place reserved marinade in a small saucepan. Add cream and pan drippings if desired. Bring to a boil. Reduce heat; simmer, uncovered, for 5-10 minutes or until slightly thickened. Serve with pork.

Nutrition Facts: 4 ounces cooked pork equals 393 calories, 21 g fat (7 g saturated fat), 77 mg cholesterol, 582 mg sodium, 25 g carbohydrate, trace fiber, 23 g protein.

HAM WITH RUBY-RED GLAZE

CHEAT IT!

Yield: 8-10 servings.

I have used this recipe for over 40 years and it is still a favorite with my family. Kids love the glaze with mashed potatoes.
beverly payne // el sobrante, california

1	**boneless fully cooked ham (about 4 pounds)**
3/4	**cup packed brown sugar**
3/4	**cup creamy French salad dressing**

Place the ham on a rack in a shallow roasting pan. Cover and bake at 325° for 1-1/2 hours.

In a small microwave-safe bowl, combine the brown sugar and salad dressing. Cover and microwave on high for 30-60 seconds or until sugar is dissolved. Pour 1/4 cup over the ham.

Bake, uncovered, 30-40 minutes longer or until a meat thermometer reads 140°. Let stand for 10 minutes before slicing. Serve with remaining glaze.

EDITOR'S NOTE: This recipe was tested in a 1,100-watt microwave.

Nutrition Facts: 6 ounces ham equals 341 calories, 15 g fat (3 g saturated fat), 92 mg cholesterol, 2,045 mg sodium, 19 g carbohydrate, 0 fiber, 34 g protein.

>> HOW TO:

STUD HAM WITH CLOVES

With a sharp knife, make diagonal cuts in a diamond pattern about 1/2 in. deep in the surface of the ham. Push a whole clove into the point of each diamond for a pretty presentation.

APPLE-STUFFED PORK ROAST

Yield: 2 servings.

My husband doesn't usually like healthy meals, but this pretty entree is one of his all-time favorites.

melissa holtz // covington, kentucky

- **1 pork tenderloin (3/4 pound)**
- **Dash salt**
- **Dash pepper**
- **1/2 cup chopped peeled tart apple**
- **1/4 cup soft bread crumbs**
- **2 tablespoons chopped celery**
- **1 tablespoon chopped green onion**
- **1 tablespoon raisins**
- **1 tablespoon chopped walnuts**
- **Dash ground nutmeg**
- **2 tablespoons unsweetened apple juice, *divided***

SAUCE:
- **2 teaspoons cornstarch**
- **1/8 teaspoon ground cinnamon**
- **1/2 cup unsweetened apple juice**

Cut a lengthwise slit down center of tenderloin to within 1/2 in. of bottom; open so meat lies flat. Cover with plastic wrap; flatten to 1/2-in. thickness. Remove wrap; sprinkle meat with salt and pepper.

In a small bowl, combine the apple, bread crumbs, celery, onion, raisins, walnuts and nutmeg. Sprinkle with 1 tablespoon apple juice; toss to coat. Spoon over pork. Roll up jelly-roll style, starting with a long side; tie roast with kitchen string and secure the ends with toothpicks.

Place on a rack in a shallow roasting pan coated with cooking spray. Drizzle with 1-1/2 teaspoons apple juice. Bake, uncovered, at 375° for 30 minutes. Brush with remaining

>> HOW TO:

STUFF A TENDERLOIN

1. Cut a lengthwise slit down the center of the tenderloin to within 1/2 in. of bottom.
2. Open tenderloin so it lies flat. If using a tenderloin 1 pound or larger, make another lengthwise slit down the center of each half to within 1/2 in. of bottom.
3. Cover with plastic wrap. Flatten to the thickness directed in the recipe.

4. Remove plastic wrap. Layer or stuff as recipe directs.
5. Roll up jelly-roll style, starting with a long side. Tie roast at 1-1/2-in. to 2-in. intervals with kitchen string.

apple juice. Bake 20-25 minutes longer or until the meat juices run clear and a meat thermometer reads 160°. Let stand for 5 minutes before slicing.

Meanwhile, in a small saucepan, combine cornstarch and cinnamon. Gradually whisk in apple juice until smooth. Bring to a boil; cook and stir for 1-2 minutes or until thickened. Serve with pork.

Nutrition Facts: 1 serving equals 314 calories, 8 g fat (2 g saturated fat), 95 mg cholesterol, 181 mg sodium, 23 g carbohydrate, 1 g fiber, 36 g protein. Diabetic Exchanges: 5 lean meat, 1 starch, 1 fat, 1/2 fruit.

INDIVIDUAL BEEF WELLINGTONS

Yield: 6 servings.

A savory mushroom-wine sauce is draped over golden puff pastry that encases tender filet mignon. Wow your guests this holiday season.
taste of home cooking school

- 6 **beef tenderloin steaks (1-1/2 to 2 inches thick and 8 ounces *each*)**
- 4 **tablespoons butter, *divided***
- 3 **sheets frozen puff pastry, thawed**
- 1 **egg, lightly beaten**
- 1/2 **pound sliced fresh mushrooms**
- 1/4 **cup chopped shallots**
- 2 **tablespoons all-purpose flour**
- 1 **can (10-1/2 ounces) condensed beef consomme, undiluted**
- 3 **tablespoons port wine**
- 2 **teaspoons minced fresh thyme**

In a large skillet, brown steaks in 2 tablespoons butter for 2-3 minutes on each side. Remove and keep warm.

On a lightly floured surface, roll each puff pastry sheet into a 14-in. x 9-1/2-in. rectangle. Cut each into two 7-in. squares (discard scraps). Place a steak in the center of each square. Lightly brush pastry edges with water. Bring opposite corners of pastry over steak; pinch seams to seal tightly. Cut four small slits in top of pastry.

Place in a greased 15-in. x 10-in. x 1-in. baking pan. Brush with egg. Bake at 400° for 25-30 minutes or until pastry is golden brown and meat reaches desired doneness (for medium-rare, a meat thermometer should read 145°; medium, 160°; well-done, 170°).

Meanwhile, in the same skillet, saute mushrooms and shallots in remaining butter for 3-5 minutes or until tender. Combine flour and consomme until smooth; stir into mushroom mixture. Bring to a boil; cook and stir for 2 minutes or until thickened. Add wine and thyme; cook 2 minutes longer. Serve with beef.

Nutrition Facts: 1 serving equals 1,122 calories, 64 g fat (21 g saturated fat), 201 mg cholesterol, 928 mg sodium, 75 g carbohydrate, 10 g fiber, 59 g protein.

WINES FOR THE CELEBRATION

- Serve the Individual Beef Wellingtons or the Beef Tips with Caramelized Onion Casserole (page 118) with a lighter-bodied red wine like Merlot, French Burgundy, Cabernet Franc or Pinot Noir.
- With its spicy flavor, Beef Roast au Poivre (page 120) needs a more assertive wine like red Zinfandel, Bordeaux or Cabernet Sauvignon.
- Serve either pork roast with Chardonnay or Sauvignon Blanc.
- The sweetly glazed hams will pair perfectly with a light and fruity wine like Riesling or white Zinfandel. Or if serving ham for brunch, consider a sparkling wine or the Mimosas on page 30.

POULTRY

GREEK ROASTED CHICKEN AND POTATOES

Yield: about 8-10 servings.

You'll find this meal is a nice one to prepare for company or to serve your family for Sunday dinner. All you need with it is a tossed salad and some crusty French bread.
pella visnick // dallas, texas

1 roasting chicken (6 to 7 pounds)	4 to 6 baking potatoes, peeled and quartered
Salt and pepper to taste	1/4 cup butter, melted
2 to 3 teaspoons dried oregano, *divided*	3 tablespoons lemon juice
	3/4 cup chicken broth

Place chicken breast side up on a rack in a roasting pan. Sprinkle with salt and pepper and half the oregano. Arrange potatoes around the chicken; sprinkle with salt and pepper and the remaining oregano. Pour butter and lemon juice over chicken and potatoes. Add chicken broth to pan.

Bake, uncovered, at 350° for 2 to 2-1/2 hours or until a meat thermometer reads 180°, basting frequently with pan drippings. Cover and let stand for 10 minutes before carving. If desired, thicken pan drippings for gravy.

Nutrition Facts: 1 serving equals 425 calories, 24 g fat (8 g saturated fat), 120 mg cholesterol, 214 mg sodium, 16 g carbohydrate, 2 g fiber, 36 g protein.

CHICKEN TIPS

TO PURCHASE THE BEST CHICKEN:
- Skin color ranges from white to deep yellow; skin color is an indication of the chicken's diet and not an indicator of freshness.
- Packages should be cold and have no holes or tears.
- Purchase chicken by the "sell-by" date.

TO BE SAFE:
- At the store, put the chicken package in a plastic bag to keep it from leaking onto other groceries.
- When you get home, freeze chicken immediately or use within 2 days.
- Wash your hands or anything else that comes into contact with uncooked poultry.
- Cook chicken breasts to an internal temperature of 170°, whole poultry and dark meat to 180°, and ground chicken to 165° or until no longer pink and juices run clear.

TO DEFROST IN THE REFRIGERATOR:
- Place a tray under the package to catch any liquid or juices.
- For bone-in parts or a small whole chicken, allow 1 to 2 days.
- For a large whole chicken, allow 24 hours for every 4 pounds.

TO DEFROST IN COLD WATER:
- Chicken must be in leakproof plastic bag.
- Submerge wrapped chicken in cold tap water.
- Change the water every 30 minutes.
- Allow 30 minutes of thawing time for every pound.

COMMON CHICKEN TERMS

ROASTER:
A chicken between 3 and 5 months old that weighs 5 to 7 pounds.

BROILER/FRYER:
A chicken about 7 weeks old that weighs 2-1/2 to 4-1/2 pounds.

CORNISH GAME HEN:
A small broiler/fryer that is less than 30 days old and weighs 1-1/2 to 2 pounds.

SPLIT CHICKEN:
A broiler/fryer that was cut lengthwise in half.

CHICKEN QUARTER:
A quarter of the chicken, usually sold as the leg quarter. The leg quarter contains the drumstick, thigh and portion of the back. The breast quarter contains the breast, wing and portion of the back.

BASTED OR SELF-BASTED:
The chicken has been injected or marinated with a solution of water, broth or stock that contains a fat, such as butter, as well as spices and flavor enhancers.

FREE RANGE OR FREE ROAMING:
The poultry was not confined to a chicken house but was allowed outside to forage for food.

SUNDAY'S BEST CHICKEN

Yield: 6 servings.

I am the busy mom of four and a nursing student, so weeknight dinners are often rushed. Sunday dinners are very important to our family, and everyone loves when I make this old-fashioned chicken recipe.

amy jenkins // mesa, arizona

- 2 **to 3 medium lemons**
- 2 **fresh rosemary sprigs**
- 1 **roasting chicken (6 to 7 pounds)**
- 1 **tablespoon olive oil**
- 2 **tablespoons minced fresh rosemary**
- 1 **tablespoon coarsely ground pepper**
- 1-1/2 **teaspoons salt**

Finely grate the peel from the lemons to measure 2 tablespoons; set aside. Coarsely chop 2 lemons; place chopped lemons and rosemary sprigs in the chicken cavity. Save remaining lemon for another use.

Place chicken on a rack in a shallow roasting pan; brush with oil. Combine the minced rosemary, pepper, salt and lemon peel; rub over chicken.

Bake, uncovered, at 350° for 2 to 2-1/2 hours or until a meat thermometer reads 180°, basting occasionally with drippings. (Cover loosely with foil if chicken browns too quickly.)

Let stand for 10 minutes before carving. Discard lemons and rosemary sprigs.

Nutrition Facts: 1 serving equals 555 calories, 34 g fat (9 g saturated fat), 179 mg cholesterol, 801 mg sodium, 3 g carbohydrate, 1 g fiber, 57 g protein.

ROAST CHICKEN WITH OYSTER STUFFING

Yield: 6 servings (4 cups stuffing).

The aroma of this moist, golden-brown chicken is almost as wonderful as its flavor, and the oyster stuffing is to die for!

joann jensen // lowell, indiana

- 1 **can (8 ounces) whole oysters**
- 1 **celery rib, chopped**
- 1 **small onion, chopped**
- 1/4 **cup butter, cubed**
- 2 **tablespoons minced fresh parsley**
- 1/2 **teaspoon Italian seasoning**
- 3 **cups cubed bread, lightly toasted**
- 1 **roasting chicken (6 to 7 pounds)**
- 1/4 **cup butter, melted**
- 1 **to 2 teaspoons paprika**

Drain oysters, reserving liquid; coarsely chop oysters. Set aside. In a small skillet, saute celery and onion in butter until tender. Stir in parsley and Italian seasoning. Place bread cubes in a large bowl; add the butter mixture, oysters and 1/4 cup reserved oyster liquid.

Just before baking, loosely stuff chicken with stuffing. Place breast side up on a rack in a large roasting pan; tie drumsticks together. Combine the melted butter and paprika; spoon over the chicken.

Bake, uncovered, at 350° for 2 to 2-1/2 hours or until a meat thermometer reads 180° for chicken and 165° for stuffing, basting occasionally with pan drippings. (Cover loosely with foil if chicken browns too quickly.)

Cover chicken and let stand for 10 minutes before removing stuffing and carving. Skim fat and thicken pan juices if desired.

Nutrition Facts: 8 ounces cooked chicken with 2/3 cup stuffing equals 738 calories, 48 g fat (19 g saturated fat), 239 mg cholesterol, 447 mg sodium, 12 g carbohydrate, 1 g fiber, 61 g protein.

>> HOW TO:

STUFF A CHICKEN

1 Tuck wings under chicken. Loosely stuff chicken with stuffing, allowing about 3/4 cup per pound of poultry. To ensure even cooking, do not overstuff the bird.

2 Tie the drumsticks together and season the bird as directed in the recipe. Place on a rack in a shallow roasting pan.

RUBY CHICKEN

Yield: 2 servings.

Treat a loved one to this tender chicken topped with plump cranberries and simmered in a spicy orange sauce.
kathy mead // gwinn, michigan

- **3 tablespoons all-purpose flour**
- **1/4 teaspoon salt**
- **2 bone-in chicken breast halves (8 ounces *each*)**
- **1 tablespoon butter**
- **1/2 cup fresh *or* frozen cranberries**
- **1/3 cup sugar**
- **1/3 cup orange juice**
- **2 tablespoons chopped onion**
- **1/2 teaspoon grated orange peel**
- **1/8 teaspoon ground ginger**
- **1/8 teaspoon ground cinnamon**

In a large resealable plastic bag, combine flour and salt; add the chicken. Seal bag and shake to coat. In a nonstick skillet, brown chicken in butter.

Meanwhile, in a small saucepan, combine the remaining ingredients. Bring to a boil over medium heat. Pour over chicken. Cover and simmer for 35-40 minutes or until a meat thermometer reads 170°.

Nutrition Facts: 1 chicken breast half with 1/2 cup sauce equals 517 calories, 16 g fat (6 g saturated fat), 126 mg cholesterol, 448 mg sodium, 51 g carbohydrate, 2 g fiber, 41 g protein.

KEY LIME CHICKEN THIGHS

Yield: 4 servings.

I've been cooking since I was a girl, and I like trying new recipes. The lime juice here is a nice change of pace from the lemon juice used in many chicken dishes.
idella koen // metolius, oregon

- **8 bone-in chicken thighs, skin removed (6 ounces *each*)**
- **3 tablespoons butter**
- **2 to 3 tablespoons key lime juice *or* lime juice**
- **12 to 16 drops hot pepper sauce**
- **1 teaspoon brown sugar**
- **1 teaspoon chicken bouillon granules**
- **1/2 teaspoon salt**
- **1/2 teaspoon poultry seasoning**
- **1/2 teaspoon dried rosemary, crushed**
- **1/4 to 1/2 teaspoon pepper**
- **1/4 teaspoon paprika**

Place chicken in a greased 13-in. x 9-in. baking dish. Dot with butter; sprinkle with lime juice and pepper sauce. Combine remaining ingredients; sprinkle evenly over chicken.

Bake, uncovered, at 425° for 30 minutes or until a meat thermometer reads 180°.

Nutrition Facts: 1 serving equals 460 calories, 27 g fat (11 g saturated fat), 196 mg cholesterol, 712 mg sodium, 2 g carbohydrate, trace fiber, 48 g protein.

>> HOW TO:

CUT UP A WHOLE CHICKEN

1 Pull the leg and thigh away from the body. With a small sharp knife, cut through the skin to expose the joint.

2 Cut through joint, then cut skin around thigh to free leg. Repeat with other leg.

3 Separate drumstick from thigh by cutting skin at the joint. Bend drumstick to expose joint; cut through joint and skin.

4 Pull wing away from the body. Cut through skin to expose joint. Cut through joint and skin to separate wing from body. Repeat.

5 Cut through the ribs along each side of the backbone with a kitchen or poultry shears; discard backbone.

6 Hold chicken breast in both hands (skin side down) and bend it back to snap breastbone. Turn over. With a knife, cut in half along breastbone. Breastbone will remain attached to one of the halves.

OVEN-FRIED PARMESAN CHICKEN

Yield: 4 servings.

Everyone will call you a gourmet cook when you serve this tasty chicken. Don't tell them how easy it is to prepare.
bessie suffield // florence, kansas

> 6 **tablespoons butter, melted**
> 5 **tablespoons dry bread crumbs**
> 3 **tablespoons grated Parmesan cheese**
> 3 **tablespoons cornmeal**
> 3/4 **teaspoon salt**
> 3/4 **teaspoon dried oregano**
> 1/4 **teaspoon garlic powder**
> 1 **broiler/fryer chicken (3 to 4 pounds), cut up**

Place butter in a shallow bowl. In another shallow bowl, combine the bread crumbs, cheese, cornmeal, salt, oregano and garlic powder. Dip chicken in butter, then roll in crumb mixture.

Place the chicken in a greased 15-in. x 10-in. x 1-in. baking pan. Bake, uncovered, at 375° for 40-45 minutes or until juices run clear.

Nutrition Facts: 1 serving equals 595 calories, 40 g fat (17 g saturated fat), 180 mg cholesterol, 872 mg sodium, 12 g carbohydrate, 1 g fiber, 45 g protein.

Transfer 1 tablespoon of drippings from the skillet to a small saucepan; stir in flour until smooth. Gradually stir in the milk, salt and pepper. Bring to a boil; cook and stir for 2 minutes or until thickened. Serve with chicken.

Nutrition Facts: 1 serving equals 679 calories, 51 g fat (17 g saturated fat), 149 mg cholesterol, 630 mg sodium, 19 g carbohydrate, 1 g fiber, 35 g protein.

OREGANO CHICKEN

Yield: 2 servings.

It's so easy to prepare this dish that you will be sure to make it often. The simple seasonings make chicken breasts a real treat. Line your baking pan with foil for fast cleanup.

taste of home cooking school

- 2 **bone-in chicken breast halves (10 ounces *each*)**
- 3/4 **teaspoon crushed garlic**
- 3/4 **teaspoon lemon-pepper seasoning**
- 1/2 **teaspoon dried oregano**
- 1 **tablespoon olive oil**

Rub chicken with garlic; sprinkle with lemon-pepper and oregano. In a large skillet over medium heat, brown chicken, skin side down, in oil for 5 minutes.

Transfer to a shallow baking pan. Bake, uncovered, at 400° for 30-35 minutes or until a meat thermometer reads 170°.

Nutrition Facts: 1 chicken breast half equals 369 calories, 17 g fat (4 g saturated fat), 139 mg cholesterol, 291 mg sodium, 1 g carbohydrate, trace fiber, 49 g protein.

CHICKEN WITH COUNTRY GRAVY

Yield: 2 servings.

My mother, grandson and I came up with our version of oven-fried chicken. We tweaked the ingredients until the gravy was perfect and the chicken was nicely seasoned.

linda foreman // locust grove, oklahoma

- 2 **tablespoons butter**
- 2 **tablespoons canola oil**
- 1/4 **cup all-purpose flour**
- 1/4 **teaspoon paprika**

Dash each seasoned salt, garlic powder, salt and pepper

- 2 **chicken leg quarters**

GRAVY:

- 1 **tablespoon all-purpose flour**
- 2/3 **cup milk**
- 1/4 **teaspoon salt**
- 1/4 **tablespoon pepper**

Place butter and oil in a large ovenproof skillet. Place in a 425° oven for 5 minutes. Meanwhile, in a large resealable plastic bag, combine flour and seasonings; add the chicken, one piece at a time. Seal bag and toss to coat.

Carefully place chicken, skin side down, in hot skillet. Bake, uncovered, for 15-20 minutes on each side or until a meat thermometer reads 180°. Remove and keep warm.

COLA BARBECUED CHICKEN

Yield: 8 servings.

I'm always looking for fun, great-tasting foods that will feed a crowd. To reduce the sugar content of this recipe, I sometimes use diet cola.

mildred dieffenbach // womelsdorf, pennsylvania

1 **can (12 ounces) cola**	1 **tablespoon Worcestershire sauce**
1 **can (6 ounces) tomato paste**	
2 **tablespoons finely chopped onion**	1/4 **teaspoon salt**
	2 **broiler/fryer chickens (3 pounds *each*), cut in half**
1 **tablespoon red wine vinegar**	

In a small saucepan, combine the cola, tomato paste, onion, vinegar, Worcestershire sauce and salt. Bring to a boil. Reduce heat; simmer, uncovered, for 15 minutes. Set aside 1/2 cup for basting; cover and refrigerate.

Carefully loosen the skin of the chicken; brush remaining sauce under skin. Cover and refrigerate for 30 minutes.

Prepare grill for indirect heat, using a drip pan. Moisten a paper towel with cooking oil; using long-handled tongs, lightly coat the grill rack. Place chicken over drip pan and grill, uncovered, over indirect medium heat for 25 minutes on each side or until chicken juices run clear, basting occasionally with reserved sauce.

Nutrition Facts: 1 serving equals 408 calories, 21 g fat (6 g saturated fat), 131 mg cholesterol, 225 mg sodium, 10 g carbohydrate, 1 g fiber, 42 g protein.

CHEAT IT: Substitute 1-1/4 cups of your favorite barbecue sauce for the cola mixture in this recipe.

>> HOW TO:

HALVE A CHICKEN

1 Using a large knife or kitchen shears, carefully cut out and remove the backbone.

2 Resting the area near the tip of the knife on the cutting board for leverage, cut through the breastbone in a firm motion. Or use kitchen shears to carefully cut through the breastbone.

3 Rearrange the skin to neatly cover the chicken breast during cooking.

SLOW-COOKED THAI PEANUT CHICKEN

Yield: 8 servings.

Have a taste for Thai? Throw together this peanutty chicken dish in your kitchen and save the trip to an Asian restaurant.
blair lonergan // rochelle, virginia

- 1 **cup all-purpose flour**
- 8 **boneless skinless chicken thighs (about 2 pounds)**
- 3/4 **cup creamy peanut butter**
- 1/2 **cup orange juice**
- 1/4 **cup orange marmalade**
- 2 **tablespoons sesame oil**
- 2 **tablespoons soy sauce**
- 2 **tablespoons teriyaki sauce**
- 2 **tablespoons hoisin sauce**
- 1 **can (14 ounces) light coconut milk,** *divided*
- 1 **cup uncooked basmati rice**
- 3/4 **cup water**
- 1/2 **cup chopped salted peanuts**

Place flour in a large resealable plastic bag. Add chicken, a few pieces at a time, and shake to coat. Transfer to a greased 4– or 5-qt. slow cooker.

In a small bowl, combine the peanut butter, orange juice, marmalade, oil, soy sauce, teriyaki sauce, hoisin sauce and 3/4 cup coconut milk; pour over chicken. Cover and cook on low for 4-5 hours or until chicken is tender.

In a small saucepan, bring the rice, water and remaining coconut milk to a boil. Reduce heat; cover and simmer for 15-20 minutes or until rice is tender. Fluff with a fork. Serve with chicken and sauce; sprinkle with peanuts.

Nutrition Facts: 1 serving equals 616 calories, 32 g fat (9 g saturated fat), 76 mg cholesterol, 665 mg sodium, 49 g carbohydrate, 3 g fiber, 34 g protein.

LEMON CHICKEN TORTELLINI

Yield: 6 servings.

This recipe freezes really well, so I toss extra helpings in the freezer for those hectic days that need fast meals.

lorraine caland // thunder bay, ontario

- 1 package (19 ounces) frozen cheese tortellini
- 1 pound boneless skinless chicken breasts, cut into 1-in. pieces
- 2 tablespoons butter
- 1/2 small sweet red pepper, julienned
- 2 garlic cloves, minced
- 3 cups reduced-sodium chicken broth, *divided*
- 1/3 cup all-purpose flour
- 1/2 teaspoon salt
- 1/4 teaspoon pepper
- 2 teaspoons grated lemon peel
- 1/2 teaspoon hot pepper sauce, optional
- 1 package (6 ounces) fresh baby spinach
- 6 tablespoons shredded Parmesan cheese

Cook tortellini according to package directions. Meanwhile, in a large skillet, saute chicken in butter until no longer pink. Remove and keep warm. In the same pan, cook red pepper until crisp-tender. Add garlic; cook 1 minute longer. Add 2 cups broth; bring to a boil.

Combine the flour, salt, pepper and remaining broth until smooth; gradually stir into the pan. Bring to a boil; cook and stir for 2 minutes or until thickened. Stir in the chicken, lemon peel and pepper sauce if desired. Add spinach; cook just until wilted. Drain tortellini; toss with sauce. Sprinkle with cheese.

Nutrition Facts: 1-1/3 cups equals 358 calories, 13 g fat (6 g saturated fat), 69 mg cholesterol, 883 mg sodium, 32 g carbohydrate, 2 g fiber, 29 g protein.

CHICKEN STRAWBERRY SPINACH SALAD

Yield: 2 servings.

This pretty spinach salad topped with grilled chicken, strawberries and almonds features a delectable sweet poppy seed dressing. Made in moments, it's a refreshing lunch or light supper for two.

ginger ellsworth // caldwell, idaho

- 3/4 pound boneless skinless chicken breasts, cut into strips
- 1/4 cup reduced-sodium chicken broth
- 1/4 cup poppy seed salad dressing, *divided*
- 2 cups fresh baby spinach
- 1 cup torn romaine
- 1 cup sliced fresh strawberries
- 1/4 cup sliced almonds, toasted

Place chicken on a double thickness of heavy-duty foil (about 18 in. x 15 in.). Combine broth and 1 tablespoon poppy seed dressing; spoon over chicken. Fold edges of foil around chicken mixture, leaving center open. Grill, covered, over medium heat for 10-12 minutes or until chicken is no longer pink.

In a salad bowl, combine the spinach, romaine and strawberries. Add the chicken and remaining poppy seed dressing; toss to coat. Sprinkle with almonds.

Nutrition Facts: 2 cups equals 438 calories, 22 g fat (3 g saturated fat), 104 mg cholesterol, 386 mg sodium, 18 g carbohydrate, 5 g fiber, 39 g protein.

BUFFALO CHICKEN SALAD

Yield: 4 servings.

Delicious and, even better, quick! This salad is a summer staple. Sometimes we grill the chicken outside, then cut it up and toss it with the hot sauce. You've gotta have that kick!

cori cooper // boise, idaho

- 1 **pound boneless skinless chicken breasts, cut into 1/2-inch cubes**
- 1 **tablespoon olive oil**
- 2 **tablespoons Louisiana-style hot sauce**
- 1/4 **teaspoon salt**
- 1/4 **teaspoon pepper**
- 1 **bunch romaine, chopped**
- 2 **celery ribs, chopped**
- 1 **cup shredded carrots**
- 1/2 **cup fat-free ranch salad dressing**

In a large nonstick skillet, saute chicken in oil until no longer pink; drain. Stir in the hot sauce, salt and pepper.

In large bowl, combine the romaine, celery and carrots. Divide among four plates. Top with chicken. Serve with ranch dressing.

Nutrition Facts: 1 serving equals 229 calories, 7 g fat (1 g saturated fat), 63 mg cholesterol, 644 mg sodium, 16 g carbohydrate, 3 g fiber, 25 g protein. Diabetic Exchanges: 3 lean meat, 1 starch, 1 vegetable, 1/2 fat.

ZIPPY PAPRIKA CHICKEN

Yield: 4 servings.

Here's a unique entree that's reminiscent of the classic Hungarian paprika chicken dish. You'll like this modern twist.

jennifer shaw // dorchester, massachusetts

- 2 **tablespoons paprika**
- 1 **to 2 tablespoons Southwest marinade mix**
- 1/8 **teaspoon salt**
- 1/8 **teaspoon pepper**
- 4 **boneless skinless chicken breast halves (4 ounces *each*)**
- 2 **tablespoons olive oil**
- 1/4 **cup water**
- 2 **tablespoons soy sauce**
- 5 **teaspoons lemon juice**
- 1/2 **cup sour cream**

In a large resealable plastic bag, combine the paprika, marinade mix, salt and pepper; add chicken. Seal bag and shake to coat; refrigerate for 10 minutes.

In a large skillet, cook chicken in oil over medium heat for 5-6 minutes on each side or until a meat thermometer reads 170°. Remove and keep warm.

Add the water, soy sauce and lemon juice to skillet; cook for 1-2 minutes, stirring to loosen browned bits. Remove from the heat; stir in sour cream until blended. Serve with chicken.

EDITOR'S NOTE: This recipe was tested with McCormick Grill Mates Southwest Marinade seasoning packet.

Nutrition Facts: 1 chicken breast half with 2 tablespoons sauce equals 263 calories, 15 g fat (5 g saturated fat), 83 mg cholesterol, 769 mg sodium, 4 g carbohydrate, 1 g fiber, 25 g protein.

GINGER CHICKEN

Yield: 4 servings.

Ginger and soy sauce lend an Asian flair to this hearty and healthy main dish.

ben haen // baldwin, wisconsin

- 1 **egg white, lightly beaten**
- 1 **tablespoon reduced-sodium soy sauce**
- 1 **teaspoon cornstarch**
- 1/8 **teaspoon white pepper**
- 1 **pound boneless skinless chicken breasts, cut into 1-inch pieces**

SAUCE:

- 1/2 **teaspoon cornstarch**
- 2 **tablespoons rice vinegar**
- 2 **tablespoons reduced-sodium soy sauce**
- 1 **teaspoon sugar**

STIR-FRY:

- 1 **tablespoon plus 2 teaspoons peanut oil,** *divided*
- 1 **medium green pepper, julienned**
- 3 **green onions, cut into 1-inch lengths**
- 1/2 **cup canned bamboo shoots, finely chopped**
- 2 **to 3 teaspoons minced fresh gingerroot**
- 1/4 **cup slivered almonds, toasted**

Hot cooked rice, optional

In a large resealable plastic bag, combine the egg white, soy sauce, cornstarch and pepper. Add chicken; seal bag and turn to coat. Refrigerate for 30 minutes. For sauce, combine the cornstarch, vinegar, soy sauce and sugar until smooth; set aside.

Drain chicken and discard marinade. In a large skillet or wok, stir-fry chicken in 1 tablespoon oil until no longer pink. Remove and keep warm.

Stir-fry green pepper and onions in remaining oil for 2 minutes. Add bamboo shoots and ginger; stir-fry 3-4 minutes longer or until vegetables are crisp-tender.

Stir sauce mixture and add to the pan. Bring to a boil; cook and stir for 2 minutes or until thickened. Add chicken and heat through. Sprinkle with almonds. Serve with rice if desired.

Nutrition Facts: 1 cup equals 248 calories, 12 g fat (2 g saturated fat), 63 mg cholesterol, 748 mg sodium, 7 g carbohydrate, 2 g fiber, 28 g protein. Diabetic Exchanges: 3 lean meat, 1-1/2 fat, 1/2 starch.

SIMPLE SALSA CHICKEN

Yield: 2 servings.

My husband and I prefer our food a little spicier than our children, so one evening I baked plain chicken for the kids and created this dish for us. My husband liked it so well that it is now a regular menu item at our house.

jan cooper // troy, alabama

- 2 **boneless skinless chicken breast halves (5 ounces** *each***)**
- 1/8 **teaspoon salt**
- 1/3 **cup salsa**
- 2 **tablespoons taco sauce**
- 1/3 **cup shredded Mexican cheese blend**

Place chicken in a shallow 2-qt. baking dish coated with cooking spray. Sprinkle with salt. Combine salsa and taco sauce; drizzle over chicken. Sprinkle with cheese.

Cover and bake at 350° for 25-30 minutes or until a meat thermometer reads 170°.

Nutrition Facts: 1 chicken breast half (prepared with reduced-fat cheese) equals 226 calories, 7 g fat (3 g saturated fat), 92 mg cholesterol, 628 mg sodium, 3 g carbohydrate, trace fiber, 34 g protein. Diabetic Exchanges: 5 lean meat, 1 fat.

CHICKEN 'N' VEGGIE KABOBS

Yield: 8 kabobs.

I threw this recipe together for a party, and it was a huge success. Everyone commented on the meat's tenderness.

becky wiesmore // rochester, new york

- 1 **pound boneless skinless chicken breasts, cut into 1-inch cubes**
- 1 **cup Italian salad dressing,** *divided*
- 1/4 **cup olive oil**
- 1 **teaspoon garlic salt**
- 1/2 **teaspoon dried rosemary, crushed**
- 1 **medium zucchini, cut into 1/2-inch slices**
- 1 **yellow summer squash, cut into 1/2-inch slices**
- 2 **medium onions, quartered**
- 1 **medium sweet red pepper, cut into 1-inch pieces**
- 2 **cups cherry tomatoes**

In a small resealable plastic bag, combine chicken and 1/2 cup salad dressing. Seal bag and turn to coat; refrigerate for 15 minutes. Meanwhile, in a large resealable plastic bag, combine the oil, garlic salt and rosemary; add vegetables. Seal bag and turn to coat.

Drain and discard marinades. On eight metal or soaked wooden skewers, alternately thread chicken and vegetables.

Grill kabobs, uncovered, over medium-hot heat for 12-15 minutes or until juices run clear, turning and basting occasionally with remaining salad dressing.

Nutrition Facts: 2 kabobs equals 445 calories, 30 g fat (4 g saturated fat), 63 mg cholesterol, 1,169 mg sodium, 18 g carbohydrate, 4 g fiber, 26 g protein.

HERB CHICKEN WITH HONEY BUTTER

Yield: 4 servings.

When the family could use a heartwarming meal, make this delicious chicken. You'll love how the honey's sweetness mixes perfectly with the herbs. It's a wonderful combination!
taste of home cooking school

- 1   egg, lightly beaten
- 3/4 cup seasoned bread crumbs
- 2   tablespoons dried parsley flakes
- 1   teaspoon Italian seasoning
- 3/4 teaspoon garlic salt
- 1/2 teaspoon poultry seasoning
- 4   boneless skinless chicken breast halves (6 ounces *each*)
- 3   tablespoons butter

HONEY BUTTER:

- 1/4 cup butter, softened
- 1/4 cup honey

Place egg in a shallow bowl. In another bowl, combine the bread crumbs and seasonings. Dip chicken in egg, then coat with crumbs.

In a large skillet over medium heat, cook chicken in butter for 4-5 minutes on each side or until a meat thermometer reads 170°. Meanwhile, combine butter and honey. Serve with chicken.

Nutrition Facts: 1 serving equals 488 calories, 25 g fat (14 g saturated fat), 173 mg cholesterol, 676 mg sodium, 28 g carbohydrate, 1 g fiber, 37 g protein.

CHICKEN WITH SUN-DRIED TOMATO BUTTER: Combine 1/3 cup butter, 1/4 cup Parmesan cheese, 2 tablespoons sun-dried tomato pesto and 1/4 teaspoon pepper. Substitute for the honey butter.

PINEAPPLE TERIYAKI CHICKEN

Yield: 4 servings.

I like to marinate this moist chicken entree overnight, then pop it on the grill in for a breezy taste of the islands that my family and friends really love.
vicki roberts // jacksonville, florida

- 1   can (20 ounces) sliced pineapple
- 1/2 cup teriyaki sauce
- 4   boneless skinless chicken breast halves (4 ounces *each*)
- 4   slices provolone cheese (1 ounce *each*)

Drain pineapple, reserving juice; refrigerate pineapple. In a small bowl, combine teriyaki sauce and reserved juice. Pour 3/4 cup marinade into a large resealable plastic bag; add chicken. Seal bag and turn to coat. Refrigerate for 8 hours or overnight. Cover and refrigerate remaining marinade for basting.

Drain and discard marinade. Grill chicken, covered, over medium heat or broil 4 in. from the heat for 4-6 minutes on each side or until a meat thermometer reads 170°, basting frequently with some of the reserved marinade.

Grill eight pineapple slices for 2 minutes on each side or until lightly browned, basting with remaining marinade (save remaining pineapple for another use).

Top each piece of chicken with cheese and two pineapple slices. Grill, covered, for 1-2 minutes or until cheese is melted.

Nutrition Facts: 1 serving equals 305 calories, 10 g fat (6 g saturated fat), 82 mg cholesterol, 1,289 mg sodium, 19 g carbohydrate, 1 g fiber, 32 g protein.

BLACKENED CHICKEN

Yield: 4 servings.

This spicy standout packs a one-two punch of flavor. The grilled chicken is basted with a peppery white sauce, and there's always plenty of extra sauce left over for dipping.
stephanie kenney // falkville, alabama

- 1 tablespoon paprika
- 4 teaspoons sugar, *divided*
- 1-1/2 teaspoons salt, *divided*
- 1 teaspoon garlic powder
- 1 teaspoon dried thyme
- 1 teaspoon lemon-pepper seasoning
- 1 teaspoon cayenne pepper
- 1-1/2 to 2 teaspoons pepper, *divided*
- 4 boneless skinless chicken breast halves (4 ounces *each*)
- 1-1/3 cups mayonnaise
- 2 tablespoons water
- 2 tablespoons cider vinegar

In a small bowl, combine the paprika, I teaspoon sugar, 1 teaspoon salt, garlic powder, thyme, lemon-pepper, cayenne and 1/2 to 1 teaspoon pepper; sprinkle over both sides of chicken. Set aside.

In another bowl, combine the mayonnaise, water, vinegar and remaining sugar, salt and pepper; cover and refrigerate 1 cup for serving. Save remaining sauce for basting.

Grill the chicken, covered, over indirect medium heat for 4-6 minutes on each side or until a thermometer reads 170°, basting frequently with remaining sauce. Serve with the reserved sauce.

Nutrition Facts: 1 cooked chicken breast equals 704 calories, 62 g fat (9 g saturated fat), 100 mg cholesterol, 1,465 mg sodium, 7 g carbohydrate, 1 g fiber, 27 g protein.

PESTO-OLIVE CHICKEN

CHEAT IT!

Yield: 4 servings.

Give weeknight dining a lift with this hearty, dressed-up chicken entree. You will find many of the ingredients right in your pantry.
cristy king // bridgeport, west virginia

- 4 boneless skinless chicken breast halves (6 ounces *each*)
- 1/2 cup prepared pesto
- 2 jars (4-1/2 ounces *each*) sliced mushrooms, drained
- 1 can (4-1/2 ounces) chopped ripe olives
- 1 cup (4 ounces) shredded provolone cheese

Flatten chicken slightly. Place in an ungreased 13-in. x 9-in. baking dish. Spoon pesto over chicken; top with mushrooms and olives.

Bake, uncovered, at 400° for 15 minutes. Sprinkle with cheese. Bake 1-2 minutes longer or until cheese is melted and chicken is no longer pink.

Nutrition Facts: 1 serving equals 490 calories, 29 g fat (10 g saturated fat), 124 mg cholesterol, 1,117 mg sodium, 8 g carbohydrate, 3 g fiber, 49 g protein.

≫ HOW TO:

BONE CHICKEN BREASTS

Insert a small boning or paring knife between the ribs and breast meat. Pressing the knife along the bones, cut to remove the meat. If desired, remove the skin by pulling it from the breast meat.

CHICKEN PICCATA

Yield: 2 servings.

I usually serve this with rice or pasta, but it takes longer to cook those than it does the chicken!

carol cottrill // rumford, maine

- 2 **boneless skinless chicken breast halves** (4 ounces *each*)
- 2 **tablespoons all-purpose flour**
- 1/4 **teaspoon salt**
- 1/8 **teaspoon pepper**
- 1 **tablespoon canola oil**
- 2 **tablespoons white wine** *or* **reduced-sodium chicken broth**
- 1 **garlic clove, minced**
- 1/3 **cup reduced-sodium chicken broth**
- 1 **tablespoon lemon juice**
- 1-1/2 **teaspoons capers**
- 1-1/2 **teaspoons butter**
- 2 **thin lemon slices**

Flatten chicken to 1/2-in. thickness. In a large plastic resealable bag, combine the flour, salt and pepper; add the chicken, one piece at a time. Seal bag and toss to coat.

In a skillet, cook chicken in oil until no longer pink. Remove and set aside. Add wine and garlic to pan; cook and stir 30 seconds.

Add the broth, lemon juice and capers. Bring to a boil; cook until slightly thickened. Stir in butter and lemon slices. Return chicken to the pan; heat through.

Nutrition Facts: 1 serving equals 259 calories, 13 g fat (3 g saturated fat), 70 mg cholesterol, 530 mg sodium, 9 g carbohydrate, 1 g fiber, 24 g protein. Diabetic Exchanges: 3 lean meat, 1-1/2 fat, 1/2 starch.

PORK MEDALLIONS PICCATA: Cut 1/2 pound pork tenderloin into 4 slices and flatten to 1/2-in. thickness; substitute for the chicken. Proceed as directed. Sprinkle with parsley.

>> HOW TO:

FLATTEN A CHICKEN BREAST

Place a chicken breast inside a resealable plastic bag or under plastic wrap. Lightly pound chicken with a meat mallet to flatten evenly.

CHICKEN PARMIGIANA

Yield: 2 servings.

For years, my husband ordered Chicken Parmigiana at restaurants. Then I found this recipe in our local newspaper, adjusted it for two and began making this at home. Now it's his favorite.

iola butler // sun city, california

- 1 can (15 ounces) tomato sauce
- 2 teaspoons Italian seasoning
- 1/2 teaspoon garlic powder
- 1 egg
- 1/4 cup seasoned bread crumbs
- 3 tablespoons grated Parmesan cheese
- 2 boneless skinless chicken breast halves (4 ounces *each*)
- 2 tablespoons olive oil
- 2 slices part-skim mozzarella cheese

In a small saucepan, combine the tomato sauce, Italian seasoning and garlic powder. Bring to a boil. Reduce heat; cover and simmer for 20 minutes.

Meanwhile, in a shallow bowl, lightly beat the egg. In another shallow bowl, combine bread crumbs and Parmesan cheese. Dip chicken in egg, then coat with crumb mixture.

In a large skillet, cook chicken in oil over medium heat for 5 minutes on each side or until a meat thermometer reads 170°. Top with mozzarella cheese. Cover and cook 3-4 minutes longer or until cheese is melted. Serve with tomato sauce.

Nutrition Facts: 1 serving equals 444 calories, 26 g fat (8 g saturated fat), 166 mg cholesterol, 1,496 mg sodium, 23 g carbohydrate, 3 g fiber, 29 g protein.

Cheat It: Substitute 2 cups of your favorite marinara for the homemade sauce in this recipe. Serve the chicken over angel hair pasta for a quick, satisfying meal.

CITRUS-BAKED CORNISH HENS

Yield: 4 servings.

The mustard and citrus in this dish provide a double zing of gorgeous flavor. Here's a special entree that's definitely worthy of a special occasion.

mary-lynne mason // janesville, wisconsin

- 4 Cornish game hens (20 to 24 ounces *each*)

SAUCE:
- 1/4 cup apricot preserves
- 2 tablespoons grated onion
- 1 tablespoon butter
- 1 tablespoon Dijon mustard
- 1 garlic clove, minced

Juice and grated peel of 1 lemon
Juice and grated peel of 1 orange

Tie legs of hens together; turn wing tips under backs. In a small saucepan, combine all the sauce ingredients. Simmer 5 minutes. Spoon half of the sauce over hens.

Place the hens breast side up on a rack in a large roasting pan. Bake at 350° for 1-1/4 hours or until a meat thermometer reads 180°, brushing hens occasionally with the remaining sauce.

Nutrition Facts: 1 hen equals 762 calories, 49 g fat (13 g saturated fat), 349 mg cholesterol, 459 mg sodium, 18 g carbohydrate, 1 g fiber, 60 g protein.

CHICKEN CORDON BLEU

Yield: 6 servings.

Christmas Eve wouldn't be complete without my dad's Chicken Cordon Bleu! My husband tries all year to talk Dad into making this scrumptious main dish for other occasions. It's a definite family favorite.

vickie lemos // modesto, california

- 6 **boneless skinless chicken breast halves (4 ounces** *each*)
- 3 **thin slices fully cooked ham, halved**
- 3 **slices Swiss cheese, halved**
- 1/2 **cup all-purpose flour**
- 1/2 **teaspoon salt**
- 1/4 **teaspoon paprika**
- 1 **egg**
- 2 **tablespoons milk**
- 3/4 **cup dry bread crumbs**
- 3 **tablespoons butter**
- 1 **cup chicken broth**
- 2 **tablespoons dried parsley flakes**

Hot cooked rice

- 1 **can (10-3/4 ounces) condensed cream of chicken soup, undiluted**
- 1/2 **cup sour cream**

Flatten chicken breast to 1/4-in. thickness; layer each with one piece of ham and one piece of cheese. Roll up each jelly-roll style, starting with a short side; secure with toothpicks.

In a shallow bowl, combine the flour, salt and paprika. In another bowl, beat egg and milk. Place bread crumbs in a third bowl. Dredge chicken in flour mixture, dip in egg mixture, then roll in bread crumbs.

In a skillet over medium heat, brown chicken in butter. Add broth and parsley. Cover and simmer over medium-low heat for 40-50 minutes or until a meat thermometer reads 170°.

Remove toothpicks. Place rice on a serving platter; top with chicken and keep warm. Combine soup and sour cream; heat through but do not boil. Serve with chicken and rice.

Nutrition Facts: 1 serving equals 316 calories, 18 g fat (10 g saturated fat), 93 mg cholesterol, 1,005 mg sodium, 23 g carbohydrate, 1 g fiber, 14 g protein.

GRILLED GAME HENS

Yield: 4 servings.

An easy overnight marinade spiced with cinnamon and cumin adds wonderful flavor to these game hens. My family enjoys them often during the summer grilling season.

marcia bland // north platte, nebraska

- 1 **cup lime juice**
- 1/2 **cup olive oil**
- 4 **garlic cloves, minced**
- 4 **teaspoons ground cumin**
- 1/2 **to 1 teaspoon ground cinnamon**

Salt and pepper to taste

- 4 **Cornish game hens (20 to 24 ounces** *each*), **halved**

In a large resealable plastic bag, combine the lime juice, oil, garlic, cumin, cinnamon, salt and pepper; add the hens. Seal bag and turn to coat. Cover and refrigerate for several hours or overnight, turning once.

Drain and discard marinade. Grill hens, covered, over medium heat for 20-25 minutes or until a meat thermometer reads 180°, turning occasionally.

Nutrition Facts: 1 hen equals 720 calories, 49 g fat (13 g saturated fat), 349 mg cholesterol, 365 mg sodium, 7 g carbohydrate, 1 g fiber, 60 g protein.

SOUTHWEST STUFFED CHICKEN

Yield: 6 servings.

A zippy cheese filling gives these tender chicken rolls a special flavor, while the golden coating enhances their appearance.

alcy thorne // los molinos, california

- **6 boneless skinless chicken breast halves (4 ounces _each_)**
- **6 ounces Monterey Jack cheese, cut into 2-inch x 1/2-inch sticks**
- **2 cans (4 ounces _each_) chopped green chilies, drained**
- **1/2 cup dry bread crumbs**
- **1/4 cup grated Parmesan cheese**
- **1 tablespoon chili powder**
- **1/2 teaspoon salt**
- **1/4 teaspoon ground cumin**
- **3/4 cup all-purpose flour**
- **1/2 cup butter, melted**

Flatten chicken to 1/8-in. thickness. Place a cheese stick down the middle of each; top with chilies. Roll up and tuck in ends. Secure with toothpicks.

In a shallow bowl, combine the bread crumbs, Parmesan cheese, chili powder, salt and cumin. Place flour in another shallow bowl. Place butter in a third shallow bowl. Coat chicken with flour, then dip in butter and roll in crumb mixture.

Place roll-ups, seam side down, in a greased 13-in. x 9-in. baking dish. Bake, uncovered, at 400° for 25 minutes or until a meat thermometer reads 170°. Discard toothpicks.

Nutrition Facts: 1 serving equals 482 calories, 29 g fat (16 g saturated fat), 136 mg cholesterol, 794 mg sodium, 21 g carbohydrate, 1 g fiber, 33 g protein.

>> HOW TO:

MAKE ELEGANT CHICKEN ROLL-UPS

1 After flattening the chicken breast, place desired filling (about 2-3 tablespoons) in the center and roll up.

2 Secure with toothpicks. Then dip in egg mixture or butter.

3 Coat all sides of each chicken roll-up with the coating of your choice.

≫HOW TO:

MAKE AND SHAPE BISCUITS

1 Combine all dry ingredients with a fork. With a pastry blender or two knives, cut shortening into flour until mixture resembles coarse crumbs.

2 Make a well in the center of the dry mixture. Pour in the liquid all at once and mix with a fork just until dry ingredients are moistened and the mixture begins to cling together.

3 Turn onto a lightly floured surface and knead gently as the recipe directs.

4 Roll dough evenly to 1/2-in. to 3/4-in. thickness. Cut with a floured biscuit cutter, using a straight downward motion; do not twist cutter. Place biscuits on a baking sheet. Place 1 to 1-1/2 in. apart for biscuits with crusty sides or almost touching for softer-sided biscuits.

5 Gently gather trimmings into a ball. Do not knead. Roll and cut out as in Step 4.

CLASSIC CHICKEN 'N' BISCUIT POTPIE

Yield: 7 servings.

This wonderful potpie feeds a lot for very little money. Its satisfying taste is worth the extra effort.

valerie belley // st. louis, missouri

- 1 **broiler/fryer chicken (3 to 4 pounds), cut up**
- 4 **cups water**
- 3 **medium carrots, halved widthwise**
- 2 **medium onions, quartered**
- 4 **teaspoons chicken bouillon granules**
- 1 **bay leaf**
- 1/2 **pound whole fresh mushrooms**
- 2 **celery ribs, cut into 1-inch pieces**
- 3 **tablespoons butter**
- 5 **tablespoons all-purpose flour**
- 1/2 **cup milk**
- 1 **cup frozen peas**
- 1 **teaspoon dried basil**
- 1 **teaspoon salt**
- 1/4 **teaspoon pepper**

BISCUITS:

- 1-1/2 **cups all-purpose flour**
- 2 **teaspoons baking powder**
- 2 **teaspoons sugar**
- 1/4 **teaspoon salt**
- 5 **tablespoons shortening**
- 1/2 **cup milk**

Place the chicken, water, carrots, onions, bouillon and bay leaf in a Dutch oven; bring to a boil. Reduce heat; cover and simmer for 25 minutes. Add mushrooms and celery; simmer 15 minutes longer or until chicken is tender.

Remove chicken; allow to cool. Strain the

broth, reserving vegetables; skim fat. Set aside 2 cups broth (save remaining broth for another use). Discard bay leaf. Remove meat from bones; discard bones. Chop vegetables and cut chicken into bite-size pieces.

In a large saucepan, melt butter. Stir in flour until smooth; gradually add the milk and reserved broth. Bring to a boil; cook and stir fo 2 minutes or until thickened. Stir in the chicken, cooked vegetables, peas and seasonings. Pour into a greased 2-qt. baking dish; set aside.

For biscuits, in a large bowl, combine the flour, baking powder, sugar and salt. Cut in shortening until mixture resembles coarse crumbs. Stir in milk just until moistened.

Turn onto a lightly floured surface; knead 8-10 times. Pat or roll out to 1/2-in. thickness; cut with a floured 2-1/2-in. biscuit cutter.

Place biscuits on top of chicken mixture. Bake, uncovered, at 400° for 25 minutes or until golden brown.

Nutrition Facts: 1 cup chicken mixture with 1 biscuit equals 521 calories, 27 g fat (9 g saturated fat), 90 mg cholesterol, 935 mg sodium, 38 g carbohydrate, 4 g fiber, 31 g protein.

SO-EASY CHICKEN POTPIE

CHEAT IT!

Yield: 2 servings.

I actually created this recipe when I was a girl. Since then, I've found it's a good way to use up the second pastry when I make a one-crust pie. When I tell my husband, "It's chicken potpie tonight," he lights up and thinks that I've worked in the kitchen all day!

marva vandivier // battle ground, washington

- 2 **medium carrots, sliced**
- 1 **medium potato, peeled and cubed**
- 1 **small onion, chopped**
- 1 **celery rib, chopped**
- 1 **can (10-3/4 ounces) condensed cream of chicken soup, undiluted**
- 1 **cup cubed cooked chicken**
- 1/2 **cup frozen peas, thawed**

Pastry for single-crust pie (9 inches)

Place the carrots, potato, onion and celery in a large saucepan and cover with water. Reduce heat; cover and cook for 15-20 minutes or until tender. Drain. Stir in soup and chicken. Gently stir in peas.

Pour into a greased 1-1/2-qt. deep baking dish. Roll out pastry to fit top of dish; place over filling. Trim, seal and flute edges. Cut slits in the pastry.

Bake at 350° for 50 minutes or until the crust is golden and the filling is bubbly.

Nutrition Facts: 1 serving equals 903 calories, 42 g fat (16 g saturated fat), 95 mg cholesterol, 1,702 mg sodium, 96 g carbohydrate, 7 g fiber, 33 g protein.

CREATE YOUR OWN SIGNATURE POTPIE

Try these ideas to make a potpie that's uniquely yours:

- Add a topping of whole wheat pie crust, breadstick dough, refrigerated biscuits, dollops of drop biscuits or corn muffin batter.
- Make a sauce that starts with bottled gravy, canned soup or leftover gravy for a hurry-up potpie; use butter, flour and broth for a traditional potpie.
- Use canned or frozen assorted vegetables or cooked veggies that you have on hand. Consider a root vegetable potpie that uses turnips, carrots and rutabaga.
- Make a large batch of filling and freeze half for an easy-to-make potpie in the future. Just be sure not to use milk products in the filling, as they do not freeze well.

CORDON BLEU CASSEROLE

Yield: 6 servings.

I often roast a turkey just to have leftovers for this creamy casserole. It makes such a pretty and special presentation.
joyce paul // qu'appelle, saskatchewan

- 2 **cups cubed fully cooked ham**
- 4 **cups cubed cooked turkey**
- 1 **cup (4 ounces) shredded Swiss cheese**
- 1 **large onion, chopped**
- 1/3 **cup butter**
- 1/3 **cup all-purpose flour**
- 1/8 **teaspoon ground mustard**
- 1/8 **teaspoon ground nutmeg**
- 1-3/4 **cups milk**

TOPPING:

- 1-1/2 **cups soft bread crumbs**
- 1/2 **cup shredded Swiss cheese**
- 1/4 **cup butter, melted**

In a large nonstick skillet, cook ham for 4-5 minutes or until browned; drain and pat dry. In a greased 2-qt. baking dish, layer the turkey, cheese and ham; set aside.

In a large saucepan, saute onion in butter until tender. Stir in the flour, mustard and nutmeg until blended. Gradually stir in milk. Bring to a boil; cook and stir for 2 minutes or until thickened. Pour over ham.

Combine topping ingredients; sprinkle over the top. Bake, uncovered, at 350° for 25-30 minutes or until golden brown and bubbly.

Nutrition Facts: 1 cup equals 601 calories, 37 g fat (20 g saturated fat), 178 mg cholesterol, 1,008 mg sodium, 18 g carbohydrate, 1 g fiber, 48 g protein.

CHICKEN NOODLE CASSEROLE

Yield: 6 servings.

Everyone who tries this comforting, cheesy combination asks for the recipe. It's so simple to make that sometimes I feel like I'm cheating.
kay pederson // yellville, arkansas

- 1 **can (10-3/4 ounces) condensed cream of chicken soup, undiluted**
- 1/2 **cup mayonnaise**
- 2 **tablespoons lemon juice**
- 2 **cups cubed cooked chicken**
- 1 **small onion, chopped**
- 1/4 **cup chopped green pepper**
- 1/4 **cup chopped sweet red pepper**
- 1 **cup (4 ounces) shredded Monterey Jack cheese, *divided***
- 1 **cup (4 ounces) shredded sharp cheddar cheese, *divided***
- 12 **ounces medium egg noodles, cooked and drained**

In a large bowl, combine the soup, mayonnaise and lemon juice. Stir in the chicken, onion, peppers, 1/2 cup Monterey Jack cheese and 1/2 cup cheddar cheese. Add noodles and toss to coat.

Transfer to a greased 2-qt. baking dish. Bake, uncovered, at 350° for 30-35 minutes. Sprinkle with remaining cheeses. Bake 10 minutes longer or until vegetables are tender and cheese is melted.

Nutrition Facts: 1 cup equals 629 calories, 34 g fat (12 g saturated fat), 143 mg cholesterol, 752 mg sodium, 47 g carbohydrate, 2 g fiber, 32 g protein.

>> HOW TO:

MAKE CHICKEN ENCHILADA LASAGNA IN NO TIME

1 In a large skillet, cook onion and garlic in oil over medium heat until tender.

2 Stir in chicken and enchilada sauce; cook until slightly thickened.

3 In a small bowl, combine the eggs, ricotta cheese and cilantro.

4 Spread some of the chicken mixture into a greased 13-in. x 9-in. baking dish. Layer with some noodles, ricotta mixture, chicken mixture and shredded cheese. Repeat layers twice. Top with remaining noodles, sauce and shredded cheese.

5 Cover and bake as directed.

CHICKEN ENCHILADA LASAGNA

Yield: 10-12 servings.

No-cook lasagna noodles shorten the prep time in this amazing entree. I make it with rotisserie chicken when time is short. You'll love the combination of cuisines in this one.

valonda seward // hanford, california

  1 **cup chopped onion**
  1 **tablespoon canola oil**
  1 **garlic clove, minced**
  4 **cups cubed cooked chicken**
  3 **cans (10 ounces *each*) enchilada sauce**
  2 **eggs**
  1 **carton (15 ounces) ricotta cheese**
1/2 **cup minced fresh cilantro**
 12 **no-cook lasagna noodles**
  4 **cups (16 ounces) shredded Mexican cheese blend**

In a large skillet, cook onion in oil over medium heat until tender. Add garlic; cook 1 minute longer. Stir in chicken and enchilada sauce. Bring to a boil. Reduce heat; simmer, uncovered, 5 minutes or until slightly thickened. In a small bowl, combine the eggs, ricotta cheese and cilantro.

Spread 3/4 cup chicken mixture into a greased 13-in. x 9-in. baking dish. Layer with three noodles, 2/3 cup ricotta mixture, 3/4 cup chicken mixture and 1 cup shredded cheese. Repeat layers twice. Top with remaining noodles, sauce and shredded cheese.

Cover and bake at 375° for 30 minutes. Uncover; bake 10-15 minutes longer or until bubbly. Let stand for 10 minutes before cutting.

Nutrition Facts: 1 piece equals 396 calories, 22 g fat (12 g saturated fat), 124 mg cholesterol, 757 mg sodium, 23 g carbohydrate, 2 g fiber, 30 g protein.

SPINACH AND TURKEY SAUSAGE LASAGNA

Yield: 12 servings.

My sausage lasagna proves you can layer on great taste while keeping a luscious comfort food light. My husband even likes this version better than the traditional tomato-based version.

lynette randleman // buffalo, wyoming

  3 tablespoons butter
1/3 cup all-purpose flour
1/2 teaspoon salt
1/4 teaspoon pepper
  3 cups fat-free milk
  3 ounces reduced-fat cream cheese, cubed
3/4 cup grated Parmesan cheese
  1 pound Italian turkey sausage links, casings removed and crumbled
  1 medium onion, chopped
  4 garlic cloves, minced
  1 teaspoon dried oregano
  1 teaspoon dried marjoram
1/2 teaspoon fennel seed, crushed
  1 jar (7 ounces) roasted sweet red peppers, drained and chopped
1/2 cup white wine *or* reduced-sodium chicken broth
  2 packages (10 ounces *each*) frozen chopped spinach, thawed and squeezed dry

3/4 cup 2% cottage cheese
1/4 teaspoon ground nutmeg
  9 lasagna noodles, cooked, rinsed and drained
1/2 cup shredded part-skim mozzarella cheese

In a large saucepan, melt butter. Stir in flour, salt and pepper until smooth; gradually stir in milk. Bring to a boil; cook and stir for 1-2 minutes or until thickened. Stir in cream cheese until melted. Stir in Parmesan cheese just until melted. Remove from the heat; set aside.

In a large nonstick skillet coated with cooking spray, cook sausage and onion over medium heat until sausage is no longer pink. Add the garlic, oregano, marjoram and fennel; cook 1 minute longer.

Add roasted peppers and wine. Bring to a boil. Reduce heat; simmer, uncovered, for 3-5 minutes or until liquid is reduced to 3 tablespoons. Remove from the heat; set aside.

In a small bowl, combine the spinach, cottage cheese and nutmeg. Spread 1/2 cup cheese sauce in a 13-in. x 9-in. baking dish coated with cooking spray. Top with three noodles, half of the sausage mixture, half of the spinach mixture and 1 cup sauce; repeat layers. Top with the remaining noodles and sauce. Sprinkle with the mozzarella cheese.

Cover and bake at 375° for 40 minutes. Uncover; bake 15-20 minutes longer or until heated through and top is lightly browned. Let stand for 10 minutes before cutting.

Nutrition Facts: 1 piece equals 279 calories, 11 g fat (6 g saturated fat), 43 mg cholesterol, 664 mg sodium, 27 g carbohydrate, 3 g fiber, 19 g protein. Diabetic Exchanges: 2 lean meat, 1-1/2 starch, 1 vegetable, 1 fat.

TURKEY MEAT LOAF

Yield: 6 servings.

I switched up my mom's classic meat loaf recipe with ground turkey instead of beef, and the addition of chopped bell peppers. My turkey loaf is a favorite at church potlucks.

john cotti-diaz // converse, texas

  1 egg, lightly beaten
  1 can (8 ounces) tomato sauce, *divided*
  1 cup soft bread crumbs
1/4 cup finely chopped onion
1/4 cup finely chopped green pepper

1/4 cup finely chopped sweet red pepper

1-1/2 teaspoons garlic powder

1/4 teaspoon salt

1/8 teaspoon pepper

1-1/2 pounds lean ground turkey

1 can (10-3/4 ounces) reduced-sodium condensed tomato soup, undiluted

2 tablespoons brown sugar

2 tablespoons cider vinegar

2 tablespoons ketchup

2 tablespoons prepared mustard

In a large bowl, combine the egg, 1/2 cup tomato sauce, bread crumbs, onion, peppers, garlic powder, salt and pepper. Crumble turkey over mixture and mix well.

In an 11-in. x 7-in. baking dish coated with cooking spray, pat the turkey mixture into a 9-in. x 4-in. loaf. Bake, uncovered, at 350° for 30 minutes; drain if necessary.

Meanwhile, combine the soup, brown sugar, vinegar, ketchup, mustard and remaining tomato sauce. Pour 1/2 cup over meat loaf. Bake 20-30 minutes longer or until a meat thermometer reads 165° and juices run clear. Warm remaining sauce; serve with meat loaf.

Nutrition Facts: 1 slice with 2 tablespoons sauce equals 282 calories, 11 g fat (3 g saturated fat), 125 mg cholesterol, 736 mg sodium, 21 g carbohydrate, 2 g fiber, 23 g protein. Diabetic Exchanges: 3 lean meat, 1-1/2 starch.

FABULOUS TACO SALAD

Yield: 4 servings.

Everyone loves a good taco salad. This one is like eating decadent Mexican food while keeping the calories under control.
anna yeatts // pinehurst, north carolina

1 pound extra-lean ground turkey

1 medium onion, finely chopped

1 teaspoon olive oil

3 garlic cloves, minced

4 plum tomatoes, chopped

1/4 teaspoon salt

1/4 teaspoon pepper

1/4 cup minced fresh cilantro

6 cups torn romaine

1/2 cup shredded reduced-fat Mexican cheese blend

1/2 cup salsa

In a large nonstick skillet over medium heat, cook turkey and onion in oil until meat is no longer pink. Add garlic; cook 1 minute longer. Stir in the tomatoes, salt and pepper; cook for 3-4 minutes or until tomatoes are tender. Remove from the heat; stir in cilantro.

Divide romaine among four plates; top each with 3/4 cup turkey mixture, 2 tablespoons cheese and 2 tablespoons salsa.

Nutrition Facts: 1 serving equals 224 calories, 6 g fat (2 g saturated fat), 55 mg cholesterol, 467 mg sodium, 11 g carbohydrate, 3 g fiber, 35 g protein. Diabetic Exchanges: 4 lean meat, 2 vegetable, 1 fat.

CHICKEN FLORENTINE MEATBALLS

Yield: 6 servings.

Served over squash with a chunky mushroom-tomato sauce, these tender meatballs are tops in flavor.

diane nemitz // ludington, michigan

- 2 **eggs, lightly beaten**
- 1 **package (10 ounces) frozen chopped spinach, thawed and squeezed dry**
- 1/2 **cup dry bread crumbs**
- 1/4 **cup grated Parmesan cheese**
- 1 **tablespoon dried minced onion**
- 1 **garlic clove, minced**
- 1/4 **teaspoon salt**
- 1/8 **teaspoon pepper**
- 1 **pound ground chicken**
- 1 **medium spaghetti squash**

SAUCE:

- 1/2 **pound sliced fresh mushrooms**
- 2 **teaspoons olive oil**
- 1 **can (14-1/2 ounces) diced tomatoes, undrained**
- 1 **can (8 ounces) tomato sauce**
- 2 **tablespoons minced fresh parsley**
- 1 **garlic clove, minced**
- 1 **teaspoon dried oregano**
- 1 **teaspoon dried basil**

In a large bowl, combine the first eight ingredients. Crumble chicken over mixture and mix well. Shape into 1-1/2-in. balls.

Place meatballs on a rack in a shallow baking pan. Bake, uncovered, at 400° for 20-25 minutes or until no longer pink. Meanwhile, cut squash in half lengthwise; discard seeds. Place squash cut side down on a microwave-safe plate. Microwave, uncovered, on high for 15-18 minutes or until tender.

For sauce, in a large nonstick skillet, saute mushrooms in oil until tender. Stir in the remaining ingredients. Bring to a boil. Reduce heat; simmer, uncovered, for 8-10 minutes or until slightly thickened. Add meatballs and heat through.

When squash is cool enough to handle, use a fork to separate strands. Serve with meatballs and sauce.

EDITOR'S NOTE: This recipe was tested in a 1,100-watt microwave.

Nutrition Facts: 3 meatballs with sauce and 2/3 cup squash equals 303 calories, 12 g fat (3 g saturated fat), 123 mg cholesterol, 617 mg sodium, 31 g carbohydrate, 7 g fiber, 22 g protein.

SAUSAGE MARINARA

Yield: 6 servings.

Not only does this sauce freeze well, but it's a family favorite. I like to keep a few batches in the freezer. Then I simply cook the pasta, reheat the sauce and dinner is ready.
christi gillentine // tulsa, oklahoma

- 1 **pound turkey Italian sausage links, casing removed**
- 1 **medium onion, thinly sliced**
- 1 **medium sweet red pepper, julienned**
- 1 **medium green pepper, julienned**
- 1 **teaspoon olive oil**
- 1 **can (15 ounces) crushed tomatoes**
- 1 **cup chicken broth**
- 1/3 **cup tomato paste**
- 3 **to 4 teaspoons sugar**
- 1-1/2 **teaspoons dried basil**
- 1/4 **teaspoon garlic powder**

Hot cooked pasta

Crumble sausage into a skillet. Add the onion, peppers and oil. Cook over medium heat until sausage is no longer pink and vegetables are tender; drain. Add the tomatoes, broth, tomato paste, sugar, basil and garlic powder; heat through. Serve with pasta.

Nutrition Facts: 3/4 cup (prepared with reduced-sodium chicken broth and 3 teaspoons sugar; calculated without pasta) equals 195 calories, 8 g fat (2 g saturated fat), 41 mg cholesterol, 675 mg sodium, 16 g carbohydrate, 3 g fiber, 16 g protein. Diabetic Exchanges: 2 lean meat, 1 starch.

CHICKEN LETTUCE WRAPS

Yield: 2 servings.

Bundle up a tasty blend of garden flavors with these delightful wraps. Sweet and hot accents set them apart.
taste of home test kitchen

- 3 **tablespoons chicken broth**
- 2 **tablespoons plus 2 teaspoons reduced-sodium soy sauce,** *divided*
- 1 **tablespoon sherry** *or* **additional chicken broth**
- 1-1/2 **teaspoons cornstarch**
- 1/2 **pound ground chicken**
- 1 **teaspoon canola oil**
- 1/4 **cup shredded carrot**
- 1 **teaspoon minced fresh gingerroot**
- 1/3 **cup plum** *or* **seedless raspberry preserves**
- 2 **teaspoons hoisin sauce**
- 1/8 **teaspoon hot pepper sauce**
- 1 **green onion, thinly sliced**
- 4 **Bibb** *or* **Boston lettuce leaves**

In a small bowl, combine the broth, 2 tablespoons soy sauce, sherry and cornstarch; set aside. In a large skillet, cook chicken in oil over medium heat until meat is no longer pink; drain. Add carrot and ginger; cook and stir for 2-3 minutes or until carrot is tender.

Meanwhile, for dipping sauce, combine the preserves, hoisin sauce, pepper sauce and remaining soy sauce; set aside. Stir cornstarch mixture; add to chicken. Cook and stir until thickened, about 2 minutes. Remove from the heat; stir in green onion.

Divide the chicken mixture among lettuce leaves. Fold lettuce over the filling. Serve with the dipping sauce.

Nutrition Facts: 2 wraps with 3 tablespoons dipping sauce (prepared with reduced-sodium broth) equals 354 calories, 12 g fat (3 g saturated fat), 75 mg cholesterol, 1,025 mg sodium, 43 g carbohydrate, 1 g fiber, 20 g protein.

>>HOW TO:

MAKE PAN GRAVY

1 To avoid lumpy gravy, first make a roux (pronounced "roo"), which is a mixture of flour and fat (such as butter or pan drippings) that's cooked over low heat and used to thicken sauces. A roux can be white, blond or brown, depending on how long it's allowed to cook.

2 Make sure the butter is completely melted before adding the flour. Test it by sprinkling in a pinch of flour. If it slowly starts to bubble, whisk in the rest of the flour. Whisk the butter and flour constantly until the mixture is blended and smooth.

3 Gradually whisk or stir in the chicken broth. Bring the mixture to a boil, whisking constantly until the gravy is thickened, about 2 minutes.

TURKEY CUTLETS WITH PAN GRAVY

Yield: 4 servings.

Using cutlets or any boneless meat speeds up cooking time for this quick entree. You can use thin boneless, skinless chicken breasts as well.

margaret wilson // sun city, california

1	**teaspoon poultry seasoning**	2	**tablespoons canola oil**
1/2	**teaspoon seasoned salt**	2	**tablespoons butter**
1/4	**teaspoon pepper,** *divided*	1/4	**cup all-purpose flour**
1	**package (17.6 ounces) turkey breast cutlets**	2	**cups chicken broth**

Combine the poultry seasoning, seasoned salt and 1/8 teaspoon pepper. Sprinkle over turkey. In a large skillet, cook cutlets in batches in oil for 2-3 minutes on each side or until turkey is no longer pink. Remove meat to a serving platter and keep warm.

In the same skillet, melt butter and stir in flour until smooth. Gradually stir in chicken broth. Bring to a boil; cook and stir for 2 minutes or until thickened. Remove from the heat; season with remaining pepper. Serve with turkey.

Nutrition Facts: 1 serving equals 286 calories, 14 g fat (5 g saturated fat), 95 mg cholesterol, 782 mg sodium, 7 g carbohydrate, trace fiber, 32 g protein.

SAUSAGE AND PUMPKIN PASTA

Yield: 4 servings.

Flavored with pumpkin and white wine, this delightful pasta with Italian turkey sausage makes a stress-free weekday meal that's special enough to serve to company.

katie wollgast // florissant, missouri

- 2 **cups uncooked multigrain bow tie pasta**
- 1/2 **pound Italian turkey sausage links, casings removed**
- 1/2 **pound sliced fresh mushrooms**
- 1 **medium onion, chopped**
- 4 **garlic cloves, minced**
- 1 **cup reduced-sodium chicken broth**
- 1 **cup canned pumpkin**
- 1/2 **cup white wine *or* additional reduced-sodium chicken broth**
- 1/2 **teaspoon rubbed sage**
- 1/4 **teaspoon salt**
- 1/4 **teaspoon garlic powder**
- 1/4 **teaspoon pepper**
- 1/4 **cup grated Parmesan cheese**
- 1 **tablespoon dried parsley flakes**

Cook pasta according to package directions.

Meanwhile, in a large nonstick skillet coated with cooking spray, cook the sausage, mushrooms and onion over medium heat until meat is no longer pink. Add the garlic; cook 1 minute longer. Stir in the broth, pumpkin, wine, sage, salt, garlic powder and pepper. Bring to a boil. Reduce heat; simmer, uncovered, for 5-6 minutes or until slightly thickened.

Drain pasta; add to the skillet and heat through. Just before serving, sprinkle with cheese and parsley.

Nutrition Facts: 1-3/4 cups equals 348 calories, 9 g fat (2 g saturated fat), 38 mg cholesterol, 733 mg sodium, 42 g carbohydrate, 7 g fiber, 23 g protein. Diabetic Exchanges: 2-1/2 starch, 2 lean meat, 1 vegetable, 1/2 fat.

taste of home
COOKING SCHOOL
SECRET

SWEET, SPICY JERK SEASONING

Jerk seasoning is a blend of hot peppers, onion, garlic and thyme mixed with sweet spices, such as allspice and cinnamon. As with any spice blend, each will vary according to the manufacturer's recipe.

If you can't find jerk seasoning, mix up your own batch with spices you have on hand. Your goal: A flavor that's hot and slightly sweet.

Try serving the Jerk Turkey Tenderloins with coconut rice for a delectable fusion of cuisines. Cook rice according to package directions, but substitute light coconut milk for some or all of the water. Add Mojito Marinated Fruit (page 207) and a refreshing drink like Sparkling Strawberry Lemonade (page 32) for an impromptu tropical getaway!

JERK TURKEY TENDERLOINS

Yield: 5 servings (2 cups salsa).

This is best with fresh pineapple, however, on particularly busy days, I have used canned pineapple tidbits in an effort to speed up the preparation.
holly bauer // west bend, wisconsin

- 1 **package (20 ounces) turkey breast tenderloins**
- 1/2 **teaspoon seasoned salt**
- 2 **tablespoons olive oil**
- 1 **tablespoon dried rosemary, crushed**
- 1 **tablespoon Caribbean jerk seasoning**
- 1 **tablespoon brown sugar**

SALSA:
- 1-1/2 **cups cubed fresh pineapple**
- 1 **medium sweet red pepper, chopped**
- 1/4 **cup chopped red onion**
- 1/4 **cup minced fresh cilantro**
- 1 **jalapeno pepper, seeded and minced**
- 2 **tablespoons lime juice**
- 2 **garlic cloves, minced**
- 1/4 **teaspoon salt**
- 1/8 **teaspoon pepper**

Sprinkle tenderloins with seasoned salt. Combine the oil, rosemary, jerk seasoning and brown sugar. Rub over tenderloins. Broil 3-4 in. from the heat for 7-9 minutes on each side or until a meat thermometer reads 170°.

Meanwhile, in a large bowl, combine the salsa ingredients. Serve with turkey.

EDITOR'S NOTE: We recommend wearing disposable gloves when cutting hot peppers. Avoid touching your face.

Nutrition Facts: 3 ounces cooked turkey with 1/3 cup salsa equals 216 calories, 7 g fat (1 g saturated fat), 56 mg cholesterol, 503 mg sodium, 12 g carbohydrate, 2 g fiber, 27 g protein. Diabetic Exchanges: 3 lean meat, 1 vegetable, 1 fat, 1/2 fruit.

Cheat It: Substitute a fruity salsa from the deli for the homemade salsa.

HONEY-DIJON TURKEY CUTLETS

Yield: 4 servings.

In the mood for a taste of turkey, but don't have time to prepare a whole bird? Here's the perfect solution! These savory slices and easy-to-prepare herb glaze offer the goodness of turkey without the hassle.

taste of home cooking school

- 1 package (17.6 ounces) turkey breast cutlets
- 1 tablespoon canola oil
- 1/2 cup chicken broth
- 1/2 cup apple juice
- 1 tablespoon honey
- 1 tablespoon Dijon mustard
- 1/2 teaspoon salt
- 1/4 teaspoon *each* dried basil, dried rosemary, crushed and garlic powder
- 1 tablespoon cornstarch
- 1 tablespoon water

In a large skillet, brown turkey slices on each side in oil. In a small bowl, combine the broth, apple juice, honey, mustard, salt, basil, rosemary and garlic powder; pour over turkey. Bring to a boil. Reduce heat; cover and simmer for 8 minutes or until the turkey is no longer pink.

Combine cornstarch and water until smooth; stir into skillet. Bring to a boil; cook and stir for 2 minutes or until thickened.

Nutrition Facts: 1 cooked turkey slice equals 213 calories, 4 g fat (1 g saturated fat), 78 mg cholesterol, 570 mg sodium, 11 g carbohydrate, trace fiber, 31 g protein. Diabetic Exchanges: 4 lean meat, 1 starch, 1 fat.

BROCCOLI TURKEY CASSEROLE

CHEAT IT!

Yield: 6 servings.

All ages go for this scrumptious meal-in-one. It takes just a handful of ingredients to put together. Try adding dried cranberries to the stuffing mix for more color and flavor.

jenn schlachter // big rock, illinois

- 1-1/2 cups water
- 1 package (6 ounces) turkey stuffing mix
- 2 cups cubed cooked turkey
- 1 cup frozen broccoli florets, thawed
- 1 can (10-3/4 ounces) condensed broccoli cheese soup, undiluted
- 1 cup (4 ounces) shredded cheddar cheese

In a small saucepan, bring water to a boil. Stir in stuffing mix. Remove from the heat; cover and let stand for 5 minutes.

Meanwhile, layer turkey and broccoli in a greased 11-in. x 7-in. baking dish. Top with soup. Fluff stuffing with a fork; spoon over soup. Sprinkle with cheese.

Bake, uncovered, at 350° for 30-35 minutes or until heated through.

Nutrition Facts: 1-1/3 cups equals 315 calories, 13 g fat (6 g saturated fat), 66 mg cholesterol, 1,025 mg sodium, 25 g carbohydrate, 2 g fiber, 23 g protein.

HONEY-APPLE TURKEY BREAST

CHEAT IT!

Yield: 12-14 servings.

I found this recipe in a diabetics' cookbook, and I really like the honey flavor. The sweetness comes through when I use the leftovers in casseroles and soups, too.
rita reinke // wauwatosa, wisconsin

- 3/4 **cup thawed apple juice concentrate**
- 1/3 **cup honey**
- 1 **tablespoon ground mustard**
- 1 **bone-in turkey breast (6 to 7 pounds)**

In a small saucepan, combine the apple juice concentrate, honey and mustard. Cook over low heat for 2-3 minutes or just until blended, stirring occasionally.

Place turkey breast on a rack in a foil-lined shallow roasting pan; pour honey mixture over the top.

Bake, uncovered, at 325° for 2 to 2-1/2 hours or until a meat thermometer reads 180°, basting with pan juices every 30 minutes. (Cover loosely with foil if turkey browns too quickly.) Cover and let stand for 15 minutes before carving.

Nutrition Facts: 1 serving equals 213 calories, 4 g fat (1 g saturated fat), 78 mg cholesterol, 570 mg sodium, 11 g carbohydrate, trace fiber, 31 g protein. Diabetic Exchanges: 4 lean meat, 1 starch, 1 fat.

CLASSIC TURKEY GRAVY

Yield: 2 cups.

Making gravy is very simple when you have the right proportions of ingredients. This recipe is delicious. You will want to serve it at every holiday dinner.

virginia watson // kirksville, missouri

Drippings from 1 roasted turkey

1 to 1-1/2 cups turkey *or* chicken broth

1/4 cup all-purpose flour

Salt and white pepper to taste

Pour turkey drippings into a 2-cup measuring cup. Skim fat, reserving 2 tablespoons; set aside. Add enough broth to the drippings to measure 2 cups.

In a small saucepan, combine flour and reserved fat until smooth. Gradually stir in the drippings mixture. Bring to a boil; cook and stir for 2 minutes or until thickened. Season with salt and white pepper to taste.

Nutrition Facts: 1/4 cup equals 45 calories, 3 g fat (1 g saturated fat), 4 mg cholesterol, 127 mg sodium, 3 g carbohydrate, trace fiber, 1 g protein.

>> HOW TO:

MAKE NO-FUSS GRAVY

1 After pouring drippings in a measuring cup or fat separator, skim the fat, reserving 2 tablespoons. Add enough broth to drippings to measure 2 cups.

2 Combine flour and reserved fat in a saucepan until smooth over medium heat.

3 Gradually stir in the drippings mixture. Bring to a boil and stir until thickened. Add seasonings to taste.

>> HOW TO:

SEASON TURKEY UNDER THE SKIN

1   With your fingers, carefully loosen skin from both sides of the turkey breast. Spread half of the mixture over the meat under the skin.

2   Smooth skin over meat and secure to underside of breast with toothpicks. Spread remaining mixture over turkey skin.

CRANBERRY-GLAZED TURKEY BREAST

Yield: 12 servings.

This golden brown turkey breast is just four ingredients away! And with its low sodium, fat and cholesterol levels, you can feel good about serving it. It's simply delicious.
audrey petterson // maidstone, saskatchewan

- 1-1/4 **cups jellied cranberry sauce**
- 2/3 **cup thawed unsweetened apple juice concentrate**
- 2 **tablespoons butter**
- 1 **bone-in turkey breast (5 to 6 pounds)**

In a small saucepan, bring the cranberry sauce, apple juice concentrate and butter to a boil. Remove from the heat; cool.

Carefully loosen skin of turkey breast. Set aside 1/2 cup sauce for basting and 3/4 cup for serving. Spoon remaining sauce onto the turkey, rubbing mixture under and over the skin.

Place turkey on a rack in a shallow roasting pan. Bake, uncovered, at 325° for 1-1/2 to 2 hours or until a meat thermometer reads 170°, basting occasionally with reserved sauce. Cover and let stand for 10 minutes before carving. Warm reserved 3/4 cup sauce; serve with the turkey.

Nutrition Facts: 1 serving equals 244 calories, 3 g fat (1 g saturated fat), 103 mg cholesterol, 91 mg sodium, 17 g carbohydrate, trace fiber, 36 g protein. Diabetic Exchanges: 5 lean meat, 1 starch.

HERB 'N' SPICE TURKEY BREAST

Yield: 12 servings.

This nicely seasoned turkey breast is a terrific accompaniment to roasted goose during the holidays. Or prepare it throughout the year for a delicious dinner on its own.

taste of home test cooking school

- 3 tablespoons canola oil
- 1 tablespoon brown sugar
- 1 teaspoon salt
- 1/2 teaspoon rubbed sage
- 1/2 teaspoon dried thyme
- 1/2 teaspoon dried rosemary, crushed
- 1/4 teaspoon pepper
- 1/8 to 1/4 teaspoon ground allspice
- 1 bone-in turkey breast (5 to 6 pounds)

In a small bowl, combine the oil, brown sugar, salt, sage, thyme, rosemary, pepper and allspice. With fingers, carefully loosen the skin from both sides of turkey breast.

Spread half of the brown sugar mixture under the skin. Secure skin to underside of breast with toothpicks. Spread the remaining brown sugar mixture over the skin.

Line the bottom of a large shallow roasting pan with foil. Place turkey breast side up on a rack in prepared pan.

Bake, uncovered, at 325° for 2 to 2-1/2 hours or until a meat thermometer reads 170°. (Cover loosely with foil if turkey browns too quickly.) Cover and let stand for 15 minutes before carving.

Nutrition Facts: 1 serving equals 253 calories, 12 g fat (3 g saturated fat), 87 mg cholesterol, 243 mg sodium, 1 g carbohydrate, trace fiber, 34 g protein.

>> HOW TO:

CARVE A WHOLE TURKEY

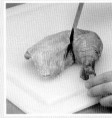

1. Place bird on a carving board and remove any stuffing. Pull drumstick away from the body and cut between the thigh joint and body to remove leg. Repeat.
2. To separate the drumstick and thigh, cut through the connecting joint.
3. Holding the drumstick by the end, slice meat. Cut thigh meat parallel to the bone.

4. Hold bird with a meat fork and make a cut into the breast above the wing area.
5. Slice down from the top of the breast into the cut made in Step 4. Slice meat 1/4 in. thick. Repeat Steps 4 and 5 on other side of bird.
6. To remove wings, cut through connecting joints by the wing bones and backbone.

tasteofhome COOKING SCHOOL SECRET

TURKEY DAY MADE EASY!

To save time on Thanksgiving Day, bake your stuffing separately in pans instead of in the turkey. While stuffed turkey may feel traditional, leaving your bird unstuffed has some advantages:

- The turkey will require less prep work to get it ready for the oven, which leaves you more free time in the morning.
- The bird will cook for less time.
- Just before dinner, you'll be busy making gravy, warming the bread, plating the side dishes and carving the turkey. Not having to remove the stuffing from the turkey will save you a step.

Whether you prefer a traditional sausage stuffing, a California-style artichoke dressing or classic Southern corn bread, you'll find the perfect dressing on pages 226-229.

CITRUS-ROSEMARY RUBBED TURKEY

Yield: 13-15 servings.

This easy, well-seasoned turkey is sure to be a timeless favorite. My family treasures this recipe.
della stamp // long beach, california

- 2 tablespoons minced fresh rosemary *or* 2 teaspoons dried rosemary, crushed
- 1-1/2 teaspoons grated fresh *or* dried orange peel
- 1-1/2 teaspoons grated fresh *or* dried lemon peel
- 1 teaspoon salt
- 1 teaspoon onion powder
- 1 teaspoon garlic powder
- 1 teaspoon pepper
- 1/4 cup olive oil
- 1 turkey (13 to 15 pounds)

In a small bowl, combine the first seven ingredients. Place turkey, breast side up, on a rack in a roasting pan; pat dry. Brush with oil; rub rosemary mixture over turkey.

Bake, uncovered, at 325° for 2-3/4 to 3-1/4 hours or until a meat thermometer reads 180°, basting occasionally with pan drippings. (Cover loosely with foil if turkey browns too quickly.) Cover and let stand for 20 minutes before carving.

Nutrition Facts: 1 serving equals 493 calories, 25 g fat (7 g saturated fat), 212 mg cholesterol, 307 mg sodium, 1 g carbohydrate, trace fiber, 63 g protein.

SEAFOOD

COMFORTING TUNA CASSEROLE

Yield: 2 servings.

Sometimes I use sliced stuffed olives instead of pimientos in this recipe I got from my mother. dorothy coleman // hobe sound, florida

- 1-3/4 **cups uncooked wide egg noodles**
- 6 **teaspoons butter,** *divided*
- 4 **teaspoons all-purpose flour**
- 1/4 **teaspoon salt**

Dash pepper

- 3/4 **cup 2% milk**
- 1 **package (3 ounces) cream cheese, softened**

- 1 **pouch (3 ounces) white water-packed tuna**
- 2 **tablespoons diced pimientos**
- 2 **teaspoons minced chives**
- 2 **slices Muenster cheese (3/4 ounce** *each***)**
- 2 **tablespoons soft bread crumbs**

Cook noodles according to package directions. Meanwhile, in a small saucepan, melt 5 teaspoons butter. Stir in the flour, salt and pepper until blended; gradually add milk. Bring to a boil; cook and stir for 1-2 minutes or until thickened. Reduce heat; add the cream cheese, tuna, pimientos and chives. Cook and stir until cheese is melted.

Drain noodles. Spread 1/4 cup tuna mixture into a 3-cup baking dish coated with cooking spray. Layer with half of the noodles, 1/2 cup tuna mixture and one slice of cheese. Repeat layers.

In a small microwave-safe bowl, melt remaining butter; stir in bread crumbs. Sprinkle over top of casserole. Bake, uncovered, at 350° for 20-25 minutes or until bubbly.

Nutrition Facts: 1-1/2 cups equals 493 calories, 26 g fat (15 g saturated fat), 118 mg cholesterol, 941 mg sodium, 37 g carbohydrate, 2 g fiber, 28 g protein.

FISH & SEAFOOD

TO PURCHASE THE BEST FISH:

- Fresh fillets or steaks should have firm, elastic, moist-looking flesh with shiny, bright skin.
- Whole fish should have eyes that are not sunken or cloudy, and a firm, springy body.
- Fresh fish should have a mild smell.
- Frozen fish should be solidly frozen with no freezer burn.

TO BE SAFE:

- Prepare fresh fish within 1 to 2 days of purchase.
- Put fresh fish in the coldest section of your refrigerator.
- To freeze, wrap in freezer paper, heavy-duty foil or heavy-duty plastic bags.
- Fatty fish can be frozen for 3 months; lean fish for up to 6 months.

TO DEFROST IN THE REFRIGERATOR:

- Place a tray under the package to catch any liquid or juices.
- Allow 12 or more hours for a 1-pound package.

TO DEFROST IN COLD WATER:

- Place fish or shellfish in a leakproof package or bag.
- Submerge the wrapped seafood in cold tap water.
- Change the water every 30 minutes.
- Allow 1 to 2 hours per pound.

TUNA NOODLE SKILLET

CHEAT IT!

Yield: 6 servings.

Enjoy the comforting flavor of tuna noodle casserole in minutes with this creamy stovetop version that's made with Alfredo sauce and frozen peas.

ruth simon // buffalo, new york

- **2 jars (16 ounces *each*) Alfredo sauce**
- **1 can (14-1/2 ounces) chicken broth**
- **1 package (16 ounces) wide egg noodles**
- **1 package (10 ounces) frozen peas**
- **1/4 teaspoon pepper**
- **1 can (12 ounces) solid white water-packed tuna, drained and flaked**

In a large skillet over medium heat, bring Alfredo sauce and broth to a boil. Add noodles; cover and cook for 7-8 minutes.

Reduce heat; stir in peas and pepper. Cover and cook 4 minutes longer or until noodles are tender. Stir in tuna; heat through.

Nutrition Facts: 1-2/3 cups equals 470 calories, 12 g fat (6 g saturated fat), 101 mg cholesterol, 736 mg sodium, 67 g carbohydrate, 5 g fiber, 24 g protein.

TUNA CASSEROLE STIR-IN IDEAS

- Pimientos, peas and chopped onion
- Chopped zucchini, green onions, tomato and shredded cheddar
- Frozen cut green beans, sliced mushrooms and shredded Swiss
- Chopped onion, green pepper, peas and grated Parmesan
- Velveeta, black olives and pimientos; sprinkle with crushed potato chips and paprika

LINGUINE IN CLAM SAUCE

Yield: 4-6 servings.

I make this quite often for family celebrations. It's a favorite. The zucchini adds such a nice touch to this traditional dish. ken vouk // willowick, ohio

- 1 **package (1 pound) linguine**
- 1 **large onion, finely chopped**
- 2 **tablespoons olive oil**
- 1 **medium zucchini, diced**
- 1 **garlic clove, minced**
- 3 **cans (6-1/2 ounces *each*) chopped clams**
- 1/2 **pound sliced fresh mushrooms**
- 2 **teaspoons chicken bouillon granules**
- 1 **teaspoon minced fresh basil**
- 1/8 **teaspoon pepper**

Shredded Parmesan cheese

Cook linguine according to package directions. Meanwhile, in a large skillet, saute onion in oil until tender. Add zucchini; cook for 2 minutes or until crisp-tender. Stir in garlic; cook 1 minute longer.

Drain clams, reserving 1/2 cup juice. Add the clams, mushrooms, bouillon, basil, pepper and reserved juice to the skillet. Bring to a boil. Reduce heat; simmer, uncovered, for 5 minutes or until vegetables are tender. Drain linguine; top with clam mixture. Sprinkle with cheese.

Nutrition Facts: 1 serving equals 377 calories, 7 g fat (1 g saturated fat), 16 mg cholesterol, 674 mg sodium, 64 g carbohydrate, 4 g fiber, 18 g protein.

TUNA ZUCCHINI CAKES

Yield: 3 servings.

This is a great combination of seafood and a bountiful garden vegetable. People like its nice color and texture...not to mention the wonderful flavor! billie blanton // kingsport, tennessee

- 1/2 **cup finely chopped onion**
- 1 **tablespoon butter**
- 1 **can (6-1/2 ounces) light water-packed tuna, drained and flaked**
- 1 **cup shredded zucchini**
- 2 **eggs, lightly beaten**
- 1/3 **cup minced fresh parsley**
- 1 **teaspoon lemon juice**
- 1/2 **teaspoon salt**
- 1/8 **teaspoon pepper**
- 1 **cup seasoned bread crumbs, *divided***
- 2 **tablespoons canola oil**

In a large saucepan, saute onion in butter until tender. Remove from the heat. Add the tuna, zucchini, eggs, parsley, lemon juice, seasonings and 1/2 cup bread crumbs. Stir until well combined. Shape into six 1/2-in.-thick patties; coat with remaining bread crumbs.

In a large skillet, heat oil. Cook the patties for 3 minutes on each side or until golden brown.

Nutrition Facts: 2 cakes equals 400 calories, 19 g fat (5 g saturated fat), 170 mg cholesterol, 1,261 mg sodium, 31 g carbohydrate, 3 g fiber, 26 g protein.

CURRY SHRIMP LINGUINE

CHEAT IT!

Yield: 6 servings.

Curry, cilantro and coconut milk make this dish exciting and different. It's also delicious prepared with Thai rice noodles or spaghetti.

jana rippee // anacortes, washington

- **1 package (16 ounces) linguine**
- **3 teaspoons curry powder**
- **1 can (14 ounces) light coconut milk**
- **1/2 teaspoon salt**
- **1/4 teaspoon pepper**
- **1-1/4 pounds uncooked medium shrimp, peeled and deveined**
- **1/3 cup minced fresh cilantro**

Cook linguine according to package directions. Meanwhile, in a large skillet over medium heat, toast curry powder for 2 minutes, stirring frequently. Stir in the milk, salt and pepper.

Bring to a boil. Add the shrimp; cook for 5-6 minutes or until shrimp turn pink. Drain the linguine; toss with the shrimp mixture and the cilantro.

Nutrition Facts: 1-1/2 cups equals 405 calories, 8 g fat (4 g saturated fat), 115 mg cholesterol, 327 mg sodium, 58 g carbohydrate, 3 g fiber, 26 g protein.

SZECHUAN SHRIMP SALAD

Yield: 8 servings.

This dish is surprisingly healthy for as yummy as it is! Leftovers also keep well in the refrigerator for a satisfying lunch. tish stevenson // grand rapids, michigan

- **10 ounces uncooked thin spaghetti**
- **1/3 cup canola oil**
- **1/3 cup honey**
- **2 tablespoons rice vinegar**
- **2 tablespoons sesame oil**
- **2 tablespoons soy sauce**
- **1 tablespoon minced fresh gingerroot**
- **1/2 teaspoon crushed red pepper flakes**
- **1 pound cooked medium shrimp, peeled and deveined**
- **1 package (10 ounces) julienned carrots**
- **2 cups fresh sugar snap peas**
- **1 large sweet red pepper, sliced**
- **1/2 cup sliced green onions**
- **3 tablespoons minced fresh cilantro**
- **3/4 cup coarsely chopped dry roasted peanuts**

Cook spaghetti according to package directions. Meanwhile, in a small bowl, whisk the canola oil, honey, vinegar, sesame oil, soy sauce, ginger and pepper flakes; set aside.

Drain spaghetti; rinse in cold water. Place in a large bowl. Add the shrimp, carrots, peas, red pepper, onions and cilantro. Drizzle with dressing; toss to coat. Sprinkle with peanuts. Chill until serving.

Nutrition Facts: 1-1/2 cups equals 462 calories, 21 g fat (2 g saturated fat), 86 mg cholesterol, 455 mg sodium, 49 g carbohydrate, 5 g fiber, 22 g protein.

GRAPEFRUIT SHRIMP SALAD

Yield: 4 servings.

A simple combination of shrimp, avocado and grapefruit add up to one simply fabulous salad. joanne beaupre // manchester, connecticut

- 1 **head Bibb *or* Boston lettuce**
- 1 **large grapefruit, peeled and sectioned**
- 1 **medium ripe avocado, peeled and thinly sliced**
- 1 **pound cooked medium shrimp, peeled and deveined**

CITRUS VINAIGRETTE:

- 2 **tablespoons orange juice**
- 2 **tablespoons red wine vinegar**
- 1 **tablespoon olive oil**
- 2 **teaspoons Dijon mustard**
- 1/4 **teaspoon salt**

Place lettuce on four serving plates. Arrange the grapefruit, avocado and shrimp over lettuce. In a small bowl, whisk the vinaigrette ingredients. Drizzle over each salad.

Nutrition Facts: 1 serving equals 266 calories, 12 g fat (2 g saturated fat), 221 mg cholesterol, 445 mg sodium, 14 g carbohydrate, 4 g fiber, 26 g protein. Diabetic Exchanges: 3 lean meat, 2 fat, 1 vegetable, 1/2 fruit.

>> HOW TO:

SECTION CITRUS FRUIT

1. Cut a thin slice off the bottom and top of the fruit. Rest the fruit, cut side down, on a cutting board. With a sharp paring knife, remove the peel and white pith from the fruit.

2. Hold the fruit over a bowl and slice between the membrane of a section and the fruit until the knife reaches the center. Turn the knife and follow the membrane so the fruit is released. Repeat until all the sections are removed.

2-3 minutes. Carefully stir in 1 cup heated broth. Cook and stir until all of the liquid is absorbed.

Add remaining broth, 1/2 cup at a time, stirring constantly. Allow liquid to absorb between additions. Cook just until risotto is creamy and rice is almost tender, about 20 minutes.

Add the spinach, shrimp, cheese and pepper; cook and stir until shrimp turn pink.

Nutrition Facts: 1-1/4 cups equals 405 calories, 8 g fat (4 g saturated fat), 187 mg cholesterol, 906 mg sodium, 47 g carbohydrate, 2 g fiber, 35 g protein. Diabetic Exchanges: 4 lean meat, 2-1/2 starch, 1 vegetable, 1 fat.

SHRIMP 'N' SPINACH RISOTTO

Yield: 4 servings.

I enjoy concocting new, healthy recipes and spinach is one of the few vegetables that my husband will eat. This creamy risotto makes a great meal-in-one, but doubles as a side dish as well.
jennifer neilsen // williamston, north carolina

- 3-1/4 to 3-3/4 cups reduced-sodium chicken broth
- 1-1/2 cups chopped fresh mushrooms
- 1 small onion, chopped
- 1 tablespoon butter
- 3 garlic cloves, minced
- 1 cup uncooked arborio rice
- 1 package (6 ounces) fresh baby spinach, coarsely chopped
- 1 pound cooked medium shrimp, peeled and deveined
- 1/2 cup shredded Parmesan cheese
- 1/4 teaspoon pepper

In a small saucepan, heat broth and keep warm. In a large nonstick skillet, saute mushrooms and onion in butter until tender, about 3 minutes. Add garlic; cook 1 minute longer. Add rice; cook and stir for

SCALLOPS IN SAGE CREAM

Yield: 4 servings.

I didn't want to hide the ocean freshness of the scallops I bought on the dock from a local fisherman, so I used simple but perfect ingredients to showcase them.
joan churchill // dover, new hampshire

- 1-1/2 pounds sea scallops
- 1/4 teaspoon salt
- 1/8 teaspoon pepper
- 3 tablespoons olive oil, *divided*
- 1/2 cup chopped shallots
- 3/4 cup heavy whipping cream
- 6 fresh sage leaves, thinly sliced

Hot cooked pasta, optional

≫ HOW TO:

CUT CHIFFONADE

For a pretty presentation, make long, even strips of leafy herbs and vegetables like basil, sage and spinach with this technique. Stack the leaves neatly in the same direction, then roll the stack lengthwise into a tight cigar shape. Slice across the rolled leaves to create thin strips.

Sprinkle scallops with salt and pepper. In a large skillet, saute scallops in 2 tablespoons oil for 1-1/2 to 2 minutes on each side or until firm and opaque. Remove and keep warm.

In the same skillet, saute shallots in remaining oil until tender. Add cream; bring to a boil. Cook and stir for 30 seconds or until slightly thickened.

Return scallops to the pan; heat through. Stir in sage. Serve with pasta if desired.

Nutrition Facts: 1 serving equals 408 calories, 28 g fat (12 g saturated fat), 117 mg cholesterol, 441 mg sodium, 9 g carbohydrate, trace fiber, 30 g protein.

MINI SCALLOP CASSEROLES

Yield: 4 servings.

Tiny and tender bay scallops take center stage in these miniature dishes. They're reminiscent of potpies, very creamy and packed with flavorful veggies in every bite.

vivian manary // nepean, ontario

> 3 **celery ribs, chopped**
>
> 1 **cup sliced fresh mushrooms**
>
> 1 **medium green pepper, chopped**
>
> 1 **small onion, chopped**
>
> 2 **tablespoons butter**
>
> 1/3 **cup all-purpose flour**

> 1/4 **teaspoon salt**
>
> 1/4 **teaspoon pepper**
>
> 2 **cups fat-free milk**
>
> 1 **pound bay scallops**

TOPPING:

> 1 **cup soft bread crumbs**
>
> 1 **tablespoon butter, melted**
>
> 1/4 **cup shredded cheddar cheese**

In a large skillet, saute the celery, mushrooms, green pepper and onion in butter until tender. Stir in the flour, salt and pepper until blended; gradually add the milk. Bring to a boil; cook and stir for 2 minutes or until thickened.

Reduce heat; add the scallops. Cook, stirring occasionally, for 3-4 minutes or until scallops are firm and opaque.

Divide mixture among four 10-oz. ramekins or custard cups. In a small bowl, combine crumbs and butter; sprinkle over the scallop mixture.

Bake, uncovered, at 350° for 15-20 minutes or until bubbly. Sprinkle with cheese; bake 5 minutes longer or until cheese is melted.

Nutrition Facts: 1 serving equals 332 calories, 12 g fat (7 g saturated fat), 70 mg cholesterol, 588 mg sodium, 27 g carbohydrate, 2 g fiber, 28 g protein. Diabetic Exchanges: 3 lean meat, 2 fat, 1 starch, 1 vegetable, 1/2 fat-free milk.

PESTO SCALLOPS VERMICELLI

Yield: 2 servings.

Quick and easy with a gourmet flavor, this seafood entree seasons tender bay scallops with garlic, oregano and pesto sauce, then tosses them with pasta.

marilyn lustgarten // wentzville, missouri

- 4 ounces uncooked vermicelli
- 2 tablespoons butter
- 1/2 teaspoon garlic powder
- 1/4 teaspoon dried oregano
- 1/8 teaspoon pepper
- 1/2 pound bay scallops
- 2 tablespoons white wine *or* chicken broth
- 3 tablespoons prepared pesto

Cook vermicelli according to package directions. Meanwhile, in a large skillet, melt butter. Stir in the garlic powder, oregano and pepper. Add scallops and wine; cook and stir over medium heat for 5-6 minutes or until scallops are firm and opaque.

Reduce heat to low. Stir in pesto; heat through. Drain vermicelli; toss with the scallop mixture.

Nutrition Facts: 1-1/4 cups equals 536 calories, 24 g fat (10 g saturated fat), 76 mg cholesterol, 481 mg sodium, 47 g carbohydrate, 3 g fiber, 31 g protein.

taste of home
COOKING SCHOOL SECRET

SMART SUBSTITUTIONS

One of cooking's many pleasures is learning to improvise and make do with what you have on hand. Save money and time when making Creamy Scallop Crepes (shown above, recipe on opposite page) with substitutions like these:

- Use 2 whole eggs in the crepe batter instead of 2 whites plus 1 egg. You will save cracking 1 egg and won't have extra yolks hanging around.

- If you don't have wine or broth for the filling, substitute 1/2 teaspoon chicken bouillon granules and 1/2 cup water. Voila! No open or partial cans.

- Evaporated milk lends rich creaminess without added fat to this dish. To make your own, cook 1-2/3 cups of low- or no-fat milk in a small heavy saucepan until it is reduced to 2/3 cup. Or you could substitute 2/3 cup heavy cream or half-and-half for the evaporated milk, but you'd be increasing the fat content.

CREAMY SCALLOP CREPES

Yield: 6 servings.

This Swiss cheese and scallop-filled crepe recipe is award-winning. For extra flavor, add 1/4 teaspoon fresh dill weed to the crepe batter before refrigerating.

doreen kelly // hatboro, pennsylvania

2 egg whites	1/8 teaspoon white pepper
1 egg	1 pound sliced fresh mushrooms
1-1/2 cups fat-free milk	4 green onions, sliced
1 cup all-purpose flour	2 tablespoons butter
1/2 teaspoon salt	1/4 cup all-purpose flour
FILLING:	2/3 cup fat-free evaporated milk
1 pound bay scallops	1/2 cup shredded reduced-fat Swiss cheese
1/2 cup white wine *or* reduced-sodium chicken broth	

In a small bowl, beat the egg whites, egg and milk. Combine flour and salt; add to milk mixture and mix well. Cover and refrigerate for 1 hour.

Coat an 8-in. nonstick skillet with cooking spray; heat. Stir crepe batter; pour 2 tablespoons into center of skillet. Lift and tilt pan to coat bottom evenly. Cook until top appears dry; turn and cook 15-20 seconds longer. Remove to a wire rack. Repeat with remaining batter, coating skillet with cooking spray as needed. When cool, stack crepes with waxed paper or paper towels in between.

In a large nonstick skillet, bring the scallops, wine and pepper to a boil. Reduce heat; simmer for 3-4 minutes or until scallops are firm and opaque. Drain, reserving cooking liquid; set liquid and scallops aside.

In the same skillet, saute mushrooms and onions in butter until almost tender. Sprinkle with flour; stir until blended. Gradually stir in evaporated milk and reserved cooking liquid. Bring to a boil; cook and stir for 2 minutes or until thickened. Remove from the heat. Stir in cheese and scallops.

Spread 1/3 cup filling down the center of each crepe; roll up and place in a 13-in. x 9-in. baking dish coated with cooking spray. Cover and bake at 350° for 12-15 minutes or until heated through.

Nutrition Facts: 2 filled crepes equals 319 calories, 8 g fat (4 g saturated fat), 79 mg cholesterol, 463 mg sodium, 32 g carbohydrate, 2 g fiber, 27 g protein. Diabetic Exchanges: 3 lean meat, 2 starch, 1 fat.

>> HOW TO:

MAKE A CREPE

1 Add batter: Spoon 2-3 Tbsp. crepe batter into a hot, greased skillet.

2 Swirl: Lift pan to gently swirl the batter so it evenly coats the skillet.

3 Flip: With a non-metal spatula, carefully loosen the crepe and turn it over. It's perfectly OK to use your fingers if necessary.

EASY CRAB CAKES

Yield: 4 servings.

Canned crabmeat makes these delicate patties simple enough for busy weeknight dinners. For something different, try forming the crab mixture into four larger patties instead of eight smaller cakes.
charlene spelock // apollo, pennsylvania

- 2 cans (**6 ounces** *each*) crabmeat, drained, flaked and cartilage removed
- 1 cup seasoned bread crumbs, *divided*
- 1 egg, lightly beaten
- 1/4 cup finely chopped green onions
- 1/4 cup finely chopped sweet red pepper
- 1/4 cup reduced-fat mayonnaise
- 1 tablespoon lemon juice
- 1/2 teaspoon garlic powder
- 1/8 teaspoon cayenne pepper
- 1 tablespoon butter

In a large bowl, combine the crab, 1/3 cup bread crumbs, egg, onions, red pepper, mayonnaise, lemon juice, garlic powder and cayenne.

Divide mixture into eight portions; shape into 2-in. balls. Roll in remaining bread crumbs. Flatten to 1/2-in. thickness.

In a large nonstick skillet, cook crab cakes in butter for 3-4 minutes on each side or until golden brown.

Nutrition Facts: 2 crab cakes equals 295 calories, 12 g fat (3 g saturated fat), 142 mg cholesterol, 879 mg sodium, 23 g carbohydrate, 1 g fiber, 23 g protein. Diabetic Exchanges: 3 lean meat, 1-1/2 starch, 1-1/2 fat.

CRAB CAKE-STUFFED PORTOBELLOS

Yield: 6 servings.

Served as an appetizer or a light main dish, these stuffed mushrooms are pretty and delicious. Canned crabmeat becomes absolutely elegant.
jennifer coduto // kent, ohio

- 6 large portobello mushrooms
- 3/4 cup finely chopped sweet onion
- 2 tablespoons olive oil, *divided*
- 1 package (**8 ounces**) cream cheese, softened
- 1 egg
- 1/2 cup seasoned bread crumbs
- 1/2 cup plus 1 teaspoon grated Parmesan cheese, *divided*
- 1 teaspoon seafood seasoning
- 2 cans (**6-1/2 ounces** *each*) lump crabmeat, drained
- 1/4 teaspoon paprika

Remove stems from mushrooms (discard or save for another use); set caps aside. In a small skillet, saute onion in 1 tablespoon oil until tender. In a small bowl, combine the cream cheese, egg, bread crumbs, 1/2 cup cheese and seafood seasoning. Gently stir in the crab and the onion.

Spoon 1/2 cup crab mixture into each mushroom cap; drizzle with remaining oil. Sprinkle with paprika and remaining cheese. Place in a greased 15-in. x 10-in. x 1-in. baking pan.

Bake, uncovered, at 400° for 15-20 minutes or until mushrooms are tender.

Nutrition Facts: 1 stuffed mushroom equals 346 calories, 22 g fat (11 g saturated fat), 138 mg cholesterol, 695 mg sodium, 14 g carbohydrate, 2 g fiber, 23 g protein.

CRAB CAKE SERVING IDEAS

Dress up your crab cakes with these accompaniments and serving ideas:

- Lemon wedges, cocktail sauce or tartar sauce
- A side dish of veggie fries, mac 'n' cheese or buttered green beans
- Coleslaw or Macaroni Coleslaw (page 209) and sliced tomatoes
- Toasted dinner rolls, baby lettuce and Easy "Roasted" Garlic Mayo (page 186) to make Crab Po' Boy Sliders

TUNA WITH WASABI SAUCE

Yield: 4 servings.

Wasabi mayonnaise can be found in the Asian section of your local supermarket. Wasabi, an Asian plant similar to horseradish, has a fiery flavor. Add some plain mayonnaise to make a milder sauce.
taste of home cooking school

1/4	cup reduced-sodium teriyaki sauce
1	tablespoon rice vinegar
2	teaspoons sesame oil
4	tuna steaks (**8 ounces** *each*)
1/2	cup wasabi mayonnaise
2	tablespoons chopped green onion
2	teaspoons lemon juice

In a large resealable plastic bag, combine the teriyaki sauce, vinegar and oil; add tuna. Seal bag and turn to coat; refrigerate for up to 1 hour. Meanwhile, in a small bowl, combine the mayonnaise, onion and lemon juice until blended. Refrigerate until serving.

Drain and discard marinade. Moisten a paper towel with cooking oil; using long-handled tongs, lightly coat the grill rack. Grill tuna, covered, over medium heat or broil 4 in. from the heat for 5-6 minutes on each side or until medium-rare or until slightly pink in the center. Serve with wasabi sauce.

Nutrition Facts: 1 tuna steak with about 2 tablespoons sauce equals 458 calories, 25 g fat (4 g saturated fat), 112 mg cholesterol, 341 mg sodium, 1 g carbohydrate, trace fiber, 53 g protein.

LOW COUNTRY GRILL

Yield: 6 servings.

Grilling is one of my family's favorite ways of cooking. This recipe contains many different ingredients but they come together quickly.
alaina showalter // clover, south carolina

2	tablespoons olive oil	1/3	cup butter, melted
1	teaspoon salt, *divided*	1	pound smoked kielbasa or Polish sausage
1	teaspoon garlic powder, *divided*	3	medium ears sweet corn, cut in half
1	teaspoon seafood seasoning, *divided*	1-1/2	pounds uncooked medium shrimp, peeled and deveined
12	small red potatoes, quartered		

In a large bowl, combine the oil with 1/4 teaspoon each of salt, garlic powder and seafood seasoning. Add potatoes; toss to coat. Spoon onto a greased double thickness of heavy-duty foil (about 18 in. square).

Fold foil around the potatoes and seal tightly. Grill, covered, over medium heat for 30-35 minutes or until tender, turning once. Set aside and keep warm.

In a small bowl, combine the butter with remaining salt, garlic powder and seafood seasoning. Grill kielbasa and corn, covered, over medium heat for 10-12 minutes or until kielbasa is heated through and corn is tender, turning occasionally and basting corn with half of the butter mixture. Keep warm.

Thread shrimp onto four metal or soaked wooden skewers; grill, covered, over medium heat for 3-4 minutes on each side or until shrimp turn pink, basting with remaining butter mixture. Slice kielbasa into six pieces before serving. Carefully open foil from the potatoes to allow steam to escape.

Nutrition Facts: 1 serving equals 566 calories, 37 g fat (15 g saturated fat), 215 mg cholesterol, 1,536 mg sodium, 26 g carbohydrate, 3 g fiber, 32 g protein.

HONEY GRILLED SHRIMP

CHEAT IT!

Yield: 8 servings.

My husband was given this super-simple recipe by a man who sold shrimp at the fish market. It's now become our absolute favorite shrimp recipe.

lisa blackwell // henderson, north carolina

- 1 **bottle (8 ounces) Italian salad dressing**
- 1 **cup honey**
- 1/2 **teaspoon minced garlic**
- 2 **pounds uncooked medium shrimp, peeled and deveined**

In a small bowl, combine the salad dressing, honey and garlic; set aside 1/2 cup. Pour remaining marinade into a large resealable plastic bag; add the shrimp. Seal bag and turn to coat; refrigerate for 30 minutes. Cover and refrigerate reserved marinade for basting.

Drain and discard marinade. Thread shrimp onto eight metal or soaked wooden skewers. Moisten a paper towel with cooking oil; using long-handled tongs, lightly coat the grill rack.

Grill, uncovered, over medium heat or broil 4 in. from the heat for 1 to 1-1/2 minutes on each side. Baste with reserved marinade. Grill or broil 3-4 minutes longer or until shrimp turn pink, turning and basting frequently.

Nutrition Facts: 1 serving equals 175 calories, 5 g fat (1 g saturated fat), 168 mg cholesterol, 383 mg sodium, 14 g carbohydrate, trace fiber, 18 g protein. Diabetic Exchanges: 3 lean meat, 1 starch, 1 fat.

≫ HOW TO:

OIL A GRILL GRATE

To oil a hot grill grate to prevent foods from sticking, fold a paper towel into a small pad and moisten it with cooking oil. Holding the pad with long-handled tongs, rub it over the grate.

>>HOW TO:

GRILL A WHOLE SALMON FILLET

1 Prepare the salmon according to the recipe, leaving the skin on (this makes it easier to remove the fish from the grill). Lightly oil the hot grill to prevent sticking, then place the whole fillet, skin side down, onto the grill. Cover and cook until done. There is no need to turn the fillet during cooking.

2 With a spatula, gently remove the salmon to a serving platter. The cooked fish easily separates from the skin, which makes serving up portions of the fillet quite simple.

HICKORY BARBECUED SALMON WITH TARTAR SAUCE

Yield: 8 servings (1 cup sauce).

Guests of all ages love this succulent seafood dish. The idea to use hickory chips came from my dad. He always prepared his salmon this way.
linda chevalie // battle ground, washington

1/2 **cup butter, cubed**	**TARTAR SAUCE:**
2 **garlic cloves, minced**	1 **cup mayonnaise**
1 **salmon fillet (3 pounds)**	1/4 **cup chopped sweet pickles**
2 **medium lemons, thinly sliced**	1 **teaspoon finely chopped onion**
2 **cups soaked hickory chips**	3/4 **teaspoon ground mustard**
	1/4 **teaspoon Worcestershire sauce**

In a small saucepan, combine butter and garlic; cook and stir over medium heat until butter is melted. Drizzle 2 tablespoons butter mixture over salmon; top with lemon slices. Set aside remaining butter mixture for basting.

Moisten a paper towel with cooking oil; using long-handled tongs, lightly coat the grill rack. Add wood chips to grill according to manufacturer's directions. Place salmon skin side down on grill rack. Grill, covered, over medium heat or 4 in. from the heat for 5 minutes.

Carefully spoon some reserved butter mixture over salmon. Cover and grill or broil 15-20 minutes longer or until fish flakes easily with a fork, basting occasionally with remaining butter mixture.

Meanwhile, in a small bowl, combine the tartar sauce ingredients. Serve with salmon.

Nutrition Facts: 5 ounces cooked salmon with 2 tablespoons tartar sauce equals 624 calories, 52 g fat (14 g saturated fat), 140 mg cholesterol, 381 mg sodium, 3 g carbohydrate, trace fiber, 34 g protein.

GLAZED SALMON FILLET

Yield: 6-8 servings.

My husband caught a lot of salmon when we lived in Alaska, so I was always trying new ways to prepare it. Basted with brown sugar and lemon, this fillet is perfect for company.
jerilyn colvin // foxboro, massachusetts

1-1/2 cups packed brown sugar	3/4 teaspoon cayenne pepper
6 tablespoons butter, melted	1 salmon fillet (about 2 pounds)
3 to 6 tablespoons lemon juice	Lemon-pepper seasoning
2-1/4 teaspoons dill weed	

In a small bowl, combine the first five ingredients. Remove 1/2 cup to a saucepan; simmer until heated through. Set aside remaining mixture for basting. Sprinkle salmon with lemon-pepper. Moisten a paper towel with cooking oil; using long-handled tongs, lightly coat the grill rack. Place salmon on grill with skin side down.

Grill, covered, over medium heat for 5 minutes. Brush with the reserved brown sugar mixture. Grill 10-15 minutes longer, basting occasionally. Serve with the warmed sauce.

Nutrition Facts: 1 serving equals 441 calories, 21 g fat (8 g saturated fat), 90 mg cholesterol, 170 mg sodium, 41 g carbohydrate, trace fiber, 23 g protein.

GINGERED HONEY SALMON: Combine 1/2 cup orange juice, 1/2 cup soy sauce, 1/3 cup honey, 2 chopped green onions, and 1-1/4 teaspoons each of garlic powder and ground ginger. Set aside 1/2 cup for basting; marinate salmon fillet in remaining mixture for 1 hour. Grill as directed, basting occasionally with reserved mixture.

SALMON WITH CREAMY TARRAGON SAUCE: Lightly brush salmon fillet with olive oil; season with salt and pepper. Grill as directed. Combine 2 cups plain yogurt, 1/2 cup chopped green onions, 2 tablespoons mayonnaise, 1 tablespoon lime juice, 2 teaspoons dried tarragon and hot sauce to taste; serve with salmon.

taste of home COOKING SCHOOL SECRET

TASTY, NUTRITIOUS GRILLED SALMON

A whole salmon fillet from the grill makes for easy, impressive entertaining. Once it's on the grill, there's no need to turn the fillet. And since it is grilled with the skin on, it stays perfectly intact. This is a great way to try something new on the grill.

TASTE THE WILD

Wild salmon is prized for its health benefits and nuanced, varied flavors. Wild salmon is 20% leaner than its farm-raised cousins, while being higher in heart-healthy omega-3 fatty acids. Some people prefer its flavor over farm-raised fish as well.

Wild salmon is available fresh from May through October, when the different species make their spawning runs.

Species you may see at the fish counter include:

- King or Chinook (the largest and first to market)
- Coho (like King but smaller; harvested late into October)
- Sockeye (firm, eye-catching red flesh; as shown in Glazed Salmon Fillet at left)
- Pink (the smallest salmon; most delicately flavored)

AT THE MARKET

Convenient and affordable, farm-raised Norwegian or Atlantic salmon is available year-round. Previously frozen wild salmon may also be available.

Choose fish that is firm-fleshed and bright in color, and allow 4 to 6 ounces of uncooked weight per serving.

EASY SERVING

Serve the grilled fillet on a platter that you've garnished with fresh herbs, greens, lemons or cucumbers.

BREAD FISH

1 Combine the dry ingredients in a pie plate or shallow bowl.

2 In another pie plate or shallow bowl, whisk the egg, milk and/or other liquid ingredients.

3 Dip fish into egg mixture, then roll gently in the dry ingredients. Fry or bake as directed.

PARMESAN FISH FILLETS

Yield: 2 servings.

I love this moist and flaky fish with just a hint of Parmesan cheese. It's fast, easy to prepare and good for you, too!

paula alf // cincinnati, ohio

- 1/4 **cup egg substitute**
- 1 **tablespoon fat-free milk**
- 1/3 **cup grated Parmesan cheese**
- 2 **tablespoons all-purpose flour**
- 2 **tilapia fillets (5 ounces each)**

In a shallow bowl, combine egg substitute and milk. In another shallow bowl, combine cheese and flour. Dip fillets in egg mixture, then coat with cheese mixture.

Place on a baking sheet coated with cooking spray. Bake at 350° for 20-25 minutes or until fish flakes easily with a fork.

Nutrition Facts: 1 fillet equals 196 calories, 5 g fat (3 g saturated fat), 78 mg cholesterol, 279 mg sodium, 5 g carbohydrate, trace fiber, 33 g protein. Diabetic Exchange: 4 lean meat.

PAN-SEARED CHILI SALMON

Yield: 4 servings.

I adapted this recipe from a restaurant dish, and I make it regularly. With shortcuts like peeled baby carrots and instant brown rice, it's ready in 30 minutes from start to finish!
cheryl herrick // burlington, vermont

- **3 cups fresh baby carrots**
- **1 cup instant brown rice**
- **1 cup reduced-sodium chicken broth**
- **1/4 teaspoon pepper, *divided***
- **3 teaspoons chili powder**
- **1/2 teaspoon salt**
- **4 salmon fillets (4 ounces *each*)**
- **2 teaspoons olive oil**
- **1 tablespoon minced fresh parsley**
- **1 teaspoon butter**

Place carrots in a steamer basket; place in a small saucepan over 1 in. of water. Bring to a boil; cover and steam for 12 minutes or until crisp-tender.

Meanwhile, in a small saucepan, bring the rice, broth and 1/8 teaspoon pepper to a boil. Reduce heat; cover and simmer for 5 minutes.

Combine chili powder and salt; rub over salmon. In a large nonstick skillet coated with cooking spray, cook salmon in oil over medium-high heat for 4-6 minutes on each side or until fish flakes easily with a fork.

Remove rice from the heat; let stand for 5 minutes. Fluff with a fork. In a small bowl, combine the carrots, parsley, butter and remaining pepper. Serve with salmon and rice.

Nutrition Facts: 1 salmon fillet with 2/3 cup carrots and 1/2 cup rice equals 369 calories, 17 g fat (3 g saturated fat), 69 mg cholesterol, 620 mg sodium, 27 g carbohydrate, 4 g fiber, 26 g protein.

TROUT MEUNIERE

Yield: 4 servings.

A fabulous dinner is ready in minutes. Just pair this recipe with an easy salad.
nancy kelley // nashville, tennessee

- **4 trout fillets (6 ounces *each*)**
- **1-1/3 cups crushed saltines**
- **4 tablespoons butter, *divided***
- **1 package (2-1/4 ounces) sliced almonds**
- **2 tablespoons lemon juice**

Coat both sides of fillets with crushed saltines. In a large skillet, melt 3 tablespoons butter over medium-high heat. Cook the fillets for 3-5 minutes on each side or until fish flakes easily with a fork. Remove and keep warm.

In the same skillet, cook and stir the almonds in the remaining butter until lightly toasted. Stir in the lemon juice. Serve with trout.

Nutrition Facts: 1 serving equals 337 calories, 24 g fat (9 g saturated fat), 56 mg cholesterol, 389 mg sodium, 18 g carbohydrate, 3 g fiber, 15 g protein.

BROCCOLI-STUFFED SOLE

Yield: 8 servings.

My husband isn't big on seafood, but he dives into this dish. Lemon enhances the delicate sole, and the pretty presentation makes it special enough for company.
edna lee // greeley, colorado

- **2 tablespoons butter, melted**
- **1 to 2 tablespoons lemon juice**
- **1 teaspoon salt**
- **1/4 teaspoon pepper**
- **3 cups frozen chopped broccoli, thawed and drained**
- **1 cup cooked rice**
- **1 cup (4 ounces) shredded reduced-fat cheddar cheese**
- **8 sole *or* whitefish fillets (4 ounces *each*)**
- **Paprika**

In a small bowl, combine the butter, lemon juice, salt and pepper. In another bowl, combine the broccoli, rice, cheese and half of the butter mixture.

Spoon 1/2 cup onto each fillet. Roll up and place seam side down in a baking dish coated with cooking spray. Pour remaining butter mixture over roll-ups. Bake, uncovered, at 350° for 25 minutes or until fish flakes easily with a fork. Baste with pan drippings; sprinkle with paprika.

Nutrition Facts: 1 stuffed fillet equals 190 calories, 6 g fat (3 g saturated fat), 64 mg cholesterol, 478 mg sodium, 8 g carbohydrate, 1 g fiber, 26 g protein. Diabetic Exchanges: 3 lean meat, 1 vegetable.

SEAFOOD ENCHILADAS

Yield: 8 servings.

I received this recipe many years ago, and my family still loves it today. The crab makes it a wonderful change of pace from other weeknight fare.
donna roberts // manhattan, kansas

- **1/2 cup chopped onion**
- **1 tablespoon butter**
- **1 garlic clove, minced**
- **1 cup (8 ounces) reduced-fat sour cream**
- **3 tablespoons all-purpose flour**
- **1 cup reduced-sodium chicken broth**
- **1 can (4 ounces) chopped green chilies**
- **1 teaspoon ground coriander**
- **1/4 teaspoon pepper**
- **1 cup (4 ounces) shredded reduced-fat Mexican cheese blend, *divided***
- **2 cups coarsely chopped real *or* imitation crabmeat**
- **8 flour tortillas (6 inches), warmed**
- **1/2 cup chopped tomato**
- **1/2 cup chopped green onions**
- **1/4 cup chopped ripe olives**

In a large saucepan, cook onion in butter over medium heat until tender. Add garlic; cook 1 minute longer. Combine sour cream and flour until smooth; gradually add to onion mixture. Stir in the broth, chilies, coriander and pepper. Bring to a boil. Reduce heat; simmer, uncovered, for 2-3 minutes or until thickened. Remove from the heat; stir in 1/2 cup cheese.

Place crab in a small bowl; stir in 1/2 cup sauce. Spoon equal amounts on tortillas; roll up tightly. Place seam side down in an 11-in. x 7-in. baking dish coated with cooking spray. Top with remaining sauce. Cover and bake at 350° for 30 minutes. Uncover; sprinkle with remaining cheese. Bake 5 minutes longer or until cheese is melted. Let stand for 5 minutes. Top with tomato, green onions and olives.

Nutrition Facts: 1 enchilada equals 243 calories, 11 g fat (5 g saturated fat), 53 mg cholesterol, 662 mg sodium, 21 g carbohydrate, 1 g fiber, 16 g protein. Diabetic Exchanges: 2 fat, 1-1/2 starch, 1 very lean meat.

TILAPIA FLORENTINE

Yield: 4 servings.

Get a little more heart-healthy fish into your diet with this quick and easy entree. Topped with fresh spinach and a splash of lime, it's sure to become a favorite!

melanie bachman // ulysses, pennsylvania

> 1 **package (6 ounces) fresh baby spinach**
>
> 6 **teaspoons canola oil,** *divided*
>
> 4 **tilapia fillets (4 ounces** *each***)**
>
> 2 **tablespoons lime juice**
>
> 2 **teaspoons garlic-herb seasoning blend**
>
> 1 **egg, lightly beaten**
>
> 1/2 **cup part-skim ricotta cheese**
>
> 1/4 **cup grated Parmesan cheese**

In a large nonstick skillet, cook spinach in 4 teaspoons oil until wilted; drain. Meanwhile, place tilapia in a greased 13-in. x 9-in. baking dish. Drizzle with lime juice and remaining oil. Sprinkle with seasoning blend.

In a small bowl, combine the egg, ricotta cheese and spinach; spoon mixture over the fillets. Sprinkle with Parmesan cheese.

Bake at 375° for 15-20 minutes or until fish flakes easily with a fork.

Nutrition Facts: 1 serving equals 249 calories, 13 g fat (4 g saturated fat), 122 mg cholesterol, 307 mg sodium, 4 g carbohydrate, 1 g fiber, 29 g protein.

≫ HOW TO:

CHECK THE DONENESS OF FISH

As a general guideline, fish is cooked 10 minutes for every inch of thickness. Avoid overcooking, which can cause fish to lose its flavor and become tough.

For fish fillets, check for doneness by inserting a fork at an angle into the thickest portion of the fish and gently parting the meat. When it is opaque and flakes into sections, it is cooked completely.

Whole fish or steaks are done when the flesh is opaque and is easily removed from the bones. The juices in cooked fish are milky white.

1 pound uncooked small shrimp, peeled and deveined
1 package (8 ounces) imitation crabmeat, chopped
1/4 teaspoon white pepper, *divided*
1/2 cup all-purpose flour
1-1/2 cups 2% milk
1/2 teaspoon salt
1 cup heavy whipping cream
1/2 cup shredded Parmesan cheese, *divided*
9 lasagna noodles, cooked and drained

In a large skillet, saute onion in oil and 2 tablespoons butter until tender. Stir in broth and clam juice; bring to a boil. Add the scallops, shrimp, crab and 1/8 teaspoon pepper; return to a boil. Reduce heat; simmer, uncovered, for 4-5 minutes or until shrimp turn pink and scallops are firm and opaque, stirring gently. Drain, reserving cooking liquid; set seafood mixture aside.

In a large saucepan, melt the remaining butter; stir in flour until smooth. Combine milk and reserved cooking liquid; gradually add to the saucepan. Add salt and remaining pepper. Bring to a boil; cook and stir for 2 minutes or until thickened.

Remove from the heat; stir in cream and 1/4 cup cheese. Stir 3/4 cup white sauce into the seafood mixture.

Spread 1/2 cup white sauce in a greased 13-in. x 9-in. baking dish. Top with three noodles; spread with half of the seafood mixture and 1-1/4 cups sauce. Repeat layers. Top with the remaining noodles, sauce and cheese.

Bake, uncovered, at 350° for 35-40 minutes or until golden brown. Let stand for 15 minutes before cutting.

Nutrition Facts: 1 serving equals 373 calories, 22 g fat (12 g saturated fat), 131 mg cholesterol, 586 mg sodium, 24 g carbohydrate, 1 g fiber, 20 g protein.

SEAFOOD LASAGNA

Yield: 12 servings.

This rich, satisfying dish is loaded with scallops, shrimp and crab in a creamy sauce. I consider this the crown jewel in my repertoire of recipes.

elena hansen // ruidoso, new mexico

1 green onion, finely chopped
2 tablespoons canola oil
2 tablespoons plus 1/2 cup butter, *divided*
1/2 cup chicken broth
1 bottle (8 ounces) clam juice
1 pound bay scallops

SEAFOOD EN CROUTE

Yield: 4 servings.

This impressive recipe is surprisingly easy to prepare. It looks so elegant and it tastes divine!

alexandra armitage // nottingham, new hampshire

1 package (17.3 ounces) frozen puff pastry, thawed
4 salmon fillets (6 ounces *each*)
1/2 pound fresh sea *or* bay scallops, finely chopped

1/3 **cup heavy whipping cream**

2 **green onions, chopped**

1 **tablespoon minced fresh parsley**

1/2 **teaspoon minced fresh dill**

1/4 **teaspoon salt**

1/8 **teaspoon pepper**

1 **egg white**

1 **egg, lightly beaten**

On a lightly floured surface, roll each pastry sheet into a 12-in. x 10-in. rectangle. Cut each sheet into four 6-in. x 5-in. rectangles. Place a salmon fillet in the center of four rectangles.

In a small bowl, combine the scallops, cream, onions, parsley, dill, salt and pepper. In another bowl, beat egg white on medium speed until soft peaks form; fold into scallop mixture. Spoon about 1/2 cup over each salmon fillet.

Top each with a pastry rectangle and crimp to seal. With a small sharp knife, cut several slits in the top. Place in a greased 15-in. x 10-in. x 1-in. baking pan; brush with egg.

Bake at 400° for 20-25 minutes or until a thermometer reads 160°.

Nutrition Facts: 1 serving equals 820 calories, 47 g fat (13 g saturated fat), 124 mg cholesterol, 706 mg sodium, 72 g carbohydrate, 9 g fiber, 30 g protein.

ORANGE TILAPIA IN PARCHMENT

Yield: 4 servings.

Sweet orange juice and spicy cayenne pepper give this no-fuss dish fabulous flavor. A bonus? Cleanup is a breeze!

tiffany diebold // nashville, tennessee

1/4 **cup orange juice**

4 **teaspoons grated orange peel**

1/4 **teaspoon salt**

1/4 **teaspoon cayenne pepper**

1/4 **teaspoon pepper**

4 **tilapia fillets (6 ounces *each*)**

1/2 **cup julienned carrot**

1/2 **cup julienned zucchini**

In a small bowl, combine the first five ingredients; set aside. Cut parchment paper or heavy-duty foil into four 18-in. x 12-in. lengths; place a fish fillet on each. Top with carrot and zucchini; drizzle with reserved orange juice mixture.

Fold parchment paper over fish. Working from the bottom inside corner, fold up about 3/4 in. of the paper and crimp both layers to seal. Repeat, folding edges up and crimping, until a half-moon-shaped packet is formed. Repeat for remaining packets. Place on baking sheets.

Bake at 450° for 12-15 minutes or until fish flakes easily with a fork. Open packets carefully to allow steam to escape.

Nutrition Facts: 1 packet equals 158 calories, 2 g fat (1 g saturated fat), 83 mg cholesterol, 220 mg sodium, 4 g carbohydrate, 1 g fiber, 32 g protein. Diabetic Exchange: 5 lean meat.

VEGETARIAN

LENTIL SPAGHETTI

Yield: 8 servings.

Packed full of lentils and Italian flavors, this sauce is thick, hearty and zesty.
marie bender // henderson, nevada

- 3/4 **cup chopped onion**
- 1 **tablespoon olive oil**
- 2 **garlic cloves, minced**
- 1-1/2 **cups dried lentils, rinsed**
- 4 **cups vegetable broth**
- 1/2 **teaspoon pepper**
- 1/4 **teaspoon cayenne pepper**
- 1 **can (14-1/2 ounces) Italian diced tomatoes, undrained**
- 1 **can (6 ounces) tomato paste**
- 1 **teaspoon white vinegar**
- 1-1/2 **teaspoons dried basil**
- 1-1/2 **teaspoons dried oregano**
- 12 **ounces uncooked spaghetti**
- 1/4 **cup shredded Parmesan cheese**

In a large saucepan coated with cooking spray, saute onion in oil until tender. Add garlic; cook 1 minute longer. Stir in the lentils, broth, pepper and cayenne. Bring to a boil. Reduce heat; cover and simmer for 20-30 minutes or until lentils are tender.

Stir in the tomatoes, tomato paste, vinegar, basil and oregano. Return to a boil. Reduce heat; cover and simmer for 40-45 minutes.

Cook the spaghetti according to package directions; drain. Serve with the lentil sauce. Sprinkle with cheese.

Nutrition Facts: 3/4 cup sauce with 3/4 cup spaghetti equals 362 calories, 4 g fat (1 g saturated fat), 2 mg cholesterol, 764 mg sodium, 65 g carbohydrate, 14 g fiber, 19 g protein.

BAKED ZITI

Yield: 6 servings.

Many of my casserole recipes have been frowned upon by my children, but they give a cheer when they hear we're having this for supper. Even the leftovers are well-liked.
charity burkholder // pittsboro, indiana

- 3 **cups uncooked ziti** *or* **small tube pasta**
- 1-3/4 **cups meatless spaghetti sauce, *divided***
- 1 **cup (8 ounces) 4% cottage cheese**
- 1-1/2 **cups (6 ounces) shredded part-skim mozzarella cheese, *divided***
- 1 **egg, lightly beaten**
- 2 **teaspoons dried parsley flakes**
- 1/2 **teaspoon dried oregano**
- 1/4 **teaspoon garlic powder**
- 1/8 **teaspoon pepper**

Cook pasta according to package directions. Meanwhile, in a large bowl, combine 3/4 cup spaghetti sauce, cottage cheese, 1 cup mozzarella cheese, egg, parsley, oregano, garlic powder and pepper. Drain pasta; stir into cheese mixture.

In a greased 8-in. square baking dish, spread 1/4 cup spaghetti sauce. Top with pasta mixture and remaining sauce and mozzarella cheese.

Cover and bake at 375° for 45 minutes. Uncover; bake 5-10 minutes longer or until a thermometer reads 160°.

Nutrition Facts: 1-1/2 cups equals 289 calories, 8 g fat (4 g saturated fat), 60 mg cholesterol, 616 mg sodium, 37 g carbohydrate, 3 g fiber, 18 g protein.

MEATLESS MEXICAN LASAGNA

CHEAT IT!

Yield: 6 servings.

Your family will ask for this fun twist on lasagna again and again. Instead of traditional lasagna noodles, corn tortillas are layered with shredded cheese and a Mexican-style corn filling for a satisfying fiesta of a meal.

jean ecos // hartland, wisconsin

- **2 cups frozen corn, thawed**
- **1 can (15 ounces) black beans, rinsed and drained**
- **1 can (14-1/2 ounces) diced tomatoes with basil, oregano and garlic, undrained**
- **1 can (4 ounces) chopped green chilies**
- **3 green onions, sliced**
- **2 teaspoons dried oregano**
- **2 teaspoons ground cumin**
- **4 corn tortillas (6 inches)**
- **1-1/2 cups (6 ounces) shredded Mexican cheese blend**
- **6 tablespoons plain yogurt**

In a large bowl, combine the first seven ingredients. Place two tortillas in an 11-in. x 7-in. baking dish coated with cooking spray. Spread tortillas with half of the corn mixture; sprinkle with half of the cheese. Repeat the layers.

Bake, uncovered, at 400° for 15-20 minutes or until heated through. Let stand for 5 minutes. Garnish each serving with a dollop of yogurt.

Nutrition Facts: 1 piece equals 291 calories, 11 g fat (6 g saturated fat), 25 mg cholesterol, 781 mg sodium, 38 g carbohydrate, 6 g fiber, 14 g protein. Diabetic Exchanges: 2 starch, 1 lean meat, 1 vegetable, 1 fat.

taste of home COOKING SCHOOL SECRET

BEANS: JUST ABOUT PERFECT

Beans are an easy, affordable way to get the protein and fiber you need each day. The nutritional one-two punch of protein and fiber means that you'll stay fuller longer, which can help you eat less.

Beans are such a good source of protein, they make an excellent meat alternative for vegetarians. Bean-based recipes are also popular with non-vegetarians because they're hearty and satisfying.

Whether you're vegetarian or not, try these ideas to work beans into your diet:

- Snack on vegetarian refried beans warmed in a tortilla, or try hummus with pita wedges
- Add beans to the meat or vegetarian meat crumbles in taco or other Southwest recipes to thriftily stretch your protein source
- Sprinkle black beans or chickpeas over a salad or stir beans into soup

For a meatless veggie-bean chili the whole gang will love, check out Spicy Vegetable Chili (page 95).

ROASTED VEGGIE SOFT TACOS

Yield: 6 servings.

My husband doesn't even miss the meat in these flavorful tacos, which are now a mainstay in my menu. Roasted vegetables add a rich taste, and I love that they cook without much supervision.

shannon koene // blacksburg, virginia

- 2 medium green peppers, cut into strips
- 3 plum tomatoes, cut into wedges
- 1 medium onion, halved and sliced
- 1 tablespoon reduced-sodium taco seasoning
- 1 tablespoon olive oil
- 1 can (16 ounces) fat-free refried beans, warmed
- 6 flour tortillas (8 inches), warmed
- 3/4 cup shredded reduced-fat cheddar cheese

In a large bowl, combine the green peppers, tomatoes, onion, taco seasoning and oil. Arrange in a single layer in an ungreased 15-in. x 10-in. x 1-in. baking pan. Bake at 425° for 15-20 minutes or until tender, stirring once.

Spread about 1/4 cup refried beans over each tortilla; top with 1/3 cup vegetable mixture and 2 tablespoons cheese.

Nutrition Facts: 1 taco equals 316 calories, 8 g fat (3 g saturated fat), 10 mg cholesterol, 722 mg sodium, 48 g carbohydrate, 6 g fiber, 14 g protein.

GNOCCHI WITH WHITE BEANS

Yield: 6 servings.

Warm their hearts on chilly nights with this yummy skillet dish full of veggies, beans, gnocchi, melty cheese and Italian flavors. It makes a fast and easy meal-in-one.

julianne meyers // hinesville, georgia

- 1 medium onion, chopped
- 1 tablespoon olive oil
- 2 garlic cloves, minced
- 1 package (16 ounces) potato gnocchi
- 1 package (6 ounces) fresh baby spinach
- 1 can (15 ounces) white kidney *or* cannellini beans, rinsed and drained
- 1 can (14-1/2 ounces) Italian diced tomatoes, undrained
- 1/4 teaspoon pepper
- 1/2 cup shredded part-skim mozzarella cheese
- 3 tablespoons grated Parmesan cheese

In a large skillet, saute onion in oil until tender. Add the garlic; cook 1 minute longer. Add gnocchi; cook and stir for 5-6 minutes or until golden brown. Stir in spinach; cook until spinach is wilted.

Add the beans, tomatoes and pepper; heat through. Sprinkle with cheeses; cover and remove from the heat. Let stand for 3-4 minutes or until cheese is melted.

EDITOR'S NOTE: Look for potato gnocchi in the pasta or frozen foods section.

Nutrition Facts: 1 cup equals 307 calories, 6 g fat (2 g saturated fat), 13 mg cholesterol, 789 mg sodium, 50 g carbohydrate, 6 g fiber, 13 g protein.

GREEK PITA PIZZAS

Yield: 2 servings.

Pita breads form the quick crust for these no-fuss, petite pizzas. Enjoy them for lunch with a green salad and some fruit.
linda lacek // winter park, florida

- 2 **whole pita breads (6 inches)**
- 1 **teaspoon olive oil,** *divided*
- 4 **cups torn fresh spinach**
- 2 **tablespoons chopped green onion**
- 1 **teaspoon minced fresh dill**
- 4 **tomato slices, halved**
- 1/2 **cup crumbled feta cheese**
- 1/4 **to 1/2 cup shredded part-skim mozzarella cheese**
- 1/8 **teaspoon dried oregano**
- 1/8 **teaspoon pepper**

Place pita breads on a baking sheet. Brush each with 1/4 teaspoon oil. Broil 6 in. from the heat for 1-2 minutes or until lightly browned. Turn pitas over; brush with remaining oil. Broil 1-2 minutes longer.

In a microwave-safe dish, microwave spinach on high for 1 to 1-1/2 minutes or until wilted; drain well. Stir in onion and dill.

Top the pitas with tomatoes, spinach mixture and cheeses. Sprinkle with oregano and pepper. Bake at 450° for 7-9 minutes or until cheese is lightly browned.

Nutrition Facts: 1 pizza (prepared with reduced-fat feta cheese and 1/4 cup part-skim mozzarella) equals 295 calories, 9 g fat (4 g saturated fat), 18 mg cholesterol, 810 mg sodium, 39 g carbohydrate, 4 g fiber, 17 g protein.

MINTED RICE WITH GARBANZO CURRY

Yield: 3 servings.

Fluffy flavored rice and tender beans in a well-seasoned, aromatic sauce make this easy, meatless main dish a fitting introduction to Indian cooking.
jemima madhavan // lincoln, nebraska

- 1 **cinnamon stick (3 inches)**
- 2 **whole cloves**
- 1/8 **teaspoon cumin seeds**
- 2 **teaspoons canola oil**
- 1 **cup uncooked long grain rice**
- 2 **cups water**
- 1/2 **cup minced fresh mint**

GARBANZO CURRY:
- 1 **medium onion, chopped**
- 1 **cinnamon stick (3 inches)**
- 1 **tablespoon canola oil**
- 1 **teaspoon curry powder**
- 1 **garlic clove, minced**
- 1/4 **teaspoon minced fresh gingerroot**
- 1 **can (15 ounces) garbanzo beans** *or* **chickpeas, rinsed and drained**
- 1 **cup water**
- 1 **can (8 ounces) tomato sauce**
- 2 **tablespoons lemon juice**
- 1/2 **teaspoon salt**
- 1/2 **cup minced fresh cilantro**

In a large saucepan over medium heat, saute the cinnamon, cloves and cumin seeds in oil until aromatic, about 1-2 minutes. Add rice; cook and stir until lightly browned. Add water and mint. Bring to a boil. Reduce heat; cover and simmer for 15-20 minutes or until rice is tender.

Meanwhile, in a large skillet, saute onion and cinnamon in oil until onion is tender. Add the curry, garlic and ginger; cook 1 minute longer. Add the garbanzo beans, water, tomato sauce, lemon juice and salt; bring to a boil. Reduce heat; simmer, uncovered, for 4-6 minutes or until slightly thickened. Discard cinnamon; stir in cilantro.

Fluff rice with a fork. Discard cinnamon and cloves. Serve with garbanzo curry.

Nutrition Facts: 1 cup rice with about 3/4 cup curry equals 475 calories, 11 g fat (1 g saturated fat), 0 cholesterol, 932 mg sodium, 82 g carbohydrate, 9 g fiber, 12 g protein.

>> HOW TO:

DRAIN SPINACH

Drain spinach in a colander or mesh strainer. If the spinach was cooked, allow it to cool. With clean hands, press the spinach against the colander to squeeze out the excess water.

EASY CHILI MAC

Yield: 8 servings.

I came across this recipe in a newspaper years ago. It appeals to all ages.

cindy ragan // north huntingdon, pennsylvania

- 1 **large onion, chopped**
- 1 **medium green pepper, chopped**
- 1 **tablespoon olive oil**
- 1 **garlic clove, minced**
- 2 **cups water**
- 1-1/2 **cups uncooked elbow macaroni**
- 1 **can (16 ounces) mild chili beans, undrained**
- 1 **can (15-1/2 ounces) great northern beans, rinsed and drained**
- 1 **can (14-1/2 ounces) diced tomatoes, undrained**
- 1 **can (8 ounces) tomato sauce**
- 4 **teaspoons chili powder**
- 1 **teaspoon salt**
- 1 **teaspoon ground cumin**
- 1/2 **cup fat-free sour cream**

In a Dutch oven, saute onion and green pepper in oil until tender. Add garlic; cook 1 minute longer. Stir in the water, macaroni, beans, tomatoes, tomato sauce, chili powder, salt and cumin. Bring to a boil. Reduce heat; cover and simmer for 15-20 minutes or until macaroni is tender. Top each serving with 1 tablespoon sour cream.

Nutrition Facts: 1-1/4 cups equals 214 calories, 3 g fat (1 g saturated fat), 3 mg cholesterol, 857 mg sodium, 37 g carbohydrate, 8 g fiber, 10 g protein. Diabetic Exchanges: 2 starch, 1 lean meat, 1 vegetable.

VEGETABLE PAD THAI

Yield: 6 servings.

Classic flavors of Thailand abound in this flavorful dish featuring peanuts, tofu and noodles. Tofu adds protein to this satisfying entree.

sara landry // brookline, massachusetts

- 1 **package (12 ounces) whole wheat fettuccine**
- 1/3 **cup reduced-sodium soy sauce**
- 1/4 **cup rice vinegar**
- 2 **tablespoons brown sugar**
- 1 **tablespoon lime juice**
- **Dash Louisiana-style hot sauce**
- 1 **package (12 ounces) extra-firm tofu, drained and cut into 1/2-inch cubes**
- 3 **teaspoons canola oil,** *divided*
- 2 **medium carrots, grated**
- 2 **cups fresh snow peas, halved**
- 3 **garlic cloves, minced**
- 2 **eggs, lightly beaten**
- 2 **cups bean sprouts**
- 3 **green onions, chopped**
- 1/2 **cup minced fresh cilantro**
- 1/4 **cup unsalted peanuts, chopped**

Cook fettuccine according to package directions. Meanwhile, in a small bowl, combine the soy sauce, vinegar, brown sugar, lime juice and hot sauce until smooth; set aside.

In a large skillet or wok, stir-fry tofu in 2 teaspoons oil until golden brown. Remove and keep warm. Stir-fry carrots and snow peas in remaining oil for 1-2 minutes. Add garlic, cook 1 minute longer or until vegetables are crisp-tender. Add eggs; cook and stir until set.

Drain pasta; add to vegetable mixture. Stir vinegar mixture and add to the skillet. Bring to a boil. Add tofu, bean sprouts and onions; heat through. Sprinkle with cilantro and peanuts.

Nutrition Facts: 1-1/3 cups equals 383 calories, 11 g fat (2 g saturated fat), 71 mg cholesterol, 806 mg sodium, 61 g carbohydrate, 10 g fiber, 18 g protein.

tasteofhome
COOKING SCHOOL SECRET

TOFU'S TERRIFIC!

Tofu is a nutritional powerhouse loaded with protein, yet it contains no animal products. Its versatility and affordable price make it terrific for vegetarian meals.

There are two types of tofu: fresh and silken. Fresh tofu is a firm block ideal for slicing and adding to soups and stir-fries. It makes Vegetable Pad Thai a satisfying meat- and dairy-free meal. You'll find it in the dairy or refrigerated produce section.

Packed in water and perishable once opened, fresh tofu should be well-drained before using. To drain, wrap tofu in a clean kitchen towel and weigh it down with a heavy plate or pan to push out any excess moisture.

Silken tofu's creamy, smooth texture makes it perfect for recipes like Tofu Manicotti, or even in smoothies to provide a nutrition boost. You'll find it in the Asian or health foods section.

TOFU MANICOTTI

Yield: 5 servings.

To create a light main course, I borrowed bits from different recipes, including my mom's lasagna. No one suspects that the creamy filling is made with tofu. It's easy to prepare, and my kids love it.

carolyn diana // scottsdale, arizona

- 2 **cups meatless spaghetti sauce**
- 1 **can (14-1/2 ounces) diced tomatoes, undrained**
- 1/3 **cup finely shredded zucchini**
- 1/4 **cup finely shredded carrot**
- 1/2 **teaspoon Italian seasoning**
- 1 **package (12.3 ounces) silken firm tofu**
- 1 **cup (8 ounces) 1% cottage cheese**
- 1 **cup (4 ounces) shredded part-skim mozzarella cheese**
- 1 **tablespoon grated Parmesan cheese**
- 10 **uncooked manicotti shells**

Combine the spaghetti sauce, tomatoes, zucchini, carrot and Italian seasoning; spread 3/4 cup into a 13-in. x 9-in. baking dish coated with cooking spray.

Combine the tofu and cheeses; stuff into uncooked manicotti shells. Arrange shells in the baking dish; top with the remaining sauce mixture.

Cover and bake at 375° for 50-55 minutes or until noodles are tender. Let stand for 5 minutes before serving.

Nutrition Facts: 2 stuffed manicotti shells equals 319 calories, 7 g fat (3 g saturated fat), 16 mg cholesterol, 885 mg sodium, 42 g carbohydrate, 4 g fiber, 23 g protein. Diabetic Exchanges: 3 starch, 2 lean meat.

RUSTIC TOMATO TART

Yield: 4-6 servings.

While my husband was stationed in the service in Naples, Italy, we tried all kinds of pizzas with fresh ingredients. This rustic square-shaped version is delicious, but not at all complicated to prepare.

priscilla gilbert
indian harbour beach, florida

- 1 tablespoon cornmeal
- 1 tube (13.8 ounces) refrigerated pizza crust
- 1-1/2 teaspoons olive oil, *divided*
- 11 slices part-skim mozzarella cheese, *divided*
- 1 small zucchini, cut into 1/8-inch slices, patted dry, *divided*
- 1 small onion, sliced
- 4 plum tomatoes, cut into 1/4-inch slices
- 1/4 teaspoon salt
- 1/4 teaspoon pepper
- 1/4 cup torn fresh basil

Sprinkle cornmeal over a greased baking sheet. Unroll pizza crust; shape into a 12-in. square. Place on the baking sheet. Brush with 1 teaspoon oil. Arrange nine slices of cheese over dough to within 1 in. of edges. Cut each remaining cheese slice into four pieces; set aside.

Place half of the zucchini, about 2 in. apart, around edges of pizza. Fold edges of dough about 1 in. over zucchini. Bake at 400° for 6 minutes.

Top pizza with onion, tomatoes and remaining zucchini. Sprinkle with salt and pepper. Bake for 16 minutes or until crust is golden brown.

Arrange reserved cheese over the tomatoes; bake 4 minutes longer or until cheese is melted. Drizzle with remaining oil. Sprinkle with basil. Let stand for 5 minutes before slicing.

Nutrition Facts: 1 piece equals 363 calories, 14 g fat (7 g saturated fat), 28 mg cholesterol, 812 mg sodium, 37 g carbohydrate, 2 g fiber, 20 g protein.

VEGETARIAN PIZZA IDEAS

Top your favorite pizza crust with one of these combos:

- Pesto, tomatoes, artichoke hearts, black olives and feta cheese
- Mashed black beans, red onion, bell peppers, jalapenos and pepper Jack cheese
- Roasted red pepper puree, mushrooms and fresh mozzarella cheese
- Marinara sauce, fresh spinach and basil, kalamata olives, mozzarella and feta cheese

BISTRO MAC & CHEESE

Yield: 8 servings.

I like to serve this mac and cheese with a salad and crusty bread. It's a satisfying meal that feels upscale, but will fit just about any budget.

charlotte giltner // mesa, arizona

- 1 package (16 ounces) uncooked elbow macaroni
- 3 tablespoons butter
- 3 tablespoons all-purpose flour
- 2-1/2 cups 2% milk
- 1 teaspoon salt
- 1/2 teaspoon onion powder
- 1/2 teaspoon pepper
- 1/4 teaspoon garlic powder

- 1 cup (4 ounces) shredded part-skim mozzarella cheese
- 1 cup (4 ounces) shredded cheddar cheese
- 1 package (3 ounces) cream cheese, softened
- 1/2 cup crumbled Gorgonzola cheese
- 1/2 cup sour cream

Cook macaroni according to package directions. Meanwhile, in a Dutch oven, melt butter. Stir in flour until smooth. Gradually stir in milk and seasonings. Bring to a boil; cook and stir for 2 minutes or until thickened.

Reduce heat; add the cheeses and stir until melted. Stir in sour cream. Drain the macaroni; stir into the sauce.

Nutrition Facts: 1 cup equals 468 calories, 22 g fat (14 g saturated fat), 68 mg cholesterol, 649 mg sodium, 49 g carbohydrate, 2 g fiber, 20 g protein.

CRUMB-TOPPED BISTRO MAC: Place the prepared macaroni in a greased 3-qt. baking dish. Combine 1/3 cup seasoned bread crumbs and 2 tablespoons melted butter; sprinkle over macaroni. Bake, uncovered, at 350° for 20-25 minutes or until bubbly.

>> HOW TO:

MAKE WHITE SAUCE

1 Start a white sauce by whisking flour into melted butter over medium heat until mixture becomes smooth.

2 Gradually whisk milk into mixture until blended. Bring mixture to a boil.

CRESCENT ZUCCHINI PIE

Yield: 6 servings.

A tender, flaky crust makes this egg and zucchini based pie a special treat. The cheese, herbs and seasonings add delectable flavor.

zelda dehoedt // cedar rapids, iowa

- **1 tube (8 ounces) refrigerated crescent rolls**
- **2 teaspoons Dijon mustard**
- **4 cups sliced zucchini**
- **1 cup chopped onion**
- **6 tablespoons butter, cubed**
- **2 eggs, lightly beaten**
- **1 cup (4 ounces) shredded part-skim mozzarella cheese**
- **1 cup (4 ounces) shredded Colby-Monterey Jack cheese**
- **2 tablespoons dried parsley flakes**
- **1/2 teaspoon salt**
- **1/2 teaspoon pepper**
- **1/4 teaspoon dried basil**
- **1/4 teaspoon dried oregano**

Separate crescent dough into eight triangles and place in a greased 9-in. deep-dish pie plate with points toward the center. Press dough onto the bottom and up the sides of plate to form a crust; seal seams. Spread with mustard.

In a large skillet, saute zucchini and onion in butter until tender. In a large bowl, combine the eggs, cheeses, seasonings and zucchini mixture. Pour into crust.

Bake at 375° for 20-25 minutes or until a knife inserted near the center comes out clean. Cover edges loosely with foil if crust browns too quickly.

Nutrition Facts: 1 piece equals 413 calories, 30 g fat (16 g saturated fat), 128 mg cholesterol, 849 mg sodium, 22 g carbohydrate, 1 g fiber, 15 g protein.

HERBED MACARONI AND CHEESE

Yield: 6 servings.

This is not your ordinary, run-of-the-mill macaroni and cheese. The herbs and spices, along with rich sour cream, give the dish a wonderful flavor. It's been a favorite in our family for a very long time.
nancy raymond // waldoboro, maine

- 1 package (7 ounces) **uncooked elbow macaroni**
- 2 tablespoons **butter**
- 2 tablespoons **all-purpose flour**
- 1/2 teaspoon **Italian seasoning**
- 1/4 teaspoon **onion powder**
Salt and pepper to taste
- 1 cup **milk**
- 1/4 cup **sour cream**
- 3/4 cup **shredded cheddar cheese**, *divided*
- 1/2 cup **cubed Havarti *or* Muenster cheese**
- 2 tablespoons **grated Parmesan cheese**
- 2 tablespoons **Italian-style seasoned bread crumbs**

Cook macaroni according to package directions; drain. Place in a 1-1/2-qt. casserole and set aside.

Meanwhile, in a large saucepan, melt butter over medium heat. Stir in the flour and seasonings; gradually add milk. Bring to a boil; cook and stir for 2 minutes or until thickened. Remove pan from heat; add the sour cream, 1/2 cup cheddar cheese and Havarti cheese. Stir until melted.

Pour sauce over macaroni; stir to coat. Combine Parmesan cheese, bread crumbs and remaining cheddar; sprinkle over casserole. Bake, uncovered, at 350° for 15-20 minutes or until heated though.

Nutrition Facts: 1 cup equals 315 calories, 15 g fat (10 g saturated fat), 49 mg cholesterol, 279 mg sodium, 31 g carbohydrate, 1 g fiber, 13 g protein.

BROCCOLI TORTELLINI ALFREDO

Yield: 6 servings.

I usually make this dish for birthdays or holiday dinners. Everyone loves the combination of broccoli, cheese and tortellini.
esther mccoy // dillonvale, ohio

- 1 package (19 ounces) **frozen cheese tortellini, cooked and drained**
- 1 package (16 ounces) **frozen chopped broccoli, thawed**
- 1 jar (2 ounces) **diced pimientos, drained**
- 2 tablespoons **chopped onion**
SAUCE:
- 1 **garlic clove, minced**
- 2 tablespoons **butter**
- 2 tablespoons **all-purpose flour**
- 1/4 teaspoon **salt**
- 1/8 teaspoon **pepper**
- 1/8 teaspoon **ground nutmeg**
- 1 cup **milk**
- 1/3 cup plus 1/4 cup **grated Parmesan cheese**, *divided*

In a large bowl, combine the tortellini, broccoli, pimientos and onion; set aside. In a large saucepan, saute the garlic in butter for 1 minute. Stir in the flour, salt, pepper and nutmeg. Gradually stir in milk until blended. Bring to a boil; cook and stir for 2 minutes or until thickened. Remove from the heat; stir in 1/3 cup Parmesan cheese until melted. Fold in broccoli mixture.

Transfer to a greased 2-qt. baking dish. Cover and bake at 350° for 40-45 minutes or until hot and bubbly, stirring twice. Top with remaining Parmesan. Cover and let stand for 5 minutes or until cheese is melted.

Nutrition Facts: 1-1/2 cups equals 307 calories, 13 g fat (7 g saturated fat), 36 mg cholesterol, 551 mg sodium, 33 g carbohydrate, 4 g fiber, 16 g protein.

PORTOBELLO SPAGHETTI CASSEROLE

Yield: 3 servings.

You can't go wrong with this easy Italian-style casserole. Substitute shiitakes or plain button mushrooms for the portobellos, if you wish.

mary shivers // ada, oklahoma

- 4 **ounces uncooked spaghetti**
- 3 **portobello mushrooms, stems removed and thinly sliced**
- 1/4 **teaspoon salt**
- 1/8 **teaspoon pepper**
- 1 **tablespoon olive oil**
- 1 **egg**
- 1/4 **cup sour cream**
- 2 **tablespoons grated Parmesan cheese**
- 1 **tablespoon minced fresh parsley**
- 1-1/2 **teaspoons all-purpose flour**
- 1/4 **teaspoon garlic powder**
- 1/8 **teaspoon crushed red pepper flakes**
- 1-1/4 **cups marinara sauce**
- 3/4 **cup shredded part-skim mozzarella cheese**

Cook spaghetti according to package directions. Meanwhile, in a large skillet, saute the mushrooms, salt and pepper in oil until tender.

In a large bowl, combine the egg, sour cream, Parmesan cheese, parsley, flour, garlic powder and pepper flakes. Drain spaghetti; add to sour cream mixture.

Transfer to a 1-1/2-qt. baking dish coated with cooking spray. Top with mushrooms and marinara sauce.

Cover and bake at 350° for 30 minutes. Uncover; sprinkle with the mozzarella cheese. Bake 10-15 minutes longer or until a meat thermometer reads 160° and cheese is melted. Let stand 10 minutes before serving.

Nutrition Facts: 1 cup equals 422 calories, 16 g fat (7 g saturated fat), 103 mg cholesterol, 601 mg sodium, 48 g carbohydrate, 4 g fiber, 20 g protein.

STUFFED PORTOBELLOS

Yield: 4 servings.

I often substitute portobellos for hamburger patties, but in this open-faced recipe, they take the place of buns. My family loves this tasty, healthful dinner, and it's ready in no time.

elizabeth doss // california city, california

- 1 **can (15 ounces) white kidney** *or* **cannellini beans, rinsed and drained**
- 2 **tablespoons olive oil,** *divided*
- 1 **tablespoon water**
- 1 **teaspoon dried rosemary, crushed**
- 1 **garlic clove, peeled and halved**
- 1/4 **teaspoon salt**
- 1/4 **teaspoon pepper**
- 4 **large portobello mushrooms (4 to 4-1/2 inches), stems removed**
- 1 **medium sweet red pepper, finely chopped**
- 1 **medium red onion, finely chopped**
- 1 **medium zucchini, finely chopped**
- 1/2 **cup shredded pepper Jack cheese**

In a food processor, combine the beans, 1 tablespoon oil, water, rosemary, garlic, salt and pepper. Cover and process until pureed; set aside.

Place mushrooms on a broiler pan coated with cooking spray. Broil 4 in. from the heat for 6-8 minutes on each side or until mushrooms are tender.

Meanwhile, in a small nonstick skillet coated with cooking spray, saute the red pepper, red onion and zucchini in remaining oil until tender.

Spread about 1/3 cup reserved bean mixture over each mushroom; top with 1/2 cup vegetable mixture. Sprinkle with cheese. Broil for 2-3 minutes or until cheese is melted.

Nutrition Facts: 1 stuffed mushroom equals 252 calories, 12 g fat (4 g saturated fat), 15 mg cholesterol, 378 mg sodium, 26 g carbohydrate, 7 g fiber, 11 g protein. Diabetic Exchanges: 2 lean meat, 2 vegetable, 1 starch, 1 fat.

Cover and bake at 375° for 45 minutes or until a thermometer reads 160°. Uncover; sprinkle with the remaining mozzarella cheese. Bake 10 minutes longer or until cheese is melted. Let stand for 15 minutes before cutting.

Nutrition Facts: 1 piece equals 241 calories, 11 g fat (5 g saturated fat), 59 mg cholesterol, 651 mg sodium, 23 g carbohydrate, 3 g fiber, 13 g protein. Diabetic Exchanges: 2 vegetable, 1 starch, 1 lean meat, 1 fat.

FRESH TOMATO PASTA TOSS

Yield: 8 servings.

Dipping whole tomatoes into boiling water makes them easier to peel for this garden-fresh recipe. Shredded Italian cheese makes a great topper.

cheryl travagliante // cleveland, ohio

- **3 pounds ripe fresh tomatoes**
- **1 package (16 ounces) uncooked penne pasta**
- **2 garlic cloves, minced**
- **1 tablespoon canola oil**
- **1 tablespoon minced fresh parsley *or* 1 teaspoon dried parsley flakes**
- **1 tablespoon minced fresh basil *or* 1 teaspoon dried basil**

ZUCCHINI RED PEPPER LASAGNA

Yield: 12 servings.

No-cook lasagna noodles, prepared pesto and roasted red peppers make this gourmet-tasting dish a snap to prepare. No one will guess it came together so quickly!

taste of home cooking school

- **1 carton (15 ounces) ricotta cheese**
- **1-1/2 cups (6 ounces) shredded part-skim mozzarella cheese, *divided***
- **2 eggs**
- **3 tablespoons prepared pesto**
- **2 cups sliced zucchini**
- **2 cups sliced baby portobello mushrooms**
- **2 tablespoons canola oil**
- **2 jars (one 26 ounces, one 14 ounces) meatless spaghetti sauce**
- **9 no-cook lasagna noodles**
- **1 jar (12 ounces) roasted sweet red peppers, drained**

In a small bowl, combine the ricotta cheese, 1/2 cup mozzarella cheese, eggs and pesto; set aside. In a large skillet, saute zucchini and mushrooms in oil for 5 minutes or until crisp-tender; set aside.

Spread 1 cup spaghetti sauce in a 13-in. x 9-in. baking dish coated with cooking spray. Top with three noodles; spread 1 cup sauce to edges of noodles. Layer with half of the zucchini mixture, red peppers and cheese mixture. Top with three more noodles and another cup of sauce. Layer with remaining zucchini mixture, peppers, cheese mixture, noodles and sauce.

>> **HOW TO:**

PEEL TOMATOES

1 Wash and core tomatoes. To remove peel, place tomato in boiling water for 30 seconds. Immediately plunge in ice water.

2 Remove skin with a sharp paring knife.

2 teaspoons minced fresh oregano *or* 3/4 teaspoon dried oregano

1 teaspoon salt

1/4 teaspoon sugar

1/8 teaspoon pepper

1/4 cup heavy whipping cream

1/4 cup shredded Parmesan *or* Romano cheese

To remove peels from tomatoes, fill a large saucepan with water and bring to a boil. Place tomatoes, one at a time, in boiling water for 30 seconds. Immediately plunge in ice water. Peel skins with a sharp paring knife and discard. Chop pulp; set aside.

Cook pasta according to package directions. In a large skillet, cook garlic in oil over medium heat for 1 minute or until tender. Add the parsley, basil, oregano, salt, sugar, pepper and reserved tomato pulp. Bring to a boil; reduce heat. Add cream; heat through.

Drain pasta and transfer to a serving bowl. Pour tomato sauce over pasta; toss to coat. Sprinkle with cheese.

Nutrition Facts: 1 cup equals 277 calories, 7 g fat (0 saturated fat), 13 mg cholesterol, 244 mg sodium, 46 g carbohydrate, 0 fiber, 9 g protein.

VEGGIE PUFF PANCAKE

Yield: 4 servings.

I clipped this recipe when I was first married, but my husband was actually first to prepare it. The puffy pancake looks so beautiful and tastes even better. It wasn't until I made this dish myself that I realized how simple it really is.

mirien church // aurora, colorado

1 teaspoon butter

1/2 cup all-purpose flour

2 eggs, lightly beaten

1/2 cup milk

1/2 teaspoon salt, *divided*

2 cups fresh broccoli florets

1 cup chopped green pepper

1 cup chopped tomato

1/2 cup chopped red onion

2 tablespoons water

1/8 teaspoon pepper

1-1/2 cups (6 ounces) shredded cheddar cheese

Place butter in a 9-in. pie plate; heat in a 450° oven until melted. Carefully tilt pan to coat bottom and sides. In a large bowl, beat the flour, eggs, milk and 1/4 teaspoon salt until smooth. Pour into pie plate. Bake for 14-16 minutes or until puffed around the edges and golden brown.

Meanwhile, in a large skillet, cook the broccoli, green pepper, tomato and onion in water for 8-10 minutes or until crisp-tender; drain well. Add pepper and remaining salt.

Sprinkle 1/2 cup cheese over pancake; top with vegetables and remaining cheese. Bake 3-4 minutes longer or until cheese is melted. Cut into four wedges; serve immediately.

Nutrition Facts: 1 wedge equals 308 calories, 17 g fat (11 g saturated fat), 158 mg cholesterol, 621 mg sodium, 23 g carbohydrate, 3 g fiber, 17 g protein.

EGGPLANT PARMIGIANA

Yield: 10-12 servings.

This delicious eggplant casserole from my mom makes a wonderful meatless meal. It's a resourceful way to use up the eggplant in your garden, and the homemade marinara sauce tastes so good.

valerie belley // st. louis, missouri

- 2 **medium eggplant, peeled and cut into 1/2-inch slices**
- 2 **teaspoons salt**
- 2 **large onions, chopped**
- 2 **tablespoons minced fresh basil** *or* **2 teaspoons dried basil**
- 2 **bay leaves**
- 1 **tablespoon minced fresh oregano** *or* **1 teaspoon dried oregano**
- 1 **tablespoon minced fresh thyme** *or* **1 teaspoon dried thyme**
- 3 **tablespoons olive oil**
- 1 **can (14-1/2 ounces) diced tomatoes, undrained**
- 1 **can (12 ounces) tomato paste**
- 1 **tablespoon honey**
- 1-1/2 **teaspoons lemon-pepper seasoning**
- 4 **garlic cloves, minced**
- 2 **eggs, lightly beaten**
- 1/2 **teaspoon pepper**
- 1-1/2 **cups dry bread crumbs**
- 1/4 **cup butter,** *divided*
- 8 **cups (32 ounces) shredded part-skim mozzarella cheese**
- 1 **cup grated Parmesan cheese**

Place the eggplant in a colander; sprinkle with salt. Let stand for 30 minutes. Meanwhile, in a large skillet, saute the onions, basil, bay leaves, oregano and thyme in oil until onions are tender.

Add the tomatoes, tomato paste, honey and lemon-pepper. Bring to a boil. Reduce heat; cover and simmer for 30 minutes. Add garlic; simmer 10 minutes longer. Discard bay leaves.

Rinse the eggplant slices and pat dry with paper towels. In a shallow bowl, combine eggs and pepper; place bread crumbs in another shallow bowl. Dip the eggplant slices into eggs, then coat with the bread crumbs.

In a large skillet, cook half of the eggplant in 2 tablespoons butter for 3 minutes on each side or until lightly browned. Repeat with remaining eggplant and butter.

In each of two greased 11-in. x 7-in. baking dishes, layer half of each of the eggplant, tomato sauce and mozzarella cheese. Repeat the layers. Sprinkle with Parmesan cheese. Bake, uncovered, at 375° for 35 minutes or until a thermometer reads 160°.

Nutrition Facts: 1 serving equals 984 calories, 59 g fat (35 g saturated fat), 226 mg cholesterol, 2,164 mg sodium, 32 g carbohydrate, 6 g fiber, 81 g protein.

≫HOW TO:

PEEL AN EGGPLANT

Cut the stem end off the eggplant, and, if desired, a small slice from the bottom so the eggplant can rest flat. Remove the peel with a vegetable peeler. Eggplant peel can be tough and bitter, and is best removed in most recipes. However, some small varieties of eggplant are completely edible, including the peel.

SPINACH PHYLLO PIE

Yield: 6 servings.

This flaky phyllo pie has an excellent mix of flavors. It's a lightened-up version of that beloved Greek classic, spanakopita.
shirley kacmarik // glasgow, scotland

- 4 **eggs, lightly beaten**
- 2 **packages (10 ounces *each*) frozen chopped spinach, thawed and squeezed dry**
- 1 **cup (4 ounces) crumbled feta cheese**
- 1/2 **cup 1% cottage cheese**
- 3 **green onions, sliced**
- 1 **teaspoon dill weed**
- 1/2 **teaspoon salt**
- 1/4 **teaspoon pepper**
- 1/4 **teaspoon ground nutmeg**
- 10 **sheets phyllo dough (14 inches x 9 inches)**

Butter-flavored cooking spray

- 3 **large tomatoes, sliced**

In a large bowl, combine the first nine ingredients; set aside.

Spritz one sheet of phyllo dough with butter-flavored cooking spray. Place in an 8-in. square baking dish coated with cooking spray, allowing one end of dough to hang over edge of dish. Repeat with four more phyllo sheets, staggering the overhanging phyllo around edges of dish. (Keep remaining phyllo covered with plastic wrap and a damp towel to prevent it from drying out.)

Spoon a third of the spinach mixture into crust. Layer with half of the tomatoes, another third of the spinach mixture, remaining tomatoes and remaining spinach mixture. Spritz and layer remaining phyllo dough as before.

Gently fold ends of dough over filling and toward center of baking dish; spritz with butter-flavored spray. Cover edges with foil. Bake at 350° for 55-60 minutes or until a thermometer reads 160°. Let stand for 15 minutes before cutting.

Nutrition Facts: 1 piece equals 216 calories, 9 g fat (3 g saturated fat), 153 mg cholesterol, 652 mg sodium, 21 g carbohydrate, 5 g fiber, 15 g protein. Diabetic Exchanges: 2 medium-fat meat, 2 vegetable, 1 starch.

SIDE DISHES

FRESH & FRUITY SPINACH SALAD

Yield: 10 servings.

Fruit and spinach make a delicious combination, especially when drizzled with a lovely strawberry vinaigrette. Toasted walnuts add a fun crunch.

amy blom // marietta, georgia

- 1 **package (6 ounces) fresh baby spinach**
- 1 **medium nectarine, chopped**
- 1/2 **cup chopped fresh strawberries**
- 2 **medium kiwifruit, peeled and sliced**
- 1/2 **cup chopped walnuts, toasted**

STRAWBERRY VINAIGRETTE:

- 1/2 **cup halved fresh strawberries**
- 1 **tablespoon balsamic vinegar**
- 1 **tablespoon sugar**
- 1/4 **teaspoon salt**
- 1/8 **teaspoon dried tarragon**
- 1/8 **teaspoon pepper**
- 1/3 **cup plus 2 tablespoons olive oil**

In a large bowl, combine the spinach, nectarine, strawberries, kiwi and walnuts.

Place the first six vinaigrette ingredients in a blender; cover and process for 15 seconds. While processing, gradually add oil in a steady stream. Drizzle over salad and toss to coat.

Nutrition Facts: 3/4 cup equals 156 calories, 14 g fat (2 g saturated fat), 0 cholesterol, 74 mg sodium, 8 g carbohydrate, 2 g fiber, 2 g protein.

>> HOW TO:

PEEL A KIWIFRUIT (TWO METHODS)

1 Cut both ends from fruit. Using a spoon, scoop out the flesh.

2 Cut both ends from fruit. Using a vegetable peeler, peel off fuzzy brown skin. Cut into slices, wedges or chunks with a sharp knife.

HOT BACON ASPARAGUS SALAD

Yield: 6 servings.

This salad is so easy to make when I get home from work...but it looks like I spent an hour preparing it. It's perfect with warm rolls.

paulette balda // prophetstown, illinois

- 7 **bacon strips, diced**
- 1 **pound fresh asparagus, trimmed**
- 1/3 **cup white vinegar**
- 1 **tablespoon sugar**
- 1/2 **teaspoon ground mustard**
- 1/4 **teaspoon pepper**
- 4 **cups torn salad greens**
- 1/2 **cup sliced almonds**
- 2 **hard-cooked eggs, sliced**

In a large skillet, cook bacon over medium heat until crisp. Using a slotted spoon, remove to paper towels to drain, reserving 2-3 tablespoons drippings. Cut asparagus into 1-1/2-in. pieces; saute in drippings until crisp-tender. Add the vinegar, sugar, mustard, pepper and bacon. Cook and stir for 1-2 minutes or until heated through.

In a large salad bowl, combine salad greens and almonds. Add the asparagus mixture; toss gently. Arrange eggs over the salad.

Nutrition Facts: 1 cup equals 243 calories, 21 g fat (7 g saturated fat), 88 mg cholesterol, 227 mg sodium, 7 g carbohydrate, 2 g fiber, 8 g protein.

≫ HOW TO:

PREPARE ASPARAGUS

To prepare asparagus, rinse stalks well in cold water. Snap off the stalk ends as far down as they will easily break when gently bent, or cut off the tough white portion. If stalks are large, use a vegetable peeler to gently peel the tough area of the stalk from the end to just below the tip. If tips are large, scrape off scales with a knife.

MOJITO MARINATED FRUIT

Yield: 10 servings.

A mojito-inspired syrup marinates assorted fruits to make a uniquely refreshing salad. marcy griffith // excelsior, minnesota

- 2/3 **cup sugar**
- 1/3 **cup water**
- 1/2 **cup light rum**
- 2 **tablespoons lime juice**
- 1 **teaspoon grated lime peel**
- 2 **cups** *each* **cantaloupe, honeydew and seedless watermelon balls**
- 2 **cups cubed fresh pineapple**
- 3 **mint sprigs**

Additional mint sprigs, optional

In a small saucepan, combine sugar and water. Cook and stir over medium heat until sugar is dissolved. Remove from the heat. Stir in the rum, lime juice and peel. Cool.

In a large bowl, combine the melon, pineapple and mint. Add marinade; toss to coat. Cover and refrigerate overnight.

Discard mint. Spoon the fruit with syrup into serving cups. Garnish with additional mint if desired.

Nutrition Facts: 3/4 cup equals 128 calories, trace fat (trace saturated fat), 0 cholesterol, 8 mg sodium, 26 g carbohydrate, 1 g fiber, 1 g protein.

ARTICHOKE CAPRESE PLATTER

Yield: 10-12 servings.

The classic Italian combination of mozzarella, tomatoes and basil is dressed up with marinated artichokes. Fresh mozzarella is the key to its great taste. margaret wilson // sun city, california

- 2 **jars (7-1/2 ounces** *each***) marinated artichoke hearts**
- 2 **tablespoons red wine vinegar**
- 2 **tablespoons olive oil**
- 6 **plum tomatoes, sliced**
- 1 **pound fresh mozzarella cheese, sliced**
- 2 **cups loosely packed fresh basil leaves**

Drain artichokes, reserving 1/2 cup marinade; cut artichokes in half. In a small bowl, whisk the vinegar, oil and reserved marinade.

On a large serving platter, arrange the artichokes, tomatoes, mozzarella cheese and basil. Drizzle with vinaigrette.

Nutrition Facts: 1/2 cup equals 192 calories, 16 g fat (7 g saturated fat), 30 mg cholesterol, 179 mg sodium, 5 g carbohydrate, 1 g fiber, 7 g protein.

RANCH PASTA SALAD

Yield: 8 servings.

Any entree only gets better with a side of this veggie-filled pasta salad.

krista collins // concord, north carolina

- 3 **cups uncooked tricolor spiral pasta**
- 1 **cup chopped fresh broccoli florets**
- 3/4 **cup chopped seeded peeled cucumber**
- 1/2 **cup seeded chopped tomato**
- 1 **bottle (8 ounces) ranch salad dressing**
- 1/2 **cup shredded Parmesan cheese**

Cook pasta according to package directions; drain and rinse in cold water. In a large bowl, combine the pasta, broccoli, cucumber and tomato. Drizzle with salad dressing; toss to coat. Sprinkle with cheese.

Nutrition Facts: 3/4 cup equals 285 calories, 17 g fat (3 g saturated fat), 8 mg cholesterol, 317 mg sodium, 27 g carbohydrate, 1 g fiber, 6 g protein.

GREEN BEAN AND MOZZARELLA SALAD

Yield: 6-8 servings.

Your tailgate crowd will love this tasty salad. It's easy to make and take.

stasha wampler // clinchport, virginia

- 2 **cups cut fresh green beans (2-inch pieces)**
- 6 **plum tomatoes, sliced**
- 1 **block (8 ounces) mozzarella cheese, cubed**
- 1/2 **cup Italian salad dressing**
- 1/3 **cup minced fresh basil**
- 1/4 **teaspoon salt**
- 1/8 **teaspoon pepper**

Place beans in a small saucepan and cover with water. Bring to a boil; cook, uncovered, for 6-8 minutes or until crisp-tender. Drain and rinse in cold water.

Place beans in a large salad bowl. Add the remaining ingredients; gently toss to coat. Cover and refrigerate for 1 hour before serving.

Nutrition Facts: 3/4 cup equals 153 calories, 12 g fat (4 g saturated fat), 22 mg cholesterol, 438 mg sodium, 6 g carbohydrate, 2 g fiber, 6 g protein.

≫ HOW TO:

TRIM GREEN BEANS

To trim fresh green beans quickly, simply line up the ends of the beans; then, using a chef's knife, slice the tips off several at a time.

MACARONI COLESLAW

My friend Peggy brought this coleslaw to one of our picnics, and everyone liked it so much, we all had to have the recipe.

sandra matteson // westhope, north dakota

- 1 package (7 ounces) ring macaroni *or* ditalini
- 1 package (14 ounces) coleslaw mix
- 2 medium onions, finely chopped
- 2 celery ribs, finely chopped
- 1 medium cucumber, finely chopped
- 1 medium green pepper, finely chopped
- 1 can (8 ounces) whole water chestnuts, drained and chopped

DRESSING:

- 1-1/2 cups Miracle Whip Light
- 1/3 cup sugar
- 1/4 cup cider vinegar
- 1/2 teaspoon salt
- 1/4 teaspoon pepper

Cook macaroni according to package directions; drain and rinse in cold water. Transfer to a large bowl; add the coleslaw mix, onions, celery, cucumber, green pepper and water chestnuts.

In a small bowl, whisk the dressing ingredients. Pour over salad; toss to coat. Cover and refrigerate for at least 1 hour.

Nutrition Facts: 3/4 cup equals 150 calories, 5 g fat (1 g saturated fat), 6 mg cholesterol, 286 mg sodium, 24 g carbohydrate, 2 g fiber, 3 g protein. Diabetic Exchanges: 1 starch, 1 vegetable, 1 fat.

HOMEMADE POTATO SALAD

Yield: 8-10 servings.

This creamy potato salad is a great side on a night when you're grilling out.

patricia kile // elizabethtown, pennsylvania

- 1 tablespoon sugar
- 2 teaspoons all-purpose flour
- 1/4 teaspoon ground mustard

Pinch salt

- 1 egg, lightly beaten
- 1/3 cup water
- 1 tablespoon white vinegar
- 3/4 cup mayonnaise
- 5 large potatoes, cooked, peeled and cubed
- 4 hard-cooked eggs, chopped
- 1 cup chopped celery
- 1/4 cup chopped green onions

Salt and pepper to taste

In a small saucepan, combine the sugar, flour, mustard and salt. Combine the egg, water and vinegar; stir into dry ingredients until smooth. Cook and stir until mixture reaches 160° and coats the back of a spoon. Remove from the heat; cool slightly. Stir in mayonnaise.

In a large bowl, combine the potatoes, hard-cooked eggs, celery, onions, salt and pepper. Add the dressing; toss gently to coat. Refrigerate until serving.

Nutrition Facts: 1 serving equals 314 calories, 16 g fat (3 g saturated fat), 112 mg cholesterol, 158 mg sodium, 36 g carbohydrate, 3 g fiber, 7 g protein.

**CORE AN APPLE
(TWO METHODS)**

1 Use an apple corer to core a whole apple. Push the apple corer down into the center of a washed apple. Twist and remove the center seeds and membranes.

2 Core an apple quarter by cutting out the core with a sharp knife.

EASY TOSSED SALAD FOR TWO

Yield: 2 servings.

Apples, almonds and cranberries provide power foods galore in this quick-to-prepare, five-ingredient salad.

katie wollgast // florissant, missouri

- **4** **cups torn mixed salad greens**
- **1** **small apple, sliced**
- **1/4** **cup sliced almonds, toasted**
- **1/4** **cup dried cranberries**
- **1/4** **cup fat-free poppy seed salad dressing**

In a large bowl, combine the salad greens, apple, almonds and cranberries. Drizzle with dressing; toss to coat.

Nutrition Facts: 2-1/2 cups equals 210 calories, 6 g fat (1 g saturated fat), 5 mg cholesterol, 109 mg sodium, 36 g carbohydrate, 6 g fiber, 5 g protein.

REFRIGERATOR PICKLES

Yield: 6 cups.

These pickles are so good and easy to prepare, you'll want to keep them on hand all the time. My in-laws send over produce just so I'll make more!

loy jones // anniston, alabama

3	**cups sliced peeled cucumbers**
3	**cups sliced peeled yellow summer squash**
2	**cups chopped sweet onions**
1-1/2	**cups white vinegar**
1	**cup sugar**
1/2	**teaspoon salt**
1/2	**teaspoon celery seed**
1/2	**teaspoon mustard seed**

Place the cucumbers, squash and onions in a large bowl; set aside. In a small saucepan, combine the remaining ingredients; bring to a boil. Cook and stir just until the sugar is dissolved. Pour over cucumber mixture; allow to cool.

Cover tightly and refrigerate for at least 24 hours. Serve with a slotted spoon.

Nutrition Facts: 1/4 cup equals 43 calories, trace fat (trace saturated fat), 0 cholesterol, 50 mg sodium, 11 g carbohydrate, 1 g fiber, trace protein.

taste of home COOKING SCHOOL SECRET

PRESERVE THE SEASON'S BOUNTY: PICKLE IT

It can be a challenge to use up all the cucumbers and squash that even a small garden can produce. That's why a good pickle recipe is a gardener's best friend!

Refrigerator pickles are easy to make and don't require any special equipment. Because the vegetables are stored in a vinegary brine, they will stay well-preserved in your refrigerator for a long time to come.

For the best results, thinly slice the vegetables you'll be pickling. When storing, make sure the pickles are fully immersed in the brine.

PREPARE & FREEZE COMPOUND BUTTER (TWO METHODS)

1 Place butter on a square of parchment paper, mounding butter into a rough log shape.

2 Fold paper toward you, enclosing the butter. Press butter with a ruler to form a log, holding the edges of paper securely with the other hand. Twist edges to seal. Wrap butter in plastic and freeze. Slice off the desired portions when ready to use, then rewrap the butter and return it to the freezer.

You can also freeze scoops or rosettes of flavored butter on a parchment paper-lined baking sheet. Once frozen, arrange the butter portions on layers of paper in a freezer container. Remove the desired number of portions from the freezer when needed.

BASIL BUTTER

Yield: 4 dozen butter balls.

Make this tasty butter during the growing season and freeze it for later use. When veggies are sauteed in the butter, they taste as fresh as the herbs do when they come out of the garden.

emily chaney // penobscot, maine

    1-1/2 **cups loosely packed fresh basil leaves**
      1/2 **pound butter, softened**
        1 **teaspoon lemon juice**
        1 **teaspoon seasoned pepper**
      1/2 **teaspoon garlic salt**

In a food processor, chop basil. Add the butter, lemon juice and pepper and garlic salt; blend until smooth. Drop by half-tablespoons onto a baking sheet; freeze. Remove from baking sheet and store in freezer bags. Use to flavor chicken, fish or vegetables.

Nutrition Facts: 1 serving equals 35 calories, 4 g fat (2 g saturated fat), 10 mg cholesterol, 58 mg sodium, trace carbohydrate, trace fiber, trace protein.

GARLIC LEMON BUTTER

Yield: 1/2 cup.

This tangy flavored butter offers a nice change from plain butter and gives a refreshing new taste to an ear of corn.

margie wampler // butler, pennsylvania

- 1/2 **cup butter, softened**
- 1 **garlic clove, minced**
- 1 **teaspoon minced fresh parsley**
- 2 **to 3 teaspoons grated lemon peel**

Salt and pepper to taste

In a small bowl, mix all ingredients until smooth. Spread on hot cooked corn on the cob or toss with vegetables.

Nutrition Facts: 1 tablespoon equals 101 calories, 11 g fat (7 g saturated fat), 31 mg cholesterol, 116 mg sodium, trace carbohydrate, trace fiber, trace protein.

PANTRY BUTTER

Yield: 1/4 cup.

This butter won't only add kick to corn on the cob, it'll zip up zucchini or any other cooked vegetable. Adapt the recipe to your own tastes by adjusting the amount of chili powder.

taste of home cooking school

- 1/4 **cup butter, softened**
- 1/2 **teaspoon dried parsley flakes**
- 1/4 **teaspoon chili powder**
- 1/4 **teaspoon salt**

In a small bowl, combine the butter, parsley, chili powder and salt until smooth. Spread on hot cooked corn on the cob.

Nutrition Facts: 1 tablespoon equals 101 calories, 11 g fat (7 g saturated fat) 31 mg cholesterol, 265 mg sodium, trace carbohydrate, trace fiber, trace protein.

CHILI BUTTER

Yield: 1/4 cup.

This spicy butter will instantly give your steak a delicious Southwestern slant. Also try it with grilled potatoes.

allan stackhouse jr. // jennings, louisiana

- 1/4 **cup butter, softened**
- 1 **teaspoon chili powder**
- 1/2 **teaspoon Dijon mustard**

Dash cayenne pepper

In a small bowl, beat the butter, chili powder, mustard and cayenne until smooth. Refrigerate until serving. Serve with steak.

Nutrition Facts: 1 tablespoon equals 103 calories, 11 g fat (7 g saturated fat), 30 mg cholesterol, 102 mg sodium, 1 g carbohydrate, trace fiber, trace protein.

>> HOW TO:

GRILL CORN IN FOIL

Husk corn; place each ear on a 12-in. square piece of foil. Top with a pat of butter and a standard-size ice cube. Wrap each ear tightly and grill for about 15 minutes.

MAKE GNOCCHI

1 Rice the potatoes and sprinkle with flour. Make a well and pour in egg, salt and seasonings.

2 Roll the dough into four ropes and cut each rope into 3/4-in., thimble-sized dumplings.

3 Press each piece between your thumb and a floured fork to make grooves for catching butter or sauce.

4 Bring a large pot of water to a boil so you're ready to cook the gnocchi when shaping is complete.

GNOCCHI IN SAGE BUTTER

Yield: 4 servings.

A buttery garlic and sage sauce adds melt-in-your-mouth flavor to these homemade potato gnocchi.

taste of home cooking school

- 1 **pound russet potatoes, peeled and quartered**
- 2/3 **cup all-purpose flour**
- 1 **egg**
- 1/2 **teaspoon salt**

Dash ground nutmeg

- 2 **tablespoons butter**
- 2 **garlic cloves, thinly sliced**
- 4 **fresh sage leaves, thinly sliced**

Place potatoes in a saucepan and cover with water. Bring to a boil. Reduce heat; cover and simmer for 15-20 minutes or until tender. Drain.

Over warm burner or very low heat, stir potatoes for 1-2 minutes or until steam is evaporated. Press through a potato ricer or strainer into a small bowl; cool slightly. In a Dutch oven, bring 3 qts. water to a boil.

Using a fork, make a well in the potatoes. Sprinkle flour over potatoes and into the well. Whisk the egg, salt and nutmeg; pour into well. Stir until blended. Knead 10-12 times, forming a soft dough.

Divide dough into four portions. On a floured surface, roll portions into 1/2-in.-thick ropes; cut into 3/4-in. pieces. Press and roll each piece with a lightly floured fork. Cook gnocchi in boiling water in batches for 30-60 seconds or until they float. Remove with a strainer and keep warm.

In a large heavy saucepan, cook butter over medium heat for 3 minutes. Add garlic and sage; cook for 1-2 minutes or until butter and garlic are golden brown. Add gnocchi; stir gently to coat.

Nutrition Facts: 2/3 cup equals 232 calories, 7 g fat (4 g saturated fat), 68 mg cholesterol, 373 mg sodium, 36 g carbohydrate, 2 g fiber, 6 g protein.

TOMATO GNOCCHI WITH PESTO: Omit the nutmeg, butter, garlic and sage. Prepare gnocchi as directed, whisking 3 tablespoons tomato paste with the egg and salt. Finish making and boiling gnocchi as directed. Toss with 1/4 to 1/3 cup prepared pesto.

NEVER-FAIL SCALLOPED POTATOES

Yield: 6 servings.

Take the chill off any blustery day and make something special to accompany roasts, chops or steaks. This creamy potato dish is a lightened-up version of a classic.

agnes ward // stratford, ontario

- 2 **tablespoons butter**
- 3 **tablespoons all-purpose flour**
- 1 **teaspoon salt**
- 1/4 **teaspoon pepper**
- 1-1/2 **cups fat-free milk**
- 1/2 **cup shredded reduced-fat cheddar cheese**
- 1-3/4 **pounds potatoes, peeled and thinly sliced (about 5 medium)**
- 1 **medium onion, halved and thinly sliced**

In a small nonstick skillet, melt butter. Stir in the flour, salt and pepper until smooth; gradually add milk. Bring to a boil. Cook and stir for 2 minutes or until thickened. Remove from the heat; stir in cheese until blended.

Place half of the potatoes in a 1-1/2-qt. baking dish coated with cooking spray; layer with half of the onion and cheese sauce. Repeat the layers.

Cover and bake at 350° for 50 minutes. Uncover; bake 10-15 minutes longer or until bubbly and potatoes are tender.

Nutrition Facts: 3/4 cup equals 196 calories, 6 g fat (4 g saturated fat), 18 mg cholesterol, 530 mg sodium, 29 g carbohydrate, 3 g fiber, 7 g protein. Diabetic Exchanges: 2 starch, 1 fat.

GRILLED VEGETABLE MEDLEY

Yield: 8 servings.

This side dish is our favorite way to fix summer vegetables. Cleanup is a breeze because it cooks in foil. It goes from garden to table in under an hour and makes a great accompaniment to grilled steak or chicken.

lori daniels // beverly, west virginia

- 1/4 **cup olive oil**
- 1 **teaspoon salt**
- 1 **teaspoon dried parsley flakes**
- 1 **teaspoon dried basil**
- 3 **large ears fresh corn on the cob, cut into 3-inch pieces**
- 2 **medium zucchini, sliced**
- 1 **medium yellow summer squash, sliced**
- 1 **medium sweet onion, sliced**
- 1 **large green pepper, diced**
- 10 **cherry tomatoes**
- 1 **jar (4-1/2 ounces) whole mushrooms, drained**
- 1/4 **cup butter, cubed**

In a large bowl, combine the oil, salt, parsley and basil. Add vegetables and toss to coat. Place on a double thickness of heavy-duty foil (about 28 in. x 18 in.). Dot with butter. Fold foil around vegetables and seal tightly.

Grill, covered, over medium heat for 10-13 minutes on each side or until corn is tender. Open carefully to allow steam to escape.

Nutrition Facts: 3/4 cup equals 172 calories, 13 g fat (5 g saturated fat), 15 mg cholesterol, 421 mg sodium, 13 g carbohydrate, 3 g fiber, 3 g protein.

CREAMY NOODLES

Yield: 6 servings.

There's a lot of garlic flavor in this creamy, filling side dish. My family likes best it with grilled chicken, but it works with a variety of menus.

brenda nolen // folsom, louisiana

- 8 **ounces uncooked thin spaghetti**
- 3 **garlic cloves, minced**
- 3 **tablespoons butter,** *divided*
- 6 **ounces fat-free cream cheese, cubed**
- 3 **tablespoons reduced-fat sour cream**
- 3 **tablespoons fat-free milk**
- 3/4 **teaspoon salt**
- 1/2 **teaspoon onion powder**
- 1/4 **teaspoon Cajun seasoning**
- 1/4 **teaspoon white pepper**
- 4-1/2 **teaspoons minced fresh parsley**

Cook spaghetti according to package directions. Meanwhile, in a large saucepan, saute garlic in 1 tablespoon butter for 1 minute. Add the cream cheese, sour cream, milk, salt, onion powder, Cajun seasoning, pepper and remaining butter. Cook and stir over low heat just until smooth (do not boil). Remove from the heat.

Drain spaghetti; toss with cream sauce. Sprinkle with parsley.

Nutrition Facts: 1 cup equals 234 calories, 7 g fat (4 g saturated fat), 20 mg cholesterol, 547 mg sodium, 32 g carbohydrate, 1 g fiber, 10 g protein. Diabetic Exchanges: 2 starch, 1 lean meat, 1 fat.

FAMILY-FAVORITE BAKED BEANS

Yield: 8 servings.

Three kinds of beans and plenty of beef and bacon make this recipe irresistible.

lea ann anderson // tulsa, oklahoma

- 1/2 **pound ground beef**
- 1/2 **pound sliced bacon, diced**
- 1 **small onion, chopped**
- 1/2 **cup ketchup**
- 1/2 **cup barbecue sauce**
- 1/3 **cup packed brown sugar**
- 2 **tablespoons molasses**
- 1 **can (16 ounces) kidney beans, rinsed and drained**
- 1 **can (15-3/4 ounces) pork and beans**
- 1 **can (16 ounces) butter beans, rinsed and drained**

In a Dutch oven, cook beef over medium heat until no longer pink; drain and set aside. In the same pan, cook bacon until crisp. Remove from the heat; drain.

Return beef to the pan. Add the onion, ketchup, barbecue sauce, brown sugar and molasses. Stir in the beans.

Transfer to a greased 3-qt. baking dish. Cover and bake at 350° for 1 hour or until beans reach desired thickness.

Nutrition Facts: 3/4 cup equals 305 calories, 8 g fat (3 g saturated fat), 22 mg cholesterol, 966 mg sodium, 46 g carbohydrate, 8 g fiber, 17 g protein.

ROAST VEGETABLES

1. Cut veggies into uniform pieces so they cook evenly. If roasting several varieties at once, cut denser veggies into smaller pieces so that everything will be done at the same time. Keep chopped beets separate from other vegetables like potatoes and onions, as they may dye them.

2. Spread vegetables evenly on a shallow roasting pan, making sure they're not crowded. Drizzle with oil and sprinkle with seasonings; toss gently to coat. Roast, uncovered, until vegetables are tender, stirring occasionally.

ROASTED AUTUMN VEGETABLES

Yield: 7 servings.

This rustic, satisfying dish is good with any meat, but I especially like it with pork. Because the vegetables can be prepared in advance, I have more time to spend with my dinner guests.

shirley beauregard // grand junction, colorado

- 3 **Yukon Gold potatoes, cut into small wedges**
- 2 **medium sweet red peppers, cut into 1-inch pieces**
- 1 **small butternut squash, peeled and cubed**
- 1 **medium sweet potato, peeled and cubed**
- 1 **medium red onion, quartered**
- 3 **tablespoons olive oil**
- 2 **tablespoons balsamic vinegar**
- 2 **tablespoons minced fresh rosemary** *or* **2 teaspoons dried rosemary, crushed**
- 1 **tablespoon minced fresh thyme** *or* **1 teaspoon dried thyme**
- 1 **teaspoon salt**
- 1/2 **teaspoon pepper**

In a large bowl, combine the potatoes, red peppers, squash, sweet potato and onion. In a small bowl, whisk the oil, vinegar and seasonings. Pour over vegetables and toss to coat.

Transfer to two greased 15-in. x 10-in. x 1-in. baking pans. Bake, uncovered, at 425° for 30-40 minutes or until tender, stirring occasionally.

Nutrition Facts: 1 cup equals 152 calories, 6 g fat (1 g saturated fat), 0 cholesterol, 347 mg sodium, 24 g carbohydrate, 4 g fiber, 2 g protein. Diabetic Exchanges: 1 starch, 1 vegetable, 1 fat.

PARMESAN RISOTTO

Yield: 12 servings.

Risotto is a traditional Italian rice dish. This version features a hint of white wine and minced fresh parsley for a simple yet elegant presentation.

taste of home cooking school

8 **cups chicken broth**	1 **cup dry white wine** *or* **additional chicken broth**
1/2 **cup finely chopped onion**	1/2 **cup shredded Parmesan cheese**
1/4 **cup olive oil**	1/4 **teaspoon salt**
3 **cups arborio rice**	1/4 **teaspoon pepper**
2 **garlic cloves, minced**	3 **tablespoons minced fresh parsley**

In a large saucepan, heat broth and keep warm. In a Dutch oven, saute onion in oil until tender. Add rice and garlic; cook and stir for 2-3 minutes. Reduce heat; stir in wine. Cook and stir until all of the liquid is absorbed.

Add heated broth, 1/2 cup at a time, stirring constantly. Allow the liquid to absorb between additions. Cook just until risotto is creamy and rice is almost tender. (Cooking time is about 20 minutes.) Add remaining ingredients; heat through. Serve immediately.

Nutrition Facts: 3/4 cup equals 260 calories, 6 g fat (1 g saturated fat), 2 mg cholesterol, 728 mg sodium, 41 g carbohydrate, 1 g fiber, 6 g protein.

SAUSAGE MUSHROOM RISOTTO: Reduce olive oil to 2 tablespoons. In the Dutch oven, cook 1 pound bulk Italian sausage over medium heat until no longer pink; drain. Set aside and keep warm. Add onion, oil and 1/2 pound quartered fresh mushrooms to the pan; cook until tender. Proceed as directed.

ASPARAGUS RISOTTO: Trim 1 pound asparagus and cut into 2-in. pieces. Place in a large saucepan; add 1/2 in. of water. Bring to a boil. Reduce heat; cover and simmer for 3 minutes or until crisp-tender. Drain and set aside. Add asparagus with the Parmesan and seasonings; heat through.

ORZO WITH PARMESAN & BASIL

Yield: 4 servings.

Dried basil adds its rich herb flavor to this creamy and delicious skillet side dish that's table-ready in just minutes!

anna chaney // antigo, wisconsin

1	**cup uncooked orzo pasta**
2	**tablespoons butter**
1	**can (14-1/2 ounces) chicken broth**
1/2	**cup grated Parmesan cheese**
2	**teaspoons dried basil**
1/8	**teaspoon pepper**

In a large skillet, saute orzo in butter for 3-5 minutes or until lightly browned.

Stir in broth. Bring to a boil. Reduce heat; cover and simmer for 10-15 minutes or until liquid is absorbed and orzo is tender. Stir in the cheese, basil and pepper.

Nutrition Facts: 1/2 cup equals 285 calories, 10 g fat (5 g saturated fat), 26 mg cholesterol, 641 mg sodium, 38 g carbohydrate, 1 g fiber, 11 g protein.

CORN & PEPPER ORZO: Omit Parmesan cheese, basil and pepper. Prepare orzo as directed. In a large skillet coated with cooking spray, saute 1 chopped large red sweet pepper and 1 chopped medium onion in 1 tablespoon olive oil. Stir in 2 cups thawed frozen corn, 2 teaspoons Italian seasoning and 1/8 teaspoon salt and pepper. Drain orzo; toss with vegetable mixture.

CHIPOTLE SWEET POTATOES

Yield: 8 servings.

Try a spicy take on sweet potatoes. It's a great way to add this nutritious veggie to your diet any time of the year.

kim jones // mount juliet, tennessee

- 3 **large sweet potatoes (about 2-1/2 pounds), peeled and cut into 1/2-inch cubes**
- 1 **cup balsamic vinaigrette, *divided***
- 1/4 **teaspoon salt**
- 1/4 **teaspoon pepper**
- 1/3 **cup minced fresh cilantro**
- 3 **tablespoons honey**
- 2 **chipotle peppers in adobo sauce, minced**

Place sweet potatoes in two greased 15-in. x 10-in. x 1-in. baking pans. Drizzle with 1/2 cup vinaigrette and sprinkle with salt and pepper; toss to coat.

Bake at 400° for 25-30 minutes or until potatoes are tender, stirring once. Cool slightly; transfer to a large bowl.

In a small bowl, whisk the remaining vinaigrette, cilantro, honey and peppers. Pour over potatoes and gently stir to coat.

Nutrition Facts: 3/4 cup equals 168 calories, 5 g fat (1 g saturated fat), 0 cholesterol, 357 mg sodium, 30 g carbohydrate, 3 g fiber, 1 g protein. Diabetic Exchanges: 2 starch, 1 fat.

CHEDDAR TWICE-BAKED POTATOES

Yield: 6 servings.

Our family rarely has steak without these easy-to-fix potatoes. They're creamy and full of bacon, cheese and onion flavor.

heather ahrens // columbus, ohio

6	large baking potatoes	1	egg
8	tablespoons butter, *divided*	1/2	teaspoon salt
1/4	pound sliced bacon, diced	1/8	teaspoon white pepper
1	medium onion, finely chopped	1	cup (4 ounces) shredded
1/2	cup 2% milk		cheddar cheese

Scrub and pierce potatoes; rub each with 1 teaspoon butter. Place on a baking sheet. Bake at 375° for 1 hour or until tender.

Meanwhile, in a small skillet, cook bacon over medium heat until crisp. Remove to paper towels; drain, reserving 1 tablespoon drippings. In the drippings, saute onion until tender; set aside.

When potatoes are cool enough to handle, cut a thin slice off the top of each and discard. Scoop out pulp, leaving a thin shell. In a small bowl, mash pulp with remaining butter. Stir in the milk, egg, salt and pepper. Stir in the cheese, bacon and onion.

Spoon into the potato shells. Place on a baking sheet. Bake at 375° for 20-25 minutes or until heated through.

Nutrition Facts: 1 potato equals 563 calories, 25 g fat (15 g saturated fat), 104 mg cholesterol, 607 mg sodium, 70 g carbohydrate, 6 g fiber, 16 g protein.

≫ HOW TO:

MAKE STUFFED POTATOES

Cut a lengthwise slice from the top of each baked potato and discard. With a spoon, scoop pulp from inside the potato, leaving a 1/4-in. shell. Mash the pulp with the other ingredients and spoon into shells. Bake as directed.

NEW ENGLAND BUTTERNUT SQUASH

Yield: 5 servings.

This traditional fall treat is a favorite because it has a hint of sweetness. Even picky eaters enjoy this dish!

linda massicotte-black
coventry, connecticut

- 1 medium butternut squash
- 1/4 cup butter, melted
- 1/4 cup maple syrup
- 3/4 teaspoon ground cinnamon
- 1/4 teaspoon ground nutmeg

Cut squash in half lengthwise; discard seeds. Place cut side down in a microwave-safe dish; add 1/2 in. of water. Cover and microwave on high for 15-20 minutes or until very tender; drain.

When cool enough to handle, scoop out pulp and mash. Stir in the butter, syrup, cinnamon and nutmeg.

EDITOR'S NOTE: This recipe was tested in a 1,100-watt microwave.

Nutrition Facts: 2/3 cup equals 192 calories, 9 g fat (6 g saturated fat), 24 mg cholesterol, 72 mg sodium,

MUSHROOM WILD RICE

Yield: 10 servings.

With its nutty texture and visual appeal, this hearty side is a great choice when your menu calls for a rice dish. I've learned to make enough for leftovers to be sent home with guests.

virginia peter // winter, wisconsin

- 4 cups chicken broth
- 1-1/2 cups uncooked wild rice
- 1/2 teaspoon salt
- 1/4 teaspoon pepper
- 3 bacon strips, cut into 1/2-inch pieces
- 2 cups sliced fresh mushrooms
- 1 small onion, chopped
- 1/2 cup sliced almonds

In a large saucepan, bring broth to a boil. Stir in the rice, salt and pepper. Reduce heat to low; cover and simmer for 55 minutes or until rice is tender. Remove from the heat.

Meanwhile, in a large skillet, cook bacon over medium heat until crisp. Using a slotted spoon, remove to paper towels to drain. Saute the mushrooms, onion and almonds in drippings until vegetables are tender; stir into rice mixture. Add bacon.

Nutrition Facts: 3/4 cup equals 173 calories, 6 g fat (1 g saturated fat), 7 mg cholesterol, 568 mg sodium, 24 g carbohydrate, 2 g fiber, 6 g protein. Diabetic Exchanges: 1-1/2 starch, 1 fat.

STEAKHOUSE MUSHROOMS

Yield: 4 servings.

I got this recipe from a friend back when we were in nursing school. Whenever my husband is cooking meat on the grill, you can bet I'll be in the kitchen preparing these mushrooms.

kenda burgett // rattan, oklahoma

- 1 **pound medium fresh mushrooms**
- 1/4 **cup butter, cubed**
- 2 **teaspoons dried basil**
- 1/2 **teaspoon dried oregano**
- 1/2 **teaspoon seasoned salt**
- 1/4 **teaspoon garlic powder**
- 1 **teaspoon browning sauce, optional**

In a large skillet, saute mushrooms in butter until tender. Stir in seasonings and browning sauce if desired. Reduce heat; cover and cook, stirring occasionally, for 3-5 minutes to allow flavors to blend.

Nutrition Facts: 3/4 cup (calculated without browning sauce) equals 131 calories, 12 g fat (7 g saturated fat), 30 mg cholesterol, 276 mg sodium, 5 g carbohydrate, 2 g fiber, 4 g protein.

MUSHROOM BUYING TIPS

- Because they're grown indoors, fresh mushrooms are available year-round.
- Avoid mushrooms with cracks, brown spots, blemishes or ones that are shriveled or moist.
- If preparing a recipe that calls for wild or gourmet mushrooms (which can be expensive), you can save money by substituting white button mushrooms or baby portobellos for half of the specialty mushrooms called for.
- Use fresh mushrooms within a few days of purchase.

CORN AND BROCCOLI IN CHEESE SAUCE

Yield: 8 servings.

I sometimes like to add ham to this savory side dish. Save room in the oven by making this in your slow cooker.

joyce johnson // uniontown, ohio

1 **package (16 ounces) frozen corn, thawed**
1 **package (16 ounces) frozen broccoli florets, thawed**
4 **ounces reduced-fat process cheese (Velveeta), cubed**
1/2 **cup shredded cheddar cheese**
1 **can (10-1/4 ounces) reduced-fat reduced-sodium condensed cream of chicken soup, undiluted**
1/4 **cup fat-free milk**

In a 4-qt. slow cooker, combine the corn, broccoli and cheeses. In a small bowl, combine soup and milk; pour over vegetable mixture. Cover and cook on low for 3-4 hours or until heated through. Stir before serving.

Nutrition Facts: 3/4 cup equals 148 calories, 5 g fat (3 g saturated fat), 16 mg cholesterol, 409 mg sodium, 21 g carbohydrate, 3 g fiber, 8 g protein. Diabetic Exchanges: 1 starch, 1 medium-fat meat.

LEMON-BUTTER NEW POTATOES

Yield: 4 servings.

With an abundance of potatoes in our garden each summer, I often make this easy recipe. We love the combination of parsley, spices and lemony butter sauce. They make a great accompaniment to grilled fish.

sandra mckenzie // braham, minnesota

12 **small red potatoes**
1/3 **cup butter, cubed**
3 **tablespoons lemon juice**
1 **teaspoon salt**
1 **teaspoon grated lemon peel**
1/4 **teaspoon pepper**
1/8 **teaspoon ground nutmeg**
2 **tablespoons minced fresh parsley**

Peel a strip from around each potato. Place potatoes in a large saucepan and cover with water. Bring to a boil. Reduce heat; cover and cook for 15-20 minutes or just until tender.

Meanwhile, in small saucepan, melt butter. Stir in the lemon juice, salt, lemon peel, pepper and nutmeg. Drain potatoes and place in a serving bowl. Pour butter mixture over potatoes; toss gently to coat. Sprinkle with parsley.

Nutrition Facts: 1 serving equals 238 calories, 15 g fat (10 g saturated fat), 40 mg cholesterol, 707 mg sodium, 23 g carbohydrate, 3 g fiber, 3 g protein.

GARLIC MASHED POTATOES

Yield: 6 servings.

Garlic cloves are boiled and then mashed right along with the potatoes to give them extraordinary flavor. These potatoes are so easy you'll want to make them often.

myra innes // auburn, kansas

- 5 **large potatoes, peeled and cut into 1/2-inch cubes**
- 15 **garlic cloves, peeled and halved**
- 2 **teaspoons salt,** *divided*
- 1/2 **cup butter, softened**
- 1/2 **cup heavy whipping cream**

Place the potatoes, garlic and 1 teaspoon salt in a large saucepan and cover with water. Bring to a boil. Reduce heat; cover and cook for 10-15 minutes or until potatoes are tender. Drain.

Transfer potato mixture to a large bowl; mash. Add the butter, cream and remaining salt; beat until smooth.

Nutrition Facts: 3/4 cup equals 311 calories, 23 g fat (14 g saturated fat), 68 mg cholesterol, 959 mg sodium, 26 g carbohydrate, 3 g fiber, 3 g protein.

CREAMY PARMESAN SPINACH

Yield: 3 servings.

This recipe combines fresh baby spinach with a delicious, creamy Parmesan cheese sauce. Crushed croutons top it off and give the side dish a wonderful crunch.

priscilla gilbert // indian harbour beach, florida

- 2 **packages (6 ounces** *each***) fresh baby spinach, coarsely chopped**
- 2 **tablespoons water**
- 2 **teaspoons butter**
- 1/2 **cup heavy whipping cream**
- 2 **teaspoons grated lemon peel**
- 1/2 **teaspoon minced garlic**
- 1/8 **teaspoon crushed red pepper flakes**
- 1/2 **cup grated Parmesan cheese**
- 2/3 **cup onion and garlic salad croutons, crushed**

Place spinach and water in a Dutch oven; cover and cook for 3 minutes or until wilted. Drain and set aside.

In the same pan, melt butter. Stir in the cream, lemon peel, garlic and pepper flakes; bring to a gentle boil. Reduce heat; simmer, uncovered, for 5 minutes or until slightly reduced. Stir in cheese and spinach; heat through. Sprinkle with croutons.

Nutrition Facts: 1/2 cup equals 275 calories, 23 g fat (14 g saturated fat), 72 mg cholesterol, 444 mg sodium, 10 g carbohydrate, 2 g fiber, 9 g protein.

MAKEOVER BEST CORN BREAD DRESSING

Yield: 12 servings.

This corn bread dressing truly has a full-flavored, rustic feel that will be the perfect accompaniment to your delicious turkey dinner.

kim kreider // mount joy, pennsylvania

- 1-1/4 **cups all-purpose flour**
- 3/4 **cup yellow cornmeal**
- 1/4 **cup sugar**
- 2 **teaspoons baking powder**
- 1/2 **teaspoon salt**
- 1 **egg**
- 1 **cup fat-free milk**
- 2 **tablespoons canola oil**
- 2 **tablespoons unsweetened applesauce**

DRESSING:

- 2 **celery ribs, finely chopped**
- 1 **large onion, finely chopped**
- 1/2 **cup chopped pecans**
- 1/2 **cup reduced-fat butter**
- 6 **cups cubed day-old bread (1/2-inch cubes)**
- 2 **eggs, beaten**
- 1-1/2 **teaspoons poultry seasoning**
- 3/4 **teaspoon salt**
- 1/2 **teaspoon pepper**
- 2-1/4 **to 2-3/4 cups reduced-sodium chicken broth**

In a large bowl, combine the first five ingredients. Combine the egg, milk, oil and applesauce; stir into dry ingredients just until moistened. Transfer to a 9-in. square baking pan coated with cooking spray.

Bake at 400° for 15-18 minutes or until a toothpick inserted near the center comes out clean. Cool on a wire rack. Place cubed bread on baking sheets; bake for 5-7 minutes or until lightly browned. Cool on a wire rack. Cut corn bread into 1/2-in. cubes; set aside.

In a large skillet, saute the celery, onion and pecans in butter until vegetables are tender. Transfer to a large bowl. Stir in the corn bread, cubed bread, eggs, seasonings and enough broth to reach desired moistness (about 2-1/2 cups).

Transfer to a 13-in. x 9-in. baking dish coated with cooking spray. Cover and bake at 350° for 35 minutes. Uncover; bake 8-10 minutes longer or until a thermometer reads 160° and top is lightly browned.

EDITOR'S NOTE: This recipe was tested with Land O'Lakes light stick butter. It makes enough dressing to stuff a 12-pound turkey. If used to stuff poultry, replace the eggs in the dressing with 1/2 cup egg substitute. Bake until a meat thermometer reads 180° for poultry and 165° for dressing.

Nutrition Facts: 3/4 cup equals 267 calories, 12 g fat (4 g saturated fat), 67 mg cholesterol, 616 mg sodium, 33 g carbohydrate, 2 g fiber, 8 g protein.

ARTICHOKE STUFFING

Yield: 16 servings.

This recipe is so good with turkey! Sometimes I also make a half-batch to serve with roasted chicken.
lorie verkuyl // ridgecrest, california

- 1 loaf (1 pound) sourdough bread, cut into 1-inch cubes
- 1/2 pound sliced fresh mushrooms
- 2 celery ribs, chopped
- 1 medium onion, chopped
- 2 tablespoons butter
- 3 to 4 garlic cloves, minced
- 2 jars (6-1/2 ounces *each*) marinated artichoke hearts, drained and chopped
- 1/2 cup grated Parmesan cheese
- 1 teaspoon poultry seasoning
- 1 egg
- 1 can (14-1/2 ounces) chicken broth

Place bread cubes in two ungreased 15-in. x 10-in. x 1-in. baking pans. Bake at 350° for 15 minutes or until lightly browned.

In a large skillet, saute the mushrooms, celery and onion in butter until tender. Add garlic; cook 1 minute longer. Stir in the artichokes, cheese and poultry seasoning. Transfer to a large bowl; stir in bread cubes.

In a small bowl, whisk egg and broth until blended. Pour over the bread mixture and mix well.

Transfer to a greased 3-qt. baking dish (dish will be full). Cover and bake at 350° for 30 minutes. Uncover; bake 5-15 minutes longer or until a thermometer reads 160°.

Nutrition Facts: 3/4 cup equals 139 calories, 6 g fat (2 g saturated fat), 18 mg cholesterol, 384 mg sodium, 17 g carbohydrate, 1 g fiber, 5 g protein.

tasteofhome COOKING SCHOOL SECRET

START YOUR OWN THANKSGIVING TRADITION

Whether you prefer a classic sausage dressing, a Southern-style version that starts with homemade corn bread, or a California-inspired vegetable artichoke dressing, you're sure to find a new favorite among these recipes.

For convenience, these festive side dishes cook separately from the bird, either in baking dishes or in a slow cooker. If you prefer to stuff your turkey with one of these recipes, allow 3/4 cup of stuffing per pound of bird. Be careful not to overstuff the turkey and to allow extra time for the turkey to bake. The finished turkey should reach 180° and the stuffing, 165°. Bake any remaining stuffing in a covered dish until a thermometer reads 160°.

For the perfect Thanksgiving turkey, see Citrus-Rosemary Rubbed Turkey, page 163. The corn bread dressing would also be excellent for Easter or other holidays with Fruit-Glazed Spiral Ham (page 119) or Ham with Ruby-Red Glaze (page 123).

Bake, uncovered, at 350° for 10 minutes. Sprinkle with the cheddar cheese, bacon and chives. Bake 5 minutes longer or until heated through and cheese is melted.

Nutrition Facts: 3/4 cup equals 433 calories, 33 g fat (22 g saturated fat), 114 mg cholesterol, 340 mg sodium, 20 g carbohydrate, 1 g fiber, 10 g protein. .

MALLOW SWEET POTATO BAKE

Yield: 12 servings.

I put a light spin on a Thanksgiving classic with this recipe. This festive looking side captures the flavors of sweet potatoes and marshmallows, but leaves the calories out!

delores nickerson // muskogee, oklahoma

- 6 **large sweet potatoes**
- 3 **tablespoons butter**

EVERYTHING MASHED POTATO CASSEROLE

Yield: 12 servings.

Here is a great dish for the holidays or to take to a covered dish event. If I need to keep it warm for a long time, I sometimes place the mixture into a slow cooker and then add the sour cream, bacon, cheese and chives.

pamela shank // parkersburg, west virginia

- 3 **pounds potatoes (about 9 medium), peeled and quartered**
- 1 **package (8 ounces) cream cheese, cubed**
- 1/2 **cup butter, cubed**
- 1/2 **cup milk**
- 1/4 **teaspoon salt**
- 1/4 **teaspoon pepper**
- 2 **cups (16 ounces) sour cream**
- 2 **cups (8 ounces) shredded cheddar cheese**
- 3 **bacon strips, cooked and crumbled**
- 1 **tablespoon minced chives**

Place potatoes in a large saucepan and cover with water. Bring to a boil. Reduce heat; cover and simmer for 15-20 minutes or until tender. Drain.

In a large bowl, mash potatoes. Beat in the cream cheese, butter, milk, salt and pepper until fluffy. Transfer to a greased 3-qt. baking dish. Spread sour cream over the top.

1 can (8 ounces) unsweetened crushed pineapple, undrained

1/2 cup dried cranberries, *divided*

1/3 cup orange juice

3/4 teaspoon salt

2/3 cup miniature marshmallows

1/3 cup chopped pecans

Scrub and pierce sweet potatoes. Bake at 400° for 45-55 minutes or until tender.

Cut potatoes in half; scoop out pulp and place in a large bowl. Stir in butter until melted. Stir in the pineapple, 1/4 cup cranberries, orange juice and salt.

Transfer to an 11-in. x 7-in. baking dish coated with cooking spray. Cover and bake at 350° for 30 minutes.

Uncover; sprinkle with marshmallows, pecans and remaining cranberries. Bake 8-10 minutes longer or just until marshmallows are puffed and lightly browned.

Nutrition Facts: 2/3 cup equals 179 calories, 5 g fat (2 g saturated fat), 8 mg cholesterol, 187 mg sodium, 32 g carbohydrate, 3 g fiber, 2 g protein. Diabetic Exchanges: 2 starch, 1 fat.

SLOW-COOKED SAUSAGE DRESSING

Yield: 8 cups.

This dressing is so delicious no one will know it's lower in fat. And best of all, it cooks effortlessly in the slow cooker, so the stove and oven are freed up for other dishes!

raquel haggard // edmond, oklahoma

1/2 pound reduced-fat bulk pork sausage

2 celery ribs, chopped

1 large onion, chopped

7 cups seasoned stuffing cubes

1 can (14-1/2 ounces) reduced-sodium chicken broth

1 medium tart apple, chopped

1/3 cup chopped pecans

2 tablespoons reduced-fat butter, melted

1-1/2 teaspoons rubbed sage

1/2 teaspoon pepper

In a large nonstick skillet, cook the sausage, celery and onion over medium heat until meat is no longer pink; drain. Transfer to a large bowl; stir in the remaining ingredients.

Transfer to a 5-qt. slow cooker coated with cooking spray. Cover and cook on low for 3-4 hours or until heated through and apple is tender, stirring once.

EDITOR'S NOTE: This recipe was tested with Land O'Lakes light stick butter.

Nutrition Facts: 2/3 cup equals 201 calories, 8 g fat (2 g saturated fat), 17 mg cholesterol, 640 mg sodium, 26 g carbohydrate, 3 g fiber, 7 g protein.

BE SMART WITH HOLIDAY LEFTOVERS

- Stock up on plastic storage bags and containers so you're prepared to store leftovers or send them home with guests.

- Promptly refrigerate leftovers; don't allow foods to stand at room temperature for over 2 hours.

- Have some go-to recipes to use up leftovers, such as Chunky Turkey Soup (page 84) or Cordon Bleu Casserole (page 148).

BREAKFAST

GOURMET SCRAMBLED EGGS

Yield: 4 servings.

Start your day off right with this special recipe for restaurant-quality eggs. A visiting friend made these one weekend. Now they're my favorite.

diana bird // jeffersonton, virginia

8 **eggs**	1 **tablespoon minced chives**
1/4 **cup shredded Parmesan cheese**	1 **tablespoon minced fresh basil**
1/4 **cup mayonnaise**	1 **tablespoon butter**

In a small bowl, whisk the eggs, cheese, mayonnaise, chives and basil. In a large skillet, heat butter over medium heat. Add egg mixture; cook and stir until completely set.

Nutrition Facts: 1 serving equals 289 calories, 25 g fat (7 g saturated fat), 439 mg cholesterol, 320 mg sodium, 1 g carbohydrate, trace fiber, 15 g protein.

>> HOW TO:

SCRAMBLE EGGS

1 Pour beaten egg mixture into prepared skillet. As eggs begin to set, gently move a spatula across the bottom and sides of pan, allowing the uncooked eggs to flow underneath.

2 Continue to cook the eggs, stirring occasionally, until the eggs are set and no visible liquid remains.

HAM & BROCCOLI FRITTATA

Yield: 4 servings.

At less than $4 for the entire dish, this is one breakfast entree that's bound to become a regular in your repertoire.

taste of home cooking school

> 6 **eggs**
>
> 1-1/4 **cups shredded Swiss cheese, *divided***
>
> 1 **cup cubed fully cooked ham**
>
> 1/4 **teaspoon pepper**
>
> 1 **cup chopped fresh broccoli**
>
> 1 **tablespoon butter**

In a small bowl, whisk the eggs, 1 cup cheese, ham and pepper; set aside. In a 10-in. ovenproof skillet, saute broccoli in butter until tender. Reduce heat; add egg mixture. Cover and cook for 4-6 minutes or until nearly set.

Uncover skillet; sprinkle with remaining cheese. Broil 3-4 in. from the heat for 2-3 minutes or until eggs are completely set. Let stand for 5 minutes. Cut into wedges.

Nutrition Facts: 1 wedge equals 321 calories, 23 g fat (11 g saturated fat), 374 mg cholesterol, 665 mg sodium, 4 g carbohydrate, 1 g fiber, 26 g protein.

CAMPER'S BREAKFAST HASH

Yield: 8 servings.

When we go camping with family and friends, I always make this hearty breakfast. It's a favorite at home, too.

linda krivanek // oak creek, wisconsin

> 1/4 **cup butter, cubed**
>
> 2 **packages (20 ounces *each*) refrigerated shredded hash brown potatoes**
>
> 1 **package (7 ounces) brown-and-serve sausage links, cut into 1/2-inch pieces**
>
> 1/4 **cup chopped onion**
>
> 1/4 **cup chopped green pepper**
>
> 12 **eggs, lightly beaten**
>
> **Salt and pepper to taste**
>
> 1 **cup (4 ounces) shredded cheddar cheese**

In a large skillet, melt butter. Add the potatoes, sausage, onion and green pepper. Cook, uncovered, over medium heat for 10-15 minutes or until potatoes are lightly browned, turning once.

Push potato mixture to the sides of pan. Pour eggs into center of pan. Cook and stir over medium heat until eggs are completely set. Season with salt and pepper. Reduce heat; stir eggs into potato mixture. Top with cheese; cover and cook for 1-2 minutes or until the cheese is melted.

Nutrition Facts: 1 cup equals 376 calories, 27 g fat (12 g saturated fat), 364 mg cholesterol, 520 mg sodium, 17 g carbohydrate, 1 g fiber, 18 g protein.

CHILE RELLENOS QUICHE

Yield: 6 servings.

To me, nothing sparks up a meal more than the smoky flavor of roasted green chilies. This is a fast and easy recipe, and I usually have the ingredients on hand, so I can always make a quick meal.

linda miritello // mesa, arizona

Pastry for single-crust pie (9 inches)

- 2 **tablespoons cornmeal**
- 1-1/2 cups (6 ounces) shredded Monterey Jack cheese
- 1 cup (4 ounces) shredded cheddar cheese
- 1 can (4 ounces) chopped green chilies
- 3 **eggs**
- 3/4 **cup sour cream**
- 1 **tablespoon minced fresh cilantro**
- 2 **to 4 drops hot pepper sauce, optional**

Line unpricked pastry shell with a double thickness of heavy-duty foil. Bake at 450° for 8 minutes. Remove foil; bake 5 minutes longer. Cool on a wire rack. Reduce heat to 350°.

Sprinkle cornmeal over bottom of pastry shell. In a small bowl, combine cheeses; set aside 1/2 cup for topping. Add chilies to remaining cheese mixture; sprinkle into crust.

In the same bowl, whisk the eggs, sour cream, cilantro and hot pepper sauce if desired. Pour into crust; sprinkle with reserved cheese mixture.

Bake for 35-40 minutes or until a knife inserted near the center comes out clean. Let stand for 5 minutes before cutting.

Nutrition Facts: 1 piece equals 444 calories, 31 g fat (18 g saturated fat), 178 mg cholesterol, 520 mg sodium, 23 g carbohydrate, 1 g fiber, 17 g protein.

>> HOW TO:

TEST BAKED EGG DISHES FOR DONENESS

Test egg dishes containing beaten eggs—like quiche, strata or custard—for doneness by inserting a knife near the center of the dish. If the knife comes out clean, the eggs are cooked.

>> HOW TO:

MAKE AN OMELET

1 Beat eggs, milk and any seasonings. Heat oil or butter in a 10-in. nonstick skillet over medium heat. Add eggs; cook until partially set. Lift edges, letting uncooked egg flow underneath.

2 Allow the eggs to set, and then sprinkle your favorite filling ingredients (such as ham, chopped green pepper, chopped tomato, shredded cheese or sliced mushrooms) over half of the omelet.

3 Fold omelet in half. Proceed as recipe directs.

CHEESY CHIVE OMELET

Yield: 1-2 servings.

This savory omelet is good fuel for a busy day.

naomi giddis // two buttes, colorado

3 eggs	Dash pepper
2 tablespoons water	1 tablespoon butter
1 tablespoon minced chives	1/4 to 1/2 cup shredded cheddar cheese
1/8 teaspoon salt	

In a small bowl, beat eggs and water. Stir in the chives, salt and pepper. In a small skillet, melt butter over medium heat; add egg mixture. As eggs set, lift edges, letting the uncooked portion flow underneath.

Just before eggs are completely set, sprinkle cheese over half of the omelet; fold in half. Cover and remove from the heat. Let stand for 1-2 minutes or until cheese is melted.

Nutrition Facts: 1 serving equals 213 calories, 17 g fat (9 g saturated fat), 349 mg cholesterol, 385 mg sodium, 2 g carbohydrate, trace fiber, 12 g protein.

HAM & SWISS OMELET: Substitute 1/8 teaspoon pepper for the chives. Sprinkle the egg mixture with 1/2 cup cubed cooked ham and 1/4 cup shredded Swiss cheese.

BACON AND CHEESE BREAKFAST PIZZA

Yield: 6 servings.

An area firefighter shared this recipe with me. It's good for breakfast and even a light dinner. As a busy college student, I'm a big fan of this easy recipe.
dina davis // madison, florida

Pastry for single-crust pie (**9 inches**)

- 1/2 **pound bacon, cooked and crumbled**
- 2 **cups (8 ounces) shredded Swiss cheese**
- 4 **eggs, lightly beaten**
- 1-1/2 **cups (12 ounces) sour cream**
- 2 **tablespoons chopped fresh parsley**

Roll pastry to fit a 12-in. pizza pan. Bake at 425° for 5 minutes. Sprinkle bacon and cheese evenly over crust.

In a large bowl, beat eggs, sour cream and parsley until smooth; pour over pizza. Bake for 20 to 25 minutes or until pizza is puffy and lightly browned.

Nutrition Facts: 1 slice equals 595 calories, 40 g fat (21 g saturated fat), 248 mg cholesterol, 1,509 mg sodium, 22 g carbohydrate, trace fiber, 32 g protein.

PINEAPPLE SUNRISE SMOOTHIES

Yield: 2 servings.

Brighten up your morning with a burst of tropical fruit flavor in this fiber-rich and fun smoothie.
diana mueller // las vegas, nevada

- 1 **can (14 ounces) unsweetened pineapple tidbits**
- 1 **small ripe banana, sliced**
- 3/4 **cup fresh *or* frozen raspberries**
- 2 **tablespoons sugar**
- 2 **ice cubes**

Drain pineapple, reserving juice and 1 cup pineapple (refrigerate remaining pineapple for another use). In a blender, combine the pineapple juice, pineapple, banana, raspberries, sugar and ice; cover and process until smooth. Stir if necessary. Pour into chilled glasses; serve immediately.

Nutrition Facts: 1-1/2 cups equals 205 calories, 1 g fat (trace saturated fat), 0 cholesterol, 18 mg sodium, 56 g carbohydrate, 6 g fiber, 1 g protein.

>> HOW TO:

DICE A MANGO

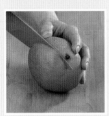

1 Wash fruit. Lay fruit on the counter, then turn so the top and bottom are now the sides. Using a sharp knife, make a lengthwise cut as close to the long, flat seed as possible to remove each side of the fruit. Trim fruit away from the seed.

2 Score each side of the fruit lengthwise and widthwise, without cutting through the skin.

3 Using your hand, push the skin up, turning the fruit out. Cut fruit off at the skin with a knife.

MANGO BANANA SMOOTHIES

Yield: 2 servings.

Toasted wheat germ is a healthy bonus in this refreshing smoothie. The chilly orange and mango flavors really hit the spot!

verna puntigan // spartanburg, south carolina

- 1/2 **cup orange juice**
- 1/2 **cup vanilla yogurt**
- 1 **cup chopped peeled mango**
- 1 **medium ripe banana, sliced and frozen**
- 2 **tablespoons honey**
- 2 **teaspoons toasted wheat germ**
- 1 **teaspoon chopped crystallized ginger**

Place all ingredients in a blender; cover and process for 1-2 minutes or until smooth. Pour into chilled glasses; serve immediately.

Nutrition Facts: 1-1/4 cups equals 271 calories, 1 g fat (trace saturated fat), 1 mg cholesterol, 47 mg sodium, 66 g carbohydrate, 3 g fiber, 5 g protein.

ISLAND FRUIT SALAD

Yield: 8 servings.

I like to serve this side with any breakfast main dish. With pina colada yogurt and toasted coconut, the fruit medley brings a hint of the tropics to the table.

krista frank // rhododendron, oregon

- **2 medium ripe bananas, sliced**
- **1 medium mango, peeled and cubed**
- **4 kiwifruit, peeled and cubed**
- **1 can (20 ounces) unsweetened pineapple tidbits, drained**
- **3/4 cup (6 ounces) reduced-fat pina colada yogurt**
- **1/2 cup flaked coconut, toasted**

In a large serving bowl, combine the bananas, mango, kiwi, pineapple and yogurt; toss to coat. Sprinkle with coconut. Serve with a slotted spoon.

Nutrition Facts: 1/2 cup equals 134 calories, 3 g fat (2 g saturated fat), 1 mg cholesterol, 37 mg sodium, 27 g carbohydrate, 4 g fiber, 3 g protein. Diabetic Exchanges: 2 fruit, 1/2 fat.

tasteofhome COOKING SCHOOL SECRET

TASTE THE TROPICS WITH MANGOES

Juicy and sweet, mangoes add exotic flavor and beautiful, bright orange color to fruit smoothies, salads and desserts. Keep these tips in mind when purchasing mangoes:

- Choose plump fruit with a sweet, fruity fragrance. Avoid those that are bruised or very soft.

- Ripe mangoes have green-yellow skin with a pronounced red blush; unripened mangoes are firm and green with just a hint of red.

- To ripen a mango, let it stand at room temperature and out of sunlight. Once ripened, refrigerate the mango.

- Though they are available year-round, you can get the lowest prices during the height of summer, when mangoes are in season.

BLUEBERRY OATMEAL

Yield: 2 servings.

I love homemade oatmeal, and this comforting breakfast dish tastes more like dessert. It's good for you, too.
lesley robeson // casper, wyoming

- 1-3/4 cups 2% milk
- 1 cup quick-cooking oats
- 1/8 teaspoon salt
- 1/3 cup packed brown sugar
- 1/2 teaspoon ground cinnamon
- 3/4 cup fresh or frozen unsweetened blueberries, thawed

In a small saucepan, bring milk to a boil. Stir in oats and salt. Cook over medium heat for 1-2 minutes or until thickened, stirring occasionally. Stir in brown sugar and cinnamon. Divide between two serving bowls; top with blueberries.

Nutrition Facts: 1 cup equals 455 calories, 7 g fat (3 g saturated fat), 16 mg cholesterol, 271 mg sodium, 89 g carbohydrate, 7 g fiber, 13 g protein.

RASPBERRY OATMEAL: Substitute 3/4 cup raspberries for the blueberries.

MY FAVORITE GRANOLA

Yield: 4 cups.

I first made this granola when I was a teenager, and I have never since found a granola I like as much. I sometimes add fresh fruit to it, but it's also delicious just as it is.
sarah wilson // republic, washington

- 2-1/2 cups old-fashioned oats
- 1/2 cup flaked coconut
- 1/3 cup chopped walnuts
- 1/3 cup sunflower kernels
- 2 tablespoons toasted wheat germ
- 1/4 teaspoon salt
- 1/3 cup water
- 1/3 cup canola oil
- 3 tablespoons brown sugar
- 2 tablespoons honey

In a large bowl, combine the first six ingredients; set aside. In a small saucepan, combine the water, oil, brown sugar and honey. Cook and stir over medium heat for 2-3 minutes or until heated through. Pour over oat mixture and toss to coat.

Transfer to a greased 15-in. x 10-in. x 1-in. baking pan. Bake at 300° for 30-40 minutes or until golden brown, stirring once. Cool on a wire rack. Store in an airtight container.

Nutrition Facts: 1/2 cup equals 311 calories, 19 g fat (3 g saturated fat), 0 cholesterol, 115 mg sodium, 32 g carbohydrate, 4 g fiber, 7 g protein.

CHILI 'N' CHEESE GRITS

Yield: 6-8 servings.

Although I live in the city, I'm really a country cook at heart. Most of our friends laugh about eating grits, but they're pleasantly surprised when they try my recipe.
rosemary west // las vegas, nevada

- 2 **cups water**
- 2 **cups milk**
- 1 **cup grits**
- 2 **egg yolks**
- 1 **cup (4 ounces) shredded cheddar cheese,** *divided*
- 1/4 **cup butter, cubed**
- 1 **can (4 ounces) chopped green chilies, drained**
- 1 **teaspoon salt**

In a large saucepan, bring water and milk to a boil. Add grits; cook and stir over medium heat for 5 minutes or until thickened.

In a small bowl, beat egg yolks. Stir a small amount of hot grits into yolks; return all to the pan, stirring constantly.

Add 3/4 cup cheese, butter, chilies and salt. Pour into a greased 1-1/2-qt. baking dish. Sprinkle with remaining cheese. Bake, uncovered, at 350° for 30-35 minutes or until a thermometer reads 160°.

Nutrition Facts: 1-1/2 cups equals 228 calories, 13 g fat (8 g saturated fat), 92 mg cholesterol, 526 mg sodium, 20 g carbohydrate, 1 g fiber, 8 g protein.

taste of home
COOKING SCHOOL SECRET

GIVE GRITS A GO!

Nutritious and satisfying, grits are a long-beloved staple in Southern cooking. Introduce them to your table with ideas like these:

- Cook the grits according to package directions and, as in the South, top them with a simple pat of butter.
- Stir grated Parmesan cheese, salt and pepper into cooked grits for an Italian-inspired take on the classic.
- For richness, cook the grits with milk or stir a little Mascarpone cheese or heavy cream into your grits.
- Stir crumbled cooked breakfast sausage into the grits; season to taste with hot sauce. Serve alongside your favorite eggs.
- Grits don't have to be just for breakfast. Serve the Chili 'n' Cheese Grits with Honey Grilled Shrimp (page 177) or Chicken with Country Gravy (page 132) for an unforgettable Southern dinner.

BUSY DAY BACON MUFFINS

CHEAT IT!

Yield: 9 muffins.

Tender and filled with the irresistible flavor of bacon, these simple muffins will disappear in a hurry. Serve them with breakfast, soup or a salad.
gracie shrader // trenton, georgia

- 6 **bacon strips, diced**
- 2 **cups biscuit/baking mix**
- 2 **tablespoons sugar**
- 1 **egg**
- 2/3 **cup milk**

Cook bacon according to package directions; drain. Meanwhile, in a large bowl, combine biscuit mix and sugar. In a small bowl, combine egg and milk. Stir into dry ingredients just until moistened. Fold in bacon.

Fill greased muffin cups three-fourths full. Bake at 400° for 13-15 minutes or until a toothpick inserted near the center comes out clean. Serve warm.

Nutrition Facts: 1 muffin equals 161 calories, 7 g fat (2 g saturated fat), 30 mg cholesterol, 448 mg sodium, 20 g carbohydrate, trace fiber, 5 g protein.

BREAKFAST IN BREAD

Yield: 1 loaf.

I enjoy making this delicious bread since it's very easy and a nice change of pace from sweet quick breads. It's a never-fail treat that my friends always enjoy.
joyce brown // warner robins, georgia

- 6 **eggs**
- 3/4 **cup milk**
- 1-1/2 **cups all-purpose flour**
- 2-1/2 **teaspoons baking powder**
- 1/2 **teaspoon salt**
- 6 **bacon strips, cooked and crumbled**
- 1 **cup diced fully cooked ham**
- 1 **cup** *each* **shredded Monterey Jack, Swiss and sharp cheddar cheese**

In a large bowl, beat eggs until foamy. Stir in milk. Combine the flour, baking powder and salt. Gradually add to egg mixture and mix well. Stir in bacon, ham and cheese. Pour into a greased 9-in. x 5-in. loaf pan.

Bake at 350° for 50-60 minutes or until a toothpick inserted near the center comes out clean. Serve warm.

Nutrition Facts: 1 slice equals 324 calories, 18 g fat (10 g saturated fat), 192 mg cholesterol, 735 mg sodium, 19 g carbohydrate, 1 g fiber, 20 g protein.

BANANA PANCAKE FOR ONE

Yield: 1 pancake.

Get a delicious start to the day with this tender and hearty pancake. Try coconut or almond extract in place of the vanilla. carmen bolar // bronx, new york

- 1/4 **cup plus 1 tablespoon all-purpose flour**
- 1/2 **teaspoon baking powder**
- 1 **medium ripe banana, mashed**
- 1 **egg, lightly beaten**
- 1/2 **teaspoon vanilla extract**

Maple syrup or spreadable fruit, optional

In a small bowl, combine the flour and baking powder. Combine the banana, egg and vanilla; stir into the dry ingredients just until moistened.

Pour batter onto a hot griddle coated with cooking spray; turn when bubbles form on top. Cook until the second side is golden brown. Serve with syrup or spreadable fruit if desired.

Nutrition Facts: 1 pancake equals 323 calories, 6 g fat (2 g saturated fat), 212 mg cholesterol, 272 mg sodium, 57 g carbohydrate, 4 g fiber, 12 g protein.

SAVORY APPLE-CHICKEN SAUSAGE

Yield: 8 patties.

These easy-to-make sausage patties taste great and make an elegant brunch dish. The recipe is easily doubled or tripled for a crowd, and the sausage freezes well whether it's cooked or raw.
angela buchanan // longmont, colorado

- 1 **large tart apple, peeled and diced**
- 2 **teaspoons poultry seasoning**
- 1 **teaspoon salt**
- 1/4 **teaspoon pepper**
- 1 **pound ground chicken**

In a large bowl, combine the apple, poultry seasoning, salt and pepper. Crumble chicken over mixture and mix well. Shape into eight 3-in. patties.

In a large skillet coated with cooking spray, cook patties over medium heat for 5-6 minutes on each side or until a meat thermometer reads 165° and juices run clear.

Nutrition Facts: 1 sausage patty equals 92 calories, 5 g fat (1 g saturated fat), 38 mg cholesterol, 328 mg sodium, 4 g carbohydrate, 1 g fiber, 9 g protein. Diabetic Exchange: 1 medium-fat meat.

HIGH-RISE APPLE PANCAKE

Yield: 2 servings.

If you want to fix something special for a weekend breakfast or Sunday brunch, whip up this delicious pancake filled with warm cinnamon-sugar apple slices.
wanda nelson // woodruff, wisconsin

- 1/4 **cup all-purpose flour**
- 1/4 **cup 2% milk**
- 1 **egg, lightly beaten**
- 1-1/2 **teaspoons plus 2 tablespoons sugar,** *divided*
- 1/8 **teaspoon salt**
- 1-1/2 **teaspoons plus 2 tablespoons butter,** *divided*
- 3 **cups chopped peeled apples**
- 1/8 **teaspoon ground cinnamon**

In a small bowl, whisk the flour, milk, egg, 1-1/2 teaspoons sugar and salt until smooth.

Place 1-1/2 teaspoons butter in a 7-in. pie plate; place in a 400° oven for 2-3 minutes or until melted. Pour batter into pan. Bake for 18-20 minutes or until the edges are lightly browned.

Meanwhile, in a saucepan, melt the remaining butter over medium heat. Saute the apples, cinnamon and remaining sugar until apples are tender. Spoon into pancake. Serve immediately.

Nutrition Facts: 1 serving equals 390 calories, 18 g fat (10 g saturated fat), 147 mg cholesterol, 339 mg sodium, 54 g carbohydrate, 4 g fiber, 6 g protein.

taste of home COOKING SCHOOL SECRET

PUFF PANCAKES IMPRESS!

The High-Rise Apple Pancake will puff up beautifully golden brown in the oven, then quickly fall once it's removed. Topped with sweet-spiced apples, it makes a special breakfast for two.

Also known as Dutch babies, puff pancakes can be topped with a variety of fruits. Or simply sprinkle the pancake with confectioners' sugar and a bit of lemon juice. Either way, these gorgeous cakes are as impressive as a souffle without the work and worry!

To make a larger Dutch baby, double the batter and bake the pancake in a 9-in. pie plate.

PANCAKES ON THE GO

Yield: about 9 pancakes.

Brown sugar wakes up your taste buds while oats add stick-to-your-ribs texture to carry you through until lunchtime. These pancakes are so nicely sweet, they don't need syrup.
karen ann bland // gove, kansas

- 1/2 **cup all-purpose flour**
- 1/2 **cup whole wheat flour**
- 1/2 **cup plus 2 tablespoons quick-cooking oats**
- 1/3 **cup packed brown sugar**
- 1/2 **teaspoon baking soda**
- 1/2 **teaspoon salt**
- 1 **egg**
- 1-1/3 **cups buttermilk**
- 2 **tablespoons canola oil**

In a large bowl, combine the first six ingredients. In another bowl, whisk the egg, buttermilk and oil; gradually stir into dry ingredients and mix well.

Pour batter by 1/3 cupfuls onto a lightly greased hot griddle; turn when bubbles form on top of pancakes. Cook until the second side is golden brown.

Nutrition Facts: 2 pancakes equals 269 calories, 8 g fat (2 g saturated fat), 45 mg cholesterol, 450 mg sodium, 42 g carbohydrate, 3 g fiber, 8 g protein.

>> HOW TO:

PREPARE PANCAKES

1 Use a measuring cup to pour batter onto a hot griddle or skillet, 5-6 in. apart, making sure to leave enough room between pancakes for expansion.

2 Turn pancakes over when edges become dry and bubbles that appear on top begin to pop.

OVERNIGHT RAISIN FRENCH TOAST

Yield: 12 servings.

I love the convenience of make-ahead recipes, and this is one I turn to all the time. I like to sprinkle cinnamon and sugar on top before serving.

stephanie weaver // sligo, pennsylvania

  1 loaf (1 pound) cinnamon-raisin bread, cubed
  1 package (8 ounces) cream cheese, cubed
  8 eggs
1-1/2 cups half-and-half cream
  1/2 cup sugar
  1/2 cup maple syrup
  2 tablespoons vanilla extract
  1 tablespoon ground cinnamon
  1/8 teaspoon ground nutmeg

Place half of the bread cubes in a greased 13-in. x 9-in. baking dish. Top with cream cheese and remaining bread. In a large bowl, whisk the remaining ingredients. Pour over top. Cover and refrigerate overnight.

Remove from the refrigerator 30 minutes before baking. Cover and bake at 350° for 30 minutes. Uncover; bake 15-20 minutes longer or until a knife inserted near the center comes out clean.

Nutrition Facts: 1 piece equals 305 calories, 14 g fat (7 g saturated fat), 177 mg cholesterol, 197 mg sodium, 36 g carbohydrate, 3 g fiber, 10 g protein.

BEAR'S BREAKFAST BURRITOS

Yield: 12 servings.

Everyone loves these hearty burritos. It's so convenient to freeze some and bake them for a lazy Saturday morning breakfast.

larry & sandy kelley // grangeville, idaho

  2 packages (22-1/2 ounces *each*) frozen hash brown patties
 15 eggs
  2 tablespoons chili powder
  2 tablespoons garlic salt
  1 tablespoon ground cumin
1/2 pound uncooked chorizo *or* bulk spicy pork sausage
  6 jalapeno peppers, seeded and minced
  1 large green pepper, chopped
  1 large sweet red pepper, chopped
  1 large onion, chopped
  1 bunch green onions, chopped
  3 cups salsa
 12 flour tortillas (12 inches), warmed
  4 cups (16 ounces) shredded Monterey Jack cheese

Sour cream, optional

Cook hash browns according to package directions; crumble and keep warm. Meanwhile, in a large bowl, whisk the eggs, chili powder, garlic and cumin. Set aside.

Crumble chorizo into a large skillet; add the jalapenos, peppers and onions. Cook and stir over medium heat until meat is no longer pink; drain. Add reserved egg mixture; cook and stir over medium heat until eggs are set. Stir in salsa.

Spoon 1/2 cup hash browns and 1/2 cup egg mixture off center on each tortilla; sprinkle with 1/3 cup cheese. Fold sides and ends over filling and roll up. Wrap each burrito in waxed paper and foil. Serve warm with sour cream if desired. Cool remaining burritos to room temperature; freeze for up to 1 month.

TO USE FROZEN BURRITOS: Remove foil and waxed paper. Place burritos 2 in. apart on an ungreased baking sheet. Bake, uncovered, at 350° for 50-55 minutes or until heated through.

EDITOR'S NOTE: We recommend wearing disposable gloves when cutting hot peppers. Avoid touching your face.

Nutrition Facts: 1 burrito equals 584 calories, 27 g fat (12 g saturated fat), 290 mg cholesterol, 2,151 mg sodium, 58 g carbohydrate, 9 g fiber, 27 g protein.

PEAR-MASCARPONE FRENCH TOAST

Yield: 8 servings.

My twist on French toast features a spiced pear and cheese filling. This dish is great for Sunday breakfast or brunch with the family and is elegant enough for company. emily butler // canton, ohio

2 **medium pears, peeled and finely chopped**	1/8 **teaspoon plus** 1/4 **teaspoon ground cinnamon,** *divided*
4 **tablespoons butter,** *divided*	8 **slices French bread (1 inch thick)**
1 **carton (8 ounces) Mascarpone cheese**	4 **eggs**
2 **tablespoons sugar**	3/4 **cup milk**
2 **teaspoons minced fresh gingerroot**	1/4 **teaspoon vanilla extract**
	Maple syrup, optional

In a small saucepan, cook pears in 1 tablespoon butter over medium heat for 2-3 minutes or just until tender. Remove from the heat; cool completely. In a small bowl, beat cheese. Stir in the sugar, ginger, 1/8 teaspoon cinnamon and pears. Cut a pocket in the side of each slice of bread. Carefully fill each pocket with about 1/4 cup of pear mixture.

In a shallow bowl, whisk the eggs, milk, vanilla and remaining cinnamon. Carefully dip both sides of bread in egg mixture (be careful not to squeeze out filling).

In a large skillet, melt remaining butter over medium heat. Cook stuffed bread on both sides until golden brown. Serve with syrup if desired.

Nutrition Facts: 1 serving equals 321 calories, 23 g fat (12 g saturated fat), 159 mg cholesterol, 238 mg sodium, 23 g carbohydrate, 2 g fiber, 8 g protein.

EGGS BENEDICT CASSEROLE

Yield: 12 servings (1-2/3 cups sauce).

Here's a dish as special as eggs Benedict, but without the fuss. Simply assemble it the night before. The hollandaise is surprisingly easy, and it holds up well.
sandie heindel // liberty, missouri

3/4	pound Canadian bacon, chopped
6	English muffins, split and cut up
8	eggs
2	cups 2% milk
1	teaspoon onion powder
1/4	teaspoon paprika
4	egg yolks
1/2	cup heavy whipping cream
2	tablespoons lemon juice
1	teaspoon Dijon mustard
1/2	cup butter, melted

Place half of the bacon in a greased 13-in. x 9-in. baking dish; top with English muffins and remaining bacon. In a large bowl, whisk the eggs, milk and onion powder; pour over the top. Cover and refrigerate overnight.

Remove from the refrigerator 30 minutes before baking. Sprinkle with paprika. Cover and bake at 375° for 35 minutes. Uncover; bake 10-15 minutes longer or until a knife inserted near the center comes out clean.

In a double boiler or metal bowl over simmering water, constantly whisk the egg yolks, cream, lemon juice and mustard until mixture reaches 160° or is thick enough to coat the back of a spoon. Reduce heat to low. Slowly drizzle in warm melted butter, whisking constantly. Serve immediately.

Nutrition Facts: 1 serving with about 2 tablespoons sauce equals 286 calories, 19 g fat (10 g saturated fat), 256 mg cholesterol, 535 mg sodium, 16 g carbohydrate, 1 g fiber, 14 g protein.

>> HOW TO:

JUDGE DONENESS OF HOLLANDAISE

Egg-rich sauces and custards are fully cooked when the mixture is thickened and coats the back of a spoon. To determine doneness, dip a spoon in the mixture and run your finger across the back of the spoon. The cooked mixture will hold a firm line and not run down onto the stripe you've made. A mixture that's not fully cooked will be too thin to hold the line.

BAKING

BANANA CHOCOLATE CHIP COOKIES

Yield: 3 dozen.

These soft cookies have a cake-like texture and lots of banana flavor that folks will absolutely love.

vicki raatz // waterloo, wisconsin

- 1/3 **cup butter, softened**
- 1/2 **cup sugar**
-   1 **egg**
- 1/2 **cup mashed ripe banana**
- 1/2 **teaspoon vanilla extract**
-   1 **cup all-purpose flour**
-   1 **teaspoon baking powder**
- 1/4 **teaspoon salt**
- 1/8 **teaspoon baking soda**
-   1 **cup (6 ounces) semisweet chocolate chips**

In a small bowl, cream butter and sugar until light and fluffy. Beat in the egg, banana and vanilla. Combine the flour, baking powder, salt and baking soda; gradually add to creamed mixture and mix well. Stir in chocolate chips.

Drop by tablespoonfuls 2 in. apart onto baking sheets coated with cooking spray. Bake at 350° for 9-11 minutes or until edges are lightly browned. Remove to wire racks to cool.

Nutrition Facts: 1 cookie equals 66 calories, 3 g fat (2 g saturated fat), 10 mg cholesterol, 51 mg sodium, 9 g carbohydrate, trace fiber, 1 g protein. Diabetic Exchanges: 1/2 starch, 1/2 fat.

>> HOW TO:

SHAPE DROP COOKIES (TWO METHODS)

1 Fill a teaspoon or tablespoon with dough. Use another spoon or small rubber spatula to push the mound of dough off the spoon onto a cool baking sheet. Place dough 2 to 3 in. apart or as recipe directs.

2 An ice cream scoop is a perfect utensil for making uniformly sized drop cookies. (A 1 tablespoon-sized ice cream scoop will result in a standard-size 2-in. cookie.) Just scoop the dough, even off the top with a flat-edge metal spatula and release onto a baking sheet.

10 TIPS FOR BAKING SUCCESS

The aroma and fantastic flavor of fresh-baked breads, coffee cakes and cookies just can't be beat. With a little practice, you'll find that baking can be a real pleasure. Family and friends will feel pampered enjoying your sensational creations. In this chapter, you'll find chip-packed cookies, gooey brownies, tempting breakfast treats, tender yeast breads and so much more! Follow these pointers to ensure baking success every time.

1. READING IS FUNDAMENTAL

Read the entire recipe before you begin. If you are not familiar with a technique or term, refer to a cooking reference or search for information on the Internet. Visit *tasteofhome.com* for how-to videos, articles and tips on baking.

3. PREP INGREDIENTS BEFORE MIXING

Prepare all the ingredients. Let butter soften, separate eggs, chop nuts, etc.

Too firm—butter is too hard to cream.

Butter is softened just right.

2. CHECK OUT INGREDIENTS

Assemble all of the ingredients for the recipe.

Gather all the ingredients before you begin. If you're missing an ingredient, look at the Ingredient Substitutions chart on the inside back cover of this book. You may have a substitution. If not, a trip to the store will be necessary.

4. GET THE OVEN READY

Position oven rack before preheating the oven.

Position the oven rack so the baking pan will be in center of the oven, or position the oven rack as the recipe directs. Preheat the oven. For yeast breads, preheat the oven during the final rise time.

5. SELECT AND PREP PANS

Use the type of pan and the size of pan stated in the recipe. Generally, pans are filled two-thirds to three-fourths full.

This pan is too full.

Use an 8-in. x 4-in. x 2-in. loaf pan filled two-thirds plus a muffin pan for extra batter, a larger 9-in. x 5-in. x 3-in. loaf pan or several 5-3/4-in. x 3-in. x 2-in. loaf pans.

Grease the pan as the recipe directs with shortening or cooking spray.

Grease and flour the pan if the recipe directs. For yeast breads, prepare pans before shaping the dough.

6. MEASURE WITH PRECISION

Accurately measure the ingredients. Use a liquid measuring cup for wet ingredients, such as milk, honey, molasses, corn syrup, water, juice or oil. Before measuring sticky ingredients like molasses or corn syrup, coat the inside of the measuring tool with cooking spray. This will make cleanup easier.

Check level of liquid at your eye level.

Fill dry ingredients to the rim and sweep off excess with the flat edge of a metal spatula or knife.

Dry measuring cups allow ingredients to be measured right to the rim of the cup. They are used to measure dry and packable ingredients like flour, sugar, chocolate chips, nuts, shortening and sour cream.

Wet and dry ingredients should be filled to the rim of the spoon.

Measuring spoons are used to measure both liquid and dry ingredients. It's nice to have two sets when baking. Use one set for measuring the liquid ingredients and the other for dry.

7. MIX IT UP

Follow the mixing directions as they are written. Altering the method may affect how the final baked good looks and/or tastes.

Cream until light and fluffy.

Fold lighter-weight ingredients into heavier ones with a rubber spatula.

Use a sturdy wooden spoon to stir chips, nuts and dried fruit into heavy batters.

8. START THE TIMER

Most recipes give a range for the baking time. Set a kitchen timer for the low end of the time range immediately after the food has been placed in the oven.

Set the timer for the shortest time given in the recipe.

9. CHECK DONENESS

Check for doneness at the shortest time given in the recipe using the stated doneness test. If the baked good does not test done, continue baking and check again.

The toothpick is clean; the cake is done.

The toothpick has crumbs on it; the cake needs more baking time.

10. TAKE TIME TO COOL OFF

A wire rack is used for cooling baked goods because it allows air to circulate around the food, which prevents moist, soggy spots. Many cookies can be immediately removed from the baking pan to a wire rack.

Carefully transfer to wire rack to cool.

Cool most baked goods for 10 minutes before removing from the pan.

Other foods like cakes and quick bread loaves need to rest for 10 minutes in their pan. The resting time helps prevent these items from crumbling when they are removed. Still other items—angel food cakes and chiffon cakes baked in tube pans—are cooled completely in their pan. Some baked goods are delicious warm, but others need to be cooled completely for frosting or easy slicing.

CHOCOLATE LOVER'S DREAM COOKIES

Yield: 3-1/2 dozen.

These rich chocolate cookies with white chocolate chips are scrumptious.

paula zsiray // logan, utah

- 6   **tablespoons canola oil**
- 1/4 **cup butter, softened**
- 3/4 **cup packed brown sugar**
- 1/2 **cup sugar**
- 2   **eggs**
- 1   **teaspoon vanilla extract**
- 1-1/4 **cups all-purpose flour**
- 1/2 **cup baking cocoa**
- 1/4 **teaspoon baking powder**
- 1   **cup white baking chips**
- 1   **cup (6 ounces) semisweet chocolate chips**

In a large bowl, beat the oil, butter and sugars until well blended. Add eggs, one at a time, beating well after each addition. Beat in vanilla. Combine the flour, cocoa and baking powder; gradually add to oil mixture and mix well. Stir in chips.

Drop by rounded tablespoonfuls 2 in. apart onto ungreased baking sheets. Bake at 350° for 12-15 minutes or until edges begin to brown. Cool for 1 minute before removing from pans to wire racks.

Nutrition Facts: 1 cookie equals 112 calories, 6 g fat (3 g saturated fat), 14 mg cholesterol, 19 mg sodium, 15 g carbohydrate, 1 g fiber, 1 g protein.

CHOCOLATE PECAN COOKIES: Omit white baking chips. Stir in 1 cup chopped pecans along with the semisweet chips.

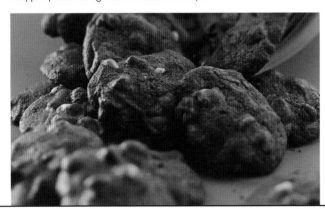

CHEWY OATMEAL COOKIES

Yield: about 5 dozen.

I packed chocolate chips, raisins, nuts and cinnamon into my oatmeal cookies. Our kids love them!

janis plageman // lynden, washington

- 1   **cup butter, softened**
- 1   **cup sugar**
- 1   **cup packed brown sugar**
- 2   **eggs**
- 1   **tablespoon molasses**
- 2   **teaspoons vanilla extract**
- 2   **cups all-purpose flour**
- 2   **cups quick-cooking oats**
- 1-1/2 **teaspoon baking soda**
- 1   **teaspoon ground cinnamon**
- 1/2 **teaspoon salt**
- 1   **cup *each* raisins and chopped pecans**
- 1   **cup (6 ounces) semisweet chocolate chips**

In a large bowl, cream butter and sugars until light and fluffy. Add the eggs, molasses and vanilla; beat well. Combine the flour, oats, baking soda, cinnamon and salt; gradually add to creamed mixture and mix well. Stir in the raisins, pecans and chocolate chips. Drop by tablespoonfuls 2 in. apart onto greased baking sheets.

Bake at 350° for 9-10 minutes or until lightly browned. Cool for 2 minutes before removing to a wire rack.

Nutrition Facts: 1 cookie equals 103 calories, 4 g fat (3 g saturated fat), 15 mg cholesterol, 77 mg sodium, 16 g carbohydrate, 1 g fiber, 1 g protein.

ROCKY ROAD BROWNIES

Yield: 2-1/2 dozen.

When my daughter was in college, she kept a batch of these fudgy brownies around when studying for final exams. With a blend of chocolate chips, marshmallows and nuts, they always earn high marks! phyllis crawford // natrona heights, pennsylvania

- 4 ounces unsweetened chocolate, chopped
- 1 cup butter, cubed
- 2 cups sugar
- 4 eggs
- 1 teaspoon vanilla extract
- 1 cup all-purpose flour
- 2 cups miniature marshmallows
- 1 cup chopped pecans *or* walnuts
- 1-1/2 cups semisweet chocolate chips, *divided*

In a microwave, melt unsweetened chocolate and butter; stir until smooth. Cool.

In a large bowl, beat the sugar, eggs, vanilla and chocolate mixture until smooth. Add flour and mix well. Fold in marshmallows, nuts and 1/2 cup chocolate chips.

Spread into a greased 13-in. x 9-in. baking pan. Sprinkle with remaining chocolate chips. Bake at 350° for 40-45 minutes or until top is set. Cool on a wire rack. Cut into bars.

Nutrition Facts: 1 brownie equals 214 calories, 13 g fat (6 g saturated fat), 45 mg cholesterol, 73 mg sodium, 25 g carbohydrate, 1 g fiber, 2 g protein.

JUMBO CHOCOLATE CHIP COOKIES

Yield: 1 dozen.

These cookies are sure to impress anyone you serve them to. The white candy coating adds a wonderful flavor and makes them look so delicious. jackie ruckwardt // cottage grove, oregon

- 1/2 cup butter, softened
- 1/2 cup sugar
- 1/2 cup packed brown sugar
- 1 egg
- 1 teaspoon vanilla extract
- 1-1/4 cups all-purpose flour
- 1/2 teaspoon baking soda
- 1/2 teaspoon baking powder
- 1/2 teaspoon salt
- 1-1/3 cups flaked coconut
- 1/2 cup semisweet chocolate chips
- 1/4 cup milk chocolate chips
- 2-1/2 ounces white candy coating, optional

In a large bowl, cream butter and sugars until light and fluffy. Beat in egg and vanilla. Combine the flour, baking soda, baking powder and salt; gradually add to creamed mixture and mix well. Stir in coconut and chips. Shape 3 tablespoonfuls of dough into a ball; repeat with remaining dough.

Place balls 3 in. apart on ungreased baking sheets. Bake at 350° for 12-18 minutes or until lightly browned. Remove to wire racks to cool.

In a microwave, melt candy coating if desired. Dip one end of cooled cookies in candy coating. Allow excess to drip off. Place on waxed paper; let stand until set.

Nutrition Facts: 1 cookie equals 292 calories, 15 g fat (10 g saturated fat), 38 mg cholesterol, 261 mg sodium, 39 g carbohydrate, 1 g fiber, 3 g protein.

PEANUT BUTTER KISS COOKIES

Yield: 2 dozen.

These cookies are great for the little ones, and they keep adults guessing as to how they can be made with only five ingredients.
dee davis // sun city, arizona

- 1 **cup peanut butter**
- 1 **cup sugar**
- 1 **egg**
- 1 **teaspoon vanilla extract**
- 24 **milk chocolate kisses**

In a large bowl, cream peanut butter and sugar until light and fluffy. Add the egg and vanilla; beat until blended.

Roll into 1-1/4-in. balls. Place 2 in. apart on ungreased baking sheets. Bake at 350° for 10-12 minutes or until the tops are slightly cracked.

Immediately press one chocolate kiss into the center of each cookie. Cool for 5 minutes before removing from pans to wire racks.

EDITOR'S NOTE: This recipe does not contain flour. Reduced-fat or generic brands of peanut butter are not recommended for this recipe.

Nutrition Facts: 1 cookie equals 123 calories, 7 g fat (2 g saturated fat), 10 mg cholesterol, 57 mg sodium, 13 g carbohydrate, 1 g fiber, 3 g protein.

GINGERBREAD SANDWICH TREES

Yield: 2 dozen.

Fun and festive, these cookie sandwich trees are an easy holiday treat!
steve foy // kirkwood, missouri

3/4 **cup butter, softened**	1-1/4 **teaspoons ground ginger**
1 **cup packed brown sugar**	1/4 **teaspoon salt**
1 **egg**	**M&M's miniature baking bits**
3/4 **cup molasses**	3/4 **cup vanilla frosting**
4 **cups all-purpose flour**	1/4 **cup confectioners' sugar**
3 **teaspoons pumpkin pie spice**	**Green food coloring, optional**
1-1/2 **teaspoons baking soda**	

In a large bowl, cream butter and brown sugar until light and fluffy. Add egg and molasses. Combine the flour, pumpkin pie spice, baking soda, ginger and salt; gradually add to creamed mixture and mix well. Cover and refrigerate for 2 hours or until easy to handle.

On a lightly floured surface, roll dough to 1/8-in. thickness. Cut with a floured 3-in. tree shaped cookie cutter. Place 2 in. apart on ungreased baking sheets. Gently press baking bits into half of the cookies.

Bake at 325° for 8-10 minutes or until edges are firm. Remove to wire racks to cool completely.

In a small bowl, combine frosting and confectioners' sugar until smooth; tint green if desired. Spread over the bottoms of plain cookies; top with decorated cookies.

Nutrition Facts: 1 cookie (calculated without M&M's miniature baking bits) equals 236 calories, 8 g fat (4 g saturated fat), 24 mg cholesterol, 174 mg sodium, 39 g carbohydrate, 1 g fiber, 2 g protein.

CRANBERRY SWIRL BISCOTTI

Yield: about 2-1/2 dozen.

A friend of mine who is known for her excellent cookies shared this recipe with me. These biscotti are so pretty, you'll want to give some as gifts. And they're delightful for entertaining served with either coffee or tea.

lisa kilcup // gig harbor, washington

- 2/3 cup dried cranberries
- 1/2 cup cherry preserves
- 1/2 teaspoon ground cinnamon
- 1/2 cup butter, softened
- 2/3 cup sugar
- 2 eggs
- 1 teaspoon vanilla extract
- 2-1/4 cups all-purpose flour
- 3/4 teaspoon baking powder
- 1/4 teaspoon salt

GLAZE:

- 3/4 cup confectioners' sugar
- 1 tablespoon 2% milk
- 2 teaspoons butter, melted
- 1 teaspoon almond extract

In a food processor, combine the cranberries, preserves and cinnamon. Cover and process until smooth; set aside.

In a large bowl, cream butter and sugar until light and fluffy. Beat in eggs and vanilla. Combine the flour, baking powder and salt; gradually add to creamed mixture and mix well.

Divide dough in half. On a lightly floured surface, roll each portion into a 12-in. x 8-in. rectangle. Spread each with cranberry filling; roll up jelly-roll style, starting with a short side.

Place seam side down 4 in. apart on a lightly greased baking sheet. Bake at 325° for 25-30 minutes or until lightly browned.

Carefully transfer logs to a cutting board; cool for 5 minutes. With a serrated knife, cut into 1/2-in. slices. Place 2 in. apart on lightly greased baking sheets. Bake 15 minutes longer or until centers are firm and dry. Remove to wire racks.

In a small bowl, combine glaze ingredients; drizzle over warm biscotti. Cool completely. Store in an airtight container.

Nutrition Facts: 1 cookie equals 120 calories, 4 g fat (2 g saturated fat), 23 mg cholesterol, 58 mg sodium, 20 g carbohydrate, trace fiber, 1 g protein.

>> HOW TO:

CHECK QUICK BREADS FOR DONENESS

Insert a toothpick near the center of the bread. If the toothpick comes out clean—without any crumbs—the bread is done.

ZUCCHINI BREAD

Yield: 2 loaves (12 slices each).

I like this bread because it's lighter and fluffier than most zucchini breads. Plus, it's a great way to put that abundant vegetable to good use!
kevin bruckerhoff // columbia, missouri

- 2 cups sugar
- 1 cup canola oil
- 3 eggs
- 2 teaspoons vanilla extract
- 3 cups all-purpose flour
- 1 teaspoon salt
- 1 teaspoon baking soda
- 1/4 teaspoon baking powder
- 1 teaspoon ground cinnamon
- 2 cups shredded zucchini (about 2 medium)
- 1/2 cup chopped nuts
- 1 teaspoon grated lemon peel

In a large bowl, beat the sugar, oil, eggs and vanilla until well blended. Combine the flour, salt, baking soda, baking powder and cinnamon; stir into sugar mixture just until moistened. Stir in the zucchini, nuts and lemon peel.

Transfer to two greased 8-in. x 4-in. loaf pans. Bake at 350° for 55-65 minutes or until a toothpick inserted near the center comes out clean. Cool for 10 minutes before removing from pans to wire racks to cool completely.

Nutrition Facts: 1 slice equals 229 calories, 11 g fat (1 g saturated fat), 26 mg cholesterol, 165 mg sodium, 29 g carbohydrate, 1 g fiber, 3 g protein.

MINI ZUCCHINI LOAVES: Transfer batter to four greased 5-3/4-in. x 3-in. x 2-in. loaf pans. Bake at 350° for 35-40 minutes or until a toothpick inserted near the center comes out clean. Cool as directed.

CHOCOLATE ZUCCHINI BREAD: Omit lemon peel and nuts. Reduce flour to 2-3/4 cups. Add 1/3 cup baking cocoa to flour mixture. Stir in 1 cup semisweet chocolate chips with zucchini. Bake as directed.

ZUCCHINI APPLE BREAD: Omit lemon peel. Reduce sugar to 1 cup; add 1 cup brown sugar. Add 1/4 teaspoon ground nutmeg with cinnamon. Reduce zucchini to 1-1/2 cups. Add 1 cup grated peeled tart apple with zucchini and nuts. Bake as directed.

IRISH SODA BREAD

Yield: 1 loaf (16 slices).

This tender loaf that's dotted with golden raisins is great any time of year, though it's popular on St. Patrick's Day. It also makes great toast in the morning.

carol fritz // fulton, illinois

- 4 **cups all-purpose flour**
- 1 **tablespoon sugar**
- 1-1/2 **teaspoons baking soda**
- 1 **teaspoon baking powder**
- 1/2 **teaspoon salt**
- 1/4 **cup cold butter**
- 1 **cup golden raisins**
- 1-3/4 **cups buttermilk**

In a large bowl, combine the flour, sugar, baking soda, baking powder and salt. Cut in butter until mixture resembles coarse crumbs. Add raisins. Stir in buttermilk just until moistened. Turn onto a lightly floured surface; gently knead 6-8 times.

Place on an ungreased baking sheet; pat into a 7-in. round loaf. Using a sharp knife, cut a 1-in. cross about 1/4 in. deep on top of the loaf. Bake at 375° for 40-45 minutes or until golden brown. Cool on a wire rack.

Nutrition Facts: 1 slice equals 181 calories, 3 g fat (2 g saturated fat) 9 mg cholesterol, 265 mg sodium, 33 g carbohydrate, 1 g fiber, 4 g protein. Diabetic Exchanges: 1-1/2 starch, 1/2 fruit, 1/2 fat.

GINGER CURRANT SCONES

Yield: 4 scones.

I add loads of currants to my flaky, attractive scones. Served warm with a drizzle of honey, these gingery treats are a welcome addition to breakfast or brunch.

sheila parker // reno, nevada

- 1-1/2 **cups all-purpose flour**
- 1/3 **cup sugar**
- 1 **teaspoon baking powder**
- 1/2 **teaspoon baking soda**
- 6 **tablespoons cold butter, cubed**
- 1/2 **cup buttermilk**
- 3/4 **cup dried currants**
- 1/2 **teaspoon minced fresh gingerroot**
- 2 **teaspoons honey**

In a small bowl, combine the flour, sugar, baking powder and baking soda. Cut in butter until mixture resembles coarse crumbs. Add buttermilk just until moistened. Stir in currants and ginger. Turn onto a floured surface; knead 10 times.

Pat or roll out to 1-in. thickness; cut with a floured 2-1/2-in. biscuit cutter. Place 2 in. apart on a baking sheet coated with cooking spray.

Bake at 375° for 20-25 minutes or until golden brown. Drizzle with honey. Serve warm.

Nutrition Facts: 1 scone equals 485 calories, 18 g fat (11 g saturated fat), 46 mg cholesterol, 414 mg sodium, 77 g carbohydrate, 3 g fiber, 7 g protein.

CHEESY PESTO BREAD

CHEAT IT!

Yield: 6-8 servings.

I topped a prebaked pizza crust with pesto and cheese for dinner one night when I was in a rush. Now it's expected whenever I make pasta and salad. It's great heated up for lunch the next day, too. karen grant // tulare, california

- 1 prebaked 12-inch pizza crust
- 3 tablespoons prepared pesto
- 1/8 teaspoon garlic salt
- 1 cup (4 ounces) shredded mozzarella cheese
- 1/2 cup shredded Parmesan cheese

Place crust on a pizza pan or baking sheet. Spread with pesto; sprinkle with garlic salt and cheeses. Bake at 325° for 12-15 minutes or until cheese is melted. Cut into wedges.

Nutrition Facts: 1 slice equals 221 calories, 10 g fat (4 g saturated fat), 17 mg cholesterol, 505 mg sodium, 22 g carbohydrate, 1 g fiber, 11 g protein.

JALAPENO CORN MUFFINS

Yield: 8 muffins.

Honey butter tastes so yummy spread over these hot and snappy muffins. They're delicious with soups, stews and chili. mary thomas // hugo, minnesota

- 1/2 cup all-purpose flour
- 1/2 cup cornmeal
- 4-1/2 teaspoons brown sugar
- 1/2 teaspoon baking powder
- 1/4 teaspoon salt
- 1/4 teaspoon baking soda
- Dash pepper
- 1 egg
- 1/3 cup sour cream
- 1/4 cup 2% milk
- 1 tablespoon canola oil
- 1 can (8-3/4 ounces) whole kernel corn, drained
- 1/2 to 1 jalapeno pepper, minced

HONEY BUTTER:

- 1/4 cup butter, softened
- 2 tablespoons honey

In a small bowl, combine the first seven ingredients. In another bowl, combine the egg, sour cream, milk and oil. Stir into dry ingredients just until moistened. Stir in corn and jalapeno.

Coat muffin cups with cooking spray; fill two-thirds full with batter. Bake at 400° for 14-16 minutes or until a toothpick comes out clean. Combine honey butter ingredients. Serve with muffins.

EDITOR'S NOTE: We recommend wearing disposable gloves when cutting hot peppers. Avoid touching your face

Nutrition Facts: 1 muffin with 2 teaspoons honey butter (prepared with reduced-fat sour cream and reduced-fat butter) equals 175 calories, 7 g fat (3 g saturated fat), 40 mg cholesterol, 277 mg sodium, 24 g carbohydrate, 1 g fiber, 4 g protein.

ZUCCHINI CHEDDAR BISCUITS

Yield: 16 biscuits.

My husband grows a big garden, and our squash crop always seems to multiply! We give squash to everyone but still have plenty left over for making jelly, relish, pickles, brownies and these delightful biscuits.

jean moore // pliny, west virginia

- 1 **large onion, chopped**
- 1/4 **cup butter**
- 2-1/2 **cups biscuit/baking mix**
- 1 **tablespoon minced fresh parsley**
- 1/2 **teaspoon dried basil**
- 1/2 **teaspoon dried thyme**
- 3 **eggs**
- 1/4 **cup 2% milk**
- 1-1/2 **cups shredded zucchini**
- 1 **cup (4 ounces) shredded cheddar cheese**

In a large skillet, saute onion in butter until tender. In a large bowl, combine the biscuit mix, parsley, basil, thyme and onion mixture. In another bowl. whisk eggs and milk. Stir into biscuit mixture just until combined. Fold in zucchini and cheese.

Drop by 1/4 cupfuls 2 in. apart onto greased baking sheets.

Bake at 400° for 10-14 minutes or until golden brown. Serve warm. Refrigerate leftovers.

Nutrition Facts: 1 biscuit equals 148 calories, 9 g fat (4 g saturated fat), 55 mg cholesterol, 315 mg sodium, 13 g carbohydrate, 1 g fiber, 4 g protein.

>> HOW TO:

MAKE MUFFINS

1 In a large bowl, combine the dry ingredients with a fork.

2 Beat the eggs and combine with the liquid ingredients.

3 Make a well in the dry ingredients and pour egg mixture into the well all at one time.

4 With a spoon or spatula, stir the ingredients together just until moistened. Fill greased or paper-lined muffin cups about two-thirds to three-fourths full, wiping off any spills.

5 Bake until golden or test for doneness by inserting a toothpick into the center of the muffin. If the toothpick comes out clean, the muffins are done. Cool for 5 minutes before removing from pan to a wire rack.

BLUEBERRY OATMEAL MUFFINS

Yield: 1 dozen.

These tender muffins are easy to eat on the go. Oats, blueberries and yogurt make them tasty and nutritious.

donna brockett // kingfisher, oklahoma

1-1/4 **cups all-purpose flour**	1/4 **teaspoon baking soda**
1 **cup quick-cooking oats**	1/4 **teaspoon ground nutmeg**
1/2 **cup packed brown sugar**	1 **egg, lightly beaten**
2 **teaspoons baking powder**	1 **cup (8 ounces) plain yogurt**
1/2 **teaspoon salt**	1/4 **cup butter, melted**
1/2 **teaspoon ground cinnamon**	1 **cup fresh blueberries**

In a large bowl, combine the first eight ingredients. Combine the egg, yogurt and butter; stir into dry ingredients just until moistened. Fold in blueberries.

Coat muffin cups with cooking spray or use paper liners; fill three-fourths full with batter. Bake at 400° for 18-22 minutes or until a toothpick inserted near the center comes out clean. Cool for 5 minutes before removing from pan to a wire rack. Serve warm.

Nutrition Facts: 1 muffin equals 167 calories, 6 g fat (3 g saturated fat), 31 mg cholesterol, 249 mg sodium, 26 g carbohydrate, 1 g fiber, 4 g protein. Diabetic Exchanges: 1-1/2 starch, 1 fat.

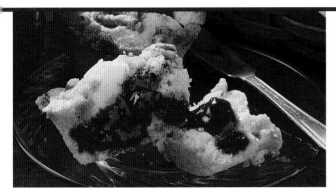

RASPBERRY STREUSEL MUFFINS

Yield: 1 dozen.

You can make these muffins in minutes for those unexpected guests, or for a quick breakfast or an afternoon snack.

rosemary smith // fort bragg, california

MUFFINS:

- 1-1/2 **cups all-purpose flour**
- 1/2 **cup sugar**
- 2 **teaspoons baking powder**
- 1/2 **cup milk**
- 1/2 **cup butter, melted**
- 1 **egg, lightly beaten**
- 1 **cup fresh *or* frozen raspberries, *divided***

PECAN STREUSEL TOPPING:

- 1/4 **cup chopped pecans**
- 1/4 **cup brown sugar**
- 1/4 **cup all-purpose flour**
- 2 **tablespoons butter, melted**

In a large bowl, combine the flour, sugar and baking powder. In a small bowl, combine the milk, butter and egg. Stir milk mixture into flour mixture just until moistened.

Spoon about 1 tablespoon batter into each of 12 greased muffin cups. Divide half of the raspberries among cups; top with remaining batter, then remaining raspberries.

For topping, combine ingredients until mixture resembles moist crumbs; sprinkle over muffins. Bake at 375° for 20-25 minutes or until a toothpick inserted near the center comes out clean. Let stand 5 minutes; carefully remove from pans. Serve warm.

Nutrition Facts: 1 muffin equals 234 calories, 12 g fat (6 g saturated fat), 45 mg cholesterol, 176 mg sodium, 29 g carbohydrate, 1 g fiber, 3 g protein.

PEACHY CHEESE DANISH

Yield: 4 servings.

I've prepared these rich sweet rolls for morning and late-night munching, but they're delicious any time.

carolyn kyzer // alexander, arkansas

- 1 **tube (8 ounces) refrigerated crescent rolls**
- 4 **ounces cream cheese, softened**
- 1/4 **cup sugar**
- 2 **tablespoons lemon juice**
- 8 **teaspoons peach preserves *or* flavor of your choice**

GLAZE:

- 1/4 **cup confectioners' sugar**
- 1/2 **teaspoon vanilla extract**
- 1 **to 2 teaspoons milk**

Separate dough into four rectangles; seal perforations. On a lightly floured surface, roll each into a 7-in. x 3-1/2-in. rectangle. In a small bowl, combine cream cheese, sugar and lemon juice until smooth; spread over rectangles. Roll up from a long side; pinch edges to seal. Holding one end, loosely coil each.

Place on an ungreased baking sheet. Top each coil with 2 teaspoons preserves. Bake at 350° for 15-20 minutes or until golden brown. Remove from pan to wire rack.

For glaze, in a small bowl, combine confectioners' sugar, vanilla and enough milk to achieve desired consistency. Drizzle over warm rolls.

Nutrition Facts: 1 pastry equals 435 calories, 22 g fat (9 g saturated fat), 31 mg cholesterol, 530 mg sodium, 52 g carbohydrate, trace fiber, 6 g protein.

HOMEMADE BAGELS

Yield: 1 dozen.

Instead of going to a bakery, head to the kitchen and surprise your family with homemade bagels. For variation and flavor, sprinkle the tops with cinnamon-sugar instead of sesame and poppy seeds. Or try stirring some cinnamon and raisins into the dough.

rebecca phillips // burlington, connecticut

- 1 teaspoon active dry yeast
- 1-1/4 cups warm milk (110° to 115°)
- 1/2 cup butter, softened
- 2 tablespoons sugar
- 1 teaspoon salt
- 1 egg yolk
- 3-3/4 to 4-1/4 cups all-purpose flour

Sesame or poppy seeds, optional

In a large bowl, dissolve yeast in warm milk. Add the butter, sugar, salt and egg yolk; mix well. Stir in enough flour to form a soft dough.

Turn onto a floured surface; knead until smooth and elastic, about 6-8 minutes. Place in a greased bowl, turning once to grease top. Cover and let rise in a warm place until doubled, about 1 hour.

Punch dough down. Shape into 12 balls. Push thumb through centers to form a 1-1/2-in. hole. Stretch and shape dough to form an even ring. Place on a floured surface. Cover and let rest for 10 minutes; flatten bagels slightly.

Fill a Dutch oven two-thirds full with water; bring to a boil. Drop bagels, two at a time, into boiling water. Cook for 45 seconds; turn and cook 45 seconds longer. Remove with a slotted spoon; drain well on paper towels.

Sprinkle with sesame or poppy seeds if desired. Place 2 in. apart on greased baking sheets. Bake at 400° for 20-25 minutes or until golden brown. Remove from pans to wire racks to cool completely.

Nutrition Facts: 1 bagel equals 239 calories, 9 g fat (5 g saturated fat), 42 mg cholesterol, 288 mg sodium, 33 g carbohydrate, 1 g fiber, 5 g protein.

NO-FRY DOUGHNUTS

Yield: 2 dozen.

I like making doughnuts when I don't have to clean up a greasy mess. You'll like making baked doughnuts, too!

susie baldwin // columbia, tennessee

- 2 packages (1/4 ounce *each*) active dry yeast
- 1/4 cup warm water (110° to 115°)
- 1-1/2 cups warm milk (110° to 115°)
- 1/3 cup shortening
- 1/2 cup sugar
- 2 eggs
- 1 teaspoon salt
- 1 teaspoon ground nutmeg
- 1/4 teaspoon ground cinnamon
- 4-1/2 to 5 cups all-purpose flour
- 1/4 cup butter, melted

GLAZE:

- 1/2 **cup butter**
- 2 **cups confectioners' sugar**
- 5 **teaspoons water**
- 2 **teaspoons vanilla extract**

In a large bowl, dissolve yeast in water. Add milk and shortening; stir for 1 minute. Add sugar, eggs, salt, nutmeg, cinnamon and 2 cups flour; beat on low speed until smooth. Stir in enough remaining flour to form a soft dough (do not knead). Cover and let rise in a warm place until doubled, about 1 hour.

Punch dough down. Turn onto a floured surface; roll out to 1/2-in. thickness. Cut with a 2-3/4-in. doughnut cutter; place 2 in. apart on greased baking sheets. Brush with butter. Cover and let rise in a warm place until doubled, about 30 minutes.

Bake at 350° for 20 minutes or until lightly browned. Meanwhile, for glaze, melt butter in a saucepan. Add the confectioners' sugar, water and vanilla; cook over low heat until smooth (do not boil). Keep the glaze warm.

Dip warm doughnuts, one at a time, into glaze and turn to coat. Drain on a wire rack.

Nutrition Facts: 1 doughnut equals 233 calories, 10 g fat (5 g saturated fat), 35 mg cholesterol, 170 mg sodium, 33 g carbohydrate, 1 g fiber, 4 g protein.

CREAMY CRANBERRY COFFEE CAKE

Yield: 12 servings.

Chopped cranberries and orange peel give this coffee cake bursts of tart flavor, but a cream cheese layer on top makes it sweet and rich. It's so lovely.

nancy roper // etobicoke, ontario

- 2 **cups all-purpose flour**
- 1 **cup sugar**
- 1-1/2 **teaspoons baking powder**
- 1/2 **teaspoon baking soda**
- 1 **egg**
- 3/4 **cup orange juice**
- 1/4 **cup butter, melted**
- 1 **teaspoon vanilla extract**

- 2 **cups coarsely chopped fresh *or* frozen cranberries**
- 1 **tablespoon grated orange peel**

CREAM CHEESE LAYER:

- 1 **package (8 ounces) cream cheese, softened**
- 1/3 **cup sugar**
- 1 **egg**
- 1 **teaspoon vanilla extract**

TOPPING:

- 3/4 **cup all-purpose flour**
- 1/2 **cup sugar**
- 1/2 **cup cold butter**

In a large bowl, combine the first four ingredients. Whisk the egg, orange juice, butter and vanilla; stir into dry ingredients just until blended. Fold in the cranberries and orange peel. Pour into a greased 9-in. springform pan.

In a small bowl, beat cream cheese and sugar until smooth. Beat in egg and vanilla. Spread over batter. Combine flour and sugar; cut in butter until the mixture resembles coarse crumbs. Sprinkle over top.

Place pan on a baking sheet. Bake at 350° for 70-75 minutes or until golden brown. Cool on a wire rack for 15 minutes before removing sides of pan.

Nutrition Facts: 1 piece equals 419 calories, 19 g fat (12 g saturated fat), 87 mg cholesterol, 286 mg sodium, 57 g carbohydrate, 2 g fiber, 6 g protein.

CINNAMON ROLLS IN A SNAP

CHEAT IT!

Yield: 1 dozen.

I turned biscuit mix into hot cinnamon rolls one morning because a friend was stopping by. They were quick to make because there was no need to let them rise. My friend was so impressed.

laura mcdermott // big lake, minnesota

- 4-1/2 **cups biscuit/baking mix**
- 1-1/3 **cups milk**

FILLING:

- 2 **tablespoons butter, softened**
- 1/4 **cup sugar**
- 1 **teaspoon ground cinnamon**
- 1/3 **cup raisins, optional**

ICING:

- 2 **cups confectioners' sugar**
- 2 **tablespoons milk**
- 2 **tablespoons butter, melted**
- 1 **teaspoon vanilla extract**

In a large bowl, combine biscuit mix and milk. Turn onto a floured surface; knead 8-10 times. Roll the dough into a 12-in. x 10-in. rectangle. Spread with butter. Combine the sugar, cinnamon and raisins if desired; sprinkle over butter.

Roll up from a long side; pinch seam to seal. Cut into 12 slices; place with cut side down on a large greased baking sheet.

Bake at 450° for 10-12 minutes or until golden brown. Meanwhile, combine the icing ingredients; spread over warm rolls. Serve warm.

Nutrition Facts: 1 roll equals 330 calories, 12 g fat (5 g saturated fat), 14 mg cholesterol, 620 mg sodium, 53 g carbohydrate, 1 g fiber, 4 g protein.

>> HOW TO:

SHAPE CINNAMON ROLLS AND STICKY BUNS

1 Roll dough into a rectangle. Spread or brush with butter; sprinkle with filling. Roll up, starting from a long end, and pinch seam to seal.
2 Slice into rolls. Place cut side down in a greased baking pan.

3 Cover and let rise until doubled. Rolls will begin to touch each other.
4 Combine the glaze ingredients if desired; spoon in a thin stream over the warm rolls.

ORANGE CINNAMON ROLLS

Yield: about 2 dozen.

The orange zest, juice and nuts give the rolls great flavor. It's my favorite recipe to make on Sunday mornings.

donna taylor // southbridge, massachusetts

- 1 loaf (1 pound) frozen bread dough, thawed
- 1/4 cup butter, softened
- 1/2 cup chopped pecans
- 1/4 cup sugar
- 1/4 cup packed brown sugar
- 1 tablespoon grated orange peel
- 1 teaspoon ground cinnamon

ICING:

- 1 cup confectioners' sugar
- 1 tablespoon butter, melted
- 1/2 teaspoon vanilla extract
- 2 to 3 tablespoons orange juice

On a lightly floured surface, roll dough into a 14-in. square. Spread with butter. In a small bowl, combine the pecans, sugar, brown sugar, orange peel and cinnamon. Sprinkle over dough to within 1/2 in. of edges.

Roll up jelly-roll style; pinch seams to seal. Cut into 28 slices. Place cut side down in two greased 9-in. round baking pans. Cover and let rise in a warm place until doubled, about 40 minutes.

Bake at 350° for 14-16 minutes or until golden brown. Combine the confectioners' sugar, butter, vanilla and enough orange juice to achieve desired consistency; drizzle over warm rolls.

Nutrition Facts: 1 roll equals 110 calories, 4 g fat (1 g saturated fat), 5 mg cholesterol, 106 mg sodium, 16 g carbohydrate, 1 g fiber, 2 g protein. Diabetic Exchanges: 1 starch, 1/2 fat.

HONEY WHOLE WHEAT ROLLS

Yield: 15 rolls.

Most of the farmers in our area grow wheat, so this recipe gives me a sense of hometown pride. I bake these rolls often, especially when I'm making soup or stew.

celecia stoup // hobart, oklahoma

- 2 packages (1/4 ounce each) active dry yeast
- 1 cup warm water (110° to 115°)
- 1/4 cup butter, melted
- 1/4 cup honey
- 1 egg
- 3/4 cup whole wheat flour
- 1/2 cup old-fashioned oats
- 1 teaspoon salt
- 2-1/4 to 2-3/4 cups all-purpose flour

Additional melted butter

In a large bowl, dissolve yeast in water. Stir in the butter, honey, egg, whole wheat flour, oats, salt and 1 cup of all-purpose flour; beat until smooth. Add enough remaining all-purpose flour to form a soft dough.

Turn onto a floured surface; knead dough until smooth and elastic, about 6-8 minutes. Place in a greased bowl, turning once to grease top. Cover and let rise in a warm place until doubled, about 1 hour.

Punch dough down. Shape into 15 rolls. Place in a greased 13-in. x 9-in. baking pan. Cover and let rise until doubled, about 45 minutes.

Bake at 375° for 20 minutes or until golden brown. Brush with butter.

Nutrition Facts: 1 roll equals 149 calories, 4 g fat (2 g saturated fat), 22 mg cholesterol, 194 mg sodium, 25 g carbohydrate, 2 g fiber, 4 g protein.

Plain Rolls: Divide dough into equal pieces as recipe directs. Shape each piece into a ball, pulling edges under the smooth top. Place 1 in. to 2 in. apart on greased baking sheets. For pan rolls, place eight balls in a greased 9-in. round baking pan or 12 balls in a greased 13-in. x 9-in. x 2-in. baking pan.

Cloverleaf Rolls: Divide dough into 1-1/2-in. balls. Make each ball smooth by pulling the edges under. Place three balls smooth side up in each greased muffin cup.

S-Shaped Rolls: Divide dough into 2-in. balls. Shape each ball into a 10-in. rope. On a greased baking sheet, coil each end in opposite directions until it touches the center and forms an S-shape.

Knot-Shaped Rolls: Divide dough into 3-in. balls. Roll each ball into a 10-in. rope; tie into a knot. Tuck and pinch ends under.

CLOVERLEAF ROLLS

Yield: 2 dozen.

When I was little, my mom would most often rely on traditional from-scratch recipes like this one. My sister and I ate more than our share of these golden rolls.
brenda dufresne // midland, michigan

1 **package (1/4 ounce) active dry yeast**	3 **tablespoons sugar**
1-1/4 **cups warm milk (110° to 115°)**	1 **teaspoon salt**
1/4 **cup butter, softened**	4 **to 4-1/2 cups all-purpose flour**
1 **egg**	**Additional butter, melted**

In a large bowl, dissolve yeast in warm milk. Add the butter, egg, sugar, salt and 3 cups flour. Beat until smooth. Stir in enough remaining flour to form a soft dough.

Turn onto a floured surface; knead until smooth and elastic, about 6-8 minutes. Place in a greased bowl, turning once to grease top. Cover and let rise in a warm place until doubled, about 1 hour.

Punch the dough down and divide in half. Divide each half into 36 pieces and shape into balls. Place three balls in each of 24 greased muffin cups. Cover and let rise until doubled, about 30 minutes. Brush with additional butter.

Bake at 375° for 15-18 minutes or until lightly browned. Remove to wire racks. Serve warm.

Nutrition Facts: 1 roll equals 110 calories, 3 g fat (2 g saturated fat), 16 mg cholesterol, 127 mg sodium, 18 g carbohydrate, 1 g fiber, 3 g protein.

SOUTHWEST PRETZELS

Yield: 16 pretzels.

These fun, filling pretzels with a mild Southwestern kick are the perfect snack for watching football games. And they'll score just as high with adults as kids!
cathy tang // redmond, washington

4 **cups all-purpose flour**	1/4 **teaspoon ground cumin**
1 **tablespoon sugar**	1/4 **teaspoon cayenne pepper**
1 **package (1/4 ounce) quick-rise yeast**	1-1/2 **cups warm water (120° to 130°)**
1-1/2 **teaspoons salt**	1 **egg, lightly beaten**
1 **teaspoon dried minced onion**	**Coarse salt**
1/2 **teaspoon chili powder**	**Salsa con queso dip**

In a large bowl, combine 2 cups flour, sugar, yeast, salt, minced onion and spices. Add water. Beat just until moistened. Stir in enough remaining flour to form a soft dough.

Turn onto a floured surface; knead until smooth and elastic, about 4-6 minutes. Cover and let rest for 10 minutes. Divide dough into 16 equal portions; roll each into a 15-in. rope. Cover and let rest 10 minutes longer.

Twist into pretzel shapes. Place on greased baking sheets; brush with egg. Bake at 350° for 15 minutes. Brush again with egg; sprinkle with coarse salt. Bake 10-13 minutes longer or until golden brown. Remove to wire racks. Serve pretzels warm with dip.

Nutrition Facts: 1 pretzel (calculated without coarse salt and dip) equals 120 calories, trace fat (trace saturated fat), 4 mg cholesterol, 224 mg sodium, 25 g carbohydrate, 1 g fiber, 4 g protein. Diabetic Exchange: 1-1/2 starch.

>> HOW TO:
FORM PRETZELS

1 Roll each piece of dough into a 15-in. rope and taper the ends. Shape the rope into a circle with about 3 in. of each end overlapping.

2 Twist ends where they overlap.

3 Flip the twisted ends over the circle; place ends around the edge and pinch under.

ROASTED GARLIC BREAD

Yield: 2 loaves (10 slices each).

I came up with this recipe one very stormy morning when we lived on the beach in the Florida Panhandle. While lightning blinked over the Gulf and rain tap-tap-tapped on our balcony, the wonderful aroma of this bread baking gave me such a cozy feeling.

barb alexander // princeton, new jersey

- 2 medium whole garlic bulbs
- 2 teaspoons olive oil
- 1 package (1/4 ounce) active dry yeast
- 1 cup warm water (110° to 115°)
- 1 tablespoon sugar
- 1 teaspoon salt
- 2-1/2 to 3 cups all-purpose flour
- 2 tablespoons minced fresh sage *or* 2 teaspoons rubbed sage
- 2 teaspoons minced fresh marjoram *or* 3/4 teaspoon dried marjoram
- 1 teaspoon minced fresh rosemary *or* 1/2 teaspoon dried rosemary, crushed
- 2 tablespoons grated Parmesan cheese
- 1 tablespoon butter, melted

Remove papery outer skin from garlic (do not peel or separate cloves). Cut top off garlic bulbs; brush with oil. Wrap each bulb in heavy-duty foil. Bake at 425° for 30-35 minutes or until softened. Cool for 10-15 minutes. Squeeze softened garlic into a small bowl; set aside.

In a large bowl, dissolve yeast in warm water. Add the sugar, salt and 1 cup flour; beat until smooth. Stir in enough remaining flour to form a soft dough.

Turn onto a lightly floured surface; knead until smooth and elastic, about 6-8 minutes. Place in a bowl coated with cooking spray, turning once to coat top. Cover and let rise in a warm place until doubled, about 45 minutes. Meanwhile, add the sage, marjoram and rosemary to the reserved roasted garlic.

Punch dough down. Turn onto a lightly floured surface; divide in half. Roll each portion into a 10-in. x 8-in. rectangle. Spread garlic mixture to within 1/2 in. of edges. Sprinkle with cheese. Roll up jelly-roll style, starting with a long side; pinch seam and ends to seal.

Coat a baking sheet with cooking spray. Place loaves seam side down on pan; tuck ends under. With a sharp knife, make several slashes across the top of each loaf. Cover and let rise until doubled, about 30 minutes.

Bake at 375° for 20-25 minutes or until golden brown. Remove to wire racks; brush with butter.

Nutrition Facts: 1 slice equals 84 calories, 1 g fat (1 g saturated fat), 2 mg cholesterol, 136 mg sodium, 15 g carbohydrate, 1 g fiber, 2 g protein. Diabetic Exchanges: 1 starch.

ROSEMARY FOCACCIA

Yield: 15 servings.

With rosemary and lots of cheese, these bread squares will make an everyday dinner seem like a festive occasion. Substitute what fresh herbs you have on hand, or use 2 teaspoons of crushed dried rosemary.

shelley ross // bow, washington

- 1 loaf (1 pound) frozen bread dough, thawed
- 2 tablespoons olive oil
- 1/4 cup thinly sliced onion
- 1-1/2 teaspoons minced garlic
- 1 cup (4 ounces) shredded part-skim mozzarella cheese
- 2 tablespoons minced fresh rosemary

Roll the dough into an ungreased 15-in. x 10-in. x 1-in. baking pan; build up edges slightly. Brush with oil; top with onion, garlic, cheese and rosemary.

Bake at 400° for 15-20 minutes or until golden brown and cheese is melted. Let stand for 5 minutes before slicing.

Nutrition Facts: 1 piece (prepared with part-skim mozzarella) equals 123 calories, 5 g fat (1 g saturated fat), 6 mg cholesterol, 197 mg sodium, 16 g carbohydrate, 1 g fiber, 5 g protein. Diabetic Exchanges: 1 starch, 1 fat.

PARMESAN-RANCH PAN ROLLS

CHEAT IT!

Yield: 1-1/2 dozen.

My mom taught me this easy recipe, which is great for feeding a crowd. There is never a crumb left over. My mom used her own bread dough, but using frozen dough is my shortcut.

trisha kruse // eagle, idaho

- 2 **loaves (1 pound** *each***) frozen bread dough, thawed**
- 1 **cup grated Parmesan cheese**
- 1/2 **cup butter, melted**
- 1 **envelope buttermilk ranch salad dressing mix**
- 1 **small onion, finely chopped**

On a lightly floured surface, divide dough into 18 portions; shape each into a ball. In a small bowl, combine the cheese, butter and ranch dressing mix.

Roll balls in cheese mixture; arrange in two greased 9-in. square baking pans. Sprinkle with onion. Cover and let rise in a warm place until doubled, about 45 minutes.

Bake at 350° for 20-25 minutes or until golden brown. Remove from pans to wire racks.

Nutrition Facts: 1 roll equals 210 calories, 8 g fat (4 g saturated fat), 17 mg cholesterol, 512 mg sodium, 26 g carbohydrate, 2 g fiber, 7 g protein.

CINNAMON RAISIN BREAD

Yield: 2 loaves (16 slices each).

Slices of warm cinnamon bread and cups of hot tea are perfect for drop-in visitors to our home during the holidays.

joan ort // milford, new jersey

- 2 **packages (1/4 ounce** *each***) active dry yeast**
- 2 **cups warm water (110° to 115°)**
- 1 **cup sugar,** *divided*
- 1/4 **cup canola oil**
- 2 **teaspoons salt**
- 2 **eggs**
- 6 **to 6-1/2 cups all-purpose flour**
- 1 **cup raisins**

Additional canola oil
- 3 **teaspoons ground cinnamon**

In a large bowl, dissolve yeast in warm water. Add 1/2 cup sugar, oil, salt, eggs and 4 cups flour. Beat until smooth. Stir in enough remaining flour to form a soft dough.

Turn onto a floured surface; knead until smooth and elastic, about 6-8 minutes. Place in a greased bowl, turning once to grease top. Cover and let rise in a warm place or until doubled, about 1 hour.

Punch dough down. Turn onto a lightly floured surface; divide in half. Knead 1/2 cup raisins into each; roll each portion into a 15-in. x 9-in. rectangle. Brush with additional oil. Combine cinnamon and remaining sugar; sprinkle to within 1/2 in. of edges.

Tightly roll up, jelly-roll style, starting with a short side; pinch seam to seal. Place, seam side down, in two greased 9-in. x 5-in. loaf pans. Cover and let rise until doubled, about 30 minutes.

Brush with oil. Bake at 375° for 45-50 minutes or until golden brown. Remove from pans to wire racks to cool.

Nutrition Facts: 1 slice equals 145 calories, 2 g fat (trace saturated fat), 13 mg cholesterol, 153 mg sodium, 28 g carbohydrate, 1 g fiber, 3 g protein. Diabetic Exchanges: 2 starch.

>> HOW TO:

KNEAD, SHAPE AND BAKE YEAST LOAVES

1 Turn dough onto a lightly floured surface; shape into a ball. Fold top of dough toward you. With your palms, push with a rolling motion away from you. Turn dough a quarter turn; repeat motion until dough is smooth and elastic. Add flour to surface only as needed.

2 Place the dough in a bowl greased with butter, oil or nonstick cooking spray. Turn dough over to grease the top. This prevents the dough from drying out while rising.

3 Cover with a clean towel or plastic wrap. Place covered dough in a warm, draft-free area (80° to 85°) until doubled. (Place covered bowl on the top rack in a cold oven with a pan of hot water underneath. Or turn your oven to its lowest setting for no longer then 40 to 50 seconds. Turn off and let dough rise in the oven.)

4 Press two finders 1/2 in. into the dough. If the dents remain, the dough is doubled in size and ready to punch down.

5 To punch dough down, make a fist and push it into the center. Gather the dough to the center and shape into a ball. Place on a floured surface.

6 Divide the dough if the recipe directs; shape into balls. Roll each ball into a 12-in. x 8-in. rectangle. You will hear air bubbles "popping" as you roll the dough.

7 Dust off any loose flour that might cling to the dough. Beginning at the short end, roll up each rectangle firmly. If it's too loose, you'll see air pockets when the bread is cut. If it's too tight, the bread will crack while baking.

8 Pinch seam and each end to seal. Place seam side down in a greased pan; cover with a towel and allow to double in size in a warm, draft-free area.

9 When the dough has doubled, remove the towel; place pans several inches apart in the center of the preheated oven.

10 When bread is golden brown, test for doneness by carefully removing loaves from pans and tapping the bottom crusts. If it sounds hollow, the bread is done. You can also use a thermometer to check that bread has reached 200°. If the bread is browning too fast and it's not done, tent with foil and continue baking. Unless recipe directs otherwise, immediately remove breads from pans and cool on a wire rack.

DILL-ONION BATTER BREAD

Yield: 1 loaf (16 slices).

Because the dough doesn't require kneading, this is a very easy bread to make. The tender loaf has a pleasant dill flavor. I serve it with soups, salads and many entrees.
gloria huey // port allegany, pennsylvania

1 package (1/4 ounce) active dry yeast	1 egg
1/4 cup warm water (110° to 115°)	2 teaspoons dill seed
1 cup warm 2% milk (110° to 115°)	2 teaspoons dried minced onion
2 tablespoons butter, softened	1/2 teaspoon salt
2 tablespoons sugar	3 cups all-purpose flour

In a large bowl, dissolve yeast in warm water. Add the milk, butter, sugar, egg, dill seed, onion, salt and 1-1/2 cups flour. Beat on medium speed for 3 minutes. Stir in remaining flour (batter will be sticky). Do not knead. Cover and let rise in a warm place until doubled, about 1 hour.

Stir batter down. Spoon into a greased 9-in. x 5-in. loaf pan. Cover and let rise until nearly doubled, about 45 minutes.

Bake at 350° for 30-35 minutes or until golden brown (cover loosely with foil if top browns too quickly). Cool for 10 minutes before removing from pan to a wire rack.

Nutrition Facts: 1 slice equals 138 calories, 3 g fat (2 g saturated fat), 22 mg cholesterol, 115 mg sodium, 24 g carbohydrate, 1 g fiber, 4 g protein.

CHALLAH

Yield: 2 loaves (16 slices each).

This traditional Jewish bread is often called egg bread because it uses more eggs than most. The attractive golden color and delicious flavor make it hard to resist.

taste of home cooking school

2 **packages (1/4 ounce *each*) active dry yeast**	6 **to 6-1/2 cups all-purpose flour**
1 **cup warm water (110° to 115°)**	**TOPPING:**
1/2 **cup canola oil**	1 **egg**
1/3 **cup sugar**	1 **teaspoon cold water**
1 **tablespoon salt**	1 **tablespoon sesame *or* poppy seeds, optional**
4 **eggs**	

In a large bowl, dissolve yeast in warm water. Add the oil, sugar, salt, eggs and 4 cups flour. Beat until smooth. Stir in enough remaining flour to form a firm dough. Turn onto a floured surface; knead until smooth and elastic, about 6-8 minutes. Place in a greased bowl, turning once to grease the top. Cover dough and let rise in a warm place until doubled, about 1 hour.

Punch dough down. Turn onto a lightly floured surface; divide in half. Divide each portion into thirds. Shape each piece into a 15-in. rope.

Place three ropes on a greased baking sheet and braid; pinch ends to seal and tuck under. Repeat with remaining dough. Cover and let rise until doubled, about 1 hour.

Beat egg and cold water; brush over braids. Sprinkle with sesame or poppy seeds if desired. Bake at 350° for 30-35 minutes or until golden brown. Remove to wire racks to cool.

Nutrition Facts: 1 slice equals 137 calories, 5 g fat (1 g saturated fat), 33 mg cholesterol, 232 mg sodium, 20 g carbohydrate, 1 g fiber, 4 g protein.

>> HOW TO:

MAKE A BRAIDED LOAF

1 Place three ropes almost touching on a baking sheet. Starting in the middle, loosely bring left rope under center rope. Bring the right rope under the new center rope and repeat until you reach the end.

2 Turn the pan and repeat braiding, bringing the ropes over instead of under.

3 Press each end to seal; tuck ends under.

SWEDISH TEA RING

Yield: 1 ring (24 slices).

This showstopper will add a special touch to any holiday spread.
elsie epp // newton, kansas

1	tablespoon active dry yeast
1-1/2	cups warm water (110° to 115°)
1/4	cup sugar
1/4	cup canola oil
2	egg whites, lightly beaten
1-1/4	teaspoons salt
5-1/2 to 6	cups all-purpose flour
1/2	cup chopped walnuts
1/2	cup chopped maraschino cherries, patted dry
1/4	cup packed brown sugar
1	teaspoon ground cinnamon
2	tablespoons butter, melted

ICING:

1	cup confectioners' sugar
1 to 2	tablespoons fat-free milk

In a large bowl, dissolve yeast in warm water. Add the sugar, oil, egg whites, salt and 1 cup flour; beat until smooth. Stir in enough remaining flour to form a soft dough.

Turn onto a lightly floured surface; knead until smooth, about 6-8 minutes. Place in a bowl coated with cooking spray, turning once to coat the top. Cover and let rise until doubled, about 1 hour.

Combine the walnuts, cherries, brown sugar and cinnamon; set aside. Punch dough down; roll into an 18-in. x 12-in. rectangle. Brush with butter; sprinkle with nut mixture to within 1/2 in. of edges. Roll up jelly-roll style, starting with a long side; pinch seam to seal.

Place seam side down on a 14-in. pizza pan coated with cooking spray; pinch ends together to form a ring. With scissors, cut from outside edge two-thirds of the way toward center of ring at scant 1-in. intervals. Separate strips slightly; twist to allow filling to show. Cover and let rise until doubled, about 40 minutes.

Bake at 400° for 20-25 minutes or until golden brown. Remove from pan to a wire rack to cool. Combine icing ingredients; drizzle over tea ring.

Nutrition Facts: 1 slice equals 196 calories, 5 g fat (1 g saturated fat), 3 mg cholesterol, 142 mg sodium, 34 g carbohydrate, 1 g fiber, 4 g protein. Diabetic Exchanges: 2 starch, 1 fat.

>>HOW TO:

SHAPE A TEA RING

1 Roll dough into a rectangle. Spread filling over dough to within 1/2 in. of edges. Roll up jelly-roll style, starting with a long side; pinch seam to seal.

2 Place seam side down on a greased baking sheet; pinch ends together to form a ring.

3 With scissors, cut from outside edge to two-thirds of the way toward center of ring at 1-in. intervals.

4 Separate the cut pieces slightly, twisting each individually to allow filling to show.

DESSERTS

SOUTH CAROLINA COBBLER

Yield: 8 servings.

With peach orchards just a couple of miles from home, it's easy to treat family to this traditional Southern favorite.

mattie carter // rock hill, south carolina

- 4 **cups sliced peeled fresh *or* frozen peaches, thawed**
- 1 **cup sugar, *divided***
- 1/2 **teaspoon almond extract**
- 1/3 **cup butter, melted**
- 3/4 **cup all-purpose flour**
- 2 **teaspoons baking powder**

Pinch salt

- 3/4 **cup milk**

Vanilla ice cream, optional

In a large bowl, gently toss peaches, 1/2 cup sugar and extract; set aside. Pour butter into a 2-qt. baking dish.

In a small bowl, combine the flour, baking powder, salt and remaining sugar; stir in milk until smooth. Pour evenly over butter (do not stir). Top with peach mixture.

Bake at 350° for 50-55 minutes or until golden brown and bubbly. Serve cobbler with ice cream if desired.

Nutrition Facts: 1 serving equals 258 calories, 9 g fat (5 g saturated fat), 24 mg cholesterol, 207 mg sodium, 44 g carbohydrate, 2 g fiber, 3 g protein.

>> HOW TO:

PIT A PEACH

1 Using the indentation as a guide, cut the peach in half, cutting around the pit.

2 Twist the halves in opposite directions to separate. Using a sharp knife, loosen and remove the pit. Treat cut surfaces with lemon juice to avoid discoloration.

BLUEBERRY BUCKLE

Yield: 6 servings.

Everybody in my family loves blueberry buckle, and I enjoy how easily it comes together. It never sets me back where time is concerned, yet it's wonderfully homemade.

jacquelin traffas // sharon, kansas

- 2 **tablespoons butter, softened**
- 1/3 **cup sugar**
- 1 **egg**
- 1 **cup all-purpose flour**
- 1 **teaspoon baking powder**
- 1/4 **teaspoon salt**
- 1/4 **cup 2% milk**
- 1 **cup fresh *or* frozen blueberries**

TOPPING:

- 1/4 **cup all-purpose flour**
- 2 **tablespoons sugar**
- 3/4 **teaspoon ground cinnamon**
- 2 **tablespoons cold butter**

In a small bowl, cream butter and sugar until light and fluffy. Beat in egg. Combine the flour, baking powder and salt; gradually add to creamed mixture alternately with milk, beating well after each addition. Fold in blueberries. Spread into an 8-in. x 4-in. loaf pan coated with cooking spray.

For topping, combine flour, sugar and cinnamon in a bowl. Cut in butter until mixture resembles coarse crumbs. Sprinkle over batter.

Bake at 350° for 40-45 minutes or until a toothpick inserted near the center comes out clean. Cool for 10 minutes before removing from pan to a wire rack.

EDITOR'S NOTE: If using frozen blueberries, use without thawing to avoid discoloring the batter.

Nutrition Facts: 1 piece equals 248 calories, 9 g fat (5 g saturated fat), 57 mg cholesterol, 230 mg sodium, 38 g carbohydrate, 2 g fiber, 5 g protein.

PEACH BUCKLE: Substitute 1 cup finely chopped peeled peaches for the blueberries. Proceed as directed.

BERRY DELICIOUS RHUBARB CRISP

Yield: 9 servings.

I sometimes grate about a tablespoon of fresh orange or lemon zest and add it to the crumb mixture for an extra-bright flavor. It's a great dessert for summer nights.

shannon arthur // lucasville, ohio

1 cup all-purpose flour

1 cup packed brown sugar

3/4 cup old-fashioned oats

1/2 cup butter, melted

1-1/2 teaspoons vanilla extract, *divided*

1 teaspoon ground cinnamon

1-1/2 cups diced fresh *or* frozen rhubarb

1-1/2 cups sliced fresh strawberries

1-1/2 cups fresh blackberries

1/2 cup sugar

1 tablespoon cornstarch

1/2 cup cold water

Vanilla ice cream

In a small bowl, combine the flour, brown sugar, oats, butter, 1 teaspoon vanilla and cinnamon. Set aside 1 cup for topping; press remaining crumb mixture into a greased 8-in. square baking dish. Top with rhubarb, strawberries and blackberries.

In a small saucepan, combine sugar and cornstarch. Stir in water. Bring to a boil; cook and stir for 1-2 minutes or until thickened. Stir in remaining vanilla. Pour over fruit; sprinkle with remaining crumb mixture.

Bake at 350° for 25-30 minutes or until bubbly. Serve with ice cream.

EDITOR'S NOTE: If using frozen rhubarb, measure rhubarb while still frozen, then thaw completely. Drain in a colander, but do not press liquid out.

Nutrition Facts: 1 serving equals 329 calories, 11 g fat (7 g saturated fat), 27 mg cholesterol, 83 mg sodium, 56 g carbohydrate, 3 g fiber, 3 g protein.

APPLE DANISH PIES

Yield: 2 servings.

Prepared with an easy crescent roll crust and served in cute ramekins, these single-serving pies are fun to share with your special someone.

joanne wright // niles, michigan

1/3 cup sugar

1 tablespoon plus 1 teaspoon cornstarch

1/2 teaspoon ground cinnamon

1/8 teaspoon ground nutmeg

2 cups chopped peeled tart apples

1/4 cup unsweetened apple juice

1 tube (4 ounces) refrigerated crescent rolls

1 package (3 ounces) cream cheese, softened

2 tablespoons confectioners' sugar

1/2 teaspoon vanilla extract

GLAZE:

1/4 cup confectioners' sugar

2 teaspoons 2% milk

In a small saucepan, combine the sugar, cornstarch, cinnamon and nutmeg. Add apples and juice; toss to coat. Bring to a boil; cook and stir for 2 minutes or until thickened. Remove from the heat.

Separate crescent dough into four triangles. On a lightly floured surface, roll two triangles into 5-in. circles. Place each into a greased 8-oz. ramekin, pressing dough onto bottoms and 1/2 in. up the sides.

In a small bowl, beat cream cheese, confectioners' sugar and vanilla. Spread over dough in ramekins. Top with apple mixture. Roll out remaining crescent dough into 4-in. circles; place over filling. Cut slits in top.

Bake at 375° for 20-25 minutes or until filling is bubbly and topping is golden brown. Combine glaze ingredients; drizzle over pies. Serve the pies warm.

Nutrition Facts: 1 pie (prepared with reduced-fat cream cheese) equals 660 calories, 22 g fat (9 g saturated fat), 30 mg cholesterol, 630 mg sodium, 108 g carbohydrate, 4 g fiber, 9 g protein.

BERRY PATCH PIE

Yield: 8 servings.

Enjoy a gorgeous, made-for-summer pie with this mouthwatering recipe. Each bite bursts with sweet, juicy berries.

taste of home cooking school

Pastry for single-crust pie (9 inches)

- 3/4 **cup sugar**
- 1/4 **cup cornstarch**
- 2 **cups halved fresh strawberries**
- 1-1/2 **cups fresh raspberries**
- 1 **cup fresh blackberries**
- 1 **cup fresh blueberries**
- 1 **tablespoon lemon juice**

On a lightly floured surface, unroll pastry. Transfer to a 9-in. pie plate. Trim pastry to 1/2 in. beyond edge of plate; flute edges. Line unpricked pastry with a double thickness of heavy-duty foil. Bake at 450° for 8 minutes. Remove foil; bake 5-7 minutes longer or until golden brown. Cool on a wire rack.

Meanwhile, in a large saucepan, combine sugar and cornstarch. Stir in berries and lemon juice. Cook, stirring occasionally, over medium heat until mixture just comes to a boil; pour into prepared crust. Cool completely on a wire rack.

Nutrition Facts: 1 piece equals 250 calories, 7 g fat (3 g saturated fat), 5 mg cholesterol, 101 mg sodium, 46 g carbohydrate, 4 g fiber, 2 g protein.

BERRY PATCH LATTICE PIE: Using enough pastry for a double-crust pie, line pie plate with bottom crust. In a large bowl, combine the sugar, cornstarch, berries and lemon juice; toss to coat. Add to prepared pie plate. Make a lattice crust. Bake the pie at 400° for 45-55 minutes or until bubbly and crust is golden brown (cover edges with foil to prevent pie from overbrowning if necessary).

>>HOW TO:

CREATE A LATTICE-TOPPED PIE

1 Make pastry for a double-crust pie. Line a 9-in. pie plate with the bottom pastry and trim to 1 in. beyond the edge of plate. Roll out remaining pastry to a 12-in. circle. With a pastry wheel, pizza cutter or a sharp knife, cut pastry into 1/2-in.- to 1-in.-wide strips. Lay strips in rows about 1/2 in. to 3/4 in. apart. (Use longer strips for the center of the pie and shorter strips for the sides.) Fold every other strip halfway back. Starting at the center, add strips at right angles, lifting every other strip as the cross strips are put down.

2 Continue to add strips, lifting and weaving until lattice top is complete.

3 Trim strips even with pastry edge. Fold bottom pastry up and over ends of strips and seal. Flute edges.

FRESH CHERRY PIE

Yield: 8 servings.

This ruby-red treat is just sweet enough, with a hint of almond flavor and a good level of cinnamon. The cherries peeking out of the lattice crust makes it so pretty, too.
josie bochek // sturgeon bay, wisconsin

- 1-1/4 **cups sugar**
-   1/3 **cup cornstarch**
-     1 **cup cherry juice blend**
-     4 **cups fresh *or* frozen pitted tart cherries, thawed**
-   1/2 **teaspoon ground cinnamon**
-   1/4 **teaspoon *each* ground nutmeg and almond extract**

PASTRY:

-     2 **cups all-purpose flour**
-   1/2 **teaspoon salt**
-   2/3 **cup shortening**
-     5 **to 7 tablespoons cold water**

In a large saucepan, combine sugar and cornstarch; gradually stir in cherry juice until smooth. Bring to a boil; cook and stir for 2 minutes or until thickened. Remove from the heat. Add the cherries, cinnamon, nutmeg and extract; set aside.

In a large bowl, combine flour and salt; cut in shortening until crumbly. Gradually add cold water, tossing with a fork until a ball forms. Divide pastry in half so that one ball is slightly larger than the other.

On a lightly floured surface, roll out larger ball to fit a 9-in. pie plate. Transfer pastry to pie plate; trim 1 in. beyond edge of plate. Add filling. Roll out remaining pastry; make a lattice crust. Trim, seal and flute edges.

Bake at 425° for 10 minutes. Reduce heat to 375°; bake 45-50 minutes longer or until crust is golden brown. Cool on a wire rack.

Nutrition Facts: 1 slice equals 457 calories, 17 g fat (4 g saturated fat), 0 cholesterol, 153 mg sodium, 73 g carbohydrate, 2 g fiber, 4 g protein.

LEMON MERINGUE PIE

Yield: 8 servings.

This is my grandmother's recipe. It's a lovely, special dessert that feels like home.
merle dyck // elkford, british columbia

>   1/2 **cup sugar**
>   1/4 **cup cornstarch**

Pinch salt

>   2 **cups cold water**
>   2 **egg yolks, lightly beaten**
>   3 **tablespoons lemon juice**
>   1 **teaspoon grated lemon peel**
>   1 **teaspoon butter**

MERINGUE:

>   3 **egg whites**
>   1/8 **teaspoon cream of tartar**
>   6 **tablespoons sugar**

Pastry for single-crust pie (9 inches), baked

In a large saucepan, combine the sugar, cornstarch and salt. Stir in water until smooth. Cook and stir over medium heat until thickened and bubbly, about 2 minutes. Reduce heat; cook and stir 2 minutes longer.

Remove from the heat. Gradually stir 1 cup hot filling into egg yolks; return all to the pan. Bring to a gentle boil; cook and stir for 2 minutes. Remove from the heat. Gently stir in lemon juice, peel and butter until butter is melted. Set aside and keep warm.

For meringue, in a small bowl, beat egg whites and cream of tartar on medium speed until soft peaks form. Gradually beat in sugar, 1 tablespoon at a time, on high until stiff glossy peaks form and sugar is dissolved.

Pour filling into crust. Spread meringue over hot filling, sealing edges to crust. Bake at 350° for 15 minutes or until meringue is golden brown. Cool on a wire rack for 1 hour; refrigerate for at least 3 hours before serving.

Nutrition Facts: 1 piece equals 246 calories, 9 g fat (4 g saturated fat), 57 mg cholesterol, 145 mg sodium, 39 g carbohydrate, trace fiber, 3 g protein.

PECAN PUMPKIN PIE

Yield: 8 servings.

A rich, crispy pecan topping and maple syrup give pumpkin pie a fall-perfect, mouthwatering twist.

deborah whitley // nashville, tennessee

Pastry for single-crust pie (9 inches)

- 2 **eggs**
- 1 **can (15 ounces) solid-pack pumpkin**
- 1/2 **cup maple syrup**
- 1/4 **cup sugar**
- 1/4 **cup heavy whipping cream**
- 1 **teaspoon ground cinnamon**
- 1/2 **teaspoon ground nutmeg**

TOPPING:

- 2 **eggs, lightly beaten**
- 1 **cup chopped pecans**
- 1/2 **cup *each* sugar and maple syrup**

Additional whipped cream, optional

Line a 9-in. pie plate with pastry; trim and flute edges. In a large bowl, beat the eggs, pumpkin, syrup, sugar, cream, cinnamon and nutmeg until smooth; pour into pastry.

For the topping, in a large bowl, combine the eggs, pecans, sugar and syrup; spoon over top.

Bake at 425° for 15 minutes. Reduce the heat to 350°. Bake 40-45 minutes longer or until crust is golden brown and top of pie is set.

Cool on a wire rack for 1 hour. Refrigerate overnight or until set. Serve with whipped topping if desired.

Nutrition Facts: 1 piece (calculated without additional whipped cream) equals 481 calories, 23 g fat (6 g saturated fat), 121 mg cholesterol, 144 mg sodium, 65 g carbohydrate, 4 g fiber, 7 g protein.

>> HOW TO:

CREATE A DECORATIVE PIE CRUST

Fluted Edge: Trim pastry 1/2 in. beyond edge of pie plate. Turn overhanging pastry under to form a rolled edge. Position your thumb and index finger about 1 in. apart on the edge or the crust, pointing out. Position the index finger of your other hand between the two fingers and gently push the pastry toward the center in an upward direction. Continue around the edge.

Braided Edge: Trim pastry even with edge of pie plate. With a sharp knife, cut additional pastry into twelve 1/4-in.-wide strips; braid three strips. Brush edge of crust with water; place braid on edge and press lightly to secure. Repeat with remaining strips, attaching braids until entire edge is covered. Cover with foil to protect edges from overbrowning.

Decorative Cutouts: Trim pastry even with edge of pie plate. Cut out shapes from additional pastry, using 1-in. to 1-1/2 in. cookie cutters. Brush bottoms of cutouts with water. Place one or two layers of cutouts around edge of crust; press lightly to secure. Cover with foil to protect edges from overbrowning.

MERINGUE SHELLS
MAKE PRETTY DESSERTS

Naturally low in fat and pretty to behold, meringue shells make for an impressive lightened-up fruit dessert. (Store meringue shell between layers of waxed paper in an airtight container or resealable plastic bag for up to a day before using.)

Schaum torte is a classic Austrian dessert of meringue topped with whipped cream or ice cream and fresh strawberries. Named after the ballerina Anna Pavlova, the Australian version of this dessert, Pavlova, is the same delicate meringue shell topped with whipped cream and any variety of fresh fruit.

Though their appearance is visually stunning, meringue desserts are easy and quick to put together. To ensure a crispy meringue, assemble the dessert just before serving.

STRAWBERRY SCHAUM TORTE

Yield: 12 servings.

This low-fat recipe was handed down from my German grandma. She took great pride in serving this delicate dessert. Whenever I make it, I'm filled with warm memories of childhood.
diane krisman // hales corners, wisconsin

8	egg whites	2	cups sugar
1	tablespoon white vinegar	3	cups sliced fresh strawberries
1	teaspoon vanilla extract	1-1/2	cups whipped cream
1/4	teaspoon salt		

Place egg whites in a large bowl and let stand at room temperature for 30 minutes. Add the vinegar, vanilla and salt; beat on medium speed until soft peaks form. Gradually beat in sugar, about 2 tablespoons at a time, on high until stiff glossy peaks form and sugar is dissolved.

Spread into a greased 10-in. springform pan. Bake at 300° for 50-60 minutes or until lightly browned. Remove to a wire rack to cool (meringue will fall). Serve with strawberries and whipped cream.

Nutrition Facts: 1 piece equals 206 calories, 6 g fat (3 g saturated fat), 20 mg cholesterol, 92 mg sodium, 37 g carbohydrate, 1 g fiber, 3 g protein.

RASPBERRY LEMON PAVLOVA: Gently spread the meringue shell with 1-1/2 cups of prepared lemon curd; top with whipped cream. Substitute raspberries for the strawberries.

>> HOW TO:

BEAT MERINGUE TO STIFF PEAKS

In a large bowl, beat egg whites, vinegar, vanilla and salt on medium speed until egg whites begin to increase in volume and soft peaks form. To test for soft peaks, lift the beaters from the whites; the peaks should curl down. Gradually add sugar on high speed as you beat meringue to stiff peaks. Whites should stand straight up and cling to the beaters as shown. Avoid overbeating.

COFFEE SHOP FUDGE

Yield: 2 pounds.

This smooth, creamy fudge has an irresistible crunch from pecans. The coffee and cinnamon blend nicely to provide luscious flavor.
beth osborne skinner // bristol, tennessee

- 1 **cup chopped pecans**
- 3 **cups (18 ounces) semisweet chocolate chips**
- 1 **can (14 ounces) sweetened condensed milk**
- 2 **tablespoons strong brewed coffee, room temperature**
- 1 **teaspoon ground cinnamon**
- 1/8 **teaspoon salt**
- 1 **teaspoon vanilla extract**

Line an 8-in. square pan with foil and butter the foil; set aside. Place pecans in a microwave-safe pie plate. Microwave, uncovered, on high for 3 minutes, stirring after each minute; set aside.

In a 2-qt. microwave-safe bowl, combine the chocolate chips, milk, coffee, cinnamon and salt. Microwave, uncovered, on high for 1 minute. Stir until smooth. Stir in vanilla and pecans. Immediately spread into the prepared pan.

Cover and refrigerate until firm, about 2 hours. Remove from pan; cut into 1-in. squares. Cover and store at room temperature (70°-80°).

EDITOR'S NOTE: This recipe was tested in a 1,100-watt microwave.

Nutrition Facts: 2 ounces equals 311 calories, 18 g fat (8 g saturated fat), 11 mg cholesterol, 64 mg sodium, 39 g carbohydrate, 3 g fiber, 5 g protein.

CHERRY & ALMOND CRISPY SQUARES

Yield: 2 dozen.

This grown-up version of a kiddie favorite will please the whole party. Everyone will agree it's delicious!
taste of home cooking school

- 1 **package (10 ounces) large marshmallows**
- 3 **tablespoons butter**
- 1 **teaspoon almond extract**
- 6 **cups crisp rice cereal**
- 3 **cups salted roasted almonds,** *divided*
- 1-1/2 **cups dried cherries,** *divided*

In a Dutch oven, combine marshmallows and butter. Cook and stir over medium-low heat until melted. Remove from the heat; stir in extract. Stir in the cereal, 1 cup almonds and 1 cup cherries.

Press into a greased 13-in. x 9-in. pan. Sprinkle with remaining almonds and cherries; gently press onto cereal mixture. Cool. Cut into squares.

Nutrition Facts: 1 square equals 205 calories, 11 g fat (2 g saturated fat), 4 mg cholesterol, 137 mg sodium, 25 g carbohydrate, 2 g fiber, 5 g protein.

RUM BANANA SAUCE

Yield: 4 servings.

Remember to save room for dessert! This sauce is delicious served over ice cream. It's so good, you'll be tempted to forget the ice cream altogether! You could also try this with butter brickle or cinnamon ice cream.

katherine desrosiers // trail, british columbia

- 3/4 **cup packed brown sugar**
- 1/4 **cup butter, cubed**
- 1/4 **cup heavy whipping cream**
- 2 **tablespoons maple syrup**
- 2 **large bananas, cut into 1/2-inch slices**
- 1/2 **teaspoon rum extract**

Vanilla ice cream

In a small saucepan, combine the brown sugar, butter, cream and maple syrup. Cook and stir over medium heat for 4-5 minutes or until sauce is smooth. Stir in bananas; heat through. Remove from the heat; stir in extract. Serve with ice cream.

Nutrition Facts: 1/2 cup equals 397 calories, 17 g fat (11 g saturated fat) 50 mg cholesterol, 104 mg sodium, 63 g carbohydrate, 2 g fiber, 1 g protein.

CHOCOLATE MOUSSE WITH CRANBERRY SAUCE

Yield: 10 servings (about 1 cup sauce).

A pretty, tangy sauce complements the sweet, fudgy mousse in this outstanding dessert. Make it the day before the party—how convenient!

barbara nowakowski // north tonawanda, new york

- 2 **cups (12 ounces) semisweet chocolate chips**
- 1/4 **cup butter, cubed**
- 1 **egg yolk, lightly beaten**
- 1-1/2 **cups heavy whipping cream,** *divided*
- 1/3 **cup light corn syrup**
- 1 **teaspoon vanilla extract**

CRANBERRY SAUCE:
- 1/3 **cup cranberry juice**
- 1 **teaspoon lime juice**
- 1 **cup jellied cranberry sauce**

In a large microwave-safe bowl, melt chocolate chips and butter; stir until smooth. In a small heavy saucepan, combine the egg yolk, 1/4 cup cream and corn syrup. Cook and stir over low heat until mixture reaches 160°, about 2 minutes.

Remove from the heat; stir into the chocolate mixture. Refrigerate for 20 minutes or until cooled and slightly thickened, stirring occasionally. Line a 1-qt. bowl with plastic wrap; set aside.

In a large bowl, beat the remaining cream until it begins to thicken. Add vanilla; beat until soft peaks form. Fold into chocolate mixture. Spoon into prepared bowl. Cover and refrigerate overnight.

Place the sauce ingredients in a blender; cover and process until smooth. Transfer to a small bowl; cover and refrigerate until serving.

Just before serving, invert mousse onto a platter; remove plastic wrap. Cut into wedges; serve with cranberry sauce.

Nutrition Facts: 1 wedge with about 5 teaspoons sauce equals 405 calories, 28 g fat (17 g saturated fat), 81 mg cholesterol, 63 mg sodium, 42 g carbohydrate, 2 g fiber, 2 g protein.

LEMONADE ICEBOX PIE

Yield: 8 servings.

You will detect a definite lemonade flavor in this refreshing pie. High and fluffy, this dessert has a creamy, smooth consistency that is perfect for summer.

cheryl wilt // eglon, west virginia

- 1 **package (8 ounces) cream cheese, softened**
- 1 **can (14 ounces) sweetened condensed milk**
- 3/4 **cup thawed lemonade concentrate**
- 1 **carton (8 ounces) frozen whipped topping, thawed**

Yellow food coloring, optional

- 1 **graham cracker crust (9 inches)**

In a large bowl, beat cream cheese and milk until smooth. Beat in lemonade concentrate. Fold in whipped topping and food coloring if desired. Pour into crust. Cover and refrigerate until set.

Nutrition Facts: 1 piece equals 491 calories, 24 g fat (15 g saturated fat), 48 mg cholesterol, 269 mg sodium, 61 g carbohydrate, trace fiber, 7 g protein.

ORANGE ICEBOX PIE: Combine 3/4 cup thawed orange juice concentrate for the lemonade, add 1/2 teaspoon grated orange peel and omit food coloring.

CREAMY PINEAPPLE PIE: Substitute 1 can (8 ounces) crushed, undrained pineapple and 1/4 cup lemon juice with the milk. Fold in whipped topping. Omit cream cheese and food coloring.

COOL LIME PIE: Substitute 3/4 cup thawed lemonade and limeade concentrate for lemonade and use green food coloring instead of yellow.

EASY TIRAMISU

Yield: 8 servings.

This no-bake treat comes together quickly and can even be made the night before. Sometimes I drizzle additional chocolate syrup over the coffee and pound cake. Other times, I add sliced almonds to the topping.

nancy brown // dahinda, illinois

>   1 **package (10-3/4 ounces) frozen pound cake, thawed**
>   3/4 **cup strong brewed coffee**
>   1 **package (8 ounces) cream cheese, softened**
>   1 **cup sugar**
>   1/2 **cup chocolate syrup**
>   1 **cup heavy whipping cream, whipped**
>   2 **Heath candy bars (1.4 ounces *each*), crushed**

Cut cake into nine slices. Arrange in an ungreased 11-in. x 7-in. dish, cutting to fit if needed. Drizzle with coffee.

In a small bowl, beat cream cheese and sugar until smooth. Add chocolate syrup. Fold in whipped cream. Spread over cake. Sprinkle with crushed candy bars. Refrigerate until serving.

Nutrition Facts: 1 piece equals 520 calories, 29 g fat (17 g saturated fat), 127 mg cholesterol, 256 mg sodium, 61 g carbohydrate, 1 g fiber, 6 g protein.

PUMPKIN CREME BRULEE

Yield: 8 servings.

I've never met a creme brulee that I didn't love! I'm not a big pumpkin fan, but this is fantastic.

tamara leonard merritt // raleigh, north carolina

>   8 **egg yolks**
>   1/3 **cup plus 1/2 cup sugar, *divided***
>   3 **cups heavy whipping cream**
>   3/4 **cup canned pumpkin**
> 1-1/2 **teaspoons vanilla extract**
>   1/2 **teaspoon ground cinnamon**
>   1/4 **teaspoon *each* ground ginger, nutmeg and cloves**

In a small bowl, whisk egg yolks and 1/3 cup sugar. In a small saucepan, heat cream over medium heat until bubbles form around sides of pan. Remove from the heat; stir a small amount of hot cream into egg yolk mixture. Return all to the pan, stirring constantly. Stir in the pumpkin, vanilla and spices.

Transfer to eight 6-oz. ramekins or custard cups. Place ramekins in a baking pan; add 1 in. of boiling water to pan. Bake, uncovered, at 325° for 25-30 minutes or until centers are just set (mixture will jiggle). Remove ramekins from water bath; cool for 10 minutes. Cover and refrigerate for at least 4 hours.

If using a creme brulee torch, sprinkle with remaining sugar. Heat sugar with the torch until caramelized. Serve immediately.

If broiling the custards, place ramekins on a baking sheet; let stand at room temperature for 15 minutes. Sprinkle with remaining sugar. Broil 8 in. from the heat for 4-7 minutes or until sugar is caramelized. Refrigerate for 1-2 hours or until firm.

Nutrition Facts: 1 creme brulee equals 452 calories, 38 g fat (22 g saturated fat), 327 mg cholesterol, 43 mg sodium, 26 g carbohydrate, 1 g fiber, 5 g protein.

WHITE CHOCOLATE CREME BRULEE

Yield: 2 servings.

If you like classic creme brulee, you have to try this version. Dressed up with white chocolate, it's a special romantic treat.

carole resnick // cleveland, ohio

- 3 **egg yolks**
- 6 **tablespoons sugar,** *divided*
- 1 **cup heavy whipping cream**
- 2 **ounces white baking chocolate, finely chopped**
- 1/4 **teaspoon vanilla extract**

In a small bowl, whisk egg yolks and 2 tablespoons sugar; set aside. In a small saucepan, combine the cream, chocolate and 2 tablespoons sugar. Heat over medium-low heat until chocolate is melted and mixture is smooth, stirring constantly.

Remove from the heat. Stir in vanilla. Stir a small amount of hot filling into egg yolk mixture; return all to the pan, stirring constantly.

Pour into two 10-oz. ramekins. Place in a baking pan. Add 1 in. of boiling water to pan. Bake, uncovered, at 325° for 50-55 minutes or until centers are just set (mixture will jiggle). Remove from water bath. Cool for 10 minutes. Refrigerate for at least 4 hours.

If using a creme brulee torch, sprinkle with remaining sugar. Heat sugar with the torch until caramelized. Serve immediately.

If broiling the custards, place ramekins on a baking sheet; let stand at room temperature for 15 minutes. Sprinkle with remaining sugar. Broil 8 in. from the heat for 4-7 minutes or until sugar is caramelized. Refrigerate for 1-2 hours or until firm.

Nutrition Facts: 1 creme brulee equals 854 calories, 62 g fat (36 g saturated fat), 488 mg cholesterol, 86 mg sodium, 70 g carbohydrate, 0 fiber, 9 g protein.

tasteofhome COOKING SCHOOL SECRET

CREME BRULEE SUCCESS

Translated from the French as "burned cream," this super-rich restaurant treat is actually easy to make at home.

To achieve a beautiful "burned cream" contrast between the rich, creamy baked custard and crisply burned sugar top, be sure to start with a well-chilled dessert.

Lightly sprinkle the tops of the custards with plain granulated sugar. As with flouring a cake pan, you may tilt and tap the ramekins to ensure the custards are coated with a thin, even coating of sugar. If desired, you may use a 50-50 mix of granulated and brown sugars, though we've found that regular granulated sugar produces the best results.

If you're lucky enough to have a creme brulee torch, simply caramelize the tops with light sweeping movements over the custards. You can also broil the custards, though this will take a bit more planning and will yield a crust that isn't quite as crispy as brulee-and-serve.

Refer to the recipe for specific directions. Or, simply enjoy your baked custards with no sugar topping at all!

STRAWBERRY & WINE SORBET

Yield: 1 quart.

Bright and refreshing, this grown-up treat tastes like you're biting into a just-picked strawberry. White wine and lemon juice enhance its not-too-sweet flavor.

donna lamano // olathe, kansas

- 3/4 **cup sugar**
- 1/2 **cup water**
- 1-1/2 **pounds fresh strawberries, hulled**
- 1 **cup white wine**
- 1/2 **cup honey**
- 1/4 **cup lemon juice**

In a small saucepan, bring sugar and water to a boil. Cook and stir until sugar is dissolved; set aside to cool.

Place the remaining ingredients in a food processor; add sugar syrup. Cover and process for 2-3 minutes or until smooth. Strain and discard seeds and pulp. Transfer puree to a 13-in. x 9-in. dish. Freeze for 1 hour or until edges begin to firm. Stir and return to freezer. Freeze 2 hours longer or until firm.

Just before serving, transfer to a food processor; cover and process for 2-3 minutes or until smooth.

Nutrition Facts: 2/3 cup equals 254 calories, trace fat (trace saturated fat), 0 cholesterol, 4 mg sodium, 59 g carbohydrate, 2 g fiber, 1 g protein.

1-2-3 BLACKBERRY SHERBET

Yield: 1 quart.

My mom gave me this recipe, which was a favorite when I was growing up. Now when I make it, my mouth is watering before I'm finished!

lisa eremia // irwin, pennsylvania

- 4 **cups fresh *or* frozen blackberries, thawed**
- 2 **cups sugar**
- 2 **cups buttermilk**

In a food processor, combine blackberries and sugar; cover and process until smooth. Strain and discard seeds and pulp. Stir in the buttermilk.

Transfer puree to a 13-in. x 9-in. dish. Freeze for 1 hour or until edges begin to firm. Stir and return to freezer. Freeze 2 hours longer or until firm.

Just before serving, transfer to a food processor; cover and process for 2-3 minutes or until smooth.

Nutrition Facts: 1/2 cup equals 249 calories, 1 g fat (trace saturated fat), 2 mg cholesterol, 60 mg sodium, 60 g carbohydrate, 4 g fiber, 3 g protein.

WATERMELON GRANITA

Yield: 8 servings.

Say a sweet "ciao" to summer with this light and airy Italian treat! Serve it in pretty glasses garnished with wedges of melon or mint sprigs.

taste of home cooking school

 1-1/4 **cups sugar**
 1-1/4 **cups water**
   6 **cups cubed watermelon**
Small watermelon wedges, optional

In a small saucepan, bring sugar and water to a boil. Cook and stir until sugar is dissolved; set aside. In a blender, process watermelon in batches until smooth. Strain; discard pulp and seeds. Transfer to an 8-in. square dish; stir in sugar mixture. Cool to room temperature.

Freeze for 1 hour; stir with a fork. Freeze 2-3 hours longer or until completely frozen, stirring every 30 minutes. Stir granita with a fork just before serving; spoon into dessert dishes. Garnish with melon wedges if desired.

Nutrition Facts: 2/3 cup equals 151 calories, 0 fat (0 saturated fat), 0 cholesterol, 4 mg sodium, 41 g carbohydrate, 1 g fiber, trace protein.

≫ HOW TO:

MAKE GRANITA

Granitas, or ices, are simple to make and don't require an ice cream freezer. The mixture of water, sugar and a liquid flavoring needs to be scraped often as it freezes to produce its characteristic crystalline texture.

PEANUT BUTTER PARFAITS

Yield: 2 servings.

You're sure to enjoy these pretty, old-fashioned treats that feel like they came from an ice cream stand.

mildred sherrer // fort worth, texas

- 1/2 **cup packed light brown sugar**
- 3 **tablespoons milk**
- 2 **tablespoons light corn syrup**
- 2 **teaspoons butter**
- 2 **tablespoons creamy peanut butter**

Vanilla ice cream

- 1/4 **cup peanuts**

In a small heavy saucepan, combine the brown sugar, milk, corn syrup and butter. Cook and stir over medium heat until sugar is dissolved and mixture is smooth, about 4 minutes.

Remove from the heat; stir in peanut butter until smooth. Cool to room temperature. Spoon half into two parfait glasses; top with ice cream. Repeat layers. Sprinkle with peanuts.

Nutrition Facts: 1 parfait equals 514 calories, 22 g fat (6 g saturated fat), 13 mg cholesterol, 172 mg sodium, 77 g carbohydrate, 2 g fiber, 9 g protein.

BLACK FOREST CHEESECAKE

Yield: 6-8 servings.

I take this popular cheesecake to every gathering. I created the recipe more than 10 years ago and my family has been asking for it ever since.

christine ooyen // winnebago, illinois

- 1 **package (8 ounces) cream cheese, softened**
- 1/3 **cup sugar**
- 1 **cup (8 ounces) sour cream**
- 2 **teaspoons vanilla extract**
- 1 **carton (8 ounces) frozen whipped topping, thawed**
- 1 **chocolate crumb crust (8 inches)**
- 1/4 **cup baking cocoa**
- 1 **tablespoon confectioners' sugar**
- 1 **can (21 ounces) cherry pie filling**

In a large bowl, beat cream cheese and sugar until smooth. Beat in sour cream and vanilla. Fold in whipped topping. Spread half of the mixture evenly into crust. Fold cocoa and confectioners' sugar into remaining whipped topping mixture; carefully spread over cream cheese layer. Refrigerate for at least 4 hours.

Cut into slices; top each slice with cherry pie filling. Refrigerate leftovers.

Nutrition Facts: 1 slice equals 469 calories, 24 g fat (15 g saturated fat), 50 mg cholesterol, 213 mg sodium, 54 g carbohydrate, 2 g fiber, 5 g protein.

EASY GRASSHOPPER ICE CREAM PIE

Yield: 8 servings.

This quick pie is such an ego booster! My family compliments me the entire time they're eating it. A big hit at work potlucks, too, it's good to the last crumb.

kim murphy // albia, iowa

- 4 **cups mint chocolate chip ice cream, softened**
- 1 **chocolate crumb crust (8 inches)**
- 5 **cream-filled chocolate sandwich cookies, chopped**
- 1/3 **cup Junior Mint candies**

Chocolate hard-shell ice cream topping

Spread ice cream into crust. Sprinkle with cookies and candies; drizzle with ice cream topping. Freeze until firm. Remove from the freezer 15 minutes before serving.

Nutrition Facts: 1 piece equals 374 calories, 19 g fat (9 g saturated fat), 25 mg cholesterol, 182 mg sodium, 47 g carbohydrate, 1 g fiber, 4 g protein.

BE AN ICE CREAM PIE ARTIST

Whip up a crowd-pleasing frozen treat in no time with these ideas:

- Start with a store-bought graham, chocolate crumb or shortbread crust.
- Mix chocolate ice cream with chopped pecans; top pie with caramel, whipped cream and more pecans.
- Stir chopped peanut butter cups into vanilla ice cream; drizzle top of pie with chocolate sauce.
- Top strawberry ice cream pie with lemon curd and garnish with fresh strawberries.

MAKE A CHEESECAKE CRUMB CRUST

1 Place cookies or crackers in a heavy-duty resealable plastic bag. Seal bag, pushing out as much air as possible. Press a rolling pin over the bag, crushing the cookies or crackers into fine crumbs. Or, process cookies or crackers in a food processor.

2 Use a flat-bottomed measuring cup or glass to firmly press the prepared crumb mixture onto the bottom (and up the sides if recipe directs) of a springform pan.

MAKEOVER TRADITIONAL CHEESECAKE

Yield: 16 servings.

This lightened-up dessert has all of the original's delectable flavor. It's sure to make any special event more festive. Omit the caramel and candy toppings and enjoy this one plain with coffee if you prefer.

anne addesso // sheboygan, wisconsin

- 1-3/4 **cups graham cracker crumbs**
- 2 **tablespoons confectioners' sugar**
- 1/4 **cup butter, melted**

FILLING:

- 1 **tablespoon lemon juice**
- 1 **tablespoon vanilla extract**
- 2 **cups (16 ounces) 1% cottage cheese**
- 2 **cups (16 ounces) reduced-fat sour cream, *divided***
- 2 **packages (8 ounces *each*) reduced-fat cream cheese**
- 1-1/4 **cups sugar**
- 2 **tablespoons all-purpose flour**
- 4 **eggs, lightly beaten**
- 1 **tablespoon fat-free caramel ice cream topping**
- 2 **Heath candy bars (1.4 ounces *each*), chopped**

Place a 9-in. springform pan coated with cooking spray on a double thickness of heavy-duty foil (about 18 in. square). Securely wrap foil around pan.

In a small bowl, combine graham cracker crumbs and confectioners' sugar; stir in butter. Press onto the bottom and 1 in. up the sides of prepared pan. Place on a baking sheet. Bake at 325° for 18-22 minutes or until lightly browned. Cool on a wire rack.

Place the lemon juice, vanilla, cottage cheese and 1 cup sour cream in a blender; cover and process for 2 minutes or until smooth.

In a large bowl, beat cream cheese and sugar until smooth. Beat in the remaining sour cream. Add flour and pureed cottage cheese mixture; mix well. Add eggs; beat on low speed just until combined. Pour into crust.

Place springform pan in a larger baking pan; add 3/4 in. of hot water to larger pan. Bake at 325° for 1-1/2 hours or until center is just set and top appears dull. Remove springform pan from water bath. Cool on a wire rack for 10 minutes.

Carefully run a knife around edge of pan to loosen; cool 1 hour longer. Refrigerate overnight. Remove sides of pan. Garnish with caramel topping and chopped candy.

Nutrition Facts: 1 slice equals 311 calories, 15 g fat (9 g saturated fat), 93 mg cholesterol, 369 mg sodium, 32 g carbohydrate, trace fiber, 11 g protein.

CHOCOLATE-PEANUT BUTTER CUPCAKES

Yield: 2 dozen.

Satisfy your chocolate craving with these cupcakes. The creamy frosting topped with chopped peanut butter cups is the best part.
taste of home test kitchen

- 1 **package (18-1/4 ounces) chocolate cake mix**
- 1-1/4 **cups water**
- 1/2 **cup peanut butter**
- 1/3 **cup canola oil**
- 3 **eggs**
- 24 **miniature peanut butter cups**

FROSTING:

- 6 **ounces semisweet chocolate, chopped**
- 2/3 **cup heavy whipping cream**
- 1/3 **cup peanut butter**

Additional miniature peanut butter cups, chopped

In a large bowl, combine the cake mix, water, peanut butter, oil and eggs; beat on low speed for 30 seconds. Beat on medium for 2 minutes or until smooth.

Fill paper-lined muffin cups half full. Place a peanut butter cup in the center of each cupcake. Cover each with 1 tablespoonful batter.

Bake at 350° for 18-22 minutes or until a toothpick inserted near the center of the cupcake comes out clean. Cool for 10 minutes before removing from pans to wire racks to cool completely.

Place chocolate in a small bowl. In a small saucepan, bring cream just to a boil. Pour over chocolate; whisk until smooth. Stir in peanut butter. Cool, stirring occasionally, to room temperature or until ganache reaches a spreading consistency, about 10 minutes.

Spread over cupcakes; immediately sprinkle with additional peanut butter cups. Let stand until set.

EDITOR'S NOTE: Reduced-fat or generic brands of peanut butter are not recommended for this recipe.

Nutrition Facts: 1 cupcake (calculated without additional peanut butter cups) equals 269 calories, 17 g fat (6 g saturated fat), 36 mg cholesterol, 220 mg sodium, 27 g carbohydrate, 2 g fiber, 5 g protein.

CHOCOLATE COOKIE CUPCAKES

CHEAT IT!

Yield: 2 dozen.

Basic cake mix gets a kick start with everybody's favorite chocolate sandwich cookie. There's some cookie in every bite!
mary wiebe // altona, manitoba

- 1 **package (18-1/4 ounces) white cake mix**
- 1-1/4 **cups water**
- 1/4 **cup canola oil**
- 3 **egg whites**
- 1 **cup coarsely crushed cream-filled chocolate sandwich cookies (about 9 cookies)**
- 1 **can (16 ounces) vanilla frosting**

Additional crushed cream-filled chocolate sandwich cookies

In a large bowl, combine the cake mix, water, oil and egg whites; beat on low speed for 30 seconds. Beat on high for 2 minutes. Gently fold in cookie crumbs. Fill paper-lined muffin cups two-thirds full.

Bake at 350° for 18-22 minutes or until a toothpick inserted near the center comes out clean. Cool for 10 minutes before removing from pans to wire racks to cool completely. Frost cupcakes; sprinkle with additional crushed cookies.

Nutrition Facts: 1 cupcake (calculated without additional cookies) equals 227 calories, 9 g fat (2 g saturated fat), 0 cholesterol, 214 mg sodium, 34 g carbohydrate, 1 g fiber, 2 g protein. Diabetic Exchanges: 2 starch, 1-1/2 fat.

SECRET KISS CUPCAKES

Yield: about 2-1/2 dozen.

I came up these cupcakes for a Cub Scouts meeting. You should have seen the grins when the kids bit into the chocolate kisses in the middle.
carol hillebrenner // fowler, illinois

- 3-1/3 **cups all-purpose flour**
- 2 **cups sugar**
- 1 **cup baking cocoa**
- 2 **teaspoons baking soda**
- 1 **teaspoon salt**
- 2 **cups buttermilk**
- 1 **cup butter, melted**
- 2 **eggs, lightly beaten**
- 2 **teaspoons vanilla extract**
- 30 **milk chocolate kisses**
- 1 **can (16 ounces) fudge frosting**

In a large bowl, combine the flour, sugar, cocoa, baking soda and salt. Combine the buttermilk, butter, eggs and vanilla. Add to the dry ingredients until blended.

Fill paper-lined muffin cups two-thirds full. Press a chocolate kiss into the center of each cupcake until batter completely covers candy.

Bake at 375° for 20-25 minutes or until a toothpick inserted into cupcakes comes out clean. Cool for 10 minutes before removing from pans to wire racks to cool completely. Frost cupcakes.

Nutrition Facts: 1 cupcake equals 262 calories, 11 g fat (6 g saturated fat) 32 mg cholesterol, 283 mg sodium, 38 g carbohydrate, 1 g fiber, 3 g protein.

STRAWBERRY-BANANA ANGEL TORTE

Yield: 8-10 servings.

This pretty cake is the perfect ending to a light summer meal.

millie vickery // lena, illinois

- 1 **prepared angel food cake (8 to 10 ounces)**
- 1/2 **cup sour cream**
- 1/4 **cup sugar**
- 1/4 **cup pureed fresh strawberries**
- 3/4 **cup sliced ripe bananas**
- 1/2 **cup sliced fresh strawberries**
- 1 **cup heavy whipping cream, whipped**

Halved fresh strawberries

Split cake horizontally into three layers; place bottom layer on a serving plate. In a large bowl, combine the sour cream, sugar and pureed strawberries; fold in bananas and sliced strawberries. Fold in whipped cream.

Spread a third of the filling between each layer; spread remaining filling over top. Refrigerate until serving. Garnish with halved strawberries.

Nutrition Facts: 1 serving equals 199 calories, 11 g fat (7 g saturated fat), 41 mg cholesterol, 183 mg sodium, 23 g carbohydrate, 1 g fiber, 2 g protein.

SKILLET PINEAPPLE UPSIDE-DOWN CAKE

Yield: 10 servings.

For a change of pace, you can substitute fresh or frozen peach slices for the pineapple in this old-fashioned recipe.

bernardine melton // paola, kansas

1/2 **cup butter, cubed**	1 **teaspoon vanilla extract**
1 **cup packed brown sugar**	1 **cup all-purpose flour**
1 **can (20 ounces) sliced pineapple**	1 **teaspoon baking powder**
1/2 **cup chopped pecans**	1/4 **teaspoon salt**
3 **eggs, separated**	**Maraschino cherries**
1 **cup sugar**	

Melt butter in a 9– or 10-in. ovenproof skillet. Add brown sugar; mix until sugar is melted. Drain pineapple, reserving 1/3 cup juice. Arrange about 8 pineapple slices in a single layer over sugar (refrigerate remaining slices for another use). Sprinkle pecans over pineapple; set aside.

In a large bowl, beat egg yolks until thick and lemon-colored. Gradually add sugar, beating well. Blend in vanilla and reserved pineapple juice. Combine the flour, baking powder and salt; gradually add to batter and mix well.

In a small bowl, beat egg whites on high speed until stiff peaks form; fold into batter. Spoon into skillet.

Bake at 375° for 30-35 minutes or until a toothpick inserted near the center comes out clean. Let stand for 10 minutes before inverting onto serving plate. Place cherries in centers of pineapple slices.

Nutrition Facts: 1 slice equals 380 calories, 15 g fat (7 g saturated fat), 88 mg cholesterol, 224 mg sodium, 59 g carbohydrate, 1 g fiber, 4 g protein.

CARAMEL APPLE TRIFLE

Yield: 14 servings.

Trifles are terrific because they're made in advance and feed a crowd. This whimsical version that tastes like caramel apples will delight people of all ages.

joanne wright // niles, michigan

- 3 **tablespoons butter**
- 4 **cups chopped peeled tart apples (about 5 medium)**
- 1 **cup chopped walnuts**
- 1/2 **cup packed brown sugar**
- 1 **teaspoon apple pie spice,** *divided*
- 1 **package (8 ounces) cream cheese, softened**
- 1 **jar (12-1/4 ounces) caramel ice cream topping,** *divided*
- 1 **carton (12 ounces) frozen whipped topping, thawed,** *divided*
- 2 **loaves (10-3/4 ounces** *each***) frozen pound cake, thawed and cut into 1-inch cubes**

Additional apple pie spice, optional

In a large skillet, melt butter over medium heat. Stir in the apples, walnuts, brown sugar and 1/2 teaspoon apple pie spice. Cook and stir for 8-10 minutes or until apples are tender.

In a large bowl, beat cream cheese until smooth. Beat in 1/2 cup caramel topping and remaining apple pie spice. Fold in 2 cups whipped topping.

In a 3-1/2-qt. trifle bowl or glass serving bowl, layer a third of the cake cubes, cream cheese mixture and apple mixture. Repeat layers twice. Garnish with remaining whipped topping and drizzle with remaining caramel topping. Sprinkle with additional apple pie spice if desired. Refrigerate for at least 1 hour before serving.

Nutrition Facts: 1 cup equals 472 calories, 25 g fat (14 g saturated fat), 87 mg cholesterol, 313 mg sodium, 57 g carbohydrate, 2 g fiber, 6 g protein.

CREAM CHEESE POUND CAKE

Yield: 16 servings.

Fresh fruit and a dollop of whipped cream dress up this tender pound cake—a winner with my family and friends.

richard hogg // anderson, south carolina

- 1-1/2 **cups butter, softened**
- 1 **package (8 ounces) cream cheese, softened**
- 3 **cups sugar**
- 6 **eggs**
- 2 **teaspoons vanilla extract**
- 1 **teaspoon lemon extract**
- 3 **cups all-purpose flour**
- 1/2 **teaspoon baking powder**
- 1/4 **teaspoon salt**

Confectioners' sugar, sliced fresh strawberries and whipped cream, optional

In a large bowl, cream the butter, cream cheese and sugar until light and fluffy. Add eggs, one at a time, beating well after each addition. Beat in extracts. Combine the flour, baking powder and salt; beat into creamed mixture until blended.

Pour into a greased and floured 10-in. fluted tube pan. Bake at 325° for 1-1/4 to 1-1/2 hours or until a toothpick inserted near the center comes out clean.

Cool for 10 minutes before removing from pan to a wire rack to cool completely. Garnish with confectioners' sugar, strawberries and whipped cream if desired.

Nutrition Facts: 1 slice equals 460 calories, 24 g fat (15 g saturated fat), 140 mg cholesterol, 239 mg sodium, 56 g carbohydrate, 1 g fiber, 6 g protein.

CRANBERRY-PECAN POUND CAKE: Omit lemon extract. Add 3/4 teaspoon grated orange peel with vanilla. Fold in 3/4 cup *each* dried cranberries and chopped pecans.

CLASSIC CHOCOLATE LAYER CAKE

Yield: 12 servings.

This rich, moist cake is perfect for birthdays. The buttery frosting has an unmatchable homemade taste. With a few simple variations, you can come up with different colors and flavors to suit your needs.

taste of home cooking school

2 **cups sugar**	2 **teaspoons baking soda**
1 **cup canola oil**	1 **teaspoon baking powder**
1 **cup milk**	1 **teaspoon salt**
1 **cup brewed coffee, room temperature**	**BUTTERCREAM FROSTING:**
2 **eggs**	1 **cup butter, softened**
1 **teaspoon vanilla extract**	8 **cups confectioners' sugar**
2 **cups all-purpose flour**	2 **teaspoons vanilla extract**
3/4 **cup baking cocoa**	1/2 **to 3/4 cup milk**

In a large bowl, beat the first six ingredients until well blended. Combine the flour, cocoa, baking soda, baking powder and salt; gradually beat into sugar mixture until blended. Pour into two greased and floured 9-in. round baking pans. Bake at 325° for 25-30 minutes or until a toothpick inserted near the center comes out clean. Cool in pans for 10 minutes before removing to wire racks to cool completely.

For frosting, in a small bowl, cream butter and confectioners' sugar until light and fluffy. Beat in vanilla. Add enough milk until frosting reaches desired consistency. Spread frosting between layers and over top and sides of cake.

Nutrition Facts: 1 piece equals 859 calories, 36 g fat (13 g saturated fat), 80 mg cholesterol, 621 mg sodium, 133 g carbohydrate, 2 g fiber, 5 g protein.

>> HOW TO:

EASILY FINISH A CAKE

Peaks: Press the flat side of a tablespoon or teaspoon into the frosting and pull straight up, forming a peak. Repeat over top and sides of cake.

Zigzags: Run the tines of a table fork through the frosting in a wavy motion.

Waves: Use the back of a tablespoon or teaspoon to make a small twisting motion in one direction. Then move the spoon over a little and make another twist in the opposite direction. Repeat until entire cake is covered.

SUBSTITUTIONS & EQUIVALENTS

EQUIVALENT MEASURES

3 teaspoons	=	1 tablespoon	16 tablespoons	=	1 cup
4 tablespoons	=	1/4 cup	2 cups	=	1 pint
5-1/3 tablespoons	=	1/3 cup	4 cups	=	1 quart
8 tablespoons	=	1/2 cup	4 quarts	=	1 gallon

FOOD EQUIVALENTS

Grains

Macaroni	1 cup (3-1/2 ounces) uncooked	=	2-1/2 cups cooked
Noodles, Medium	3 cups (4 ounces) uncooked	=	4 cups cooked
Popcorn	1/3 to 1/2 cup unpopped	=	8 cups popped
Rice, Long Grain	1 cup uncooked	=	3 cups cooked
Rice, Quick-Cooking	1 cup uncooked	=	2 cups cooked
Spaghetti	8 ounces uncooked	=	4 cups cooked

Crumbs

Bread	1 slice	=	3/4 cup soft crumbs, 1/4 cup fine dry crumbs
Graham Crackers	7 squares	=	1/2 cup finely crushed
Buttery Round Crackers	12 crackers	=	1/2 cup finely crushed
Saltine Crackers	14 crackers	=	1/2 cup finely crushed

Fruits

Bananas	1 medium	=	1/3 cup mashed
Lemons	1 medium	=	3 tablespoons juice, 2 teaspoons grated peel
Limes	1 medium	=	2 tablespoons juice, 1-1/2 teaspoons grated peel
Oranges	1 medium	=	1/4 to 1/3 cup juice, 4 teaspoons grated peel

Vegetables

Cabbage	1 head	=	5 cups shredded	Green Pepper	1 large	=	1 cup chopped
Carrots	1 pound	=	3 cups shredded	Mushrooms	1/2 pound	=	3 cups sliced
Celery	1 rib	=	1/2 cup chopped	Onions	1 medium	=	1/2 cup chopped
Corn	1 ear fresh	=	2/3 cup kernels	Potatoes	3 medium	=	2 cups cubed

Nuts

Almonds	1 pound	=	3 cups chopped	Pecan Halves	1 pound	=	4-1/2 cups chopped
Ground Nuts	3-3/4 ounces	=	1 cup	Walnuts	1 pound	=	3-3/4 cups chopped

EASY SUBSTITUTIONS

When you need...		Use...
Baking Powder	1 teaspoon	1/2 teaspoon cream of tartar + 1/4 teaspoon baking soda
Buttermilk	1 cup	1 tablespoon lemon juice or vinegar + enough milk to measure 1 cup (let stand 5 minutes before using)
Cornstarch	1 tablespoon	2 tablespoons all-purpose flour
Honey	1 cup	1-1/4 cups sugar + 1/4 cup water
Half-and-Half Cream	1 cup	1 tablespoon melted butter + enough whole milk to measure 1 cup
Onion	1 small, chopped (1/3 cup)	1 teaspoon onion powder or 1 tablespoon dried minced onion
Tomato Juice	1 cup	1/2 cup tomato sauce + 1/2 cup water
Tomato Sauce	2 cups	3/4 cup tomato paste + 1 cup water
Unsweetened Chocolate	1 square (1 ounce)	3 tablespoons baking cocoa + 1 tablespoon shortening or oil
Whole Milk	1 cup	1/2 cup evaporated milk + 1/2 cup water

COOKING TERMS

**HERE'S A QUICK REFERENCE FOR SOME OF THE COOKING TERMS
USED IN TASTE OF HOME RECIPES.**

baste: To moisten food with melted butter, pan drippings, marinades or other liquid to add more flavor and juiciness.

beat: A rapid movement to combine ingredients using a fork, spoon, wire whisk or electric mixer.

blend: To combine ingredients until just mixed.

boil: To heat liquids until bubbles form that cannot be "stirred down." In the case of water, the temperature will reach 212°.

bone: To remove all meat from the bone before cooking.

cream: To beat ingredients together to a smooth consistency, usually in the case of butter and sugar for baking.

dash: A small amount of seasoning, less than 1/8 teaspoon. If using a shaker, a dash would comprise a quick flip of the container.

dredge: To coat foods with flour or other dry ingredients. Most often done with pot roasts and stew meat before browning.

fold: To incorporate several ingredients by careful and gentle turning with a spatula. Used generally with beaten egg whites or whipped cream when mixing into the rest of the ingredients to keep the batter light.

julienne: To cut foods into long thin strips much like matchsticks. Used most often for salads and stir-fry dishes.

mince: To cut into very fine pieces. Used often for garlic or fresh herbs.

parboil: To cook partially, usually used in the case of chicken, sausages and vegetables.

partially set: Describes the consistency of gelatin after it has been chilled for a short amount of time. Mixture should resemble the consistency of egg whites.

puree: To process foods to a smooth mixture. Can be prepared in an electric blender, food processor, food mill or sieve.

saute: To fry quickly in a small amount of fat, stirring almost constantly. Most often done with onions, mushrooms and other chopped vegetables.

score: To cut slits partway through the outer surface of foods. Often used with ham or flank steak.

stir-fry: To cook meats and/or vegetables with a constant stirring motion in a small amount of oil in a wok or skillet over high heat.

GUIDE TO COOKING WITH POPULAR HERBS

Seasoned cooks know that a pinch of this herb and a dash of that spice can really perk up a dish. A well-stocked spice rack can be one of the quickest and least expensive ways to add flair to ordinary meals. Store dried herbs and spices in tightly closed glass or heavy-duty plastic containers. It's best to keep them in a cool, dry place; avoid storing them in direct sunlight, over the stove or near other heat sources.

For best flavor, keep dried herbs and ground spices for up to 6 months. They can be used if they are older, but the flavors might not be as intense. Whole spices can be stored for 1 to 2 years.

Select fresh herbs that are fragrant with bright, fresh-looking leaves. Avoid those with wilted, yellowing or browning leaves. Wrap fresh herbs in a slightly damp paper towel and place in a resealable plastic bag. Press as much air as possible out of the bag and seal. Store in the refrigerator for 5 to 7 days. To substitute dried herbs for fresh, use one-third of the amount. For example, if a recipe calls for 1 tablespoon fresh, use 1 teaspoon dried.

HERB		APPETIZERS SALADS	BREADS/EGGS SAUCES/CHEESE	VEGETABLES PASTA	MEAT POULTRY	FISH SHELLFISH
Basil	Available as fresh green or purple leaves or dried and crushed. Sweet flavor with hints of mint, pepper and cloves. Use for tomato sauce, pestos, chicken, meat, zucchini, summer squashes.	Green, Potato & Tomato Salads, Salad Dressings, Stewed Fruit	Breads, Fondue & Egg Dishes, Dips, Marinades, Sauces	Mushrooms, Tomatoes, Squash, Pasta, Bland Vegetables	Broiled, Roast Meat & Poultry Pies, Stews, Stuffing	Baked, Broiled & Poached Fish, Shellfish
Bay Leaves	Available as whole, fresh or dried, dull green leaves. Savory, spicy and aromatic. Use for pickles, soups, stews, meat, casseroles.	Seafood Cocktail, Seafood Salad, Tomato Aspic, Stewed Fruit	Egg Dishes, Gravies, Marinades, Sauces	Dried Bean Dishes, Beets, Carrots, Onions, Potatoes, Rice, Squash	Corned Beef, Tongue Meat & Poultry Stews	Poached Fish, Shellfish, Fish Stews
Chives	Available as fresh or freeze-dried hollow stems. Delicate and peppery, mild onion flavor. Use for potatoes, eggs, sauces, seafood, salads.	Mixed Vegetable, Green, Potato & Tomato Salads, Salad Dressings	Egg & Cheese Dishes, Cream Cheese, Cottage Cheese, Gravies, Sauces	Hot Vegetables, Potatoes	Broiled Poultry, Poultry & Meat Pies, Stews, Casseroles	Baked Fish, Fish Casseroles, Fish Stews, Shellfish
Dill	Available as fresh leaves, dried and crushed or seeds. Fresh, sweet, grassy flavor. Use for pickles, tomatoes, cucumbers, breads, fish.	Seafood Cocktail, Green, Potato & Tomato Salads, Salad Dressings	Breads, Egg & Cheese Dishes, Fish & Meat Sauces	Beans, Beats, Cabbage, Carrots, Cauliflower, Peas, Squash, Tomatoes	Beef, Veal Roasts, Lamb, Steaks, Choops, Stews, Roast & Creamed Poultry	Baked, Broiled, Poached & Stuffed Fish, Shellfish
Marjoram	Available as fresh leaves or dried and crushed. Tastes like oregano. Use for tomato dishes, meat, poultry, seafood, vegetables.	Seafood Cocktail, Green, Poultry & Seafood Salads	Breads, Cheese Spreads, Egg & Cheese Dishes, Gravies, Sauces	Carrots, Eggplant, Peas, Onions, Potatoes, Dried Bean Dishes, Spinach	Roast Meats, & Poultry, Meat & Poultry Pies, Stews & Casseroles	Baked, Broiled & Stuffed Fish, Shellfish

HERB		APPETIZERS SALADS	BREADS/EGGS SAUCES/CHEESE	VEGETABLES PASTA	MEAT POULTRY	FISH SHELLFISH
Mustard	Available ground or as seeds. Pungent, sharp, hot flavor. Use for meats, vinaigrettes, seafood, sauces.	Fresh Green Salads, Prepared Meat, Macaroni & Potato Salads, Salad Dressings	Biscuits, Egg & Cheese Dishes, Sauces	Baked Beans, Cabbage, Egg Plant, Squash, Dried Beans, Mushrooms, Pasta	Chops, Steaks, Ham, Pork, Poultry, Cold Meats	Shellfish
Oregano	Available as fresh leaves, dried and crushed or ground. Pungent, slightly bitter flavor. Use for tomato dishes, chicken, pork, lamb, vegetables.	Green, Poultry & Seafood Salads	Breads, Egg & Cheese Dishes, Meat, Poultry & Vegetable Sauces	Artichokes, Cabbage, Eggplant, Squash, Dried Beans, Mushrooms, Pasta	Broiled, Roast Meats, Meat & Poultry Pies, Stews, Casseroles	Baked, Broiled & Poached Fish, Shellfish
Parsley	Available as fresh leaves, curly or Italian (flat-leaf) or dried and flaked. Fresh, slightly peppery flavor. Use for poultry, seafood, tomatoes, pasta, vegetables.	Green, Potato, Seafood & Vegetable Salads	Biscuits, Breads, Egg & Cheese Dishes, Gravies, Sauces	Asparagus, Beets, Eggplant, Squash, Dried Beans, Mushrooms, Pasta	Meat Loaf, Meat & Poultry Pies, Stews & Casseroles, Stuffing	Fish, Stews, Stuffed Fish
Rosemary	Available as fresh leaves on stems or dried. Pungent flavor with a hint of pine. Use for lamb, poultry, pork, vegetables.	Fruit Cocktail, Fruit & Green Salads	Biscuits, Egg Dishes, Herb Butter, Cream Cheese, Marinades, Sauces	Beans, Broccoli, Peas, Cauliflower, Mushrooms, Baked Potatoes, Parsnips	Roast Meat, Poultry & Meat Pies, Stews & Casseroles, Stuffing	Stuffed Fish, Shellfish
Sage	Available as fresh leaves, dried and crushed or rubbed. Pungent, slightly bitter, musty mint flavor. Use for pork, poultry, stuffing.		Breads, Fondue, Egg & Cheese Dishes, Spreads, Gravies, Sauces	Beans, Beets, Onions, Peas, Spinach, Squash, Tomatoes	Roast Meat, Poultry, Meat Loaf, Stews, Stuffing	Baked, Poached & Stuffed Fish
Tarragon	Available as fresh leaves or dried and crushed. Strong, spicy, anise-like flavors. Use for poultry, seafood, meats, vegetables.	Seafood Cocktail, Avocado Salads, Salad Dressings	Cheese Spreads, Marinades, Sauces, Egg Dishes	Asparagus, Beans, Beets, Carrots, Mushrooms, Peas, Squash Spinach	Steaks, Poultry, Roast Meats, Casseroles & Stews	Baked, Broiled & Poached Fish, Shellfish
Thyme	Available as fresh leaves or dried and crushed. Pungent, earthy, spicy flavor. Use for meat, poultry, lentils, soups, stews.	Biscuits, Breads, Egg & Cheese Dishes, Sauces, Spreads	Biscuits, Breads, Egg & Cheese Dishes, Sauces, Spreads	Beets, Carrots, Mushrooms, Onions, Peas, Eggplant, Spinach, Potatoes	Roast Meat, Poultry & Meat Loaf, Meat & Poultry Pies, Stews & Casseroles	Baked, Broiled & Stuffed Fish, Shellfish, Fish Stews

INDEXES

ALPHABETICAL INDEX

GENERAL INDEX

HOW-TO'S, SECRETS & TIPS INDEX